"Following on his impressive study of the Greek term *ekklēsia*, Ralph Korner here engages an extremely important issue in current scholarship, too often ignored: the challenge of addressing supersessionism in the Book of Revelation."

—ELAINE PAGELS, Harrington Spear Paine Professor of Religion; Princeton University

"In this impressive and closely argued book, written with full cognizance of the latest scholarship, Korner brings a whole range of different issues and insights to bear upon key interpretative questions in the Book of Revelation. This is a very significant contribution to current debates and is essential reading for all future discussions of supersessionism."

—PAUL TREBILCO, Professor of New Testament; University of Otago, New Zealand

"In this ground-breaking study, Korner provides a carefully nuanced understanding of Revelation by focusing attention on group dynamics and nomenclature in the Roman world. He convincingly demonstrates that Revelation is supersessionist in wanting to replace the Roman imperium with a new Jewish order, yet given the thoroughly Jewish nature of the author's symbolic universe, it is 'post-supersessionist' when it comes to the Judeans themselves. A rare combination of arguments that are scholarly and accessible at the same time."

—RICHARD S. ASCOUGH, Professor, School of Religion; Queen's University

"In this important book, Ralph Korner argues that Revelation has a very clear supersessionist agenda, but not in relation to Jews and Judaism. Rather, from within a Jewish symbolic universe, Revelation targets the Roman Empire on multiple fronts, claiming that its days are counted; Rome will be replaced by the eschatological new Jerusalem. Arguing his case, Korner ingeniously brings his expertise in ancient institutions, notably those called *ekklēsiai*, to bear on several interpretive cruces, showing convincingly that reading Revelation as a Jewish text unlocks key aspects of its message. Highly recommended for anyone interested in understanding Revelation, but also more generally for those seeking to know more about what it means to read the New Testament from a late first-century Jewish perspective."

—ANDERS RUNESSON, Professor of New Testament; University of Oslo

"Ralph Korner sets forth an impressive respo
does the Book of Revelation promote a theolo

D1715622

Thankfully, Korner refuses to dodge the complexity of the problem. His careful examination of Revelation at multiple dimensions reveals an Apocalypse that promotes a thoroughly Jewish vision for following Jesus. Korner shows that Revelation's two references to the "synagogue of Satan" need not be understood as a condemnation of Jews who do not worship Jesus."

—Greg Carey, Professor of New Testament,
Lancaster Theological Seminary

"In a well-documented and superbly nuanced study Ralph J. Korner has penned a defining historical, exegetical, and socio-political critique of popular and less precise views of Revelation which continue to advance many su-persessionistic theories. He challenges contemporary readers to reconsider their understanding of the ancient writer's basic concepts such as: *ekklēsia* and synagogue, even Jew and Christian, as well as the very nature of covenant letter and apocalyptic prophecy. I highly recommend this work."

—Gerald Borchert, Senior Adjunct Professor of New Testament,
Carson-Newman University

"Has God rejected Israel and transferred his covenant to the church?—a claim based not least on the Christian Apocalypse. Korner, a specialist in its ecclesiology, argues not: the Revelation's portrayal of God's multi-ethnic people in terms of Jewish history, imagery, and literary techniques, far from displacing Israel, 'emplaces' the church within God's irrevocable covenant with Abraham's children. Korner's challenge to supersessionism in this NT book should prompt careful review of our exegetical tradition."

—Paul A. Rainbow, Professor of Bible;
Kairos Project and Sioux Falls Seminary

"Truly a work of leading-edge scholarship, a precious stone amidst all the clay (to borrow from 4 Ezra 7). Korner labors assiduously to overcome the anachronistic or erroneous understandings of terms and concepts, like *ekklēsia*, historically divested of their Jewish heritage and essence. Reestablishing the thoroughly Jewish character of the Apocalypse, he proffers that its epistolary framework may be more precisely a 'covenantal letter to the Diaspora,' and its only supersessionist agenda the proleptic and future displacement of the Roman imperium."

—Henri Louis Goulet, Academic Dean; Messianic Studies Institute,
Columbus, Ohio

Reading Revelation After Supersessionism

Series Preface

The **New Testament after Supersessionism** (NTAS) is a series that presents post-supersessionist interpretations of the New Testament. By post-supersessionism, we mean "a family of theological perspectives that *affirms God's irrevocable covenant with the Jewish people as a central and coherent part of ecclesial teaching*. It rejects understandings of the new covenant that entail the abrogation or obsolescence of God's covenant with the Jewish people, of the Torah as a demarcator of Jewish communal identity, or of the Jewish people themselves" (spostst.org). Although the field of New Testament studies has made significant strides in this direction in recent years, the volumes in this series, written by Jewish and gentile believers in Jesus, seek to advance the conversation by offering post-supersessionist readings of the New Testament that address the question of ongoing Jewish particularity, and the relationship of interdependence and mutual blessing between Jew and gentile in Messiah.

SERIES EDITORS

J. Brian Tucker
Moody Theological Seminary, Plymouth, MI

David Rudolph
The King's University, Southlake, TX

Justin Hardin
Palm Beach Atlantic University, West Palm Beach, FL

PROJECTED VOLUMES

New Testament After Supersessionism, Introductory Volume
—Justin K. Hardin, David J. Rudolph, and J. Brian Tucker

Reading Matthew After Supersessionism
—Anders Runesson

Reading Mark after Supersessionism
—Vered Hillel

Reading Luke-Acts after Supersessionism
—Mark S. Kinzer and David J. Rudolph

Reading John after Supersessionism
—Wally V. Cirafesi

Reading Romans after Supersessionism
—-J. Brian Tucker

Reading 1 Corinthians after Supersessionism
—Kar Yong Lim

Reading 2 Corinthians after Supersessionism
—James A. Waddell

Reading Galatians after Supersessionism
—Justin K. Hardin

Reading Philippians after Supersessionism
—Christopher Zoccali

Reading Ephesians and Colossians after Supersessionism
—Lionel Windsor

Reading Hebrews after Supersessionism
—David M. Moffitt

Reading 1 Peter after Supersessionism
—Kelly D. Liebengood

Reading Revelation after Supersessionism
—Ralph Korner

New Testament after Supersessionism, Supplementary Volume
—edited by Justin K. Hardin, David J. Rudolph, and J. Brian Tucker

Reading Revelation After Supersessionism

AN APOCALYPTIC JOURNEY OF
SOCIALLY IDENTIFYING JOHN'S MULTI-ETHNIC
EKKLĒSIAI WITH THE *EKKLĒSIA* OF ISRAEL

Ralph J. Korner

CASCADE *Books* • Eugene, Oregon

READING REVELATION AFTER SUPERSESSIONISM
An Apocalyptic Journey of Socially Identifying John's Multi-Ethnic *Ekklēsiai* with the *Ekklēsia* of Israel

Cascade Books
An Imprint of Wipf and Stock Publishers
199 W. 8th Ave., Suite 3
Eugene, OR 97401

www.wipfandstock.com

PAPERBACK ISBN: 978-1-7252-7465-5
HARDCOVER ISBN: 978-1-7252-7466-2
EBOOK ISBN: 978-1-7252-7467-9

Cataloguing-in-Publication data:

Names: Korner, Ralph J., author
Title: Reading Revelation after supersessionism : an apocalyptic journey of socially identifying John's multi-ethnic *ekklēsiai* with the *ekklēsia* of Israel / Ralph J. Korner.
Description: Eugene, OR: Cascade Books, 2020 | Includes bibliographical references and index.
Identifiers: ISBN 978-1-7252-7465-5 (paperback) | ISBN 978-1-7252-7466-2 (hardcover) | ISBN 978-1-7252-7467-9 (ebook)
Subjects: LCSH: Bible.—Revelation—Criticism, interpretation, etc | Jews in the New Testament | Antisemitism—Biblical teaching | Ekklēsia (The Greek word) | Gentiles in the New Testament
Classification: BS2825.52 K667 2020 (print) | BS2825.52 (ebook)

Manufactured in the U.S.A.   NOVEMBER 2, 2020

To my wife Kathy, who is an *apokalypsis* of Jesus

Table of Contents

List of Tables

Acknowledgments

THERE IS A SAYING that it takes a village to raise a child. Allow me to adapt that saying for my Acknowledgments to say that it takes a global academic village to raise a scholar. The start of my focused study of the book of Revelation began with a course at Taylor Seminary on eschatology with the now deceased Stanley J. Grenz (1990s). Years earlier, Drs. Syd Page and Benno Przybylski had enlivened within me a love of reading the NT in Greek, which formed a firmer foundation for my eschatology paper. Dr. Grenz encouraged me to expand my analysis of how visionary literary devices in chs. 18—20 facilitated an amillennial reading into a broader assessment of their effect on the entire book.

Thus, began an academic journey in all things apocalyptic which has been spurred on by many people during these more than twenty years. As I moved towards the publication of my structural findings, Dr. Benno Przybylski helped me hone my manuscript. The resultant article on the literary structure of Revelation's vision episode (2000) facilitated my acceptance into the MA in Biblical Studies program at Trinity Western University where, under the wise tutelage of my thesis advisors, Drs. James Scott and Craig Evans, my attention shifted towards an analysis of the genre of the book of Revelation.

This led to a formal debate at a TWU graduate seminar with Dr. David E. Aune (2004) over the genre of the Apocalypse. One can imagine my fear and trepidation. It was all for naught, however, as Dr. Aune turned the "debate" into a gracious and collegial conversation. He continues to inspire and encourage me with our occasional opportunities for academic updates.

With my move to doctoral studies at McMaster University, I was encouraged to put my Revelation studies on hold and move into Pauline studies. My dissertation on the word *ekklēsia*, however, has many applications for a better understanding of John's seven Roman Asia *ekklēsiai* to whom the Apocalypse is addressed. My dissertation supervisor, Dr. Anders Runesson, brought his ancient synagogue expertise to bear in shepherding my research on *ekklēsia*, especially as it relates to assessing its use as a synagogue term. This insight has immeasurably informed my perspective on the value that a Jewish heritage held not only for Paul's *ekklēsia* communities but also for John's. Drs. Richard Ascough, Phil Harland, and John Kloppenborg helped me better to contextualize my *ekklēsia* findings within associations research, which has particular application for Roman Asia. This socio-historical understanding was then immeasurably aided by the gracious interactions I was privileged to have had with Drs. Onno van Nijf (University of Groningen) and George van Kooten (University of Cambridge). Onno rooted my Roman Asia research within the inscriptional witness of the political culture and George increased my understanding of the counter-imperial message of John's New Jerusalem.

Dr. J. Brian Tucker expanded my research horizons so as also to consider the supersessionist implications (or lack thereof) of early Christ-follower communities being designated as *ekklēsiai*. My dissertation, and the resultant published volume (Brill, 2017), would have been much poorer without Brian's insights and his provision of unpublished works. Without Brian's encouragement for me to incorporate research on supersessionism into my *ekklēsia* book, this Revelation book would not only have been much the poorer for it, but probably would not even have seen the light of day (and not only because he is a co-editor of the NTAS series).

As I wrestled with how best to address the topic of supersessionism in Revelation, a serendipitous email came my way (2018) that began a conversation which became seminal for how I addressed two very troublesome passages (Rev 2:9; 3:9). Dr. Elaine Pagels shared the gift of her time and encouragement, first, by affirming the value that my *ekklēsia* book held for her and, second, by engaging in an extended conversation over, and providing some of her personal research on, the book of Revelation, not least relative to those two troublesome passages. I am indebted to her kindness and grace.

I continue to have the privilege of scholarly interaction on the book of Revelation (thanks again George!) and also of student interaction. I have learned much from my students at Taylor Seminary. Their enthusiasm invigorates me each time I teach my Revelation course. Particular thanks are due to one of my students, Caley Tse, for the gift of her graphic design skills, which crafted the Appendices on the chiastic "pyramids." Many thanks to the efficient and committed staff of Wipf and Stock and especially to Robin Parry, for their guidance throughout this publication process.

Above all else, I wish to acknowledge my deep gratitude and indebtedness to my wife Kathy, and to my children Naomi, Natasha, Daniel, and Deborah, for their belief in me and for their encouragement of me to continue to live fully into my academic calling. To God goes any glory.

Ralph Korner
March 2020

Abbreviations

ABD	*The Anchor Bible Dictionary*. 5 volumes. Edited by David Noel Freedman. New York: Doubleday, 1992.
AGRW	Ascough, Harland, Kloppenborg, *Associations in the Greco-Roman World: a Sourcebook*. Waco, TX: Baylor University Press, 2012.
ASSB	Runesson, Binder, and Olsson, *The Ancient Synagogue Sourcebook*. Leiden: Brill, 2008.
BCH	*Bulletin de correspondance hellénique* (Paris).
Arist.	Aristotle
Dem.	Demosthenes

I

Introduction: Definitions and Directions

The revelation ["apocalypse"/*apokalypsis*] of Jesus the [Jewish]
Christos/messiah, which God gave him to show his servants
what must soon take place; he made it known by sending his
angel to his servant, John, [a Jewish apocalyptic apostle-proph-
et], who testified to the word of God and to the testimony of
Jesus the *Christos*, even to all [six *vision blocks* within the vision
episode] that he saw [*eiden*]. Blessed is the one who [publicly]
reads aloud [during an *ekklēsia*/"assembly"] the words of this
[Jewish apocalyptic apostolic-]prophecy . . . for the time [of the
"Last Day" (i.e., the completion of the telescopically reiterative
sixth seal) of these "last days" (that began with the first five
seals)] is near. John to the seven *ekklēsiai* [that is, the multi-
ethnic *Christos*-following associations,] in [the Roman province
of] Asia. (Rev 1:1–4)[1]

At first glance, my adaptation of the NRSV's translation of the first four
verses of the book of Revelation may not seem to make immediate sense.
In fact, it may serve, rather, to blur any normal sense with which we usually read John's introductory comments. It is my hope, though, that by
the end of this book I will have provided sufficient definitions of, and
rationale for including, the terms (e.g., *ekklēsia*, associations, Last Day)
and concepts (e.g., *vision blocks*, telescopic reiteration)[2] used in my rather

1. Unless otherwise noted, all biblical quotations are taken from the NRSV (1989;
Division of Christian Education of the National Council of Churches of Christ in the
United States of America).

2. In its essence, "telescopic reiteration" names an organizational principle that
John uses to demonstrate that the *eschaton*, as it is concisely depicted in the sixth

1

unorthodox "amplified" translation of Rev 1:1–4 SO AS to justify my interpretative moves.

Aside from providing greater clarity with respect to terms and concepts associated with the Apocalypse, the foundational purpose of my investigative journey through Revelation is to assess the degree to which John inculcates a supersessionist perspective for his *ekklēsia* addressees. In other words, does John's extensive social identification with Judaism(s), Jewishness, and Jewish institutions reflect a literary program either (1) of *replacing* Israel with the remnant of Israel, that is, Jewish and non-Jewish followers of the Jewish *Christos*, or (2) of *emplacing* the multi-ethnic associations of John's *Christos*-followers *further within* Israel, without thereby superseding the legitimacy of Israel as a national identity for ethnic Jews who do not follow Jesus as the Jewish *Christos*. Two passages in Revelation are particularly challenging in arguing for option 2 (i.e., emplacement within Israel). They each contain statements about people who claim to be Jews "and are not" and who are said to be "a synagogue of Satan" (2:9; 3:9). Their exegetical and socio-historical analysis follows in chapter 4.

It is important at this point to clarify what I mean by "social identification," particularly as it relates to John's *ekklēsia* communities and a Jewish heritage. Social identification "denotes individuals' psychological bond with their ingroup."[3] It is "psychologically relevant and socially consequential" in that "those who identify highly with their ingroup think of themselves in terms of their group membership, feel close to the group, are committed to the group, and act on behalf of the group."[4] There are two primary cognitive pathways that facilitate a person's process of socially identifying with an ingroup: (1) self-stereotyping and (2) self-anchoring.[5] Self-stereotyping describes how one's "personal self" moves to the backseat, so to speak, as one's "social self" takes the driver's seat through assimilation of an ingroup's identity. Self-anchoring describes the opposite side of the "social identification coin" in that "information about the *personal* self-concept is used as an anchor to define an

---

seal (6:12–17), is progressively expanded upon in the first six trumpets (8:2—9:21; cf. also 11:1–14) and brought to summation in the seven bowls (15:5—16:21), with the seventh bowl reiterating the "Last Day" sixth seal events.

3. Veelen, et al., "An Integrative Model," 3. See also the seminal study by H. Tajfel and J. C. Turner, "An Integrative Theory of Intergroup Conflict," 33–47.

4. Veelen, et al., "An Integrative Model," 3.

5. Veelen, et al., "An Integrative Model," 4.

ingroup."[6] In other words, one's "perception that 'the group is like me'" actually puts pressure on the ingroup to re-shape its social dynamic towards that individual's self-perception.

In this study it will become clear that John's self-stereotyping predominantly identifies himself socio-ethnically with the Jewish people. Indicators of his psychological bond with that ingroup is reflected not least in his use of Jewish theology, terminology, imagery, and literary genres for the communication of his apocalyptically prophetic message. Additionally, it will be seen that John uses self-anchoring to influence how his predominantly Jewish *ekklēsia* communities re-imagine their theology, terminology, imagery, and literary history. This is particularly evident in his transformation of the common Jewish *topos* of an eschatological Jerusalem into a new Jerusalem that is not only a place but also a people ("the bride of the Lamb"), who in fact are that place (21:9–10). Thus, John's depiction of his seven *ekklēsiai* as a city within which the Lord God eternally dwells would immeasurably have strengthened their resilience under social pressure, and even persecution—irrespective of the social conditions they might encounter in Roman Asia they can be sure that the Lord God will not, and in fact cannot, ever leave them or forsake them.

Stephen Spence provides an appropriate nuance when he notes that social identification with Jewish practices and ideology, at most, speaks only to some of the *internal* dynamics operating within *Christos*-followers, that is, that they inculcated a Jewish *ethos*. Social interaction, however, goes one step further from internal dynamics to actual external interactions on a social basis by *Christos*-followers with a Jewish synagogal community.[7] Evidence of social interaction reinforces a perception of inter-community respect and cooperation between a *Christos*-following community and a non-Jesus following Jewish community, which then lessens the prospect of an underlying supersessionist ideology being endemic to that Christ-follower community.

When it comes to the book of Revelation, there is one very clear supersessionist agenda therein, however. But it does not necessarily relate to the *intra*-Jewish dialogue (or diatribe) between Jews in Roman Asia (*Christos*-following and non-*Jesus*-following). Rather, the thoroughly Jewish character of John's symbolic universe clearly communicates, from

6. Veelen, et al., "An Integrative Model," 4 [author's emphasis].

7. Spence, *Parting of the Ways*, 8–11, 61–63.

as many perspectives as possible, a supersessionist agenda relative to a *non-Jewish* entity, the Roman *imperium*. John pictures the city of Rome and its religio-political *imperium* as being visibly superseded in the future, and perhaps even invisibly in John's present, by an eschatological Jewish city known as "the New Jerusalem" (chs. 21 and 22).

In John's cosmic apocalyptic drama, the Roman *imperium* is cast as the primary earthly antagonist against God and his multi-ethnic people. In order to make sure that his listening (and reading) audience is able to identify Rome as that antagonist, John employs two bizarre symbols. The first image is of a "beast" (*thērion*) with seven heads. This beast rises out of the sea to persecute God's people (13:1–11). Later on John introduces a second symbol for the *imperium*. He describes a vision of a whore called "Babylon" who rides on that seven-headed "sea beast" (17:1–18). Together, these two symbols depict the Roman government, its religio-political ideology, and perhaps even its imperial cults.[8] Thus, Revelation is supersessionist to its core—John's visionary agenda is to replace the Roman *imperium* with a Jewish recreated order (the New Jerusalem).

What is not so clear in Revelation is whether John expresses an agenda to replace "historic Judaism(s)" with his depiction of an eternal "Christian" New Jerusalem. John's extensive integration of Jewish history, motifs, tropes, imagery, mythology, literary techniques, and eschatology into his apocalyptic prophecy allows for two polar opposite conclusions: either the Apocalypse is the most expressly supersessionist book in the New Testament (*"replacement of* Israel") or it is the most comprehensively non-supersessionist book in the New Testament (*"emplacement within* Israel"). In this volume, I will argue that even though John casts the eschatological fulfillment of Christ-follower hopes within the framework of a Jewish symbolic universe, this does not necessarily mean that he intends to communicate that *Ioudaioi* (Jews/Judeans), Jewishness, and Jewish institutions are superseded by the resurrected Jewish *Christos* (the Lamb; chs. 4 and 5) and his earthly followers, not least those within the seven *ekklēsiai* ("churches") of Roman Asia (chs. 2—3).

8. I do not speak of "*the* Imperial cult" since there was no empire-wide, centralized cult of emperor worship. Rather, there were four provincial cults and four levels of imperial cults: "[1] the official cult of *deceased* emperors centred at the city of Rome ... [2] *provincial* imperial cults and temples organized by institutions that claimed to represent the civic communities of a given Roman province [e.g., the *koinon* of Asia] ... [3] *civic* imperial cults devoted to honouring the *Sebastoi* (or a particular emperor) at the city level ... [4] other *local or unofficial* shrines, monuments and expressions of honour for the emperors as gods in unofficial settings (e.g., small groups), including associations" (Harland, *Associations, Synagogues, and Congregations*, 121-25).

Definition: Post-Supersessionism

My talk of John seeking to *emplace* his *ekklēsia* communities further into their Jewish heritage fits within a theological perspective called post-supersessionism. One helpful definition of post-supersessionism reads as follows:

> a family of theological perspectives that affirms God's irrevo-
> cable covenant with the Jewish people as a central and coherent
> part of ecclesial teaching. It rejects understandings of the new
> covenant that entail the abrogation or obsolescence of God's
> covenant with the Jewish people, of the Torah as a demarcator
> of Jewish communal identity, or of the Jewish people themselves
> . . . [which] address the question of ongoing Jewish particular-
> ity, and the relationship of interdependence and mutual blessing
> between Jew and gentile in Messiah.[9]

Thus, supporters of the post-supersessionist perspective contend that the "church" does not *displace* or *replace* historic Israel, but rather is *emplaced within* Israel. A variety of academic categories fit underneath the post-supersessionist theological "umbrella," so to speak. Those categories associated with studies of the apostle Paul's writings include the so-called "Radical Perspective on Paul,"[10] also known as the "Beyond the New Perspective on Paul" (BNP)[11] and, more recently, as the "Paul within Judaism Perspective."[12] They each argue that, for Paul, Israel and the "church"—that is, the universal, multi-ethnic community of Christ-followers—are *distinct yet covenantally related* socio-religious entities.[13]

9. Cited from the webpage of the Society for Post-Supersessionist Theology (spostst.org; accessed Oct. 15, 2019), which is also the definition of post-superses-sionism cited for this Cascade book series, *The New Testament After Supersessionism*.

10. For example, Ehrensperger, *That We May Be Mutually Encouraged*, 39; Zetter-holm, *Approaches to Paul*, 127–63; Eisenbaum, *Paul Was Not a Christian*, 216.

11. For a discussion of the similarities and differences between scholars in the New Perspective and Beyond the New Perspective (BNP) "camps," see Tucker, *Remain in Your Calling*, 7–10. BNP scholars include, but are not limited to, William S. Campbell, Kathy Ehrensperger, Anders Runesson, Magnus Zetterholm, Mark Nanos, David Ru-dolph, Pamela Eisenbaum, John Gager, Stanley Kent Stowers, Lloyd Gaston, Krister Stendahl, Markus Barth, Markus Bockmuehl, and J. Brian Tucker (Tucker, *Remain in Your Calling*, 8).

12. See especially, Nanos, "Introduction," 1–29. See also, Runesson, "The Question of Terminology," 53–78.

13. David Rudolph argues for the inclusion of a Messianic Jewish perspective in Christian theology ("Messianic Jews and Christian Theology," 58–84). Rudolph

As such, so the argument goes, by faith in the Jewish Christ, gentiles *qua* gentiles share with Torah-observant Jews *qua* Jews in God's salvation history with historic Israel.[14]

William Campbell gives greater clarity as to how a post-supersessionist reading of Paul in particular lends itself to an affirmation of the continuation of social and ethnic identity among the diverse followers of the Jewish *Christos*. He states that "The church and Israel [are] related but separate entities which should not be dissolved or merged in such a way that the sub-group identity of the one is lost or unrecognized."[15] With respect to Pauline Christ-followers, Campbell argues that they would not have seen themselves as some sort of new, a-cultural, universal association that is disconnected from its Jewish roots. Rather the multi-ethnic members of Paul's *ekklēsiai* ("assemblies/communities/congregations/'churches'") would have viewed themselves as remaining Jews and other ethnicities who, while ethnically diverse, are united under the transforming influence of Christ, and who express that diverse unity within their individual cultures.[16] Campbell contends, therefore, that Paul is a non-sectarian, Jewish reformist who sought to establish groups that were *theologically united with, yet socially distinct from*, the greater

---

envisions a five-fold post-supersessionist perspective that Messianic Jews would bring to Christian theology: "(1) God's covenant fidelity to the Jewish people, (2) that Jesus was Israel's Messiah and participated in the unique identity of the God of Israel, (3) that the *besorah* (gospel) was for Jews and Gentiles, (4) that Jesus-believing Gentiles were full members of God's people without becoming Jews, and (5) that Jesus-believing Jews should continue to live as Jews in keeping with Israel's calling to be a distinct and enduring nation" (http://mjstudies.squarespace.com/about-post-supersessionist/; accessed 1.29.2015).

14. Zoccali states that Nanos and Campbell appear to presume that "while the church existed for Paul under the umbrella of Israel, in as much as it consists of Jewish and gentile Christ-followers it can equally be seen as a larger entity encompassing both Israel and the nations" (*Whom God has Called*, 135). See Nanos ("Challenging the Limits," 221) and Campbell (*Paul*, 138). For a volume that extensively explores the inter-relationship between first-century CE Jewish Christ-followers and a Jewish heritage, see Skarsaune and Hvalvik, eds., *Jewish Believers in Jesus*, esp. 3–418.

15. Campbell, *Paul*, 101. Campbell notes that one cannot merely distinguish Israel from the church in the conviction that God's purposes for historical Israel are not yet fully realized (*Paul*, 99). One must rather establish to what degree Israel and the (predominantly gentile) church universal are mutually distinct entities in Paul's theology.

16. For an assessment of Campbell's argument, see Ralph J. Korner, on-line review of William S. Campbell, *Paul and the Creation of Christian Identity*, Bryn Mawr Classical Review (2009.07.42).

synagogue community, but who still accepted Jewish ethno-religious identity markers in their worship of the Jewish *Christos*.[17]

The need for a non-supersessionist re-reading of New Testament writings generally, and of the book of Revelation specifically, comes more clearly to the fore in Kendall Soulen's observation that, "For most of the past two millennia, the church's posture toward the Jewish people has come to expression in the teaching known as supersessionism, also known as the theology of displacement."[18] This supersessionist posture is not simply a theological exercise, however. Supersessionist theology inevitably translates into attitudes and actions. Some of these attitudes and actions have resulted in anti-Judaistic, and even anti-Semitic, attacks against those of a Jewish heritage.

The book of Revelation has contributed at least two specific theological underpinnings for some of those prejudicially supersessionist dealings with people of Jewish ethnicity. The first is a *textual witness*—the sentence "those who say they are Jews and are not, but are a synagogue of Satan" (Rev 2:9; cf. also 3:9). The second is a *theoretical framework* for reading the visionary content of the Apocalypse—the linearly chronological reading of eschatological events known as dispensationalism, which has been popularized through the best-selling *Left Behind* book and movie "franchise." This interpretive approach raptures the church universal into heaven to escape the worst of God's judgments upon the earth but leaves the Jews (and all other non-*Christos*-followers) behind to endure them.

With respect to the ostensible identification of Jews with Satan, in chapter 4 I will explore the history of Christian interpretation and offer an alternative approach that aligns the identity of John's adversaries analogously with Paul's judaizing adversaries in nearby Galatia.

With respect to undermining a linear dispensational eschatology, in chapter 8, I will explore how John's use of Jewish apocalyptic and Hebrew

17. Campbell, *Paul*, 66. Campbell makes this point very clear in his analysis of Paul's discussion on the weak and the strong in Romans 14:1—15:13. Campbell states that Paul "feels obliged to make it clear that accommodation to those living a Jewish way of life, far from being in conflict with his gospel, is demanded by it, if the conviction of fellow Christ-followers so requires" ("The Addressees of Paul's Letter to the Romans," 188).

18. Soulen, *God of Israel*, 1. Justin Martyr (second century CE) is one example. In "Justin Martyr's Argument with Judaism," Gaston states that Justin believes that "his group and its social and cultural worlds . . . supersede" those of Trypho and the Jews (*Anti-Judaism in Early Christianity*, 2.77).

prophetic literary devices creates a structure for the Apocalypse that facilitates a reiterative/repetitive reading of the Apocalypse's visionary content. In essence, I will argue that the very structure of Revelation's vision episode (1:9—22:20) would have communicated to John's seven *ekklēsiai* that they were already living in the *eschaton* and that the return of their *Christos* was imminent (1:3).

Restated more specifically, I will identify how, within Revelation's reiterative structure, it is only the sixth of the first six seals that depicts the *eschaton* and *parousia* of Jesus the *Christos*. The first five seals simply relate historical events already fulfilled by 70 CE with the Jerusalem temple's destruction. The telescopic seventh seal appears, then, to reiterate in greater detail and with expansive progression the condensed "reader's digest" version of eschatological events found in the sixth seal. I call this reiterative reading strategy "telescopic reiteration." The sociological effect of this reading strategy is that God's judgments, as described within the sixth seal/seventh seal/six trumpets/seventh trumpet/seven bowls, are experienced equally by all peoples. There is no exclusive divine favor or supersessionist privilege enjoyed by Jewish and gentile followers of Jesus, the Jewish *Christos*/Messiah. However, before proceeding to my exegetical, socio-historical, and literary analyses of Revelation's content, it is important first to clarify the semantic domains of the terminology that I use throughout this volume.

Definitions:
Supersessionism, Anti-Judaism, Anti-Semitism

Terence Donaldson has succinctly identified the three-way interplay between text, action, and attitude, not least through his analysis of three interrelated but distinct terms that are used in discussions on Christian self-definition(s): supersessionism, anti-Judaism, and anti-Semitism. Donaldson provides some definitional clarification for these three terms:

> If anti-Semitism refers to hateful attitudes and actions directed toward Jewish people per se—that is, an ethnic, social, and often political phenomenon—and if anti-Judaism refers to statements and formulations designed to defend and bolster Christian claims about themselves by denouncing what were perceived as Jewish counter-claims—that is, a theological and socio-religious phenomenon—then supersessionism refers to the kind of

Christian self-understanding that might be seen to undergird such anti-Judaic rhetoric and anti-Semitic activity.[19]

Donaldson brings to the fore the importance of understanding how throughout history the foundational and formative nature of supersessionist assumptions have informed and deformed Christian attitudes and actions towards their Jewish "cousins." Donaldson gives helpful definition to the term supersessionism: "Supersession describes a situation where one entity, by virtue of its supposed superiority, comes to occupy a position that previously belonged to another, the displaced group becoming outmoded or obsolete in the process. The term thus properly applies to a completed process of (perceived) replacement."[20] In other words, broadly defined, the term "supersessionism"[21]—otherwise known as "replacement theology"[22] or "fulfillment theology"—holds that the "promises and covenants that were made with the nation of Israel . . . now allegedly belong to another group that is not national Israel."[23]

Justin Martyr's *Dialogue with Trypho the Jew* (early second century CE) is one historical example of this replacement/supersessionist theology at work in anti-Judaistic ways. Justin comments that "you Jews" (11.2) no longer are foundational to the church since it is primarily a gentile entity (11.7–23), and thus as "the true spiritual Israel" (11.5) it no longer adheres to the old law and covenant since they have become "obsolete," and have been "abrogated" and replaced by a new law and covenant (11.2–4) reflected in the appended Scriptures, which are no longer "yours, but ours" (29.2). However, even Justin realizes that this supersessionist impulse inherently accedes priority of place to the Jews (*Dial.* 23, 30). Thus, rather than grant credibility to the first covenant, Justin undermines it by suggesting to Trypho the Jew that the old Israel

19. Donaldson, "Supersessionism," 6.

20. Donaldson, "Supersessionism," 6.

21. For an extensive review of supersessionist and post-supersessionist approaches, particularly as they apply to specific books of the New Testament, see the introductory sections of each of the volumes in this series, The New Testament After Supersessionism. For example, Zoccali, *Reading Philippians After Supersessionism*, 1–14; Windsor, *Reading Ephesians and Colossians After Supersessionism*, 1–25; Tucker, *Reading Roman After Supersessionism*, 1–14.

22. Waltke ascribes to a "replacement theology" in which "national Israel and its law have been permanently replaced by the church and the New Covenant" ("Kingdom Promises as Spiritual," 274).

23. Vlach, *Has the Church Replaced Israel?* 10.

and its institutions never had divinely authorized credibility in the first place since "your circumcision of the flesh, your Sabbath days, and, in a word, all your festivals . . . were imposed upon you, namely, because of your sins and your hardness of heart" (*Dial.* 18.2).[24]

Chris Zoccali highlights two basic approaches taken by supersessionist interpreters.[25] First is the approach represented by Ernst Käsemann who sees discontinuity between the "church" and historic Israel. Thus, Torah-observance and faith in Jesus as Messiah are incompatible. Second is the general approach represented by J. D. G. Dunn. He champions the view that there is continuity in salvation history between the "church" and historic Israel.[26] Thus, Torah-observance and faith in Christ are compatible for Jews who have become Christ-followers.

There are some who would position N. T. Wright into the supersessionist camp. Wright would disagree, though. He sees his approach as reflecting a "middle view," which he calls "incorporative christology."[27] He argues that those Jews who do not believe in Jesus as their *Christos* "have not been 'replaced' or 'disinherited' or 'substituted.'"[28] His "incorporative christology" emphasizes that, for Paul, Jesus is the continuation of Israel in the latter days, and that all Christ-followers, whether messianic Jews or gentiles, together compose latter-day Israel.[29] In this regard, Wright affirms that there is only one redeemed people of God/family of Abraham and that Jesus the Jewish *Christos*/Messiah is the *only* eschatological mediator of salvation.[30] As such, he does not affirm a two covenant system (Torah and Jesus).[31]

---

24. Donaldson, "Supersessionism," 7.

25. Zoccali, *Whom God Has Called*, 23ff. See, for example, Käsemann's work *Leib und Leib Christi* (1933).

26. Dunn, *Theology of the Apostle Paul*, 508; Wright, *Climax of the Covenant*, 237; Donaldson, *Paul and the Gentiles*, 306.

27. Wright, *Paul and the Faithfulness of God*, 2.825–34.

28. Wright, *Paul and the Faithfulness of God*, 2.1212.

29. The importance of this topic to Wright is evident in the fact that he dedicates his largest chapter of his two-volume work to it (chapter 10, 268 pages) and a significant section of the next chapter (chapter 11, 225 pages) (Wright, *Paul and the Faithfulness of God*, 2.774–1042 and 2.1043–1268, respectively).

30. Wright, claims that "Paul sees Jesus . . . [as] the True Jew, the one in whom Israel's vocation has been fulfilled" (*Paul and the Faithfulness of God*, 2.830).

31. For one example of a "two-covenant" perspective, see Eisenbaum, *Paul Was Not a Christian* (2009).

Even if Wright is correct that technically his view is not super-sessionist, it would still seem to hold socio-cultural ramifications. His "incorporative christology" raises the question as to the value that Jewish ethnic identity would have held, not least within the multi-ethnic *ekklēsiai* of Paul's and John's Christ-followers. This question comes to the fore in Wright's view that all ethnicities are incorporated into the Jewish national identity "Israel" through faith in the Jewish *Christos*, Jesus of Nazareth. However, I will suggest further on that Paul in particular does not view the corporate identity "Israel" as being transferable to gentile communities of *Christos*-followers. Rather, it is his distinctive use of the term *ekklēsia* as a trans-local, corporate identity for his multi-ethnic communities (Jews and gentiles) that served to incorporate gentiles into the *qāhāl* (supra-local *ekklēsia*) of Israel, even though they are not part of the ethnic '*am* (nation/Israel) of the Jewish people.

Supersessionism, Anti-Judaism(s), Anti-Semitism in the New Testament?

Although this volume is specifically focused around an exploration of a post-supersessionist reading of the book of Revelation, there is a broader issue at stake here. Not only the book of Revelation, but the corpus of the New Testament in general, has been tied to anti-Semitic (or anti-Judaic)[32] interpretations throughout the ages, which some have claimed even formed interpretive foundations upon which were built theological justifications for the Holocaust.[33] These are high interpretive stakes indeed. But these stakes are not only planted within modern history. Ancient historical readings are also affected. James D. G. Dunn observes that if anti-Semitic "attitudes are already inseparable from the scriptures on which they are based ... [then] does the attitude of post-70 NT documents indicate that the final breach, the decisive parting of the ways between Christianity and (rabbinic) Judaism has already happened?"[34]

Any answer to Dunn's question requires a nuanced review of Jewish and "Christian" relations relative to region, historical era, source reliability

32. Feldman notes that "the term anti-semitism is an absurdity which the Jews took over from the Germans ... the more accurate term would be 'anti-Judaism'" ("Is the New Testament Anti-Semitic?" 277).

33. For example, Eckhardt, *Elder and Younger Brothers* (1967). See also the Acknowledgments section in Nanos, *Mystery of Romans* (1996).

34. Dunn, "Question of Anti-Semitism," 179.

(e.g., elite bias in literary artefacts), and in the avoidance of anachronistic terminology (e.g., Christian, Christianity[35]).[36] Two key determining factors that must converge in any discussion related to a "parting of the ways" is the substantiveness of the interplay of social identification and social interaction between Jews and *Christos*-followers. One key way in which John socially identifies his communities in Roman Asia with Judaism(s) and Jewishness is through his designation of each of his communities as an *ekklēsia* ("assembly/congregation/church"). *Ekklēsia*, as a Jewish communal designator, has deep roots, not least in the Septuagint (LXX) and in the writings of Josephus and Philo. Within Revelation, John uses *ekklēsia* twenty times and always in reference to a permanent collective designation for a *Christos*-following community.[37] One question that I will seek to clarify is the degree to which their *ekklēsia* group identity reflects not just social identification with, but perhaps even social interaction with, synagogue contexts of non-Jesus-following Jews in Roman Asia.

Supersessionism, Anti-Judaism(s), Anti-Semitism in the Book of Revelation?

When one narrows the investigative focus from the New Testament down to the book of Revelation, then two specific phrases, which I have already mentioned, stand out as Exhibit A and B, so to speak, in the libel lawsuit that John's "supersessionist prosecutors" bring against him. Post-supersessionist interpreters, or "defense attorneys" if you will, need carefully to assess whether John's phrase, "those who say they are Jews and are not" (2:9; 3:9) is inherently supersessionist. Additionally, an assessment needs to be made about how intrinsically anti-Judaistic, and even anti-Semitic, impulses are tied to John's phrase "synagogue of Satan" (2:9; 3:9).

If one accords with the view that the author of Revelation is also the author of the Gospel of John, then any conclusions reached relative to his ostensibly anti-Jewish ideology in the Gospel may have relevance for

---

35. On the topic of avoiding anachronistic designations, see, Trebilco, *Self-designations*, 3; Mason, "Jews, Judaeans, Judaizing, Judaism," 482–88; and Runesson, "Inventing Christian Identity," 59–92.

36. For alternative perspectives to the Dunn volume that provide nuanced historical investigations, see the essays in Becker and Yoshiko Reed, eds., *Ways That Never Parted* (2007).

37. Rev 1:4, 11, 20; 2:1, 7, 8, 11, 12, 17, 18, 23, 29; 3:1, 6, 7, 13, 14, 22; 22:16.

one's characterization of John's ideological agenda in Revelation. The very Jewishness of the John of Revelation and the author of the Gospel would seem to preclude any anti-Semitic agenda, at least if one concurs with Paul Rainbow's observation that "if the author was Jewish to his bones, there will be a presumption against answering positively the post-Holocaust question of possible anti-Semitism or anti-Judaism in the Fourth Gospel."[38] Paul Anderson concurs and provides extensive support for his conclusion. He concludes that "the negative references to the *Ioudaioi* in John are almost exclusively confined to particular *Judean religious authorities* who engage Jesus pointedly in adversarial ways."[39] Jonathan Bernier adds further support to Anderson's conclusion with his rebuttal of interpretations that attach anti-Semitic intentions to John's *aposynagōgos* passages in the Gospel (John 9:22; 12:42).[40]

The Jewishness of John's literary *apokalypsis* will be explored in chapter 8. However, irrespective of how extensively John identifies socially with Jewishness, if positive social interaction cannot be demonstrated between John's *ekklēsiai* and Jewish synagogue communities in Roman Asia, then no positive determination can be made as to whether the very Jewishness of John's Apocalypse is meant (1) to expropriate Jewish identity markers (textual, religious, historical) for his multi-ethnic *Christos*-followers such that they are now depicted as having *replaced* Israel in God's salvific economy (i.e., supersessionism) or (2) to reinforce a Jewish heritage for his multi-ethnic *ekklēsiai* such that they are now depicted as having been further *emplaced* within Israel.[41]

Prior to looking at some exegetical "trees" (e.g., specific phrases like "synagogue of Satan") that might inform an interpreter's conclusion relative to John's ostensible "forest" of supersessionist sentiment, I will review issues related (1) to key word definitions (e.g., anachronistic terms), (2) to foundational theological motifs (e.g., the New Jerusalem, Hebrew Bible allusions, Jewish apocalyptic tropes), (3) to Jewish literary styles (e.g., genre, chiasm, visionary organizational devices), and (4) to socio-historical backgrounds (e.g., *ekklēsiai* and Jews in Roman Asia). The combined witness of these four foci will suggest the plausibility of reading the book of Revelation through post-supersessionist rather than

38. Rainbow, *Johannine Theology*, 62.

39. Anderson, "Anti-Semitism and Religious Violence," 265–311.

40. Bernier, *Aposynagōgos* (2013).

41. The seven *poleis* in Roman Asia are Ephesos, Smyrna, Pergamon, Thyatira, Sardis, Philadelphia, and Laodicea.

through supersessionist lenses. Such plausibility, then, limits any assumptions that John displays anti-Judaistic and/or anti-Semitic sentiments. Before proceeding to a focused analysis of theological motifs and sociohistorical backgrounds, I will first engage the issue of semantic domains for terminology such as religion, Judaism(s), Jew/ishness, Christianity, Christian, and church.

Definitions: Religion, Judaism(s), Jew/ishness, Christianity, Christian, Church/*Ekklēsia*

Religion

Modern (re)constructions of ancient "Judaism" and "Christianity" imply some sort of cohesive social reality called "religion" that was somehow separable from one's ethnic, cultural, national, and familial value structures. This is an anachronistic historical reconstruction. With respect to the term "religious," Bruce Malina states that "the social institutions known as religion and economics did not exist as discrete, self-standing, independent institutions in antiquity. In antiquity, there were only two focal, freestanding social institutions: kinship and politics, yielding domestic economy, domestic religion, political economy, and political religion."[42] Anders Runesson suggests three social levels upon which "religion" "played out" in antiquity: "a. Public level (civic/state/empire concerns); b. Semi-Public level/Association level (voluntary groups/ cults and their concerns); c. Private level (domestic, familial concerns)."[43] Steve Mason identifies six aspects of "religion" that apply to each of Runesson's three social levels, which were intrinsically interconnected in everyday life in early antiquity: *ethnos*, cult, philosophy, kinship traditions/domestic worship, astrology/magic, and voluntary association (*collegia/thiasoi*).[44] Thus, unlike modern terminological usages, one can see the veracity in Brent Nongbri's claims that in antiquity there was no conceptual category that could be designated as "religious" as opposed to "secular"; *all* of ancient life was inextricably interwoven with religiosity.[45]

---

42. Malina, "Social-Scientific Approaches," 170.
43. Runesson, "Was There a Christian Mission," 213.
44. Mason, "Jews, Judaeans, Judaizing, Judaism," 482–88.
45. Nongbri, *Before Religion* (2013).

Thus, when speaking of first-century realities, the terms "Judaism" and "Christianity" are reductionist and inappropriate.

Judaism(s)

If one does choose to speak of "Judaism," then the most one can intend thereby is the definition of "common Judaism" offered by E. P. Sanders: "*common* Judaism [is] that of the ordinary priest and the ordinary people. . . . *Common* is defined as what is agreed among the parties, and agreed among the populace as a whole."[46] More specifically, Sanders states that "common Judaism" is the convergence of four beliefs among first-century CE Jews: "belief that their God was the only true God, that he had chosen them and had given them his law, and that they were required to obey it" and that "the temple was the visible, functioning symbol of God's presence with his people and it was also the basic rallying point of Jewish loyalties."[47] Barclay claims that among Jews in the Mediterranean diaspora, "common Judaism" continued the "biblical demand for 'monolatry' . . . , [that is,] Jews may worship God only according to Jewish traditions."[48]

Notwithstanding the common belief structure that undergirded the various sects within "common Judaism," the elephant in the room still needs to be addressed: "What exactly are we talking about when we talk about 'Judaism'?"[49] I have already suggested that there was no such thing as a religion that could be separated from the three social levels that were interconnected in everyday-life realities such as *ethnos*, cult, philosophy, kinship traditions/domestic worship, astrology/magic, and voluntary association (*collegia/thiasoi*).

However, the question still needs to be asked as to whether within the ethnic/cultural life of Jews/Judeans there was such a thing as a consistent, integrated religious/ritualistic category one could call "Judaism"? Many biblical studies scholars have shifted away from using the term "Judaism" and taken to talking about "Judaisms" instead. That there are "Judaisms" is true not least from a diachronic perspective on the development of Jewish ethno-religious culture throughout the centuries (e.g., Second Temple Judaism, rabbinic Judaism, medieval Judaism). A

46. Sanders, *Judaism*, 11–12.
47. Sanders, *Judaism*, 241.
48. Barclay, *Jews in the Mediterranean Diaspora*, 430.
49. Boyarin, *Judaism*, xi.

synchronic analysis of the Second Temple period reveals sectarian diversity (e.g., Pharisees, Sadducees, Essenes, Zealots, Theraputae) within the unity of what Sanders calls "common Judaism."

Despite this unified diversity, Boyarin claims it is still problematic to use the term "Judaism": "There is no word in premodern Jewish parlance that means: 'Judaism' . . . [and that] when the term *Ioudaïsmos* appears in non-Christian Jewish writing—to my knowledge only in 2 Maccabees— it doesn't mean 'Judaism', the 'religion', but the entire complex of loyalties and practices, including dress, speech *and also* sacrifice, that mark off the people of Judea (what we now call 'Jewishness')."[50] Boyarin cites the apostle Paul as a prime example. He notes that "although [Paul *nee* Saul], for sure, [is] a *Ioudaios* and remaining one forever, he only uses *Ioudaïsmos* as something from which he has distanced himself, from which he is other as it is (now) other to him; it clearly no longer has for him quite the sense it had in Maccabees."[51]

Jew/ish/ness

While Boyarin provides a succinct definition of "Jewishness" (as a definition of *Ioudaïsmos*), Mark Nanos offers a more expansive definition, one which integrates universal continuity with particularized diversity, as does Sanders in his definition of "common Judaism," that applies across the diversity of "Judaism(s)," so to speak. Nanos suggests that:

> the adjective "Jewish" is used both to refer to those who are Jews ethnically and to the behavior generally associated with the way that Jews live, albeit variously defined, such as by different interpretations of Scripture and related traditions, different views of who represents legitimate authority, and different conclusions about what is appropriate for any specified time and place. The behavior can be referred to by the adverb "Jewishly," and as the expression of "Jewishness." In colloquial terms, one who practices a Jewish way of life according to the ancestral customs of the Jews, which is also referred to as practicing "Judaism," might be called a "good" Jew.[52]

---

50. Boyarin, *Judaism*, xi [author's emphasis].

51. Boyarin, *Judaism*, xi.

52. Nanos, "Paul's Non-Jews," 27–28.

Throughout this study, I will use the term "Jew/Jewish" rather than "Judean," in contradistinction to Steve Mason's approach. Mason asserts that *Ioudaikos* is better translated as "Judean" rather than the traditional "Jewish."[53] Mason applies the same rationale to his choice to translate *Ioudaios* as "Judean" rather than as "Jew." Anders Runesson provides a judicious critique of Mason's position, particularly as it relates to (1) Mason's "terminological distinction between ancient contexts . . . and the late antique and modern situation," and (2) "the name of the place associated with Jews," that is Judea.[54]

Even within the first few verses of the book of Revelation it becomes readily apparent that the ethno-religious ideology of its epistolary and visionary content would have broadly resonated with a Jewish audience. The author socially connects his seven *ekklēsiai* with a Jewish heritage in at least three ways: through his integration of Jewish literary genres, a Jewish *polis* ("city-state"), and a Jewish temple-*polis*.

Regarding Jewish literary genres, Greg Carey notes, firstly, that "Revelation stand[s] in a tradition of Jewish visions about Imperial rule."[55] Revelation correlates with Jewish visionary literature in its theology, terminology, imagery, and apocalyptic genre.[56] Revelation is unique among apocalypses, however, in having an epistolary framework. This fact opens up the possibility, not yet suggested by scholarship, that Revelation's covenant-based *apokalypsis*[57] may also reflect another Jewish

---

53. Mason, "Jews, Judaeans, Judaizing, Judaism," 457–512.

54. Runesson, "Inventing Christian Identity," 64–70.

55. Greg Carey highlights other Jewish elements in Revelation: "John himself is Jewish. His name is Jewish. The letters to the seven churches assume that the addressees are Jewish, . . . there has been no split between the followers of Jesus and 'Judaism.' . . . John builds his Apocalypse upon the foundation of Jewish Scriptures" ("The Book of Revelation," 159).

56. The Greek word ἀποκάλυψις (Rev 1:1), from which the modern word "apocalypse" is derived, simply means "revelation." Anything formally classified as apocalyptic has primary reference to the "revelation" of heavenly mysteries. These mysteries, though, need not necessarily be of an eschatological nature. Rather, they may simply involve heavenly "revelations" of what is true throughout all of human history and not just in the *eschaton* (e.g., the tour of the heavenly luminaries in 1 *Enoch*). For a list of the formal characteristics of the literary genre "apocalypse," see Appendix in Collins, "Jewish Apocalypses," 23–44.

57. Strand explores the covenantal format of the book of Revelation in relation to ancient Hittite suzerainty-treaty formulary in Rev 1:5—22:21 ("Further Note," 251–64).

literary genre: a "covenantal letter to the Diaspora."[58] These and other correlations with Jewish literary genres will be explored in further detail in chapter 8 ("John's *Ekklēsiai*: Jewish Literary Contexts").

A second way in which Revelation socially identifies with Jewishness is in its description of a hegemonic *polis* called "the New Jerusalem." The exponential size of John's eschatological Jerusalem immeasurably reinforces Jewish Second Temple conceptions of Jerusalem's centrality as the "navel/center of the earth."[59] Additionally, the expansive New Jerusalem builds out from, yet builds way beyond, previous Jewish depictions of an ostensible eschatological New Jerusalem. The primary depictions are found in Ezekiel 40—48[60] and in the seven Dead Sea scrolls that collectively are referred to as the "Description of the New Jerusalem" (hereinafter DNJ).[61] I will explore the ethnic, religious, cultural, and political ramifications of John's New Jerusalem imagery for a Roman Asia audience in chapter 7 (John's *Ekklēsiai* as Jewish "City Writ Large").

A third way in which John socially identifies with Jewishness is in his depiction of his eschatological *polis* as a Jewish *naos* (sanctuary or temple).[62] The cubic form of John's New Jerusalem is reminiscent of the shape ascribed to the Holy of Holies in the Israelites's desert tabernacle[63]

58. Verseput, "Genre and Story," 96–110.

59. Jerusalem is called the "navel of the earth" in *Jub.* 8.19 and is said to be situated in the "middle of the earth" in 1 *En.* 26.1, *Sib. Or.* 5.249, and *Arist.* 83. In the Hebrew Bible, Jerusalem is the city that is implicit in the descriptor "the navel/center of the earth" (Isa 24:13; Ezek 38:12).

60. A square wall surrounds the outer court of the temple (40:5). It measures 500 cubits (approx. 0.25 km) on each side (42:15–20; 45:2). Beyond this, the wall of the city itself forms an immense square 4,500 cubits on each side (approx. 2 km), with three gates per side.

61. So called by J. T. Milik with respect to 1Q32 in "Description de la Jerúsalem Nouvelle (?)," 134–45 + pl. XXXI. The seven documents which together comprise the DNJ are 1Q32, 2Q24, 4Q554–555ᵃ, 5Q15 and 11Q18 (ca. early to mid-second century BCE). See further in (1) Wise, "New Jerusalem Texts," 742; and (2) Aune, "Qumran and the Book of Revelation," 2.622–48.

62. John notes that he "saw no temple in the city, for its temple is the Lord God the Almighty and the Lamb" (21:22), that holiness extends to all parts of the temple-city ("nothing unclean will enter it"; 21:27), that only the pure will enter the city (21:27; 22:3, 14, 15), and that the (chariot) throne of the God and of the Lamb is set within its midst (22:3, 4).

63. In Exod 26:15–30 the vertical boards of the tabernacle are described as being ten cubits high.

and in the Solomonic Temple in Jerusalem.[64] Beginning with Rev 21:9, 10, John symbolically depicts the people of God who represent the faith legacy of Abraham's lineage (i.e., first-covenant ethnic Jews plus the multi-ethnic followers of the Jewish *Christos*) into a metaphorical temple-*polis* (Rev 21:9, 10). In this, he positions the New Jerusalem: (1) as being the eschatological fulfillment of the Jewish hope for a renewed and purified temple;[65] (2) and as mirroring Jewish portrayals of heaven as a temple, (3) even as a replacement for "heaven" itself.[66] I will discuss further this apparent conflation of people with a Jewish eschatological city/temple in chapter 7.

Christian

Steve Friesen speaks to the problem of using the term "Christian" anachronistically when reading John's Apocalypse: "Our use of 'Christian' to describe Revelation is a powerful and pervasive retrojection that warps our analysis of the first century by subtly redefining the churches as opposed to, and superior to, Judaism."[67] Although his use of the anachronistic term "church" lessens the force of his critique, in another (earlier) article, he enacts his critique by using John's own terminology such that he uses "saints" to talk about Christ-followers and "assemblies," rather than "church," when translating *ekklēsiai.*[68]

In this book the term "Christ-followers" (a.k.a. followers of the Jewish *Christos*/Messiah) functions as a technical designation for members of the Jesus movement during the first century CE. I have chosen to use "Christ-follower" rather than "Christ-believer" because it represents not just beliefs, but also practice. I reserve use of the term "Christian" for Late Antique Christ-followers (most of whom no longer valued or understood their Jewish roots as followers of Jesus as the *Christos*/Jewish Messiah).

---

64. 1 Kgs 6:20 describes the inner sanctuary as being 20 cubits cubed. See further Briggs, *Jewish Temple* (1999).

65. See Gärtner, *Temple* (1965).

66. John locates the throne of God and of the Lamb within the New Jerusalem before which "his servants will worship him ... reign forever and ever" (Rev 21:5). Prior to the eschatological consummation of all things (6:12—22:21), John had located the throne of God "in heaven" (4:1—5:14, esp. 4:1).

67. Friesen, "Sarcasm in Revelation 2—3," 142.

68. Friesen, "Satan's Throne," 351—73.

In this respect, I would also translate the three New Testament occurrences of the Greek term *Christianos* as "Christ-follower," rather than
as "Christian" (Acts 11:26; 26:28; 1 Pet 4:16; cf. *Did.* 12.4).[69] It is of interest to note that while both the book of Revelation and the epistle of
1 Peter are addressed to Christ-followers in Asia Minor, they do not use
the same group-identity terminology. 1 Peter uses the pluralistic identity
Christianoi for his predominantly Jewish Christ-followers in diasporic
Pontus, Galatia, Cappadocia, Roman Asia, and Bithynia (1 Pet 1:1). John
uses the collective term *ekklēsia*, but never *Christianoi*, for his (predominantly Jewish) associations in Roman Asia (Rev 2—3). What might be a
potential rationale for this social-identity phenomenon?

While the absence of evidence is not necessarily evidence of absence, it is instructive to note that the term *Christianos* only occurs in
the book of Acts when other ethnicities are depicted as being allowed
entrance into a Jewish sub-group of Christ-followers whose apostolic
loyalty lies with the apostles in Jerusalem (e.g., Greeks in Antioch, 11:26;
Herod Agrippa [Idumean] and Festus [Roman] in Palestine, 26:28).[70] If
this silence represents social reality, then one can see why Paul did not
use *Christianos* as a social identity for his Christ-follower associations.
He required a group identity moniker that had no socio-religious ties
to the apostles in Jerusalem. The word *ekklēsia* would have allowed him
to keep his multi-ethnic Christ-followers socio-religiously connected to
the Jewish roots of Jerusalem-loyal Christ-followers, while at the same
time implicitly tying them to his apostolic authority and to the fulfillment of his divinely mandated mission to those of non-Jewish ethnicity.
If Paul is distinctive among the early apostles in having adopted *ekklēsia*
as an ongoing group identity, then John's use of *ekklēsia* when addressing
the seven Christ-follower associations in Roman Asia implies that those
communities had existing socio-religious ties to the apostolic authority
of Paul, rather than to Peter and/or James.[71]

---

69. *Did.* 12:4 uses *Christianos* as insider terminology to instruct an itinerant
preacher that he should live "as a *Christianos* . . . not idle" (πῶς μὴ ἀργὸς μεθ᾽ ὑμῶν
ζήσεται Χριστιανός).

70. For an extensive review of the term *Christianos*, see Trebilco, *Self-designations*,
272–97.

71. For my rationale for claiming that Paul originated the use of the term *ekklēsia*
as an ongoing group designation in the Jesus Movement, see Korner, *Origin and Meaning of* Ekklēsia, 156–73.

To what do I attribute the above thesis? In Acts we are told that the sub-group identity *Christianoi* originated in Antioch. Its genesis occurs only after the exodus of exclusively Jewish *Christos*-followers from Jerusalem to faraway regions such as Phoenicia, Cyprus, and Cyrene. They were escaping the persecution in connection with Stephen's martyrdom. Of these, some Jewish *Christos*-followers from Cyprus and Cyrene stopped telling the gospel only to Jews (11:19) and shared it with Greeks in Antioch, with the result being that "a great number of people believed and turned to the Lord" (11:20).

If that is the case, then what might have been the prior group identity of those Jewish *Christos*-followers from Jerusalem? Some scholars suggest that they self-designated pluralistically as *hoi hagioi* ("the holy ones").[72] However, it would seem that with the addition of Greeks (gentiles), their exclusively Jewish identity (*hoi hagioi*) would no longer have been tenable for this newly formed *multi-ethnic* association of *Christos*-followers in Antioch. The term *Christianoi* would have been quite fitting given the new socio-ethnic realities of the Antiochean community. First, it maintained their indelible rootedness in a Jewish heritage (i.e., followers of the Jewish Messiah/*Christos*). Second, its semantic range was broad enough to allow for gentile inclusion (i.e., *Christianos* indicates a follower of the Jewish *Christos*, while maintaining boundary permeability regarding the ethnicity of that *Christos*-follower).

However, as I have already suggested, *Christianoi* could not function universally as a group designation, especially for those *Christos*-followers committed to the gentile mission of Paul. This is true not least in respect of the fact that the *Christianoi* of Antioch held their primary apostolic allegiance with the apostles of Jerusalem (e.g., Acts 11:19; 1 Pet 4:16). Thus, Paul would have needed a new collective group identity for his gentile mission. Paul chose *ekklēsia*.[73]

---

72. For a detailed discussion of the term *hoi hagioi* and its use as a group identity by early Christ-followers loyal to, or associated with, Jerusalem, see Trebilco, *Self-designations*, 104–37. Acts and some of the Pauline epistles both imply that *hoi hagioi* is an actual sub-group designation adopted by non-Pauline communities in the early Jesus Movement (e.g., Acts 9:13; Rom 15:25, 26, 31). Trebilco argues that the Aramaic-speaking Christ-followers referenced in Acts originally chose to self-designate as *hoi hagioi* because of that term's historic association with the eschatological "people of the *hoi hagioi*" in Daniel 7 (*Self-designations*, 134).

73. This point becomes even more convincing if one grants the point that the use of *ekklēsia* in Acts is evidence of provincialism (not anachronism) on the part of the redactor (Luke?) for the sake of clearer regionally-specific communication to his

If *ekklēsia* was "free" as a Jewish communal identity in the helle-nized diaspora, as Trebilco suggests,[74] then it would have served Paul's missional needs admirably given its roots within both Greek and Jewish civic cultures.[75] Paul's use of *ekklēsia* as a sub-group designation appears to have gained traction by the late first century CE given its use by other Christ-follower sub-groups, such as the communities of Matthew (Matt 16:18; 18:17), the "elder" John (3 John 6, 9), and the "prophet" John (Rev 2–3). Given that John also addresses his letter to *ekklēsia* associations it would seem logical to assume that any scholarly findings relative to the social, political, and religious implications of Paul having designated his communities as *ekklēsiai* should also serve to inform our understand-ings of Greco-Roman and Jewish perceptions in Roman Asia of John's *ekklēsiai* to whom he addresses his "revelation of Jesus Christ."

Christianity

It is in late antiquity that we see the political mission of (the almost ex-clusively gentile) Christ-followers reach its pinnacle with the edict of Theodosius I that all subjects of the Roman empire should worship the Christian God (380 CE). Daniel Boyarin, among others, claims that this formal decree represents the birth of "religion" as a separate social catego-ry[76] and of a "religion" that is now known as "Christianity."[77] Institutional

---

benefactor, Theophilus. Theophilus's potential residence was in Macedonia, which had provincially distinct ways of naming an *ekklēsia* (i.e., *ennomos ekklēsia*; cf. Acts 19:39). See a full discussion on the phrase *ennomos ekklēsia* and its connection to the Hellenic regions of Phokis and Thessaly, near Macedonia, in Korner, *Origin and Meaning of Ekklēsia*, 159–60.

74. Trebilco, "Why Did the Early Christians," 456.

75. See further in the next section, *Ekklēsia* Usage in the First Century CE.

76. Brent Nongbri argues that the absence of the "secular" in pre-modern, non-Western contexts makes "religion" a uniquely modern, Western concept (*Before Reli-gion*, 2013). For a judicious critique of Nongbri's conceptual paradigm, see Laughlin and Zathureczky, "Anatomy," 235–36.

77. Boyarin, "Semantic Differences," 77. Boyarin's argument for the birth of "reli-gion" as a social category is not a social-scientific argument based on the differentia-tion of proscribed descriptive and prescribed redescriptive discourse (e.g., Nongbri). Rather, he bases it upon the historically specific context of the fourth century CE. See Daniel Schwartz, however, who offers fourteen examples from Josephus where the Greek word *threskia* is best translated as "religion" rather than as a religious activity such as "worship," "cult," or "ceremony" (*Judeans and Jews*, 91–99).

representation of this "religion" fell to "the c/Catholic Church"[78] (*katholikē ekklēsia*),[79] with the religious rituals being enacted within purpose-built structures that also were called "churches" (*ekklēsiai*). This fourth-century conception of *ekklēsia* as a religious organization and as religious buildings ("church"), however, was a far cry from how the word *ekklēsia* ("assembly") is used not only in the book of Revelation but in the New Testament generally.

Church/*Ekklēsia*

As I have just noted, "church" is not a helpful translation for the Greek word *ekklēsia*. The late antique addition of the concepts of "organization" and "building" to the semantic domain of *ekklēsia*, which the English word "church" also includes, makes "church" an anachronistic term. As such, in this book I will either transliterate the Greek word (as *ekklēsia*) or translate *ekklēsia* as "assembly/gathering/meeting." The civic *ekklēsia* of Classical, Hellenistic, and Imperial timeframes was a regularly convened, juridically defined event during which members of the *dēmos* (the gathered citizenry)[80] assembled at a particular time (e.g., every thirty-six or thirty-nine days [Classical Athens]) and location (e.g., agora [civic market place]) to carry out specific governmental functions as directed by the *boulē* (civic councilors). There is a long history of interaction between *boulai* and *dēmoi* within *ekklēsiai* as described in both literary and epigraphic sources. These date from the fifth century BCE into the Imperial period (27 BCE–284 CE). Literary sources include, but are not

---

78. Inscriptional occurrences of *katholikē ekklēsia* include references (1) to a building (*Pan du désert* 27; 340/1CE: ὁ κατασκευάσας ἐνταῦθα καθολικὴν ἐκκλησίαν), (2) to an institutionalized organization (*IGLSyr* 5 2126; n.d.; [ὡς ἐνετύπωσεν(?) ὁ θεοτίμητος Γρηγόρι]ος ἡμῶν πατριά[ρχης], [κατὰ τοὺς ἱεροὺς κανόνας(?) τῆς καθολικῆς ἐκκ]λησίας·), and (3) in the non-universal sense, to a regional community of Christians (*RIChrM* 235; Makedonia [Edonis], Philippoi; fourth century CE: τῆς καθολικῆς καὶ ἀποστολικῆς ἁγίας ἐκκλησίας Φιλιππησίων).

79. During the earlier patristic era, however, the term *katholikē ekklēsia* referred simply to the "worldwide church" ("universal/catholic church") (cf. Polycarp, Introduction: "The *ekklēsia* of God which dwells in Smyrna to the *ekklēsia* of God which dwells in Philomelium and to all the sojournings of the holy *catholic ekklēsia* in every place." In that same vein, see also *Smyrn.* 8:1a, 2; 16:2; 19:2.

80. When the term δῆμος (*dēmos*) occurs within an enactment formula (e.g., ἔδοξε δήμωι) that was motioned and approved before an ἐκκλησία (*ekklēsia*), δῆμος always refers to the body of the full citizenry in Athens that was gathered for the purpose of conducting civic business (Rhodes, "Epigraphical Evidence," 93).

limited to, Plato (429–347 BCE),[81] Xenophon (*c.* 430–355 BCE),[82] and Plutarch (*c.* 46–120 CE).[83] Epigraphic sources that mention *ekklēsiai* span the centuries (fifth century BCE to the early third century CE), and hail from geographically diverse regions such as the Aegean Islands (e.g., Delos),[84] central Greece (e.g., Delphi),[85] and Asia Minor (e.g., Pisidia[86] and Caria[87]).[88]

The English words "assembly/gathering/meeting" have a broad enough semantic domain to communicate the three primary meanings of *ekklēsia* found within Greek (epigraphic and literary), Jewish (literary) and Christ-follower (literary) sources: (1) a formal or informal assembly/gathering/meeting for discussion and decision-making purposes; (2) a temporary group designation (*ekklēsia*) during the duration of that group's gathering within an *ekklēsia* (assembly/gathering/meeting); and (3) only in Philo (*Virt.* 108) and in New Testament writings is *ekklēsia* used as a permanent, ongoing group designation, applicable even when they disperse at the conclusion of their *ekklēsia* ("assembly").[89] This third fact means that the Greek civic semantic domain for *ekklēsia* was insufficient by itself to fulfill Paul's need for a non-civic group identity by which to designate in an ongoing fashion his sub-group of *Christos*-followers. Only in Philo do we find extant evidence of an ancient precedent for Paul's *ekklēsia*-identity project: a non-civic, semi-public association that self-identified in an ongoing fashion as an *ekklēsia*.

But one might ask what rhetorical end this third meaning of *ekklēsia* served relative to the mission of *Christos*-followers generally, and to the gentile/Greco-Roman mission of Paul specifically? *Ekklēsia* is used in Jewish sources as a supra-local descriptor (the "assembly/congregation"

81. Plato writes about a civic *ekklēsia* thirteen times.

82. Xenophon mentions a civic *ekklēsia* twenty times.

83. Plutarch speaks of a civic *ekklēsia* 142 times.

84. For example, *IDelos* 1502 (Delos, 148/7 BCE) reads, δεδόχθαι τεῖ [βουλεῖ τοὺς λαχόν]τας προέδρους εἰς [τὴν ἐπιοῦσαν ἐκκλησίαν] χρηματίσαι περὶ [τούτων].

85. For example, *FD* III 4:47 (Delphi, 98 CE).

86. For example, *Mon. Ant.* 23.1914.259, 172 (Pisidia, Sagalassos, fourth/third century BCE).

87. For example, *BCH* 1972, 435–36 (Caria, found at Aphrodisias, second/first century BCE).

88. For discussion of *ekklēsia* mentions in Greek inscriptions, see esp. Korner, *Origin and Meaning of* Ekklēsia, 22–79.

89. See my full analysis of how *ekklēsia* was used in Greek, Jewish, and Christ-follower contexts (Korner, *Origin and Meaning of* Ekklēsia, 2017).

of Israel during their desert wanderings) and as a local descriptor (a Jewish sub-group/association, e.g., Philo, *Virt.* 108; cf. Hebrew equivalent *qāhāl* in 4QMMT, the Damascus Document [CD 7.17, 11.22, 12.6]).[90] This reality suggests the possibility also of identifying *ekklēsia* as a Jewish synagogue/community term, not only as a Greek civic term.

The Jewish and Greco-Roman backgrounds for *ekklēsia* usage are both of equal importance in providing missional relevance for Paul's communities with Greco-Roman and Jewish outsiders (and insiders). However, as just indicated, the *civic* Greek *ekklēsia* in and of itself could not provide Paul with a sufficient precedent for permanently designating a non-civic group (e.g., an association) as an *ekklēsia*. This is because there is no extant example in the inscriptional, papyrological, or literary records of a non-Jewish association self-designating collectively as an *ekklēsia*.[91] There is only one source that holds promise in this regard, and it is a Jewish literary one (*Virt.* 108). I will explore this issue more fully in chapter 6 ("*Ekklēsia* as a Jewish Synagogue Term").

The above supra-local and local Jewish usages of the term *ekklēsia* gave Paul a ready-made solution for a key ethno-religious conundrum: If gentiles could not collectively assume the designation "Israel," but yet, through faith in the Jewish *Christos*, could share in historic Israel's covenantal benefits, then Paul's designation of his multi-ethnic communities as *ekklēsiai* provided them with an inherently Jewish collective identity other than "Israel" by which he could institutionally integrate gentiles *qua* gentiles into theological continuity with Torah-observant Jews *qua* Jews.[92] In other (Hebrew) words, in analogous fashion to the supra-local identity of God's people during the desert wanderings (i.e., the *ekklēsia* of the LORD/Israel), gentiles can become part of the *qāhāl*[93]

90. Within CD, *qěhal* occurs at 7.17 ("the King is the assembly"), 11.22 ("trumpets of the assembly"), and 12.6 ("he may enter the assembly").

91. See my discussion in *Origin and Meaning of* Ekklēsia, 52–68.

92. By "gentiles qua gentiles" I mean that gentiles could become fully constituted followers of the Jewish *Christos* without being required to become Jewish proselytes and/or take up any one, or all, of the Jewish covenantal identity markers such as circumcision, dietary restrictions, and festival observances.

93. Within the ancient *qāhāl/ekklēsia* there were those who were not members of the people of Israel (*'am*). Not dissimilarly, Paul's *ekklēsiai* were comprised of individuals who belonged to the people of Israel (i.e., the ethnically defined *'am*) and of individuals who did not belong to the *'am*/ethnic Israel. This provides at least one rationale for why *ekklēsia* functioned well as a group designation for Paul's communities: *ekklēsia* had the ability to create a collective entity (in the Jewish *Christos*) without

(the socio-political *ekklēsia*/assembly [of Israel]), but not part of the *'am* (the ethnic people/nation of Israel).[94]

---

erasing distinction between Israel and the nations.

94. See further in Korner, "*Ekklēsia* as a Jewish Synagogue Term: A Response," 128.

2.

Ekklēsia *Usage in the First Century* CE

Ekklēsia: Greco-Roman Contexts and Johannine Usage

The book of Revelation is addressed to seven *ekklēsiai* of Christ-followers in the Roman province of Asia, each of which is located in a different "city-state" (*polis*).[1] These seven city-states lie within a roughly circular pattern, each being separated by about fifty miles. As such, they were ideally situated as centers of communication for John, Revelation's author, and for the apostle Paul, who ostensibly founded the *ekklēsiai* in Asia (cf. Acts 18:18—19:41). The word *ekklēsia* occurs twenty times in Revelation, always in reference to the permanent designation of a community.[2] A positive perception of Johannine *ekklēsiai* by Greco-Romans would have been enhanced if they also perceived John's associations as Jewish synagogue entities. Such a conclusion, however, would probably only hold true if the Revelation of John pre-dates the Jewish Revolt (66–74 CE). Up until that historical juncture, Jewish synagogue communities had a long diasporic history of benign and/or positive engagement with civic authorities, institutions, and practices. I will discuss the dating options for the book of Revelation in chapter three.

John's *ekklēsia* associations lived in a political era that was undergoing significant change with respect to the empowerment of the ordinary citizenry (e.g., associations) in relation to the official power structures of

1. The seven *poleis* in Roman Asia are Ephesos, Smyrna, Pergamon, Thyatira, Sardis, Philadelphia, and Laodicea.

2. Rev 1:4, 11, 20; 2:1, 7, 8, 11, 12, 17, 18, 23, 29; 3:1, 6, 7, 13, 14, 22; 22:16.

municipalities (e.g., *ekklēsiai, boulai*). Onno van Nijf calls this empowering phenomenon within the Greek East, "political culture." It began to expand exponentially with the Imperial period (27 BCE–284 CE). Political culture is an unofficial political framework through which non-elites could wield informal socio-political influence over the formal political institutions and processes. Political culture, in its essence, is the social expression of the underlying mentality and practices that inform political practice. It is particularly evident in Imperial-period inscriptions from Asia Minor *poleis* ("city-states"). Onno van Nijf identifies three non-institutional aspects of vibrant political culture: festivals, monuments of leadership (e.g., honorific inscriptions), and emotive communities.[3] As such, political culture is an informal power structure in Roman Asia that parallels the official civic power structures ("rule of law") in Greco-Roman city-states (e.g., the city elites [oligarchs], councilors [*boulai*],[4] and magistrates [*archontes*]).[5]

Community groups (associations) were key participants in the political culture of Roman Asia. Paul Foucart was one of the first to observe that "associations imitated the structure of the *polis*,"[6] which brings Kloppenborg to suggest that the moniker "city writ small" is an apt descriptor for the organizational structure and *ethos* of associations.[7] Philip Harland highlights the practice of "city" mimesis by associations in their adoption of civic titles for their associational leadership positions.

---

3. Seminal discussions of vibrant political culture in Imperial period *poleis* in Asia Minor include: (1) Nijf, *Civic World*, 215–42; (2) Zuiderhoek, "On the Political Sociology," 417–45; Zuiderhoek, *Politics of Munificence* (2009); (3) Mitchell, "Festivals, Games, and Civic Life," 183–93; and (4) Pleket, "Political Culture," 204–16. Mitchell and Pleket both argue that politics permeated cultural forms and religious life.

4. Beginning with the Classical period, members of the *boulē* (the *bouleutai*) had administrative oversight of civic, foreign, and regional affairs. They brought forward recommendations during an *ekklēsia* for ratification or revision by the *dēmos*. See further in Sinclair (*Democracy and Participation*, 105, 229) and in Hansen (*Athenian Assembly*, 220).

5. The *archontes*/magistrates in Athens were overseers of the *dikastēria* or popular courts which heard civil and criminal cases and met upwards of 200 times a year (Hansen, *Athenian Assembly*, 211).

6. Kloppenborg, "Edwin Hatch," 212–38. See also Kloppenborg, "Collegia and *Thiasoi*," 16–30. Harland (*Associations*, 106) cites Jean-Pierre Waltzing's observation (1902) that associations were, in numerous ways, "a veritable city within the city, a small country within the large one."

7. "Collegia and *Thiasoi*," 26–27. Even Roman associations (*Romaioi*) adopted a type of mini-city terminology: see Nijf, "Staying Roman—Becoming Greek" (2012).

Harland mentions "crossovers in [civic] titles such as 'overseer' or 'bishop' (*episkopos*), 'elders' (*presbyteroi*), 'servant'/'deacon' (*diakonos*), and 'patroness' (*prostatis*)."[8] Anyone familiar with Pauline writings, in particular, will note immediately that a significant crossover exists between the titles used for his *ekklēsia* officers and for Greco-Roman *polis* officials.

Associations, as "cities writ small," wielded informal power with the city elites/oligarchs through their provision of "social capital" via euergetism, also called benefaction. Zuiderhoek calls this phenomenon the "politics of redistribution."[9] Acts of munificence by individuals and associations towards the elites had as their overarching priority the avoidance of *intra-polis* conflict through preservation of the *status quo*. Euergetism served both internal and external political functions.[10]

Internally, euergetism allowed the lines of political influence between the oligarchic elite and the *dēmos* to flow in both directions. Through the provision of social capital, such as honorific inscriptions and monuments, the *dēmos* (e.g., associations) received reciprocal material and "social wealth" from the oligarchs.[11] Van Nijf argues that the public use of honorific language implicitly pressures the honorand to live up to the public impression created of him or her.[12] This "politics of redistribution" allowed associations, in particular, to play an active informal role in the process of political identity-construction, even without having any formal political offices, roles, or powers.[13]

8. Harland, *Associations*, 182 (see 299 n. 4 for his epigraphic references). Kloppenborg agrees with Edwin Hatch's suggestion that "ἐπίσκοπος ... along with ἐπιμελητής was a key title for a financial administrator in associations and in the *polis*. The terms 'elders' (πρεσβύτεροι) and 'bishops' (ἐπίσκοποι) referred to the same persons, but to different roles: as members of the council they would be called πρεσβύτεροι, but as administrators they were ἐπίσκοποι" ("Edwin Hatch," 214).

9. Zuiderhoek, "Political Sociology," 435.

10. See Zuiderhoek for his study of how high mortality rates and short lifespans affected the demography of social elites. He hypothesizes that public euergetism served an important private function for elites in memorializing their family lineage ("Oligarchs and Benefactors," 185-96).

11. Zuiderhoek notes that public rituals associated with euergetism, "did much to ease possible tensions arising from this political configuration by creating a dynamic exchange of gifts for honours which allowed the elite to present itself as a virtuous, benevolent upper class, while simultaneously allowing the demos [sic] to affirm (and thereby legitimate) or reject this image through the public allocation of honours" (Zuiderhoek, "Political Sociology," 444).

12. Nijf, *Civic World*, 73-130; Nijf, "Public Space," 217-23.

13. Plutarch, *Mor.* 814F-815A. Fear of Roman intervention is explicitly cited as the reason for dismissing an "illegal" *ekklēsia* that was hastily assembled in Ephesos

Externally, "the politics of redistribution" helped the oligarchic elite to prevent outside Roman interference in civic affairs. As long as order was maintained, Rome was not overly particular about how a *polis* self-governed. Civic disturbances, however, are widely attested throughout Roman Asia and beyond during the first two centuries CE.[14] This required an ongoing negotiation of power between the oligarchic elites and the citizenry (*dēmos*) so as to maintain the *status quo* of *pax Romana*. As an appeasement process for the expressed and perceived demands of the *dēmoi*, euergetism facilitated civic harmony.[15] Zuiderhoek states that this three-way tug of war involving imperial authorities, civic elites, and popular assemblies "helps to explain the remarkable proliferation of euergetism we see in the eastern provinces during the first two centuries."[16]

Even though the democratic freedom associated with Classical-era popular assemblies (sixth to the late fourth century BCE) had waned by the Imperial period, the political relevance of *ekklēsiai*, not least in Asia Minor, continued (e.g., Termessos).[17] Given the oversight of regional politics by Roman functionaries (e.g., governors) and of civic politics (e.g., *ekklēsiai*) by the ruling elites/oligarchs, Rome's concern over the potential for the growth of seditiousness through civic self-governance would have lessened. As such, I have argued that for a semi-public association to have used political terminology, even to have self-identified as an *ekklēsia*, would not have been seen as a seditious or counter-imperial move by Roman authorities.[18] Some of my rationale for that conclusion is as follows.

First, Richard Ascough argues that even though associations "often took their nomenclature from the civic institutions [it was] more often

---

(Acts 19:23–41, esp. vv. 39–41).

14. Zuiderhoek cites examples of civic unrest, though not of revolt, throughout the Greek East during the Imperial period ("Political Sociology," 442 n. 61).

15. Zuiderhoek even goes so far as to claim that, "to a large measure, the well-being and stable functioning of the Empire depended on the vitality of its cities, . . . [hence] euergetism's contribution to civic socio-political stability may well have been one of the keys to the survival and flourishing of the Roman imperial system as a whole during the first two centuries AD" (*Politics of Munificence*, 5).

16. Zuiderhoek, "Political Sociology," 435.

17. Van Nijf claims that second-century CE Termessos "was technically still a democracy" with a regular assembly (*ennomos ekklēsia*) in which recommendations of the *boulē* were considered by upwards of 4,500 citizens ("Public Space," 234).

18. See further in Korner, "*Ekklēsia* of Early Christ-Followers in Asia Minor," 455–99; Korner, *Origin and Meaning of Ekklēsia*, 22–80; 182–87.

not in direct competition but in the sense of 'imitation as flattery."[19] Paul, at the very least, seeks to inculcate this type of pro-*dēmokratia* impulse for his *ekklēsia* association in Galatia. In Gal 3:28, Paul reminds them that in their common commitment to the Jewish *Christos* there must be no communal stratification along gender, social, economic, and ethnic lines.

Second, civic self-depictions by associations do not necessarily express anti-Roman ideology by virtue of the fact that many inscriptional examples of associations self-presenting as "cities writ small" *pre-date* the rise of Roman hegemony in the Greek East (e.g., Roman Asia). Thus, since the original rationale for the adoption of civic terminology by semi-public associations was not anti-Roman, it would seem logical to assume that the continuation of that practice into the Imperial period also would not reflect counter-Imperial sentiments.

Third, it would seem that by ascribing his Roman Asia associations with a political identity (*ekklēsia*), John would have provided them with a political "defense mechanism" that could counter any outsider misperceptions of socio-political subversion among his communities. It would have been difficult for Roman suspicions to have been aroused over a Christ-follower association in Roman Asia, the socio-religious *praxeis* of which portrays it as a paragon of civic order and *dēmokratia*, and the very name of which situates it in the center of political culture of Asia Minor.

So how closely does John's presentation of his *ekklēsiai* mirror the positive "city writ small"/"imitation as flattery" approaches taken by other Greco-Roman and Jewish associations in Roman Asia? I have argued elsewhere that if John had simply called his associations "*ekklēsiai*," rather than also intrinsically associating them with the counter-imperial symbol of the New Jerusalem (21:9, 10),[20] then Greco-Roman outsiders, not least municipal and imperial authorities, could very well have viewed them as being positive contributors to the political culture of Roman Asia in the first century CE. This perception is discordant with the way in which John characterizes Imperial Rome, and all other gentile religio-political worldviews that are not grounded in the Jewish *Christos*. John's visionary content in the Apocalypse is highly counter-imperial, even supersessionally so (e.g., the New Jerusalem).[21] John's need to in-

19. Ascough, "Voluntary Associations," 159 n. 47.

20. See further in my chapter on John's *ekklēsiai* and political and ethnic (Jewish) contexts in Roman Asia.

21. For example, (1) the seven hills/heads on which Babylon sits (17:9) symbolically represents the historical city of Rome, which was situated among seven hills and (2) the "footprint" of the New Jerusalem (2,220 km/12,000 stadia) would have

clude the very counter-imperial New Jerusalem becomes more logical if in fact his *Christos*-followers would have perceived their *ekklēsia* title as communicating a benign, if not even positive, political stance towards imperial Rome. I will explore the counter-imperial imagery of the New Jerusalem more extensively in chapter 7 (John's *Ekklēsiai* as Jewish "City Writ Large").

Ekklēsia: Jewish Contexts and Johannine Usage

Given that Paul's *ekklēsiai* were founded in some of the same cities to whom John is later to write his "revelation of Jesus the *Christos*" (Rev 1:1), John's seven *ekklēsia* associations would have gained similar *ekklēsia*-related socio-ethnic benefits, not least with respect to their social identification with four Jewish usages of the word *ekklēsia*. The four Jewish *ekklēsia* usages serve to enhance the possibility of a post-supersessionist reading of John's Apocalypse: (1) the Hebrew *ekklēsia* of Israel in the desert, (2) the Jewish semi-public *ekklēsia* associations of Philo in Alexandria (first century CE; *Virt.* 108), (3) the Jewish public *ekklēsiai* of Judea and Galilee (2nd century BCE to 1st century CE), and (4) the multi-ethnic *ekklēsiai* of Pauline Christ-followers (first century CE). I will explore Jewish usages of the word *ekklēsia* further in chapter 6.

The Jewish author of Revelation affirms and further inculcates a Jewish heritage for his multi-ethnic *ekklēsiai* through literary and symbolic means. Literarily, the Jewish John's creative genius dips deeply and liberally into a multiplicity of Jewish literature (Hebrew Bible prophets, Second Temple writings), literary devices (chiasm, visionary devices), writing styles (rhetoric, Hebraisms), genres (prophecy, apocalypse), and symbolism. Perhaps his most obvious affirmation of the enduring value of Jewishness, into the *eschaton* and beyond, is John's vision of both a heavenly Jewish *cosmos-polis* and temple-*polis* that descends to earth in the *eschaton* (Rev 21 and 22), and perhaps even already in this present aeon at the coming of the universal *ekklēsia* on the day of Pentecost (Acts 2 and Rev 4—5).[22] I will explore these issues further in chapters 7 and 8.

---

straddled both Jerusalem and Rome as the victorious eschatological city/temple for all of eternity (22:16).

22. See chapter 7 in this book for my rationale for suggesting that inaugurated eschatology is at play relative to John's vision of the New Jerusalem, both visible (Rev 21—22) and invisible (Rev 4—5; the rainbow and twenty-four elders).

3.

Dating Considerations

Continuity between Pauline and Johannine *Ekklēsiai*?

The compositional dating the book of Revelation is by no means a *fait accompli*. It has been dated as early as Claudius (41–54 CE) or as late as Trajan (98–117 CE). However, the very early dating proposed by Epiphanius (a fourth-century bishop of Salamis) was no doubt based on a case of mistaken identity for Nero Claudius.[1] The very late dating is only suggested by authorities many centuries subsequent to the book's writing (Dorotheus, sixth century CE; Theophlact, eleventh century CE).[2] The majority of scholarship favors a compositional date for Revelation either toward the end, or immediately after the reign of Nero (68–69 CE)[3] or during that of Domitian (81–96 CE).[4]

One may wonder how an evaluation of the compositional date for the book of Revelation relates to assessing whether it inculcates supersessionist ideology. The primary issue this question illuminates is the

---

1. Guthrie, *New Testament Introduction*, 277.

2. Mounce, *Book of Revelation*, 15.

3. Minority opinion dates Revelation to Nero's reign of 54–68 CE. Scholars of this opinion include: Kooten, "The Year of the Four Emperors," 205–48; Bell, "Date of John's Apocalypse," 93–102; Rowland, *Open Heaven*, 403–407;Wilson, "Problem of the Domitianic Date," 587–605; Marshall, *Parables of War* (2001); Marshall, "Who's on the Throne?" 123–41; Slater, "Dating the Apocalypse to John," 252–58; Rojas-Flores, "Book of Revelation," 375–92; and Wilson, "Early Christians," 163–93.

4. The majority consensus is well represented by commentators such as Aune, *Revelation* (WBC 52A-C, 1997–98), Thompson, *Revelation* (1998), and Beale, *Book of Revelation* (1999).

perceived connection, or lack thereof, with the *ekklēsiai* in Roman Asia (e.g., Ephesus) and surrounding provinces/regions that the apostle Paul visited and/or corresponded with (e.g., Phrygia, Galatia). If John is writing Revelation during Nero's reign (54–68 CE), then he may be writing in the same timeframe to the same *ekklēsiai* to which Paul wrote/was writing.

In this chronological scenario, there need not be any necessary assumption of theological (e.g., non-supersessionism) or socio-religious discontinuity between the Roman Asia communities to which each was writing. For example, this would allow the possibility that John's eschatology is not discontinuous with Paul's inaugurated eschatology, especially as it is expressed in Paul's ostensible letter to the *ekklēsia* in Ephesus (e.g., Eph 2:1–10).[5] The possibility that Paul is the actual author of what many scholars consider to be a pseudepigraphic post-70 CE letter (i.e., deutero-Pauline) is championed by Douglas Campbell in his (controversial) claim that the book of Ephesians is one of Paul's earliest letters.[6] The earliest manuscript evidence for the epistle to the Ephesians does not include the phrase "to the Ephesians."[7] Thus, this (unaddressed) letter could have been meant as a circular letter, not unlike the epistolary apocalyptic prophecy that John circulated among seven *ekklēsiai* in Roman Asia. The potential addressees of the ostensible letter to the Ephesians may then also have included Pauline *ekklēsiai* in the Lycus River valley (e.g., Colossae, Hierapolis, Laodicea). It is estimated that already by 62 BCE the Jewish population in the Lycus River Valley numbered around 50,000.[8]

In Douglas Campbell's (controversial) view the *ekklēsia* in Laodicea was the first to receive Paul's "Ephesian" letter.[9] Campbell claims that Paul wrote this letter during his few months of imprisonment in Apamea

5. For a comparison of Pauline eschatology with John's millennial eschatology, see Page, "Revelation 20," 31–43. For a review of Paul's inaugurated eschatology, see esp. Ladd, *Theology of the New Testament*, 70.

6. Campbell, *Paul*, 75–90.

7. See the helpful discussion of textual variants for Eph 1:1 by Campbell, *Framing Paul*, 309–13.

8. Barclay, *Letters to the Philippians*, 93. See also Trebilco, *Jewish Communities* (1991).

9. Campbell, *Paul*, 76, 179. Campbell argues that three of Paul's epistles were composed during his imprisonment in Apamea: Ephesian, Colossians, and Philemon. Campbell identifies the "Ephesian" letter as being the letter that Paul speaks of having sent to the Laodiceans, who are just down the road from the Colossian *ekklēsia* (Col 4:16). Paul enjoins the Colossians to exchange epistles with the Laodiceans (Col 4:16).

in mid-50 CE.[10] Apamea is a city east of the Lycus Valley.[11] Given the textual correspondences between "Ephesians" and Colossians, and between Colossians and Philemon, Campbell dates all three concurrently as an interrelated cluster that were delivered by the same messenger. The Laodicean *ekklēsia* was encouraged by Paul to share his letter (Ephesians?) with the Colossians (Col 4:16). The Laodiceans are also the recipients of John's apocalyptic letter (Rev 3:14–22; cf. 1:3).

Even if one cannot demonstrate a concurrent compositional timeframe for both letters, it is nonetheless worth observing that a note of theological continuity does exist between them. Paul's eschatology in Ephesians can be said to correspond with John's eschatology. Paul implies a correlation between the corporate resurrection of God's people—past, present, and future—and Christ's resurrection in Ephesians (2:3–10; the "captives" of Eph 4:9–11). If one assumes that the twenty-four elders in Revelation's throne scene (Rev 4—5) symbolically also refer to the people of God who were corporately resurrected when the Lamb took his seat upon the heavenly throne, then John's "inaugurated eschatology" would have held a note of theological familiarity for the *ekklēsia* members in Laodicea/Ephesus, who previously had known of Paul's inaugurated eschatology.

Another rationale that is suggestive of an early dating for the Apocalypse of John is its theological and linguistic correlations with the Gospel of John.[12] Given the fact that the Gospel of John differs so significantly from the Synoptic Gospels, not least in its presentation of the cosmic dimensions of Jesus, which are also found in the book of Revelation, it begs the question as to (1) whether Revelation's "John" is the author of the Gospel, and, if so, (2) whether "John" saw his *apokalypsis* ("revelation") of Jesus before writing the Gospel. Some of the christological correlations between Revelation and the Gospel include the concepts of Jesus

---

10. See Campbell's revised Pauline timeline in *Framing Paul*, 412–14.

11. For an extensive review of Campbell's rationale in identifying Paul's imprisonment in Apamea, see his book, *Framing Paul*, 254–338 (ch. 5).

12. I wish to acknowledge with gratitude the research work done for me on correlations between Revelation and the Gospel of John by my MTS student Caley Tse (2018). She has noted many more correlations than I list here.

(1) as light,[13] (2) as Logos/Word,[14] (3) as very God,[15] (4) as judge,[16] (5) as heavenly messenger,[17] and (6) as sacrificial lamb.[18] Theologically, both books openly exhibit dualism[19] and share a motif of division.[20] Henry Barclay Swete provides an extensive review of linguistic correlations such as similar words (e.g., testify, sign, word), similar word constructions, phrases, parallelisms, explanations, antithetical statements, and common use of the article for emphasis.[21] There is also one particular literary correlation of note with respect to how each book uses the clause "after this/after these things" to demarcate major transitions in the narratological flow of the text (see chapter 8).

A common authorship for the Apocalypse and the Gospel of John also receives reinforcement if one assumes an an earlier compositional date for the Apocalypse (e.g., 60s CE). Such a scenario allows time for John to have honed his Greek skills away from the "solecisms" (problematic grammar) and "barbarous idioms," as Eusebius called them (*Eccl.*

13. Jesus as light: *Revelation*: 1:14–16; 2:18; 21:23; 22:16; *Gospel of John*: 1:4, 5, 7, 8, 9; 3:19–21;8:12; 9:5; 11:9–10; 12:35–36; 12:46.

14. Jesus as Logos/Word—the creative power and wisdom of God: Rev 19:13 and John 1:1–3.

15. Jesus's divinity: *Revelation*: Jesus worshiped (5:6, 8–14 (Cf. Rev 4:11; 7:9–12). Richard Bauckham sees Jesus's deity confirmed in these texts: Rev 1:8, 17; 21:6; 22:13 (*Theology of the Book of Revelation*, 54, 55); *Gospel of John*: Jesus with God (John 1:1, 18; 8:16; 14:23; 17:5; (2) Jesus as God (John 1:1, 18; 5:18; 8:19, 58; 10:30, 33; 14:9; 20:28).

16. Jesus as judge: *Revelation*: (1) a correcting judge (2:4–5, 12, 14–16, 20–23; 3:1–3, 5); (2) a rewarding judge (2:2, 3, 7, 9–11, 13, 17, 19, 24–28; 3:4, 5, 8–12); (3) the cosmic judge (6:17; 19:11, 15 [cf. 14:14–20]; 22:12); *Gospel of John*: 5:22–20.

17. Jesus as heavenly messenger: *Revelation*: herald to the seven *ekklēsiai* of Roman Asia (chs. 2—3), at the center of the throne (5;6, 7:9, 17); *Gospel of John*: sent from heaven by God (3:13, 31; 6:32, 33, 38, 41, 50, 51, 58; 8:23; 17:5) with God's message (1:14; 3:34; 5:19, 23, 37; 7:17; 8:16, 28, 38, 42; 12:49, 50; 14:10, 24; 16:27, 28; 17:25; 20:21 [cf. 6:46; 10:32, 37; 14:31]) and will return to heaven (13:1, 3; 14:2, 12, 28; 16:10, 28; 20:17).

18. Jesus as sacrificial lamb: *Revelation*: 5:6, 8, 12, 13; 6:1, 3, 5, 7, 16; 7:9, 10, 14, 17; 12:11; 13:8; 14:1, 4, 10; 15:3; 17:14; 19:7, 9; 21:9; *Gospel of John*: 1:29, 35. Exodus 12 and Isa 53:7 are also important for context.

19. Andreas Köstenberger notes the following dualism themes in the Gospel, which are also evident in Revelation: light/darkness, life/death, spirit/flesh, above/below, truth/falsehood, and believe/unbelief (*A Theology of John's Gospel and Letters*, 282–83).

20. For discussion on the ascent/descent motif as division, see Meeks, "Man from Heaven," 67. On division, see Rev 1:11, 12; 2:36; 7:43; 9:16; 10:19.

21. Swete, *Apocalypse of St. John*, 120–30.

Hist. 7.25.24–27), towards the more polished Greek evident in the Gospel of John (and the Johannine epistles) (without needing thereby to assume John's use of an amanuensis).

Pre-70 CE Composition: Neronic

The stronger arguments in favor of an early date focus on four factors: (1) the measurement of the temple (11:1), (2) Babylon as Jerusalem (11:8), (3) the number 666 (13:18), and (4) the seven kings (17:10–11).

Regarding the measurement of the temple, in 11:1–2, John is given a reed and is told, "Go and measure the temple of God and the altar." It is claimed that this instruction presupposes the existence of the literal Herodian temple of Jerusalem in the pre-70 CE era. However, since Revelation is highly symbolic in nature, there are at least two other options for the temple reference in 11:1–2. First, the angel could be referencing a future rebuilt temple in post-70 CE Jerusalem. Second, given that John is never said actually to enter the temple, the temple measured by the angel could simply have existed within a vision. This would be similar to John's later vision of the New Jerusalem and an angel's citation of the measurements of the city and its walls (21:9—22:20).

Regarding an identification of Jerusalem as "Babylon," Revelation could then be dated beginning with the start of the Jewish Revolt in 66 CE. Chapter 18 would then be seen as being descriptive of its impending destruction in 70 CE. There are two primary reasons for correlating Jerusalem with Babylon. First, 11:8 connects "the great city" with the place "where their Lord was crucified." In subsequent chapters "the great city" is also identified with "Babylon" (18:10, 16, 18, 19, 21; cf. 14:8; 17:5). Second, Babylon's adornment with "fine linen and purple and scarlet . . . gold, precious stones, and pearls" (18:16; cf. 17:4) can be seen as an allusion to the Israelite high priest's garb. If so, then Revelation is using Babylon imagery to describe an apostate Israel. This seems to be affirmed in 11:8 with the statement that "the great [apostate] city . . . is called spiritually Sodom and Egypt."

Regarding an early historical referent for the two symbolic statements "666" and "seven kings," Caesar Nero is one person who fits within a pre-70 CE compositional date. If one uses the ancient practice of gematria (the practice of attaching historical significance to symbolic

numbers),[22] then the numerical value of the Hebrew letters which transliterate the Greek phrase *nerōn kēsar* (Nero Caesar) is 666 (or 616).[23]

There are at least four objections brought against the use of gematria
to correlate Nero with the Beast of Rev 13. First, this approach naively
assumes that John's Greek readership had knowledge of Hebrew and the
system of gematria. Second, if they did, then gematria would point most
directly towards the word (Sea) "Beast" (13:1) and not to a specific person such as "Nero." Bauckham points out that "the Greek word *thērion*
(beast), when transliterated into Hebrew as *nwyrt*, has the numerical
value 666 (t = 400 + r = 200 + y = 10 + w = 6 + n = 50)."[24] Third, the
transliteration of Hebrew gives some latitude in the selection of vowels
and even consonants. For example, there are three Hebrew equivalents
available for the Greek letter *s*. This linguistic reality mitigates against
any expectation of precision one might have in assuming that there is
only one numerical value available per letter in a word or phrase. Fourth,
and probably most significantly, it would seem that putting forward a
gematriac formulation as the primary meaning of the number 666 misses
the essential function of any number in Revelation—numbers are used
symbolically with no necessary historical referent in time and space. The
number 666 may simply function as a cryptogram that emphasizes the
fact that the triple digit 666 falls short of the "tripled perfection" implicit
in the threefold repetition of the number 7, which symbolizes perfection
and completion. In this regard, the tripled 6 may even be symbolic of the
"unholy trinity" (the Beast, the False Prophet, and the Dragon), who are
a "parody of the divine trinity of three sevens . . . [such that] six repeated
three times indicates the completeness of sinful incompleteness found in
the beast."[25]

Nero and the Nero *redivivus* myth may be behind John's mention
of the "seven hills" (17:9) that are symbolic of seven Roman kings: "five

---

22. See Bauckham's chapter entitled "Nero and the Beast" in his book *Climax of Prophecy*, 384–452.

23. The Hebrew letters that transliterate *nerōn kēsar* are נרון קסר [νέρων κέσαρ]
nun, resh, waw, nun + qof, samekh, resh = 50+200+6+50+100+60+200 = 666 (Bauckham, *Climax of Prophecy*, 387). Papyrus 115 (P. Oxyrhynchus. 4499; c. 225–275 CE)
records the number of the Beast as being 616. If one transliterates "Caesar Nero" (*nerō
kēsar*) into Hebrew letters then it adds up to 616 (*rsq wrn* [nun, resh, waw + qof,
samekh, resh]). One minor problem with this hypothesis is that Greek grammar does
not require a *nu* (ν) in the phrase νέρων κέσαρ.

24. Bauckham, *Climax of Prophecy*, 389. Popular gematria associated the numerical value of Nero's name in Greek with the phrase "he murdered his mother," both
phrases of which total "1,005."

25. Beale, *Revelation*, 733.

have fallen, one is, the other has not yet come" (17:10). Most commentators agree that the "seven hills" refer to the city of Rome itself, which was situated on seven hills. Those who favor an early date for Revelation see the "seven kings" as referring to seven Caesars, the sixth one being the one "who is" reigning during John's day.

In this scenario, the first "king" is the first official "king" of Rome (post-Republican era), which would be either Julius Caesar or Octavian/Augustus. This then would make the sixth king either Nero or Galba, respectively. There is little evidence to guide us to a certain conclusion on this point. Beale retorts that if Nero is the sixth king and if Jerusalem is the "Babylon" described in 11:8 ("where also their Lord was crucified"), then Galba, the seventh king would have died prior to the destruction of Jerusalem, since he reigned only from Oct. 68–Jan 69 CE. Such a scenario runs contrary to the chronology of chs. 17—18.[26] There are many in scholarship, however, who equate the Nero *redivivus*/Nero *rediturus* (13:14) legend with the eighth king, who "is one of them," that is, the seven kings (17:11).[27]

Nero, thus, best fulfills two statements if John is writing during "the year of the four emperors" right after Nero's death (68–69 CE): (1) he could be "the Beast . . . who was, and is not, and is about to ascend from the bottomless pit" (17:8) since Nero has died but is expected as Nero *redivivus* to return from the east with the Parthians; and (2) he could be one of the five kings "who have fallen," which then makes Galba the sixth king "who is living," and the other emperors during 68–69 CE together being envisioned as the seventh king "who has not yet come" (17:10). The conflation of the last three emperors into one reference becomes more understandable with the observation that even after Otho and Vitellius were confirmed as regents, each of their short reigns was overlapped by the movement of legions loyal to the next emperor to be confirmed (Vitellius and Vespasian, respectively). The struggle to establish a lasting dynasty in Rome finally took hold with Vespasian's acknowledgment as emperor on December 21, 69 CE, and the concomitant establishment of the stable Flavian dynasty.

---

26. Beale, *Revelation*, 22.

27. For example, Thompson, *Revelation*, 162–63. The Nero *redivivus* legend that was propagated by some Romans asserts that Nero will return to power with the help of the Parthians to whom he escaped after his ostensible assassination (attempt) (e.g., Suetonius, *Nero* 57). John's mention in 13:14 of the "beast that had been wounded by the sword yet had lived" is seen by some scholars as a cryptic reference to the Nero *redivivus* legend.

One implication of a pre-70 CE dating relative to a post-supersessionist reading of Revelation is that one can then (controversially) suggest some sort of contemporaneous connectivity between John's and Paul's Roman Asia *ekklēsiai* (not least in Ephesus and Laodicea) and perhaps (more controversially) as both reflecting similar, if not even the same, audiences.[28] If any of this is deemed possible, then conclusions reached relative to Paul's post-supersessionist ideology for his *ekklēsiai*, may have some transferability to John's *ekklēsiai*, not least how John might view the terms "Israel" and "Jew."[29] My previously published perspective on Paul's *ekklēsia* ideology is summarized as follows:

> [Paul believed that] gentiles could not collectively assume the designation "Israel," but yet, through faith in the Jewish *Christos*, could share in historic Israel's covenantal benefits. . . . [Thus] Paul's designation of his multi-ethnic communities as *ekklēsiai* provided them with an inherently Jewish collective identity other than "Israel" by which he could institutionally integrate gentiles qua gentiles into theological continuity with Torah-observant Jews qua Jews[30] (i.e., those who are part of the *qahal*, but not of the *'am*[31]).[32]

Post-70 CE Composition: Domitian

The majority view dates Revelation's composition sometime during the reign of Domitian (81–96 CE). Some of the primary reasons in favor of a

28. The book of Acts records that Paul himself established at least one *ekklēsia* in Roman Asia, in the *polis* of Ephesus (Acts 19:1–8; cf. 20:17–38). (Deutero-)Paul names at least one other *ekklēsia* in Roman Asia which was loyal to Paul's apostolic authority (Laodicea; Col 4:16). Paul, who potentially writes four decades before John, also speaks of a regional affiliation of *ekklēsiai* in the Roman province of Asia (1 Cor 16:19), although Paul does not give the exact number. These *"ekklēsiai* of Asia" send greetings to the Christ-followers in Corinth (1 Cor 16:19).

29. See especially the section "Pauline Supersessionism? 'So-Called Jew' and 'Israel of God'" in chapter 4. See also some of my earlier publications: Korner, *"Ekklēsia* as a Jewish Synagogue Term: Some Implications,"* 53–78; Korner, *"Ekklēsia* as a Jewish Synagogue Term: A Response,"* 127–36; Korner, *Origin and Meaning of* Ekklēsia (2017).

30. See p. 25 n. 92 for my definition of what I mean by the phrase "gentiles qua gentiles."

31. Within the ancient *qāhāl/ekklēsia* there were those who were not members of the people of Israel (*'am*). *Ekklēsia* functioned well as a group designation for John's communities since it had the ability to create a collective entity (in the Jewish *Christos*) without erasing distinction between Israel and the nations.

32. Korner, *"Ekklēsia* as a Jewish Synagogue Term: A Response,"* 127.

post-70 CE dating include factors such as Babylon being identified with Rome, patristic comments, and the lived realities experienced by Revelation's addressees like emperor worship, persecution by outsiders, and the allusion in chapter 13 to the Nero *redivivus* legend.

With respect to an identification of Rome as "Babylon," one finds key textual support for this in 17:18 where Babylon is called "the woman ... [who] is the great city that rules over the kings of the earth," a very apt description of Rome given its position of world dominance during John's day. If the Apocalypse is dated post-70 CE, then this terminology would have been especially *apropos* for a Jewish audience, given that it was not until after the destruction of Jerusalem that Jewish commentators began to call Rome "Babylon."[33]

Regarding patristic sources, their comments relative to the dating of the Apocalypse have favored the time of Domitian. The most important of these are Irenaeus,[34] Victorinus of Pettau,[35] Eusebius,[36] Jerome,[37] and possibly Clement of Alexandria[38] and Origen.[39] The clearest and earliest witness to the late date is Irenaeus, who in a discussion of the Antichrist in Revelation writes: "We will not, however, incur the risk of pronouncing positively as to the name of the Antichrist; for if it were necessary that his name should be distinctly revealed in this present time, it would have been announced by him who beheld the Apocalypse. For it was seen not very long ago, but almost in our day, toward the end of Domitian's reign."[40]

When it comes to the lived realities of John's *ekklēsiai*, emperor worship was prevalent in Roman Asia. It appears to be presupposed in the passages where the Beast is worshiped (13:3–4, 12). Emperor worship

33. See 4 *Ezra* 3.1–2, 28–31; 2 *Bar.* 10.1–3; 11.1; 67.7; *Sib. Or.* 5.143, 159–60 (Charlesworth, ed., *The Old Testament Pseudepigrapha*, vol. 1). Just as Babylon had destroyed Jerusalem and its temple in the sixth century BCE, so also Rome did in the first century CE, thus becoming analogously known as "Babylon" to post-70 CE Jewish writers.

34. Irenaeus, *Haer.* 5.30.3.

35. Victorinus, *Apocalypse* 10.11 (304 CE).

36. Eusebius, *Hist. Eccl.* 3.18.1; 3.20.9; 3.23.1 (260–340 CE).

37. Jerome, *Vir. Ill.* 9.

38. Clement, *Quis Div.* 42.

39. Matt 16:6.

40. In Eusebius, *Hist.Eccl.* 3.18.3; 5.8.6. Some commentators state that rather than "it [i.e., the Apocalypse] was seen" Irenaeus's comments should read "he [John] was seen," thus indicating only that John was seen during Domitian's reign not that he necessarily also saw the Revelation during that same time period (e.g., Gentry, *Before Jerusalem Fell*, 46–67).

had its beginning already during the time of Julius Caesar (who accepted worship as a god for political purposes). However, its official status became particularly predominant during the post-70 CE reign of Domitian (who made failure to honor the emperor as a god punishable as a political offense). This late first-century historical reality for the Asia Minor churches would also then have left open the possibility of imperial persecution.

The universal persecution of Christians for their refusal to worship the Dragon and his Beast, as described in Revelation (e.g., 12:18; 13:7, 15), is seen as a symbolic window into the plight of the Christian community during the time of Revelation's composition. Thus, the argument is made that the compositional date of the Apocalypse should correlate to the date of officially sanctioned imperial persecution. Documented persecution did not arise first until the reign of Nero. Under his reign, however, persecution was neither universal (persecution was primarily localized in Rome) nor based on imperial claims to divinity (persecution was used to scapegoat Christians for the burning of Rome). This leaves the reign of Domitian as the most relevant compositional timeframe for Revelation.

J. B. Lightfoot convincingly championed the claim that Domitian's reign was the first to officially sanction the widespread persecution of Christians[41] and, in the process, to lend support to a later dating (although the "Cambridge Three" [Lightfoot, Westcott, and Hort] all favored an earlier date).[42] However, subsequent investigation has called into question the literary claims of Pliny the Younger, Tacitus, and Suetonius (all three are ca. 60–120 CE) to the effect that Domitian was a detestable and incompetent autocrat whose reign was one of terror.[43] Additionally, Kloppenborg notes that Pliny's letter may be historically suspect given that "his letter to Trajan shows heavy dependence on Livy's account of the

---

41. His claims are based on Roman literary witnesses which originate from the reign of Domitian. Cf. *Apostolic Fathers: Clement, Ignatius, and Polycarp* (2 parts in 5 vols.; London: Macmillan, 1889–90), 104–15 (cited in Aune, *Revelation 1–5*, lxvi).

42. See, for example, Lightfoot, *Biblical Essays*, 132 (cited in Aune, *Revelation 1–5*, lvii).

43. Aune (*Revelation 1–5*, lxvii–lxviii) explains that "Much of the Latin literary evidence that presented this image of Domitian was the product of a relatively tight circle of politician-writers associated with the senatorial aristocracy with which Domitian was frequently in conflict. . . . The propagandistic views of this circle, and of later writers who accepted their party line . . . have been widely accepted . . . [by] modern historians."

Bacchanalia conspiracy . . . where he described the early-second-century arrival of the Bacchic cults in Rome a 'contagion.'"[44] He suggests that this literary strategy is meant implicitly "to assure Trajan that the *Christianoi* do not pose a real threat."[45] Nevertheless, it would appear that the storm clouds of persecution were sufficiently recognizable on the horizon that John's use of the imperial cult imagery in chapter 13 could be seen as a reasonable projection of existing conditions during Domitian's reign.

The description of the Beast whose fatal wound was healed (13:3–4) is used by some to connect the biblical Beast with the Nero *redivivus*[46] legend that expected Nero to return after his disappearance/death and lead a Parthian army against the Roman Empire.[47] Given Nero's death in 68 CE, it would have taken some time for this legend to take root in popular myth, thus favoring a turn-of-the-century compositional date for Revelation. However, due to the differences in which the Nero *redivivus* myth is portrayed, its validity as a basis for dating Revelation is questioned, even by some who hold that the legend is reflected in Rev 13:3–4 and 17:8.[48]

Richard Bauckham, while not directly legitimizing the Nero *redivivus* legend as being the only historical backdrop for the Beast, does see John possibly using it as a christological parody in the Apocalypse such that the Beast's resurrection in chapter 13 is an event distinct from his *parousia* in chapter 17. Thus, through his resurrection (13:3–4) the Beast enhances his kingly status (analogous to Christ's exaltation and glorification) while in his *parousia* he destroys "Babylon" (17:16), the enemy of God (as Christ will at his *parousia*). Bauckham claims that this theological confluence "indicates that John has constructed a *history* for the beast which parallels that of Christ,"[49] which in his estimation lends further credence to a later dating of Revelation.

44. Kloppenborg, *Christ's Associations*, 328.

45. Kloppenborg, *Christ's Associations*, 329.

46. Bauckham, *Climax of Prophecy*, 421.

47. For an extensive treatment of the background to the Nero *redivivus* legend as well as its possible implications for the Apocalypse, see Bauckham, *Climax of Prophecy*, esp. 40–52.

48. See Bauckham, *Climax of Prophecy*, 414–23.

49. Bauckham, *Climax of Prophecy*, 437.

The Dating Implications for Revelation's Compositional History

David Aune contends that the book of Revelation is comprised of two separate genres that reflect a threefold compositional history for the book: (1) the writing of the apocalyptic body of Revelation (4:1—22:6 [or 9]); (2) the composition of the prophetic framing sections (1:9—3:22 and 22:6 [or 10]–21); and (3) the redaction of both sections into a literary unity bounded by epistolary elements. Aune sees a pre-70 CE compositional date for the apocalyptic section and a late first-century date for the prophetic framework and final redaction.

Even if, contrastingly, one holds that Revelation is reflective of only a single genre, the weight of evidence would still appear to support a later dating of the Apocalypse. A later date addresses the theological conundrum of having to explain how the destruction of Jerusalem as "Babylon" (11:8; 17:16—18:24) failed to usher in the expected consummation (19:1—22:21). A later date also gives the message of the Apocalypse a greater sense of relevance and immediacy for the later first-century *ekklēsiai* that appeared to experience increased levels of persecution. However, ultimately, neither dating scenario is inherently at odds with the content of, or interpretive approaches to, the book of Revelation.

4

Supersessionist and Anti-Judaistic Passages in Revelation?

Asia Minor and Jewish Demographics

SINCE JOHN IS SO steeped in a Jewish heritage, and uses that ethnic framework for communicating to his audience, one can assume with great probability that John's audience also was deeply steeped in a Jewish heritage. This assumption gains reinforcement in the fact that there was a large Jewish population in Roman Asia, not least in the Lycus River Valley. There are two problematic passages, though, in which John appears to impugn the Jewish communities of two cities wherein are found two of his seven *ekklēsiai* ("churches"/communities/congregations). In this chapter, I will attempt to assess how John may have intended, and/or how his intended audience may have perceived, his use of two potentially anti-Judaistic statements—(1) "those who claim to be Jews but are not" and (2) "the synagogue of Satan" (Rev 2:9; 3:9).

Asia Minor: History of Jewish Settlement

Paul Trebilco's study of Jewish communities in Asia Minor is a seminal review of ancient literary and epigraphic evidence. During the time of Antiochus III, approximately 10,000 pro-Seleucid Jews emigrated from Mesopotamia and Babylon to settle "among an unspecified number of sites" in Lydia and Phrygia in Asia Minor.[1] They "were granted land for

1. Trebilco, *Jewish Communities*, 6.

homes, farming and agriculture, very favorable exemptions from tax and as much grain as was needed to ensure that the settlements flourished and became permanent."[2] By 139–138 BCE there were Jews in the kingdoms of Pergamum, Cappadocia, and in cities within Caria (Myndos, Halicarnassus, Cnidus), Lycia (Phaselis), and Pamphylia (Side).[3] The roots of the Jewish community in Sardis go back to at least 200 BCE, with its influence continuing, and growing, well into the third century CE.[4] The city of Acmonia, which is located in the conventus of Apamea, was a regional military and commercial center with a considerable population.[5] The strength of its Jewish community is evidenced through the synagogue building constructed (c. 50–60's CE) by Julia Severa, an *archiereia* of the Imperial cult at Acmonia, and a patroness of the Jewish community. This synagogue is the earliest synagogue in Asia Minor attested by an inscription.

Throughout Asia Minor, the Romans granted a variety of privileges to Jewish communities, further solidifying their longevity and success in Asia Minor.[6] Trebilco postulates that since the "paucity of references to hostility in the literary sources between the cities in Asia Minor and their Jewish communities from 2 CE onwards is significant . . . we can suggest that in many cities in Asia Minor a tradition of tolerance and positive interaction was established between the city and its Jewish community."[7]

In addition to the large population of ethnic Jews, Hirschberg states that "the group of 'God-fearers' was very strongly represented, especially in Asia Minor."[8] He notes further that often God-fearers "occupied high social positions and were therefore an important factor for the social integration of the Jews. Losing even one Godfearer to the Christian community could bring about a substantial loss of social prestige to the

2. Trebilco, *Jewish Communities*, 6.

3. Trebilco, *Jewish Communities*, 7.

4. Trebilco, *Jewish Communities*, 57.

5. Acmonia was also prestigious: it held a high priesthood of the Imperial cult and enjoyed the status as Neokrate. Jews most likely first came in 205 BCE.

6. Roman privileges extended to Jews included: "the right to be organised as a community, to administer their own finances, to observe the Sabbath and to be exempt from duties such as military service that conflicted with the full observance of Jewish Law, . . . [even though] local opposition from the cities in which the Jews lived [was not uncommon]" (Trebilco, *Jewish Communities*, 8). The opposition was particularly significant at least from 49 BCE to 2 CE (Trebilco, *Jewish Communities*, 183).

7. Trebilco, *Jewish Communities*, 57.

8. Hirschberg, "Jewish Believers in Asia Minor," 221.

group."[9] It is this large group of God-fearers which provides a socio-historical backdrop for a new non-supersessionist way of interpreting John's ostensibly pejorative clause "those who say they are Jews and are not."[10]

Apamea: Jewish Flood Tradition

Apamea, a *polis* just east of Roman Asia had a particularly vibrant Jewish community. Its Jewish populace exerted significant socio-political and cultural influence even well into the third century CE, as is evidenced by coins that depict Noah and the Ark. Earlier in the third century BCE, the city of Celaenae was relocated by the Seleucids and renamed Apamea. During this move large numbers of Jews were also transplanted. Apamea sat astride a major east-west trading route, and as such, it became a city of significant economic importance, second only to Ephesus, until the turn of the second century CE. It was relatively near to three *Christos*-follower communities connected with Paul (Laodicea, Colossae, Hierapolis), with at least one of them receiving John's Apocalypse (Laodicea). As already indicated, Douglas Campbell claims that Paul wrote his epistles to the Colossians and Laodiceans during an imprisonment in Apamea.[11]

Second century CE numismatic evidence from Apamea demonstrates the extent to which its populace, and even civic leaders, had already adopted (and adapted) the Noachic flood tradition. This then suggests the possibility of this Jewish tradition already being extant in the first century CE.[12] The city of Apamea minted a series of coins which bear images of Noah and the Ark.[13] This integration of biblical images onto imperial coinage is unique in antiquity. One side of the coin depicts two people who are situated both inside, and to the left of, an ark. Above the ark are two birds, a raven and a dove. The dove is holding an olive branch in its claws.

9. Hirschberg, "Jewish Believers in Asia Minor," 221.

10. See my discussion in this chapter in the section entitled "Judaizing Non-Pauline Gentile *Christos*-followers."

11. For an extensive review of Campbell's rationale in identifying Paul's imprisonment in Apamea, see his book, *Framing Paul*, 254–338.

12. For a full discussion of Greek flood traditions and their correlation with the Noachic Flood account, see Korner, "Great Earthquake," 161–67. See also, Hillhorst, "The Noah Story," 57.

13. Trebilco, *Jewish Communities*, 86–88.

The inscription on the inside of the ark reads ΝΩΕ (Noah). This inscription confirms that the local flood legend associated with the figures of Deucalion and Pyrhha is not being commemorated, nor are the four local (Phrygian) flood legends.[14] The ark on the coin is a rectangular box-like structure. The two figures (Noah and his wife?) are depicted standing on dry ground with their right arms raised in an "orans" gesture as an expression of gratitude for salvation.

Does this coin also imply that the Ark's resting place was Apamea? The ostensibly indigenous Jewish *Sibylline Oracles* reinforce such an assumption. In Book III, which dates to the second century BCE,[15] Sibylla describes her journey with Noah as his daughter-in-law.[16] She identifies the Ark's landing place as "a certain tall lofty mountain on the dark mainland of Phrygia. It is called Ararat."[17] This "Mt. Ararat," in contrast to the Mt. Ararat in Armenia, is identified as a hill near "the great river Marsyos" (also Marsyas). The river Marsyas is in the immediate vicinity of Apamea. This associates the Ark's landing place with the hill of Celaenae (3,660 ft. high) where Apamea also is located.

Apamea's nickname is *kibōtos* ("box, crate") due to its economic influence. However, *kibōtos* is also the same word used in the LXX for Noah's Ark.[18] This fact makes more understandable why the Jewish *Sibylline Oracles*, and even the Jewish populace of Apamea, associated the Ark's resting place with the hill of Celaenae near the city nicknamed *kibōtos*, that is, Apamea. By contrast, a Greco-Roman readership would most likely not have associated Deucalion's ark with Apamea since the Deucalion flood legend used the word *laranx* instead of *kibōtos* for Deucalion's ark.[19] Additionally, Asia Minor residents would not have associated any other ark with Apamea either, since local Phrygian flood traditions were devoid of ark traditions.

---

14. Trebilco notes that each of the four Phrygian flood legends is missing an ark, along with some other important biblical features (*Jewish Communities*, 87–89, 91).

15. E. Isaac, "1 *Enoch*," OTP, 1:354.

16. *Sib. Or.* 3.823–27.

17. *Sib. Or.* 1.261–62.

18. The word *kibōtos* is also found in the book of Revelation. It is mentioned in the third storm theophany, which occurs within the context of the seventh trumpet/third woe (11:15–19; cf. 8:13; 11:14). It is not Noah's *kibōtos* though, but the Ark of the Covenant (11:19; ἡ κιβωτὸς τῆς διαθήκης αὐτοῦ).

19. Trebilco (*Jewish Communities*, 224 n. 35) notes that "it is possible that the translators of the Septuagint used the unusual word for the Ark—κιβωτός—precisely to distinguish the story from the Greek myth of Deucalion."

Given the Greek flood traditions, Hilhorst concludes that it "seems warranted that Noah was known to the Greek world of the early Empire to a serious extent."[20] Thus, if the Jewish and/or Greco-Roman audience of Revelation would have perceived an allusion to the Noachic earthquake ("fountains of the great deep opened up"; Gen 7:11) in relation to John's final, eschatological "great earthquake" (Rev 6:12; 11:13; 16:19), then the Apocalypse's message of inescapable divine judgment would have had even greater relevance for a first-century CE Asia Minor audience.

Greco-Roman familiarity with Noachic literary traditions notwithstanding, it is the geological history of Asia Minor, particularly in Roman Asia and Phrygia, that would have maximized the relevance of John's "great earthquake" for his readership, especially for those in Sardis, Philadelphia, and Laodicea. Tacitus (*Ann.* 2.47.3–4) notes that the great earthquake of 17 CE was particularly devastating for Sardis and Philadelphia, and to such a degree that Philadelphia required, and received, imperial exemption from paying taxes for a five-year period. Laodicea experienced a similarly destructive earthquake in 60 CE.

Devastating earthquakes were also known outside of Roman Asia. Apamea experienced an earthquake in 88 BCE. Beyond Asia Minor, "great" earthquakes" also occurred in Cyprus (76 CE) and in Pompeii (79 CE). Bauckham suggests that the eruption of Vesuvius, which destroyed Pompeii, "would have included both an earthquake and a hail of stones quite adequate to the description in Rev. xvi 21." The *Sibylline Oracles* record *ex-eventu* prophecies of the earthquakes in Cyprus and Asia Minor (4.107–13, 129f).

As has become evident through socio-historical data, there was a significant populace of Jews and God-fearers in Asia Minor in John's day. It seems that at least one of John's *ekklēsiai* encountered stiff opposition from a Jewish synagogue community (Smyrna). Given that socio-political scenario, it is not surprising that the majority of interpreters default to seeing a supersessionist, and even anti-Judaistic, attitude at play in John's letters to the *ekklēsiai* in Smyrna and in Philadelphia, both of which are dealing with "a synagogue of Satan." What are the interpretive options that have been identified so far for understanding John's problematic terminology?

20. Hillhorst, "The Noah Story," 65.

Pauline Supersessionism?
"So-Called Jew" and "Israel of God"

Given the possibility that the seven *ekklēsiai* of Revelation were the same communities as (60s CE), or continuous with (90s CE), Paul's addressees, I would suggest there is warrant for postulating some continuity between Paul's and John's use of similar phraseology: "so-called Jew" (Rom 2:17) and "those who say they are Jews and are not" (Rev 2:9; 3:9). If so, then it opens up the possibility that a related ideology to the one identified by Paul to his Galatian addressees (cf. 1:10; 6:15) is also behind John's pejorative term "synagogue of Satan" (2:9; 3:9). This possibility increases due to the geographical proximity of Galatia to Roman Asia, irrespective of whether Paul's addressees are from the Roman province of Galatia (the South Galatian theory) or are ethnic Galatians (the north Galatia theory). It would not seem improbable that the ideology of Paul's Galatian trouble-makers may have spread to Roman Asia's *ekklēsiai* in at least Smyrna and Philadelphia. In a previous work, I suggest that Paul's reference to the "so-called Jew" (Rom 2:17) does not target ethnic Jews, and thus, does not affirm malleability for Jewish ethnicity.[21] In other words, Paul is not broadening the semantic domain for the term "Jew" to include non-Jews, circumcised or not. Rather, I suggest that Paul is targeting a *gentile* God-fearing convert to Judaism who later became a God-fearing *Christos*-follower. For Paul then refer to him as "so-called Jew" affirms in a different way the non-malleability of Jewish identity: no gentile, even a full Jewish convert, could truly be considered an ethnic Jew/Judean. In the ensuing discussion I review in more detail my argument for the gentile identity of the "so-called Jew" in Romans 2.

"So-Called Jew" (Rom 2:17–29)

If one agrees with the majority consensus that in Rom 2:17–29 Paul addresses an ethnic Jew, then Paul has expanded the semantic boundaries of the word "Jew" (*Ioudaios*) to now include circumcised non-Jews.[22] There are dissenting voices, however. Matthew Thiessen, building upon the

---

21. For my complete discussion of Rom 2:17–29, see Korner, *Origin and Meaning of* Ekklēsia, 216–20.

22. See, for example, Dunn, *Romans*, 448–49.

work of Runar M. Thorsteinsson,[23] argues that "Paul addresses a gentile, specifically a gentile who has judaized [i.e., undergone genital circumcision] and now thinks of himself as a Jew."[24]

Thiessen extends Thorsteinsson's research by asking under what circumstance ethnic Jews would consider a circumcised gentile convert to "Judaism" as being uncircumcised. His answer is that a circumcised gentile has not followed "the entirety of the law of circumcision"[25] which requires a male to be circumcised on the eighth day—a gentile convert's circumcision is always after the eighth day.[26] Thus, if one accords with Thiessen's argument, Paul is not redefining the term "Jew" in Rom 2:17–29, but rather is speaking to a gentile proselyte who self-proclaims as being a Jew by virtue of his circumcision. In other words, Paul is not changing the definition of what it means to be a Jew; he is reconfirming the definition of a Jew (for a male, at least) as being someone who is circumcised *on the eighth day*. Thus, circumcised gentiles who now think of themselves as being Jews would never be considered as such by Jews. Could this same conclusion also be extended to the ethnic demarcator "Israel"? In other words, would a Jew consider a gentile as being part of socio-ethnic Israel? Some have identified evidence in that direction from Paul's letter to the Galatians wherein he uses the term "Israel of God" (Gal 6:16).

"Israel of God" (Galatians 6:16)

There are a number of "ecclesiological" interpreters of Gal 6:16 who argue that Paul uses the term "Israel of God" in reference to the universal, multiethnic "church of God," which is comprised both of Jews and gentiles.[27]

---

23. Thorsteinsson, *Paul's Interlocutor* (2003).

24. Thiessen, "Gentile Circumcision," 390–91.

25. Thiessen, "Gentile Circumcision," 385.

26. Thiessen writes that, "according to the legislation of Gen 17:12 and Lev 12:3, Jewish circumcision is distinct from the circumcision of other nations in that it occurs on the eighth day after birth. Covenantal circumcision is not merely any form of circumcision, but specifically circumcision on the eighth-day" ("Gentile Circumcision," 387).

27. Zoccali helpfully provides an extensive list of scholars, who, to varying degrees, also hold the ecclesiological position (*Whom God Has Called*, 73, n. 37).

Such commentators include N. T. Wright, [28] James Dunn,[29] and Terence Donaldson.[30] Wright uses Rom 2:17–29 as a precedent for also suggesting malleability in Paul's use of "Israel of God" such that it can include gentile followers of the Jewish *Christos*.[31] However, if Thiessen is correct then the "so-called Jew" of Rom 2:17–29 is not a malleable term, which then lessens the force of Wright's (supersessionist) argument for "Israel of God." William Campbell notes an additional challenge with assuming ethnic boundary permeability for the term "Israel of God." He notes that if "gentiles are so designated, even if only in association with Jewish Christ-followers, they may then separate from Jewish Christ-followers and yet retain the title to Israel and her heritage independently, a possibility Paul warns against in Rom. 11."[32]

There are at least four ways to read the phrase "the Israel of God" in such a way as to maintain its reference only to people of Jewish ethnicity: (1) historical Israel as a whole;[33] (2) Jewish Christ-followers (cf. Rom 9:6);[34] (3) the total elect from historical Israel;[35] and (4) that segment of Jewish Christ-followers who require circumcision of gentile Christ-followers.[36] However, ecclesiological interpreters disagree with all four and instead see the multi-ethnic universal "church" (*ekklēsia*) as being Paul's referent for the "Israel of God."

28. Wright, *Climax of the Covenant*, 689–90; Wright, *Paul and the Faithfulness of God*, 2.1146.

29. Dunn, *Epistle to the Galatians*, 345. Dunn allows for the fact that Jews who do not believe in Jesus as the *Christos* continue to retain the identity of "the Israel of God." Dunn then qualifies this with his understanding that what is implicit in Gal 6.16 is Paul's hope that such Jewish unbelief ultimately will translate into a belief in his *Christos*.

30. Donaldson, *Paul and the Gentiles*, 237–38. Donaldson is careful, though, along with Dunn, to note that Paul does not deny to the unbelieving segment of the Jewish nation the identity of "Israel" in the full covenantal sense, despite the fact that they are presently disobedient to God's messianic purposes.

31. Wright, *Paul and the Faithfulness of God*, 2.1146.

32. Campbell, *Paul*, 49.

33. Davies, "Paul and the People of Israel," 10.

34. For example, John Murray claims that "in Rom 9:6 Paul writes of 'an Israel within ethnic Israel'" (*Epistle to the Romans*, 2.9).

35. Mussner, *Der Galaterbrief*, 417; Bruce, *Epistle to the Galatians*, 275; Burton, *Critical and Exegetical Commentary*, 357; and Richardson, *Israel in the Apostolic Church*, 82–83.

36. See Schrenk, "Was bedeutet 'Israel Gottes'?" 81–94; Robinson, "Distinction," 29–44; Betz, *Galatians*, 323.

The *crux interpretum* in Gal 6:16 is the syntactically awkward phrase εἰρήνη ἐπ' αὐτοὺς καὶ ἔλεος καὶ ἐπὶ τὸν Ἰσραὴλ τοῦ θεοῦ (e.g., "peace upon them [i.e., "those who walk by this rule"] and mercy and/also/even upon the Israel of God").[37] And the *crux interpretum* for this Greek clause revolves around the translation of the second καὶ.[38] If one reads the second καὶ as an ascensive/adjunctive καὶ (e.g., "also"), then two different *Christos*-follower sub-groups could be in view here, with only one being called "the Israel of God." The resulting translation reads, "Peace upon them [i.e., 'those who walk by this rule'] and mercy also upon the Israel of God [i.e., 'those who do not walk by this rule']." More specifically, the two sub-groups are differentiated by their adherence to Paul's rule for his diasporic (e.g., Galatia and Roman Asia) *ekklēsiai*: (1) "those who walk by this rule" are his *ekklēsia* of Galatian Christ-followers who do not require circumcision of gentiles; and (2) "also the Israel of God" are those Galatian Jewish and/or gentile Christ-followers who do require circumcision of gentiles (e.g., "the circumcision faction" in Syrian Antioch; Gal 2:11–12). I would not, however, characterize this judaizing faction of *Christos*-followers ("Israel of God") as being members of Pauline *ekklēsiai*. Rather, I would view them as having their sectarian allegiance centered in the apostolic community in Jerusalem.[39]

My exegetical conclusion gains reinforcement through the literary arrangement of Paul's letter to the Galatians. In the salutation/exordium (1:1–10) Paul engages polemically with those who mandate circumcision for gentile followers of the Jewish *Christos* ("let that one be accursed"; 1:8, 9). I would suggest that Paul's prayer for "mercy also upon the Israel of God" (6:16) creates an implicit *inclusio* with 1:1–10 such that 6:16 adds a conciliatory nuance ("mercy") to his original "prayer" of imprecation upon one segment of "the Israel of God," that is, the judaizing sub-group of *Christos*-followers originally referenced in 1:1–10.

Thus, to summarize, in the final verse of the *inclusio* (6:16) Paul prays the benediction of peace (*shalom*) upon "those who follow this rule" (i.e., his *ekklēsia*; 6:16a). "This rule" is that gentiles wishing to become Christ-followers must not be circumcised (6:11–15). This prayer of peace, then, explicitly excludes the judaizing Jewish Christ-followers since they do not

37. Gal 6:16 reads, καὶ ὅσοι τῷ κανόνι τούτῳ στοιχήσουσιν, εἰρήνη ἐπ' αὐτοὺς καὶ ἔλεος καὶ ἐπὶ τὸν Ἰσραὴλ τοῦ θεοῦ.

38. For a full review of the exegetical options see Korner, *Origin and Meaning of Ekklēsia*, 221–28.

39. Betz, *Galatians*, 323.

follow "this rule." By excluding the unrepentant Judaizers from his *shalom*, Paul thereby avoids contradicting his "prayer" at the beginning that they be accursed (1:8, 9). However, these Judaizers are still fellow followers of the Jewish *Christos*, notwithstanding their misunderstanding of the gospel of grace. Thus, Paul concludes with a prayer for mercy upon them (*chesed/ eleos*; 6:16). Susan Eastman notes that by praying for God's mercy upon judaizing Jewish *Christos*-followers (i.e., the Galatian sub-group of the "circumcision faction" of Syrian Antioch; Gal 2:12), Paul "nips in the bud," so to speak, any schismatic attitudes and actions that may have arisen among his Galatian *ekklēsiai* members given his less than conciliatory language towards those self-same Judaizers (1:8, 9).[40]

Identifying the "Israel of God" not least with Jewish *Christos*-followers also finds a parallel in 1 Peter. "Peter," the ostensible author, writes his letter to diasporic Christ-followers in Asia Minor (1 Pet 1:1), the same landmass that contains the political region of Roman Asia where Revelation's addressees are located. It is tempting to see "replacement theology" at play in Peter's identification of his *Christianoi* (4:16; but not *ekklēsia*) as metaphorical partners with key Israelite institutions (living temple, royal priesthood, holy nation; 2:5, 9). Reidar Hvalvik, however, avers. He suggests instead that 1 Peter presents Jewish Christ-followers as being "equal with Israel,"[41] not as a replacement for Israel. This conclusion may also then have value for how to view John's letter to the seven *ekklēsiai* of Roman Asia (Rev 1:4). Viewing Christ-followers (whether Jewish or gentile) as being "equal with Israel" infers that John's *ekklēsiai* are presented as being non-supersessionist messianic sub-groups of pluriform Second Temple Judaism.

If one accords with my arguments for restricting the semantic domain of the terms *Ioudaios* ("Jew/Judean") and "Israel of God" to ethnic Jews, not least genealogically Jewish males circumcised on the eighth day, irrespective of whether they are messianic or non-messianic Jews, then the phrase "synagogue of Satan" used of adversarial "so-called Jewish"

40. Susan G. Eastman argues that "the Israel of God" refers to historic Israel and that Paul prays a benediction of mercy over them because of the implications of his arguments in Galatians ("Israel and the Mercy of God," 367–95).

41. Although Reidar Hvalvik uses the term "new Israel" when speaking of 1 Peter's appropriation of Israelite covenantal terminology, he does not mean thereby that Peter is "advocating a 'replacement theology.' It is not said that the believing Gentiles have *taken the place* of the Jews. What is said is that believing Gentiles are *equal with* the Israel of the Old Testament. In Christ they have now become the people of God" ("Jewish Believers and Jewish Influence," 205; author's emphasis).

sub-groups in Roman Asia could be the same lineage of opponents that Paul was dealing with in Rome—Torah-observant *gentile* converts to Judaism who now have become followers of the Jewish *Christos*, Jesus of Nazareth. Thus, this would then mean that it is *gentiles* and not Jews to whom John is referring when he uses the phrase "synagogue of Satan" (Rev 2:9; 3:9). But I am getting ahead of myself. My claim that John is using the word *synagōgē* ("synagogue") in reference to a Christ-follower sub-group is not without precedent and will be explored more fully in the next chapter.[42]

Johannine Supersessionism?
"Those Who Say They Are Jews and Are Not"

There are some socio-historical backdrops to keep in mind when seeking to interpret what John means by his clause "those who say they are Jews and are not." First, there was a history of Jewish hostility to Christ-followers, not least in Smyrna (2:9; 3:9). Commentators who provide details on this hostility include R. H. Charles,[43] Colin Hemer,[44] Eugene Boring,[45] Richard Bauckham,[46] David Aune,[47] Craig Koester,[48] Pierre Prigent,[49] Paul

---

42 See the section "'Synagogue' as *Christos*-follower Assembly."

43. Charles, *Revelation of St. John*, 1:56. Charles cites evidence of "the bitter hostility of the Jews to the Christians at Smyrna" found in the writings of *Mart. Poly.*, Ignatius, Justin, Tertullian's *Against the Jews* (*Revelation of St. John*, 1:56).

44. Hemer, *Letters to the Seven Churches*, 66.

45. Boring writes that John's phrase "alludes to 'the evident hostility that exists between Jews and Christians in Asia, . . . by John's time Christianity was already predominantly a gentile religion" (*Revelation*, 13).

46. Bauckham writes that while these phrases refer to "non-Christian Jews . . . it is important to recognize this as an intra-Jewish dispute . . . like that between the temple establishment and the Qumran community, who denounced their fellow Jews as an 'assembly of deceit, and a congregation of Belial' (I QH 2:22)" (*Theology of the Book of Revelation*, 124).

47. Aune, *Revelation 1—5*, 237–38.

48. Koester, *Revelation and the End of All Things*, 64.

49. Prigent, *Commentary on the Apocalypse*, 168.

Duff,[50] Steve Friesen,[51] Adela Yarbro Collins,[52] Lloyd Gaston,[53] and Brian Blount.[54] Craig Koester suggests that John's invectives against the Jewish synagogue communities of Smyrna and Philadelphia resulted from their denunciation of his *ekklēsiai* members to the Roman authorities for the purpose of getting them imprisoned.[55]

Koester also emphasizes that John's *Christos*-followers were "regarded as a sub-group within the Jewish community," who most likely delineated their communal boundaries through identity markers such as circumcision, kinship, dietary laws, and Sabbath observance. In this respect, Koester sees Rev 2:9 as being reflective of an *intra*-Jewish dialogue, or should one say, diatribe, given those Jewish communities's ostensible political "due diligence" strategy of seeking imprisonment for their fellow Jews out of a self-preservationist impulse that sought to avoid having Roman authorities associate their synagogue communities with *Christos*-follower associations through perceptions of "guilt by association."

Second, Hemer notes that later epigraphic evidence from Smyrna during Hadrian's reign (early second century CE) may have interpretive import, not least for Rev 2:9. An inscription lists a group of people in Smyrna as *hoi pote Ioudaioi* ("the former Jews") who had made a contribution of 10,000 drachmas to the city (123–124 CE; *IGRom* 4:1431.29; *CIJ* 2:742.29; *CIG* 3148). Two historical conclusions arise from this mention of "former Jews": (1) it confirms the presence of Jews in Smyrna after John's day and thus implies their presence during his day, and (2) scholars note that it indicates that, ever since temple destruction in 70 CE, the Jewish nation as a political entity was no longer recognized in Roman law.[56]

50. Duff, *Who Rides the Beast?* 49; Duff, "Synagogue of Satan," 163. Duff concludes that "ultimately, it is clear that John is trying to set walls between the church and synagogue" ("Synagogue of Satan," 163).

51. Friesen, "Sarcasm in Revelation 2—3," 127–44. Friesen favors an ironic reading for the phrase "synagogue of Satan," even though it is "at the mainstream Jewish communities of Smyrna and Philadelphia" ("Sarcasm in Revelation 2—3," 134).

52. A. Y. Collins, *Crisis and Catharsis* (1984). She writes the "there is no good reason to think here of Judaizers rather than actual Jews of the local synagogues" (*Crisis and Catharsis*, 85).

53. Gaston, "Jewish Communities," 21.

54. Blount, *Revelation* (2009). Blount sees the Jews of Smyrna as being allied with the Romans in persecuting Christ-followers (*Revelation*, 54).

55. Koester, *Revelation*, 64.

56. Hemer, *Letters to the Seven Churches*, 66 n. 34.

Given not least these historical backdrops, I will review five interpretive options for John's intended referent for the term *Ioudaioi* ("Jews") in Rev 2:9 and 3:9:[57] (1) non-Jesus-following ethnic Jews, (2) non-Jesus-following Judean Jews, (3) judaizing non-Pauline Jewish *Christos*-followers, (4) non-judaizing Pauline gentile *Christos*-followers,[58] and (5) judaizing non-Pauline gentile Christos-*followers*.[59] Only the first of these five perspectives lends itself to a supersessionist understanding of John's phrase "not Jews."

"Not Jews": Non-Jesus Following Ethnic Jews (Supersessionist)

While most commentators concur that John's polemical statements (2:9; 3:9) are addressed to ethnic Jews, a minority read his statements in supersessionist fashion. Colin Hemer, for one, suggests that John "insists that the true people of God is a spiritual nation, not an ethnic group . . . the Christians were now the true Jews; those who maintained a racial separation had rejected the Christ, according to John, and were of Satan." [60]

If Hemer is correct, then John is creating permeable social boundaries for what it means to be an ethnic Jew. John is saying that his semantic domain for the term "Jew" includes gentile and Jewish followers of the Jewish *Christos* but excludes non-Jesus-following ethnic Jews. Scholars

---

57. I wish gratefully to acknowledge Elaine Pagels for her gracious provision of an annotated bibliography of interpreters's responses to the phrase "synagogue of Satan" as it occurs within Rev 2:9 and 3:9.

58. Pagels, "Social History of Satan," 487–505.

59. See my discussion on Paul's intended referents for his phrase "so-called Jew" (Rom 2:17–29) in *Origin and Meaning of Ekklēsia*, 216–219. I argue that the referents are judaizing *non-Pauline gentile* Christ-followers.

60. Hemer, *Letters to the Seven Churches*, 66, n. 40. Hemer notes others whose lead he has followed in this: "So Charles, pp. 56–57; Hort, p. 25; Swete, pp. 31–32. [However], W. W. Tarn and G. T. Griggith, Hellenistic Civilization (London, 3rd edn, 1952), p. 225 offer an alternative."

who acknowledge (and support) this supersessionist conclusion include R. H. Charles,[61] G. B. Caird,[62] A. Y. Collins,[63] and Pierre Prigent.[64]

"Not Jews": Non-Jesus-Following Ethnic Jews (Non-Supersessionist)

There are at least three ways to read John's polemical statements as being addressed to ethnic Jews, but yet that he intended them as non-supersessionist comments: politically, religiously, and ethically. First, John may be saying that Jews may have lost their *political status* as "Jews" in Roman law ("not [a political entity known as] Jew"). This interpretation would require that the Hadrianic-era phrase "former Jews" was a political statement ("no longer having privileged political status under Roman law") and that this political reality was in effect already in John's day. Thus, John's not dissimilar phrase ("those who say they are Jews and are not") at the very least may be reminding the Jews of Smyrna who were hostile to his *Christos*-followers, that they had lost their trans-local privileged political identity "Jew." Hemer notes that in Smyrna, as in other Ionian cities, Jews were able to become citizens of *poleis*. Such a political privilege may have been particularly resented by non-Jews in a Greek city, not least given the Jews' attitudes to pagan environments.[65] Such a judgmental attitude against non-Jews in Smyrna seems to be evident in the earlier Jewish *Sibylline Oracles* (3.344, 365; 5:122–23, 306–7). Thus, John may be reminding the "no longer politically privileged Jews" that their primary political allegiance now is to the *polis* in which they are citizens and thus they must not privilege their religio-political Jewish heritage

61. Regarding Rev 3:9, R. H. Charles writes "Our author claims that Christians alone had the right to the name 'Jew'" (here Charles cites Rom 2:28–29 on "Jews inwardly" (*Revelation*, 1.88).

62. G. B. Caird writes that in Rev 2:9 and 3:9 "the Christians have been subjected to active hostility . . . instigated by the Jews (cf *Mart Polyc* 19:1) . . . The Jews of Philadelphia have rejected the Messiah, thereby forfeiting their right to be called Jews" (*Revelation of St. John*, 53).

63. A. Y. Collins writes that in Rev 2:9 and 3:9: "The name 'Jews' is denied to the Jewish community in Smyrna . . . (i.e.) to actual Jews of the local synagogues . . . The name 'Jews' is denied them because the followers of Jesus are held to be the true Jews" (*Crisis and Catharsis*, 85).

64. Prigent comments that "It is the Christians who form the true Israel by their intransigent faithfulness to the one God" (*Apocalypse*, 203).

65. Hemer, *Letters to the Seven Churches*, 66.

when it comes to how they settle *intra*-Jewish disputes or extra-*mural* disputes with their fellow non-Jewish *polis* citizens.

It would seem difficult, though, to use a political framework for interpreting John's corollary phrase "synagogue of Satan," unless, in concord with Hirschberg, one identifies "Satan" as a code-word for Rome and its religio-political *imperium*.[66] Then what John might be saying is that the Jews of Smyrna and Philadelphia, while no longer holding the political identity "Jew" in Roman jurisprudence, also have lost their privileged title "synagogue of YHWH" because of their religio-ethnic compromises to Greco-Roman cultural influences (Hellenism), generally, and to imperial cults, specifically, in their participation in emperor worship mandated through their involvements in professional associations (*collegia*) of various trade guilds. In this regard, the "not (political) Jews" of Smyrna and Philadelphia can be considered a "synagogue/community of satan(ic Rome)."

Second, *religiously*, John could be saying that those whom he does not consider to be Jews are those who are apostate Jews (i.e., "not [religiously faithful] Jews"). This possibility is reinforced if one reads John's statement in light of the Hadrianic-era inscriptional phrase *hoi pote Ioudaioi* ("former Jews/Judeans"). In this regard, John may be implying that "those who say they are Jews and are not" are in fact apostate because concomitant with them being granted civic citizenship they also had publicly to abandon their ancestral religion.

Third, *ethically*, Peter Hirschberg states that John "urges us to see in this polemic ['not Jews'] above all a judgment on specific Jewish behavior."[67] Thus, he sees John as criticizing these Torah-observant Jews, who are persecuting his followers of the Jewish *Christos*, for not living faithfully enough into their religious commitments of engendering *intra*-Jewish *shalom* within the *pax Romana* of Smyrna. They are "not (ethically faithful) Jews." In this fashion, Hirschberg avoids interpreting John's phrase "not Jews" as implying that John views *Christos*-followers as having superseded/replaced ethnic Jews in God's covenantal community.

66. Hirschberg, "Jewish Believers in Asia Minor," 223; 223 n. 20.
67. Hirschberg, "Jewish Believers in Asia Minor," 220.

"Not Judeans": Non-Jesus-Following Judean Jews
(Non-Supersessionist)

Steve Mason has made the controversial argument for translating the word *Ioudaioi* as the socio-political term "Judeans," rather than as the ethnic term "Jews." One implication of such a translational move is that one can mitigate any anti-Semitic connotations in references to *Ioudaioi* in the NT, especially in the Gospel of John.[68] For such a reason, Messianic Bibles and the Jesus Seminar substitute the word "Jews" with "Judeans" in the Gospel of John. If one applies Mason's logic to Rev 2:9 and 3:9 then their resulting translation would be, "Those who say that they are Judeans but are not." There are many dissenters, though, not least David Aune, who cites Solin's claim that *Ioudaios* and *Iudaeus* "almost always denote membership in a Jewish religious community and hardly ever denote ethnic or geographic origin."[69] However, the validity of Solin's observation is muted somewhat if one keeps in mind Brent Nongbri's claim that "religion" in the ancient world cannot be viewed as a separate category from one's ethnic and cultural identity.[70] If one follows Mason in translating "Jews" as "Judeans" then two non-supersessionist interpretations of John's "not Jews" comment unfold.

First, Mason's view gives extra purchase to Kraabel's argument that the Hadrianic phrase *hoi pote Ioudaioi* should be translated as "former Judeans," that is, ethnic Jews who emigrated to Roman Asia from Judea. Kraabel challenges any interpretation of the inscriptional phrase *hoi pote Ioudaioi* as referring to ethnic Jews who apostatized as a condition of being granted citizenship. He suggests that an official civic record of citizenship would be a highly inappropriate place to emphasize an act of apostasy.[71] Thus, by extrapolation, John would then be saying that those who comprise the "synagogue of Satan" are not apostate Jews ("not Jews"). This then changes John's "not Jew" from an ethnically charged term into an ethnically neutral socio-political term ("Judean"). One might then wonder if John would pejoratively call Jewish immigrants in Smyrna and Philadelphia the "synagogue of Satan"? One response might be that these

---

68. See my earlier references to the works of Paul Anderson ("Anti-Semitism and Religious Violence," 265–311) and Jonathan Bernier (*Aposynagōgos*, 2013).

69. Aune, *Revelation* 1—5, 164, citing H. Solin, "Juden und Syrer im Westlichen Teil der römischen Welt," *ANRW* II, 29.2:587–89.

70. See chapter one.

71. Kraabel, "Roman Diaspora," 455.

"former Judeans" who are persecuting his law-abiding *Christos*-followers, are doing the work of Satan through their collusion with officials from Rome ("Satan").

A second interpretive option arises if one reads *Ioudaioi* as "Judeans" through the lens of two historical presuppositions: (1) John wrote the book of Revelation during a pre-70 CE timeframe and (2) the John who wrote Revelation is the same John who wrote the Gospel of John. These two presuppositions, then, allow for an alignment of Revelation's *Ioudaioi* ("Judeans") with the Gospel of John's use of *Ioudaioi* not as a global/national reference to ethnic Jews but rather as a reference to a sub-group of ethnic Jews in Judea, such as the religio-political leadership (e.g., Sanhedrin, Sadducees). Obviously, in a post-70 CE timeframe "Judeans" would not refer to those with Sadducean roots at all, since the temple lay in ruins.

If one views "Judeans" as more generically referencing a sub-group of ethnic Jews living in Judea who hold socio-political (and even religious) authority, then perhaps Paul's diasporic experiences shed some analogous light upon the Smyrnean Christ-followers's experience of opposition from those whom John calls "not Judeans." Paul allowed himself to be flogged by diasporic Jewish ("Judean-connected"?) synagogue authorities who assumed they held an authoritative status over him. I am getting a bit ahead of myself, though, since, in chapter 6, I rehearse the research that underlies the following two historical realities. First, in the land of Judea, synagogues, especially rural ones, functioned as community centers that served all facets of Jewish life, not least the ethno-religious, social, political, economic, and judicial dimensions. Second, the word *ekklēsia* also functioned both as a public Judean and as a semi-public Egyptian synagogue term (e.g., in Sirach, 1 Maccabees, Josephus, Philo). Other Jewish synagogue terms include *synagōgē* ("synagogue/assembly/community"; Judea and diaspora) and *proseuchē* ("prayer hall"; Galilee and diaspora).[72]

These two historical realities create a better context of understanding for why Paul submitted to being flogged by diasporic Jewish synagogue authorities. It could be that some first-century diasporic Jews may have perceived Paul's diasporic trans-locally connected *ekklēsiai* as claiming to be extensions of public Judean synagogues. If so, then each Pauline *ekklēsia* could have been viewed as a diasporic "satellite" in relation to

---

72. See my full discussion in Korner, *Origin and Meaning of* Ekklēsia, 81–125.

other Judean public *ekklēsiai*, thereby implicitly laying claim to being able to express all facets of Jewish life (ethno-religious, social, political, economic, and judicial dimensions). If diasporic synagogue authorities viewed Paul's *ekklēsiai* (1) as *intra*-Jewish associations and (2) as satellites of public Judean synagogues (i.e., *ekklēsiai* of non-Jesus-following Jews), and if they also viewed Paul as being in some fashion an ambassadorial *archisynagōgos* ("synagogue ruler"), then it makes more sense as to why Paul acquiesced to allowing himself to be flogged five times by diasporic Jews (1 Cor 11:23).

If John's *ekklēsiai* also were experiencing presumptuous "Judean"-style "power plays" upon them by Jewish synagogue associations in Smyrna and Philadelphia, it is quite obvious by John's phrase "synagogue of Satan" that he was in no mood to acquiesce to their authority. He doubly reinforces that fact by also calling them "not Judeans," that is, "not Jews" who possess no inherent authority over his Christ-followers, like they might have over the synagogues in Smyrna and Philadelphia by virtue of their "deputized" authority from Judean religio-civic authorities. Furthermore, if one translates the Greek word *ho satanas* ("the satan/ Satan") in line with its usage in LXX Zech 9, then it could simply mean "the accuser."[73] This would result in John non-supersessionally identifying "those who say they are Judeans, and are not" as being "the assembly/ community of the accusers," who accuse his *Christos*-followers before the civic authorities and *ho satanas*, Rome.

"Not Jews": Judaizing Non-Pauline Jewish *Christos*-followers

Leonard Thompson postulates that it may be, in analogous fashion with Paul's struggle against judaizing Jewish *Christos*-followers in Galatia, that John also is struggling against judaizing non-Pauline Jewish *Christos*-followers.[74] This judaizing group then becomes the intended target of John's pejorative phrase "synagogue of Satan." In John's case, as in Paul's, these Torah-observant Jewish *Christos*-followers would have rooted their apostolic loyalties with the Jerusalem-centered *Christos*-followers, and in particular with James, the (half-)brother of Jesus. These "so-called Jews"

73. See pp. 78–79 (Satan and the Hebrew Bible).

74. Thompson, *Revelation*, 68–69. Thompson references Gal 2—3 and *The Book of Elchasai* in HSW 2:685. He also mentions that *synagōgē* "does not necessarily refer to a Jewish community (cf. Jas 2:2 NRSV: 'assembly'; *Herm. Man* 11.9)" (*Revelation*, 69).

would have mandated circumcision of gentile *Christos*-followers in the same fashion as did James's Jewish *Christos*-followers (Gal 2:12).

It is such a scenario that Paul views as being *anathema* in Galatians (1:6–9). Further in that letter, Paul recounts his visit to Jerusalem to confirm his gospel that gentile *Christos*-followers are not required to live Torah-observant lives. This means that gentiles were free from having to observe at least four Jewish identity markers: festival observances, dietary restrictions, Sabbath observance, and circumcision (Gal 2:1–10). Paul gives details as to the identity of those who opposed his gospel: "false believers . . . who slipped in to spy on the freedom we have in Christ Jesus" (Gal 2:4). These judaizing spies appear to have been associated with "certain people who came from James" who comprised "the circumcision faction" (Gal 2:12).

If John is referring to Jewish *Christos*-followers "who are not Jews" what did he mean? At the very least John is not making a supersessionist statement—he is not talking about non-Jesus-following ethnic Jews. But it does sound as if he is denigrating those Jewish Christ-followers's identity because of their emphasis on circumcision and other purported Jewish identity markers (festivals observance, Sabbath keeping, dietary restrictions).

One critique of this interpretive option is Aune's claim that John does not seem to struggle against "the threat of Judaizing" or give evidence of "polemic between Jews and Christians" anywhere else in his book.[75] He suggests that the "blasphemy" (2:9) "may be denunciation of Christians to local authorities by Jews[, thus] all of this is extramural."[76] However, if one assumes that later evidence from Ignatius about Smyrna and Philadelphia may also have been applicable in John's day, then Aune's observation loses some of its critical force.

"Not Jews": Non-Judaizing Pauline Gentile *Christos*-followers

David Frankfurter suggests that John is referring in 2:9 and 3:9 to Christ-follower gentiles who are non-Torah-observant, that is, non-judaizing, with the result being that they "anger John by claiming Israel's legacy while neglecting religious practices incumbent upon devout Jews."[77]

75. Aune, *Revelation* 1—5, 165.
76. Aune, *Revelation* 1—5, 165.
77. Frankfurter, "Jews or Not?" 403–25.

Frankfurter is not alone in his claim[78] that the apostolic loyalties of these gentile *Christos*-followers are usually identified as being Pauline.[79] Elaine Pagels, a notable proponent of this view,[80] is cognizant that she stands upon the shoulders of nineteenth-century members of the Tübingen school.[81] She says that these non-Torah-observant gentiles are "groups that apparently consist largely of [second-generation] gentile converts who follow Pauline or neo-Pauline teaching."[82] She points to Ignatius, who himself is a gentile Pauline convert, as being a good exemplar of the type of supersessionist teaching and separationist leadership that John is so vehemently denouncing.

If Eusebius is correct in dating (on unknown grounds) Ignatius's letters to Trajan's reign (98–117 CE), and if Revelation was written only a decade or so earlier (the 90s CE), as Pagels presumes (in line with majority consensus), then her identification of Ignatius's predominantly gentile, hyper-supersessionist, neo-Pauline communities as the rhetorical target of John's polemic against "those who [falsely] say they are Jews" makes eminent sense.

Pagels sees a Pauline connection in 2:9 and 3:9 through the non-halakhic accommodation therein to Greco-Roman cultural practices. Some examples of non-Torah-observance that she discerns include Paul's teaching found in 1 Cor 7—10 where he allows practices that are prohibited by Jews, such as eating meat sacrificed to idols and marriage to outsiders.[83] She locates this ostensible Pauline emphasis, not least on meat and idols, in references to the Nicolaitans (2:6), to the teaching of Balaam (2:14), and to the teaching of Jezebel (2:20). Pagels, not unreasonably,

---

78. For example, Buchanan writes that John's opponents "may have been Paulinists or enthusiasts . . . but they were not non-Christian Jews" (*Book of Revelation*, 92). Paul Duff identifies Helmut Koester, C. K. Barrett, John Gager, Lloyd Gaston, and Stephen Wilson as being other commentators who view John's opponents as being gentile *Christos*-followers ("The Synagogue of Satan," 151). Duff himself sees ethnic Jews as John's target ("The Synagogue of Satan," 163).

79. Frankfurter argues that "those who call themselves Jews but are not" were "Pauline and neo-Pauline proselytes to the Jesus movement who were not, in John's eyes, . . . halakically pure enough to merit this term." Two issues of halakic purity were the eating of sacrificial meat and sexual practices (Frankfurter, "Jews or not?" 403).

80. Pagels, *Revelations* (2013).

81. See for example, Gustav Volkmar (1862) and Ferdinand C. Baur (1864) (Pagels, *Revelations*, 194 n. 58).

82. Pagels, "Social History," 498.

83. Pagels, "Social History," 496.

envisions John of Patmos as being just as capable of using scathing polemic as Paul was. In John's case, however, his polemic (e.g., Balaam and Jezebel terminology) is directed in an opposite direction. It is directed against gentiles who diminish the value of a halakhic lifestyle for Jewish followers of Jesus. Thus, for example, these gentiles accommodate for the eating of meat sacrificed to idols and of mixed marriages (which John calls *porneia*). Pagels reinforces the identification of Pauline groups as the antagonists of Rev 2:9 and 3:9 by reminding the reader that John was a Jew, not a "Christian," meaning thereby the technical term *Christianos*.[84] She uses the term *Christianos* only in technical fashion as an outsider term that was "coined by Roman magistrates to refer in particular to gentile converts," and not as insider terminology used by Christ-followers themselves.[85]

On a side note, although there may be some veracity in limiting the referents for the term *Christianos* to gentiles, I would suggest that *Christianos* is not an appropriate self-designation for gentile *Pauline* Christ-followers. As previously argued, I contend that the designation *Christianos* originated in order to address a group-identity conundrum that arose when gentiles in Syrian Antioch began to respond to the gospel as it was presented by Hellenistic Jewish Christ-followers who were loyal to the Jerusalem apostles (Acts 11:26).[86] If, after this, Paul would have used *Christianoi* as a group identity for his gentile Christ-followers, then the inferred allegiance to Jerusalem assumed in the term *Christianos* would implicitly have mitigated Paul's apostolic influence over his Christ-follower communities. Paul, thus, required a new sub-group designation

84. Pagels, "Social History," 490.

85. Pagels, "Social History," 498. In this, Pagels follows Philippa Townsend, who claims that *Christianos* is a term "adapted from a self-designation current among groups of Paul's gentile converts who followed Paul's lead and called themselves *hoi tou Christou* [and was] probably coined by Roman magistrates to refer in particular to Gentile converts" ("Social History," 498).

86. Korner, *Origin and Meaning of* Ekklēsia, 152–53. I write that the descriptor *christianoi* communicates an indelible rootedness in a Jewish heritage (i.e., *Christos* as the Jewish Messiah), but it has a semantic range broad enough to allow for gentile inclusion (i.e., *christianoi* simply indicates followers of the *Christos*; no ethnic heritage is necessarily presumed). Thus, *Christianos* would have worked for Paul if all he needed was a group designation that implicitly affirmed the continuation of the social and ethnic identity of each of his *Christos*-followers. However, since the term *christianoi* implied communal loyalty to the Jerusalem-centered apostles, Paul needed a different group designation that would tie his Christ-follower communities to *his* apostolic authority—*ekklesia* met that need.

that allowed for the inclusion of gentiles qua gentiles and of Jews qua Jews—the term *ekklēsia*, with its linguistic roots in Greco-Roman politics and in Jewish writings (e.g., the LXX), suited his socio-religious needs well.

Critique: Non-Torah-Observant Pauline Gentile Christ-followers

There are at least four questions that could be asked of Pagels's equation of "those who say they are Jews and are not" with gentile non-Torah-observant Christ-followers who promulgate "Pauline or neo-Pauline teaching." First, it seems a logical overextension to assume that John's moralistic challenges to his *ekklēsiai* about eating meat sacrificed to idols and exhibiting *porneia* (immorality) *necessarily* applies also to the *ekklēsiai* in Smyrna and Philadelphia. These prohibitions were explicitly directed to the *ekklēsiai* of Ephesus (Nicolaitans; 2:6), of Pergamum (the teaching of Balaam; 2:14), and of Thyatira (the teaching of Jezebel; 2:20). Clearer evidence is required to suggest that all seven Asia Minor *ekklēsiai* were dealing with those two moral issues.

Second, Pagels's claim that the word *porneia* includes the semantic domain of "immorality as cultural accommodation" also bears further scrutiny. Pagels invites us to read *porneia* through the lens of a broader semantic range that metaphorically includes cultural/religious/ethical unfaithfulness to God's covenantal expectations (e.g., the Jezebel metaphor). If, through this lens, *porneia* includes the concept of mixed marriages, as some Jews in the first century assumed, then 1 Cor 7—10 could provide some insight into whether John is challenging Pauline theology/morality in Rev 2—3. However, as I understand Paul's instructions to Christ-followers who are in mixed marriages, he is not writing to address *new* marriages. Rather, he is seeking to address *pre-existing* mixed marriages. He is seeking to maintain the sanctity of the marriage covenant between religiously unequally yoked partners in such a way that the unbelieving partner is given freedom of departure without the believing partner providing any just cause for such a departure. If, for those who participated in the Jerusalem Council (Acts 15), *porneia* does include the concept of mixed marriages, then the Jerusalem apostles could have charged Paul with having accommodated to Greco-Roman culture on two counts, not least in his later directions to the Corinthians: (1) his allowing of *porneia* (mixed marriages; 1 Cor 7), and (2) his enduring commitment to being all things for all people so as to persuade some to faithful discipleship in Christ (1 Cor 9:19–21).

Third, although neo-Pauline communities, like Ignatius's, could be accused of regularly accommodating the eating of meat sacrificed to idols, could one also say the same thing of Paul's earlier communities, as Pagels seems to suggest in her exploration of 1 Cor 7—10? In his Corinthian and Roman correspondence Paul appears to favor cultural accommodation for the sake of gospel proclamation through abrogation of his commitment to the Jerusalem Council to tell his Christ-followers to abstain from blood. In Rom 14 he nuances the Jerusalem Council's clear directive by allowing the Roman Christ-followers to eat meat sacrificed to idols, but only as long as it does not defile the conscience of a fellow Christ-follower (cf. also 1 Cor 8:9). Cultural accommodation is disallowed by Paul in instances where expressions of personal freedom become a cause for a fellow Christ-follower to stumble (1 Cor 8:13). Paul's carefully nuanced instructions to the Corinthians, thus, mitigate against his Christ-followers being the target of John's invective "synagogue of Satan." If they ate meat sacrificed to idols in such a public way that John became incensed, then they were not actually following the Pauline tradition of avoiding public eating for the sake of the consciences of Jewish Christ-followers, in particular, for whom such a practice would have been *anathema*.

It should also be noted that Paul's instructions to the Roman Christ-followers about meat sacrificed to idols (Rom 14) need not *necessarily* also have been an issue that his *ekklēsia* association in Rome was dealing with. The two "denominational" communities, if you will, held separate apostolic allegiances. Paul's epistle is not addressed to Pauline-loyal Christ-followers (an *ekklēsia*) but rather to the Roman Christ-followers loyal to the Jerusalem apostles (Rom 1:7; "to the holy ones"/*hagiois*). The only *ekklēsia* in Rome is the one that met in the home of Priscilla and Aquila (Rom 16:3–5). Since Paul asks the Roman Christ-followers to greet this *ekklēsia* on his behalf, it can be assumed that his Roman epistle, with his instructions in Romans 14, is not directly intended for the *ekklēsia* under the leadership of Priscilla and Aquila.[87]

A fourth reason to reassess Pagels's connection of "those who say they are Jews and are not" with gentile non-Torah-observant Christ-followers

---

87. For a fuller discussion of my rationale for the distinction between the subgroup identities, and, thus, the apostolic allegiances, of the Roman Christ-followers and the *ekklēsia* in Rome, see Korner, *Origin and Meaning of* Ekklēsia, 151, 166 n. 54, 196 n. 174, 243, 244.

who promulgate "Pauline or neo-Pauline teaching" relates to her claim that Paul is a primary referent for John's clause "those who claim to be apostles and are not." This would hold veracity only if one reads the *porneia* that these "apostles" are promulgating as being a spiritual metaphor for non-halakhic religious compromise, since Paul was adamantly opposed to sexual immorality. One example of "other unsanctioned apostles" could be those who, analogous to the "super-apostles" that Paul lambastes in 2 Corinthians, presume a similar level of apostolic authority to Paul, or not least to those whom Paul sanctioned as "apostles" (e.g., Andronicus and Junias [Rom 16]; cf. Eph 4:11).

One could not identify the apostle James, with his judaizing Jewish Christ-followers, as being John's referent for "those who claim to be apostles and are not" (2:2)—James is a Torah-observant Jew and "those who claim to be apostles" are not. Rather, John's "false apostles" encourage behavior reflective of the Nicolaitans (2:6, 15), who, in concord with the error of Balaam, encouraged both the eating of meat sacrificed to idols and sexually immoral behavior (2:14; cf. also 2:20–21). If the Greek compound noun "Nicolaitan" (*nikē* + *laos* = victory over the people) intends an allusion to the Hebrew name Balaam ("he who consumed the people"), then one could suggest that the Nicolaitans promoted similar non-Torah-observant practices as those associated with the teaching of Balaam.

There is one final rationale for not identifying Paul (or neo-Pauline followers) as the target of John's clause "those who claim to be apostles and are not." This rationale relates to John's vision of the twelve-fold foundation of the New Jerusalem, which he symbolically identifies with "the twelve apostles of the Lamb" (21:14, 19–20). If this is a historical reference to the twelve disciples chosen by Jesus, it is hard to imagine that Judas Iscariot is included.[88] If Judas is not intended, then who is the twelfth? I would forward Paul over Matthias (Acts 1:26) for the following reason. When identifying the criteria by which an apostolic successor to Judas should be chosen, Peter missed the most essential criterion—an apostle is one who is personally chosen by Jesus. Paul was personally chosen by Jesus at his Damascus Road experience. Although Matthias

88. It may be that John intends by the number "12" a symbolic reference which may not have required an actual twelfth disciple/apostle to have been chosen. One example of this is that the term "the twelve" was "a general evocation of all Israel, rather than the embodiment of a specific hope for restoring Israel by reuniting the twelve tribes" (McKnight, "Jesus and the Twelve," 213; cf. also, Meier, "Circle of the Twelve," 635–72).

qualifies for Peter's two criteria of (1) having accompanied the other disciples since Jesus's baptism and (2) who also was a witness of Jesus's resurrection (Acts 1:21–22), Matthias fails the most crucial criterion—he was not explicitly chosen by Jesus, but rather only implicitly so through the drawing of straws. If Paul is the intended twelfth apostle of John's symbolic foundation for the New Jerusalem, then why would John target Paul's gentile Christ-followers as being "the synagogue of Satan"? This point is particularly striking if the John who wrote Revelation is also one of the eleven apostles/disciples chosen by Jesus.

"Not Jews": Judaizing Non-Pauline Gentile *Christos*-followers

There is at least one more option for the identity of "those who call themselves Jews and are not." It entails reading Rev 2:9 and 3:9 with an eye to Paul's mention of a "so-called Jew" in Rom 2:17–29. The legitimacy of such a reading gains more plausibility if one assumes a somewhat contemporaneous compositional timeframe for Paul's epistle to the Roman community of *hoi hagioi* (1:7; 50's CE) and John's apocalyptic letter to the Roman Asia *ekklēsiai* (later 60s CE, rather than in the 90s CE).

If one reads Paul's "so-called Jew" phrase through Matthew Thiessen's interpretive framework then the phrase "so-called Jew" refers to a God-fearing gentile who became a full Jewish proselyte through circumcision.[89] In John's case, his "not Jews" are ethnic gentiles who converted previously into ostensibly Jewish proselytes, who are now Torah-observant *Christos*-followers and whose apostolic loyalties lay in Jerusalem, specifically with James, the (half-)brother of Jesus. Thus, John's "so-called Jews" (purported gentile proselytes) also would have mandated circumcision of gentile *Christos*-followers in the same fashion as did James's Jewish *Christos*-followers (Gal 2:12).

Two questions need to be answered for this possibility to gain plausibility. First, is there evidence of gentile proselytes to Judaism(s) living in Smyrna and Philadelphia? Second, is there evidence of gentile proselytes to Judaism(s) in Smyrna and Philadelphia who later became *Christos*-followers and mandated that gentile (non-proselyte) *Christos*-followers become fully Torah-observant? If John accords with Paul's earlier stance against the judaizing of gentile *Christos*-followers, then it becomes readily

---

89. Thiessen, "Gentile Circumcision," 373–91. See also my discussion of Thiessen's proposal in Korner, *Origin and Meaning of* Ekklēsia, 216–20.

understandable why he is just as vociferously lambasting "those who say they are Jews and are not" in Smyrna and Philadelphia, and attributing their work to Satan, "the angel of (false) light" (cf. Paul and 2 Cor 11:14; Gal 2:12).

Hirschberg answers our first question with his observation that in Asia Minor there was a strong representation of gentile converts to Jewishness, whether proselytes (circumcised) or "Godfearers" (uncircumcised but otherwise committed to Torah-observance).[90] Hirschberg's observation opens up the possibility that our second question also can be answered in the affirmative. But for that possibility to move towards plausibility we still require evidence of *Christos*-following gentile proselytes (or God-fearers) who continued to live within a theological framework that promoted the erasure of gentile ethnic identity through the adoption of Jewish identity markers, such as circumcision. The seven letters of Ignatius, the bishop of (Syrian) Antioch, provide implicit confirmation not least of uncircumcised/gentile judaizing Christ-followers who promulagated Judaistic lifestyles for gentiles living in or around Smyrna. Given Paul's adamant opposition to Judaistic lifestyles for gentiles, we can assume that these uncircumcised/gentile Christ-followers were non-Pauline.

Ignatius makes very clear in his seven letters that he is (rabidly) supersessionist and anti-Judaistic. Four of his letters were written while he stayed in Smyrna and two of his other three letters were written to Smyrna from Troas. His most explicit prejudice against all things Jewish is expressed in his (infamous) letter to the Magnesians while in Smyrna. He writes that "it is monstrous to talk of Jesus Christ and to practice Judaism (*Ioudaïsmos*)" (*Magnesians* 10.1.3). In his letter to the Philadelphians, Ignatius lambasts "the uncircumcised" Christ-followers who "interpret Judaism" by calling them "tombstones and sepulchers" (*Philadelphians* 6.1). Dietmar Neufeld comments that there has been "a great deal of speculation about the identity of these interpreters of Judaism [with some concluding] that they are Gentile converts who have been attracted to Judaism."[91] He does caution us, though, to be aware of undue rhetoric on Ignatius's part. Nonetheless, if Ignatius can be understood to

90. Hirschberg, *Das eschatologische Israel*, 49–52.

91. Neufeld, "Christian Communities," 34. Neufeld notes two other interpretive options for the "uncircumcised interpreters": (1) "God-worshipers who are imposing their Jewish practices on other Christians"; and (2) "docetic teachers who have adopted Jewish themes" ("Christian Communities," 34).

be writing about judaizing (uncircumcised) gentile Christ-followers in his day, then it would not seem unwarranted to extrapolate that fact back to John's day not least for his *ekklēsia* in Philadelphia.

Ignatius's potential evidence of judaizing gentile *Christos*-followers accords with Pagels's assertion that "John is . . . attacking as rival prophets and teachers, followers of Jesus in Asia."[92] In another respect, however, it does not concur with her identification of those "rival prophets and teachers" as being those "who follow Pauline teaching." Rather, Ignatius's evidence, if applicable in John's day, would point to those "rival prophets and teachers" as being those who promulgate a judaizing agenda that initially began with James's Jewish Christ-followers (Gal 2) and continued to be an issue with judaizing gentile Christ-followers (not necessarily affiliated with James) in Smyrna and Philadelphia.

Ignatius's evidence of gentile judaizers brings up a corollary question: "Would John associate gentile *Christos*-followers with a *synagōgē* (synagogue) rather than with an *ekklēsia*?" I would suggest that Nazorean Christ-followers provide a precedent for assuming that other first-century CE *Christos*-followers with strong ties to a Judaistic lifestyle would self-designate corporately as a "synagogue." James's community is not necessarily as helpful of a precedent in that the "synagogue" in which they are said to have met may have been an actual synagogue building. It is in the Jewish synagogue in their city that James's Jewish *Christos*-followers met *en ekklēsia* ("in an assembly") (Jas 2:2).[93]

Johannine Anti-Judaism(s)? "The Synagogue of Satan"

When modern readers encounter the word "synagogue" it is most natural to assume that this term is making reference to a Jewish institution or congregation or building or even to "Judaism" more generally. In the ancient world of John's readership, the Greek word *synagōgē*, which underlies our English word "synagogue," simply means "assembly/gathering," much the same as does the word *ekklēsia*, which modern interpreters unfortunately continue to translate anachronistically as "church." Thus, given modern assumptions that "synagogue" refers to a Jewish entity and *ekklēsia* to a "Christian" (read "non-Jewish") entity, it is readily apparent how easy it is

92. Pagels, "Social History of Satan," 505.

93. The NRSV translates the Greek word *synagōgē* in Jas 2:2 as "assembly," which hides the connection of James' diasporic *Christos*-follower community to a "synagogue."

for a modern reader to assume that John's phrase "synagogue of Satan" is pejorative at best (i.e., anti-Jewish) and supersessionist at worst.[94]

The Meaning of "Synagogue"

There are different ways to understand what John may be communicating with his phrase "*synagōgē* of Satan." John may be using the phrase "synagogue of Satan" pejoratively to refer to non-Jesus-following Jews in general or neutrally to a specific type of association (*synodos, thiasos, Christos*-follower) in the Greco-Roman world. The first step in ascertaining his rhetorical intentions is to assess what he means by the term "synagogue," and, in particular, if he attaches any *necessary* ethnic sentiments to *synagōgē*.

"Synagogue" as Greco-Roman Assembly

Synagōgē is not necessarily a strictly Jewish term. The "*synagōgē* of *the satanas*" could refer to a Greek non-civic association or even to a civic entity. The word *synagōgē* was used to denote formal non-civic or civic gatherings. As such, it was an *ethnically neutral* term that simply means "assembly/meeting." A second-century BCE example of a non-Jewish *synagōgē*, which in this case is a *synagōgē* of the *neoi* of a *polis*, is extant in a civic honorary decree from Thessaly (*I.Thess* I 16).[95] A late first-century BCE Alexandrian papyrus records the decree of a *synodos* devoted to emperor Augustus (*SB* XXII 15460).[96] It reads, "In the twenty-fifth year of Caesar . . . at the *synagōgē* which met in the house of the *synodos* of the *archakolothoi* ('principal followers') of emperor Augustus Caesar, . . . whose *synagōgos* ('synagogue leader') is Primos and whose president

---

94. Aside from persecution in Smyrna and Philadelphia by the "synagogue of Satan," John mentions that one Christ-follower was purportedly killed in Pergamon (2:13). Even though Pergamon is identified as the location of "Satan's throne" (2:13), David Aune claims that a Jewish synagogue community is not one of the possible referents for John's polemical phrase (*Revelation* 1—5, 182–84).

95. *I.Thess* I 16 (Kierion: Sphades, c. 125 BCE; cf. *IG IX*,2 259: ἐκκλησία<ς> [γενομέ]<ν>ης ἐννόμου, [ἐμφανισμὸν] ποιησαμένων τῶν ταγῶν . . . [—] τῆς τῶν νέων συναγωγῆς).

96. *AGRW*, no. 280 (see also *AGRW*, no. 63): *SB* XXII 15460=Brashear 1993, 14–15 = Papyrus written by the same association as the inscription *BGU* IV 1137; 5 BCE (August 21).

is Ioukoundos."[97] This non-civic association appears even to be named *synagōgē*, rather than only using *synagōgē* as the name for their assembly which met in the house of the semi-public association (*synodos*).

The reality that *synagōgē* need not be translated only as "synagogue" should give pause for New Testament translators. Given the modern predilection for associating the word "synagogue" with an assembly/building/congregation of ethnic Jews, and in light of the fact that ancient usages of the word *synagōgē* do not solely refer to an assembly/building/congregation of ethnic Jews, it is perhaps more appropriate to translate "the *synagōgē* of Satan" as "the assembly/gathering of Satan." This translation serves to maintain the ethnic neutrality with which John's audience may have understood the word *synagōgē*.

"Synagogue" as Jewish Assembly

Despite the original ethnic neutrality inherent in the term *synagōgē*, the majority of commentators favor seeing "synagogue" as being a generalized reference to Jewish synagogue communities. For example, some later non-Jewish Christ-followers (e.g., Ignatius) read this verse as justification for their parting of ways with Jews. Although, in the first century CE, *synagōgē* is the favoured term for identifying gatherings of Jews or their communal buildings, it is helpful to note that, in their synagogue sourcebook, Runesson, Binder, and Olsson identify upward of twenty-two terms that were used by Jews for their public and semi-public communal entities.[98] There are two questions to address with respect John's use of *synagōgē*. First, is John using *synagōgē* with Jewish particularity or as a synonym for *ekklēsia*? If as a synonym, then one could translate *synagōgē* neutrally as "gathering/meeting/assembly." Second, if John is not using the *synagōgē* in an ethnically particularized fashion, then to what type of semi-public association is he referring: (1) one for non-Jesus-following Jews, (2) one for Jewish *Christos*-followers, (3) one for non-Jewish *Christos*-followers, or (4) one for Jewish and non-Jewish *Christos*-followers?

97. See examples of other "synagogue" terminology used by non-Jews in *AGRW*, nos. 39, 54, 63 (*archisynagōgos*) and nos. 84, 85, 87, 291 (*synagōgos*).

98. Runesson, Binder, and Olsson note that "what in English is translated 'synagogue' went under several different names in antiquity," that is, seventeen Greek terms, five Hebrew terms and three Latin terms, some of which overlap (*Ancient Synagogue*, 10, n. 21). For extensive descriptions of each term as used by Jewish communities, see Binder, *Into the Temple Courts*, 91–151.

It is clear that since the *synagōgē* of *the satanas* is not in the land of Israel, it is not a public *synagōgē*. As such, as a diasporic *synagōgē*, it can be nothing other than a semi-public association, one with trans-local connections between at least two cities (Smyrna and Philadelphia). Given this background, John is not casting aspersion upon Jews in general, or upon all Jewish synagogue communities in general, or even upon all Jews or Jewish synagogue communities in Smyrna and Philadelphia. Rather, John is casting aspersion only on *one specific sub-set* of "those who say they are Jews" within each city, the *synagōgē* who actively oppose *Christos*-followers within the Johannine (previously Pauline?) *ekklēsiai* in Smyrna and Philadelphia.

Elisabeth Schüssler-Fiorenza is one scholar who does not see anti-Jewish rhetoric as being inherent in John's phraseology. She contends that "John's identification of the synagogue as a congregation of Satan should not be misread as anti-Semitism, since the author expresses great appreciation for true Judaism . . . as a Jew."[99] She suggests that John's messages to his *ekklēsiai* in Smyrna and Philadelphia appear to reflect the conflict between Jews who could "claim the protection granted by Roman law to Judaism" and Jewish *Christos*-followers who "were less and less able to claim their political privileges and identity as Jews."[100] Paul Duff points towards John's allusion to Isa 60:14 in Rev 3:9 as an indication of "a rather benevolent treatment at the *eschaton*" for the "synagogue of Satan."[101] John's message in 3:9 can even be said to suggest benevolent treatment of the "synagogue of Satan" in his own day and age—its members's "punishment" is limited only to performing an act of humble submission before the *ekklēsia* community.

"Synagogue" as Christos-follower Assembly

At least one sub-group in the early Jesus movement explicitly self-identified collectively as *synagōgē*—the Jewish *Christos*-followers called the Nazoreans/Nazarenes of Transjordan (the east side of the Jordan).[102] Ad-

---

99. Schüssler-Fiorenza, *Revelation*, 55.

100. Schüssler-Fiorenza, *Revelation*, 55.

101. Duff, "The Synagogue of Satan," 159. Isaiah 60:14 reads (NRSV) "The descendants of those who oppressed you shall come bending low to you."

102. Elderen, "Early Christianity in Transjordan," 97–117; Kinzig, "Nazoreans," 463–87.

ditionally, some early church fathers also use *synagōgē* as a descriptor of Christ-follower assemblies: (1) Ignatius (*Pol.* 4.2: "Let the *synagōgai* be more numerous"; late first century CE), (2) the author of the *Shepherd of Hermas* (11.9: "a *synagōgē* of righteous men"; also 11.13, 14; first/second century CE), (3) Dionysius of Alexandria (mid-third century CE) who calls the assemblies *synagōgai* (Eusebius, *Hist. Eccl.* 7.9.2; 7.11.11, 12, 17),[103] and (4) Epiphanius who used the word *synagōgē* as a designation for a public meeting of Christ-followers gathered for the purpose of worship (*Haer.* 30.18.2). The epistle of James, which is addressed to the "twelve [Jewish] tribes in the diaspora [a.k.a., Asia Minor?]," appears to refer to the gathering of his Jewish *Christos*-following addressees as a *synagōgē* (Jas 2:2).

If James's phrase "your *synagōgē*" refers to the building of a Jewish synagogue community, within which his halakhic observant Christ-followers met, then his Christ-followers differentiated their "members only" meeting from other Jewish "members only" gatherings within the same synagogue building by naming their particular meeting *ekklēsia* ("assembly/gathering").[104] Given that the Nazoreans in the land self-identified collectively as *synagōgē*, it is not unreasonable to conclude that James's phrase "your *synagōgē*" may also refer to a collective identity assumed by his diasporic Jewish Christ-followers ("if a poor person comes into the midst of your gathered sub-group named *synagōgē*"; 2:2). This being the case, then James's use of the term *ekklēsia* refers to a semi-public assembly convened by the *Christos*-follower members (5:14). The use of *synagōgē* by Christ-followers continued past the first century into the patristic era.[105]

The inherent Jewishness and common commitment to Torah-observance of the Nazoreans and James's diasporic addressees provides a precedent for suggesting that, at most, John's use of the phrase "*synagōgē* of Satan" simply reflects "a parting of ways" *within* Judaism(s), but not a parting between two so-called "religions" called "Judaism" and "Christianity." Three factors suggest this: (1) the Jewishness of the literary makeup of Revelation's text (see chapter 8); (2) the probability that John's text is

---

103. Dibelius, *James*, 133.

104. Two other interpretations of the word *synagōgē* are possible: (1) a ritual assembly of Jewish Christ-followers (Bauckham, "James and the Jerusalem Community," 58) or (2) a building owned by Christ-followers and dedicated for their ritual worship assemblies (McKnight, *Letter of James*, 183). These two usages of the word *synagōgē* are anomalous with respect to other New Testament writings.

105. See Martin Dibelius (*James*, 133) and Ralph Martin (*James*, 61).

describing an inner-Jewish debate;[106] and (3) the fact that both *ekklēsia* and *synagōgē* are used as collective terminology for Jewish communities.[107]

As I will argue in my review of Jewish uses of the word *ekklēsia*,[108] *ekklēsia* is used to denote both semi-public associations[109] and public assemblies within which are addressed a broad range of issues relevant to all members of a regional community.[110] Its appropriation by *intra muros* groups within pluriform Second Temple Judaism,[111] and its subsequent adoption by Christ-follower communities in Roman Asia, both Pauline and Johannine, becomes another factor by which to problematize

106. David Aune notes that "The phrase 'synagogue of Satan' has a very close parallel in the expression . . . 'congregation of Belial,' in 1QH 2:22 and 1QM 4:9 ('Belial' is an alternative name for Satan in 2 Cor 6:15; *T. Reub.* 2:4; *Jub.* 15:33; CD 6:9), and in the LXX *synagōgē* is used to translate *'ēdâ* over 100 times. 1QS 5:1–2 has the parallel expression . . . ('congregation of the perverse men'; cf. 1QM 15:9) . . . 'congregation of wickedness.' *Barn.* 5:13 and 6:6 have the phrase 'groups/synagogues of evil people'" (*Revelation* 1—5, 164). See also Marshall, "John's Jewish (Christian?) Apocalypse," 233–56.

107. See my discussion of *ekklēsia* as a Jewish synagogue term in chapter six. See Korner, "*Ekklēsia* as a Jewish Synagogue Term: Some Implications," 53–78; Korner, "*Ekklēsia* as a Jewish Synagogue Term: A Response," 127–36; Korner, *Origin and Meaning of* Ekklēsia, 81–125.

108. See chapter 6 of this book.

109. See p. 14 where Anders Runesson helpfully clarifies the three social levels on which "religion" "played out" in antiquity ("Was There a Christian Mission," 213). Semi-public/association synagogues are for members and sympathizers only (Runesson, *Origins of the Synagogue*, 213–32). One could call these a Jewish form of Greco-Roman associations known as *thiasoi* or *collegia* (Runesson, *Origins of the Synagogue*, 354, 480). Two examples of association synagogues in the land of Israel are Philo's reference to the Essenes (*Prob.* 80—83), and the community associated with the first-century CE synagogue in Jerusalem mentioned in the Theodotus inscription (*CIJ* II 1404; see Kloppenborg, "Dating Theodotus," 243–80).

110. In his survey of first century CE sources, Lee Levine notes that the public *synagōgē* building was used for "the entire gamut of [public] activities connected with any Jewish community . . . [such] as a courtroom, school, hostel, a place for political meetings, social gatherings, housing charity funds, a setting for manumissions, meals (sacred or otherwise), and, of course, a number of religious-liturgical functions [such as public Torah reading, rituals, festival observance]" (Levine, *Ancient Synagogue*, 29).

111. In chapter 1, I clarified what I mean when I speak of "Judaism." I follow the definition of "common Judaism" offered by E. P. Sanders. "Common Judaism" is the convergence of four beliefs among first-century CE Jews: "belief that their God was the only true God, that he had chosen them and had given them his law, and that they were required to obey it" and that "the temple was the visible, functioning symbol of God's presence with his people and it was also the basic rallying point of Jewish loyalties" (*Judaism*, 241).

scholarly suggestions that early Christ-followers were "parting ways" with the *Ioudaioi* (Jews/Judeans), that is, with Judaism(s), "Jewishness," or Jewish organizational forms.

In light of the foregoing, I would suggest that John's term "synagogue of Satan" is not meant to create a bifurcation between "Christianity" and "Judaism"/*Christos*-following and non-Jesus-following Jews. Rather, one could view his term "synagogue of Satan" as having primary reference to the fact, not least, that judaizing (circumcised) gentile *Christos*-followers should not be considered as *ekklēsia* members. Rather, these gentile "so-called Jews" should be considered members of their own sectarian Torah-observant community ("a synagogue"), but one that is functionally doing the work of Satan.

Although extreme, it is not without precedent in the New Testament for a writer to ascribe the actions of *Christos*-followers to Satan. Paul identifies Satan as being able to masquerade as an angel of light (2 Cor 11:14), and perhaps even as being the "angel from heaven" (Gal 1:8) whom he curses because this angel (and its human counterpart) "perverts the gospel" by promoting Torah-observance for gentiles. Jesus speaks directly to Peter and addresses him as Satan, meaning thereby not that Peter is satanic but that at that moment he was doing the work of Satan by trying to dissuade Jesus from fulfilling his calling of going to the cross (Matt 16:23; Mark 8:33).

The Meaning of "Satan"

This preliminary conversation on Satan leads us to the need to explore more fully the interpretive options for John's use of the word *ho satanas* ("the satan"; 2:9; 3:9). Two primary semantic domains arise from a study of Jewish literary works: (1) a proper name for a living supernatural adversary of God and his people (alias "the Devil"/*ho diabolos*), and (2) a descriptive term for a forensic prosecutor/accuser of God's people similar to how it is used in Zechariah. Thomas Farrar notes that: "the closest terminological and conceptual parallels to New Testament Satanology in pre- and non-Christian Second Temple Jewish literature occur in texts that reflect mythological Satanology and that the New Testament writers show no sign of eliminating the mythological connotations of their Satanological vocabulary."[112] The strength of Farrar's study which follows is

---

112. Farrar, "New Testament Satanology," 26.

his greater precision in "admitting into evidence as possible background to New Testament Satanology only texts that can be assigned with high probability to a non-Christian Jewish provenance and a date of approximately 70 C.E. or earlier."[113]

"Satan" and the Hebrew Bible

Farrar observes that the word *satan* (שטן) generally is used in the Hebrew Bible in reference to humans with the meaning of "adversary."[114] There are four passages, however, in which *satan* refers to a celestial being.[115] In two passages the term *satan* is used as a proper noun (*ha-satan*; Job's prologue and the vision of Zech 3). Scholarly consensus locates the setting of each passage as being the divine council.[116] In 1 Kgs 22:19–23 another divine council scene unfolds, which alludes to Job 1–2. The *ha-satan* (השטן) heavenly figure therein is variously viewed as ranging in character "from 'noble' and 'good' to 'morally neutral' or ambiguous, to 'not . . . normative,' characterized by *Hinterhältigkeit*, 'insolent' or 'evil.'"[117] While some associate the role of a prosecutor with *ha satan*, it is not simply a judicial role—one must also consider the antagonism exhibited between *ha satan* and YHWH (Job 2:3; Zech 3:2).[118] Farrar summarizes the Hebrew Bible usage of *ha satan* as not referencing "the malevolent prince of demons that 'Satan' subsequently became, there is tension in the figure's relationship with Yahweh. . . . There is 'no Satan in the Old Testament' in the later

---

113. Farrar, "New Testament Satanology," 27. Literature that speaks of a "leading Suprahuman opponent" (LSO) and which meets his "date and provenance criteria and contain text-critically reliable material relevant to our study are as follows: four books of the Hebrew Bible (Numbers, Job, Zechariah, and 1 Chronicles), their LXX translations, Sirach, *Wisdom of Solomon*, the *Book of the Watchers*, the *Book of Jubilees*, the *Book of Parables*, the *Moses Fragment*, selected Qumran literature, and two pseudo-Philonic works (*On Samson* and *Biblical Antiquities*)" ("New Testament Satanology," 22).

114. For example, Hadad the Edomite (1 Kgs 11:14).

115. Num 22:22–32; Job 1—2; Zech 3:1–2; 1 Chr 21:1.

116. Day, *Adversary in Heaven*, 79; Floyd, *Minor Prophets*, 374; Japhet, *I & II Chronicles*, 375; Meyers and Meyers, *Haggai, Zechariah 1—8*, 184; White, *Yahweh's Council*, 65.

117. Farrar, "New Testament Satanology," 33.

118. The verb גער denotes YHWH's "particularly strong invective against his opponents" (Sacchi, "The Devil in Jewish Traditions," 217).

sense of the word, but there is a kernel from which later, sometimes more elaborate, Satanologies developed."[119]

The LXX translates השטן in Job and Zechariah as ὁ διάβολος ("the devil") and casts this figure as an angelic being with evil intention, unlike the Hebrew Bible's morally ambiguous "accuser."[120] Thus, the LXX forms a bridge between the Hebrew Bible's angelic "accuser" and the later "devil" of the New Testament.

"Satan" and Jewish Second Temple Writings

Second Temple Jewish writings that attest a "satan" figure include the book of *Jubilees* (mid-second century BCE) and the *Book of Parables* (1 *En.* 37—71; *ca.* Herod the Great). *Jubilees* builds upon the Watchers tradition from 1 *En.* 1—16 by describing "a combination of demonic enemies and their satanic leader [Mastema] who remains active in the heavenly court."[121] *Jubilees* designates Mastema as "prince of the spirits" (*Jub.* 10.8) and "satan/the satan" (Ethiopic lacks a definite article). *Jubilees*'s Mastema mirrors Job's השטן: "Mastema remains subordinate to God and retains access to the heavenly court. He is not God's opponent in any dualistic sense."[122] The *Book of Parables* used the term Azazel (derived from Lev 16:8–10) and foretells punishment for "the host of Azazel" for "becoming servants of (the) Satan" (1 *En.* 54.6). As master of Azazel's host, Satan would seem to be Azazel himself. Thus, in *Parables* the Satan "is a malevolent angel named Azazel who leads a host of other angels/satans. Their functions are to incite violence, accuse humans before God, and inflict punishment; yet he and his host are themselves destined for eschatological punishment."[123]

"Satan" and the Dead Sea Scrolls

The sectarian Qumran literature also includes evidence of a malevolent angelic being equivalent to *ho diabolos/ha satan*. Five times the Damascus Document (CD) uses the name Belial (Hebrew בליעל) for an archdemon

---

119. Farrar, "New Testament Satanology," 34.
120. Farrar, "New Testament Satanology," 34.
121. Ellis, "Theology of Evil," 267; cf. *Jub.* 5, 10.
122. Farrar, "New Testament Satanology," 44.
123. Farrar, "New Testament Satanology," 44.

who employs "three traps" to make the Israelites stumble: unchastity, wealth, and defilement of the sanctuary (CD 4.12–19). As in *Jubilees*, CD points to Belial as the one who empowers the Egyptian magicians who challenged Moses (CD 5.18–19). Belial also serves as the eschatological punisher of those who do evil (CD 8.1–3). Belial also appears in the War Scroll (1QM; first century BCE). Therein, Belial is given the role of leader of the sons of darkness in battle against the sons of light (1QM 1.1) and of commander of angelic subordinates ("the spirits of his lot—angels of destruction"; 1QM 13.1–6). The angelic counterpart of Belial ("the prince of the dominion of evil"; 1QM 17.5) is "the majestic angel . . . Michael" (1QM 17.6–7). The War Scroll makes sure to emphasize, though, that Belial is no match for God because God created Belial (1QM 13.11). This cosmic "duel-ism," so to speak, is also evident in the Treatise of the Two Spirits (1QS 3.13—4.26), a self-contained section within the Community Rule (1QS). Therein, the "sons of justice" are led by the "Prince of Lights," while the "sons of deceit" are led by the "Angel of Darkness" (1QS 3.20–22).

"Satan" and the New Testament

The New Testament reduces the designations for a malevolent angelic leader to primarily two names: ὁ σατανᾶς and its LXX synonym ὁ διάβολος.[124] This intentionality comes particularly to the fore in the Synoptic Gospels where Jesus affirms his challengers's belief in a prince of demons, whom they name "Beelzebul" but whom Jesus designates as ὁ σατανᾶς (Mark 3:22–30; Matt 12:24–32; Luke 11:15–22). Prior to the New Testament, there is no unambiguous reference to "Satan" as being a proper name. Farrar takes New Testament translators to task for their inconsistency in rendering ὁ διάβολος as a descriptor ("the devil") but ὁ σατανᾶς as the anarthrous "Satan." He recommends that "future translations should include the definite article with 'Satan' in most cases and should also capitalize 'Devil/Diable' to avoid creating an unwarranted semantic contrast between ὁ διάβολος and ὁ σατανᾶς."[125]

---

124. Other NT descriptors include ὁ πονηρός ("the evil one"; 12x) and ὁ ἄρχων ("the prince/ruler" [of the demons; of this world; of the power of the air]; 8x).

125. Farrar, "New Testament Satanology," 60.

Farrar also makes note of a "*conceptual* consistency in the functions and attributes assigned to the Satan,"[126] some of which are presaged in Jewish Second Temple texts. Distinctive developments include: (1) Jesus's replacement of Michael and other angelic figures with himself as Satan's dualistic counterpart (e.g., Matt 13:38–43; 2 Cor 6:15), (2) the devil's role in bringing about Jesus's death (Luke 22:3, 53; John 13:2, 27; 1 Cor 2:8); (3) the decisive defeat of Satan by Jesus, particularly through the cross (Mark 3:27 par.; Heb 2:14; 1 John 3:8; Rev 12:10–11); and (4) the very active nature of Satan that is evident in his dialoguing, disputing, lying, murdering, accusations, and scheming, among other things. The distinctive New Testament conceptions of Satan/the devil "place the burden of proof squarely on those who interpret the Satanology of particular New Testament writings non-mythologically."[127] Although numerous scholars assert the non-personal nature of *ho satanas* and *ho diabolos* usages in the New Testament, Aune counters with his assessment that "the various aliases 'ruler of this world,' 'Satan,' and 'Devil' are designations for a personal being."[128]

"Satan" in Revelation

Farrar's analysis of "Satan" usage in the New Testament does not address one other potential referent: a symbolic reference to the Roman *imperium*. Hirschberg states that "in Revelation 'Satan' is identified primarily with Rome and the worship of the emperor."[129] Following on from Klauck, Hirschberg states that "the dogmas condemned in his Seven Letters (Nicolaitans, 2:15; Balaam, 2:14; Jezebel, 2:20ff) might have been connected to a pagan way of life tolerant toward the worship of the emperor."[130] While it is clear that John symbolically depicts Rome through his Babylon the prostitute imagery (e.g., Dea Roma allusions in ch. 17), I would suggest that it is less clear that *ho satanas* functions as an allusion to Rome. Rather, John's mention of the "throne of Satan" relative to Pergamum's tribute to Zeus would seem to indicate that John's use of "Satan" is pejorative mockery against idol worship related most directly

126. See Farrar and Williams, "Talk of the Devil," 80–82, especially Table 1.

127. Farrar, "New Testament Satanology," 63.

128. Aune, "Dualism in the Fourth Gospel," 135.

129. Hirschberg, "Jewish Believers in Asia Minor," 223.

130. Hirschberg, "Jewish Believers in Asia Minor," 223, n. 20.

to the Greek pantheon. Hirschberg's suggestion that it has more global intent such that emperor worship is also implied would seem to require evidence that has a more direct correlation.

At the outset of this chapter I identified two primary meanings that may lie behind John's use of the word *ho satanas*. Although one could claim a correlation with LXX Zechariah's forensic prosecutor/accuser of God's people, it would seem the bulk of evidence suggests that John is making reference in 2:9 and 3:9 to a proper name for a supernatural adversary of God and his people (alias "the Devil"/*ho diabolos*). If the *synagōgē* of Satan in Smyrna and Philadelphia is a *Christos*-follower group, then, at the very least, John, in continuity with the Gospels (e.g., Peter) and with Paul (Galatians, Corinthians), also affirms that Christ-followers functionally can do the work of Satan. As such, one can understand why John would not want to identify that "satanic" group as an *ekklēsia*, even if that group itself self-identified as an *ekklēsia*. In the next chapter I will address in much more detail the fact (1) that the word *synagōgē* does not necessarily refer to a non-Jesus-following Jewish association and (2) that the word *ekklēsia* is one of among twenty-two different words that underly the English word "synagogue" when "synagogue" is used in reference to buildings, meetings, or group identities of non-Jesus-following Jews in the ancient Mediterranean.

Johannine Supersessionism: Hebrew Bible *Topoi*

There are two *topoi*, which have roots in the Hebrew Bible, that John recontextualizes and which figure prominently in one's assessment of John's supersessionistic intentions: (1) the seven *ekklēsiai* as seven golden lampstands (*menorot*?) and (2) the 144,000.

Seven Lampstands (1:12–13, 20)

John describes his encounter with "one like a son of man" (1:12–20)[131] who walks among "the seven lampstands (*lychniai*) [which] are the seven *ekklēsiai* [of Roman Asia]" (1:20). Aside from the seven *ekklēsiai*, Beale

131. One can read John's phrase *homoion huion anthrōpou* as a euphemism for "human being" or as a deliberate allusion to the messianic "Son of Man" figure in the Ancient of Days eschatological scene in Dan 7. The context of Rev 1:12–20 clearly connects this "one like a human being/Son of Man" with Jesus the resurrected Jewish *Christos*/Messiah (cf. 1:17–18).

adds a second metaphorical referent for John's "lampstands"—ethnic Israel. Beale, thus, supersessionally claims that John's seven *ekklēsiai* ("lampstands") replace ethnic Israel because they "represent the church as the true temple and the totality of the people of God witnessing in the period between Christ's resurrection and his final coming."[132]

Beale's metaphorical identification of ethnic Israel with John's seven "lampstands" (*lychniai*) stems from the fact that in the LXX the word *lychnia* translates the Hebrew word *menorah*. The *menorah* with its seven golden lamps was part of the furniture in the tabernacle and temple (e.g., Exod 25 [LXX vv. 30–31; HB vv. 31–32]).[133] Beale suggests that the *menorah* symbolizes Israel as a "figurative synecdoche [in which] part of the temple furniture stands for the whole temple, which by extension also represents the faithful Israel."[134] Additionally, Beale notes that "Jewish writings also understand the lampstand [*lychnia/menorah*] of Zechariah as symbolizing Israel, especially the righteous gathered from all generations at the end time."[135] Thus, Beale's logical progression moves in the following direction: given (1) that John's *ekklēsiai* are metaphorical "lampstands" (*lychniai*), and (2) that the word "lampstand" refers to a *menorah*, and (3) that a *menorah* is a synecdoche of ethnic Israel, then (4) John's *ekklēsiai* are portrayed as being a replacement for ethnic Israel. Aune provides a helpful observation that places into question Beale's supersessionist interpretation of John's "lampstands": "there is no explicit indication that John conceived of these [seven lampstands] as *branched* lampstands with seven oil lamps like the traditional Jewish menorah used as a religious symbol."[136]

If, however, one does grant Beale's interpretive assumption that John's "lampstand" is a synecdoche for "faithful Israel," there may still be a non-supersessionist way forward. In essence, this requires posturing John's *multi-ethnic ekklēsiai* not as *being* Israel, but rather as being part *of* Israel, that is, as being the *ekklēsia . . .* of Israel, so to speak. There

132. Beale, *Revelation*, 207.

133. For additional LXX translations of the Hebrew הַמְּנֹרָה (*ha menorah*) as *lychnia*, see, for example, Exod 40 (vv. 22–23, LXX; vv. 24–25, HB), 1 Chr 28:15, 2 Chr 4:7, 20–22.

134. Beale, *Revelation*, 206.

135. Beale, *Revelation*, 206. In LXX Zech 5:2 and 11 the word *lychnia* translates the Hebrew word *menorah* (HB Zech 4:2, 11).

136. Aune, *Revelation* 1—5, 89 (author's emphasis). See Aune's extensive review of Jewish traditions relative to the *menorah* (*Revelation* 1—5, 88–90).

are, thus, two assumptions that require demonstration: (1) that there is an LXX example of the phrase "*ekklēsia* of Israel," or its equivalent, and (2) that the *ekklēsia* (of ethnic Israel) connotes a regional or supra-local group identity that also includes non-Jews, whether those non-Jews are proselytes, God-fearers, or simply "resident aliens" (Heb. *gērim*).

The LXX uses *ekklēsia* only to translate the Hebrew word *qāhāl* ("assembly"), not the generally synonymous *'ēdâ*, and only beginning with Deuteronomy.[137] Regarding the collocation of ethnic Israelites with a national identity that includes the word *ekklēsia*, LXX Deut 23 provides a clear exemplar. Du Toit contends that in LXX Deut 23 the *ekklēsia* of the Lord [*kyriou*/YHWH] is "understood as a closed group with boundary markers and entrance requirements . . . the ἐκκλησία κυρίου is no longer a one-off assembly; it has acquired a permanent existence of its own and the meeting aspect has become supplementary."[138] Philo (first century CE) builds on this LXX *traditum* in his tendentious re-use of LXX Deut 23 as a new *traditio* for "the *ekklēsia* (of the Lord)" as a contemporary semi-public Jewish association that oversaw the socio-religious initiation of Egyptian proselytes in Alexandria (*Virt.* 108).[139]

Regarding the question as to whether non-Jews could be considered part of the supra-local Israelite *ekklēsia* identity, the Chronicler provides an example. In 2 Chr 30:25, the term *qāhāl* (LXX *ekklēsia*) is used both of the people of Judah *and* of the people of Israel, including the non-Jewish "resident aliens" (*gērim*/LXX *prosēlytoi*), all of whom attended King Hezekiah's celebratory Passover after the reinstatement of temple worship.[140]

---

137. The noun קָהָל occurs 122 times in the Hebrew Bible (Fabry, "קָהָל," In *TDOT* 12.549). It is only after Numbers that the LXX translates קָהָל as ἐκκλησία (68 times). From Genesis to Numbers, the LXX uses συναγωγή (*synagōgē*). There are 149 occurrences of the essentially synonymous עֵדָה (*'ēdâ*) in the Hebrew Bible. Fabry notes that "with few exceptions *'ēdâ* is indeed generally rendered as *synagōgē* 132 times," but never as *ekklēsia* ("עֵדָה," In *TDOT* 12.561).

138. Du Toit, *Paulus Oecumenicus*, 135. Du Toit claims that this is particularly true in LXX Deut 23 wherein: "the [semantic] focus [of *ekklēsia*] shifted to the *group* who attended these [*ekklēsia*] meetings" ("*Paulus Oecumenicus*," 137, author's emphasis). He also cites a similar semantic development in LXX Neh 13:1–3 where "separating those of foreign descent from the ἐκκλησία actually means excommunication from the people of Israel" (*Paulus Oecumenicus*, 135).

139. See further in the section "Egyptian Semi-Public Associations Named *Ekklēsia*? (Philo)."

140. 2 Chr 30:25 (HB): "The whole assembly of Judah [כל־קהל יהודה] the priests and the Levites, and the whole assembly that came out of Israel [וכל־הקהל הבאים מישראל], and the resident aliens who came out of the land of Israel [והגרים הבאים

The underlying Hebrew for *gērim* also allows for non-proselyte gentile participants (e.g., Lev 25:47). Interestingly, the LXX translator appears intentionally to provide a tendentious reading of the Hebrew in 2 Chr 30:25: he only gives the people of Judah/Yehuda the privilege of being called a *qāhāl* (LXX *ekklēsia*). The LXX does not translate the "*qāhāl* of Israel" as the "*ekklēsia* of Israel."[141]

There is also a potential linguistic rationale for suggesting that the LXX "*ekklēsia*" could have been perceived as having included non-Jews. During the Hellenistic era in which LXX Deuteronomy's translator(s) lived (third century BCE), the word *ekklēsia* primarily referenced the civic *ekklēsia* of *poleis* ("city-states"), which had a predominantly non-Jewish citizenry.

Given the two rationales above, at the very least a third century BCE diasporic Jew might have viewed non-Jews as being part of the *ekklēsia* of the covenantal community of Yehuda, without thereby making the ethnic identity "Israel" available to non-Jews. By metaphorical extension, then, (1) if John's new covenantal *ekklēsiai* are seen as a synecdoche of the supra-local *ekklēsia* of all multi-ethnic *Christos*-followers (i.e., the universal Body of Christ), and (2) given that the universal, multi-ethnic *ekklēsia* is rooted in its Jewish heritage (i.e., the Body of the Jewish *Christos*), then John's designation of his multi-ethnic communities as *ekklēsiai* provided them with an inherently Jewish supra-local identity other than "Israel" (i.e., *ekklēsia*), by which he could institutionally integrate gentiles qua gentiles into theological continuity with Torah-observant Jews qua Jews. In other words, gentiles can then be considered as being part of the *qāhāl* ("the *ekklēsia*"), but not as being part of the *'am* ("the ethnic people of Israel").[142] Or, if one was to restate this analogously in Pauline terms, John's lampstand imagery could be seen to function theologically in a similar fashion to Paul's imagery of *Christos*-following gentiles being grafted into the "tree" of Israel (Rom 11)—the socio-ethnic identities of non-Jewish *Christos*-followers (e.g., Greek, Scythian) remain distinct,

---

מארץ ישראל], and the resident aliens who lived in Judah, rejoiced."

141. The LXX translator of 2 Chr 30:25 removes the term *hē ekklēsia* for the members of Israel, even though the underlying Hebrew word is "the *qāhāl* of Israel": "And all the congregation (πᾶσα ἡ ἐκκλησία), the priests, and the Levites rejoiced, and all the congregation of Judah (πᾶσα ἡ ἐκκλησία Ιουδα), and they that were present of Jerusalem (οἱ εὑρεθέντες ἐξ Ισραηλ), and the strangers (οἱ προσήλυτοι) that came from the land of Israel, and those dwelling in Judah."

142. See Korner, "*Ekklēsia* as a Jewish Synagogue Term: A Response," 127.

even while being joined in covenantal union with socio-ethnic Israel through Jesus, the Jewish *Christos*.

As an aside, given my brief discussion earlier of reiteration in Revelation (at the start of chapter 1), and in anticipation of my fuller discussion later (in chapter 8), it is worth noting at this point that John transforms the *traditum* of Zechariah's two olive trees ("two anointed ones") which "feed" the golden *menorah/lychnia* (Zech 4:1–14) into a new *traditio* of two witnesses, each of whom is also called a *lychnia* ("lampstand") (Rev 11:3–13). John chronologically conjoins their "bodily resurrection" with the occurrence of a "great earthquake" (11:13) during "the second woe" (11:14), that is, the sixth trumpet (9:13–19; cf. 8:13), during which time also the implied battle of Armageddon appears to take place (9:13–19; cf. 16:12–16; sixth bowl).

144,000 (7:1–8)

John describes 144,000 who are "sealed [on their foreheads] out of every tribe of the people of Israel" (7:3, 4). The 144,000 are ostensibly comprised of 12,000 from each of the twelve tribes of Israel (7:4–8).[143] Beale notes five identifications that are possible for the 144,000:[144] (1) a literal number of a remnant of ethnic Israelites who are sealed, (2) a figurative number of ethnic Israelites who correlate with Paul's conception of the final salvation of "all [ethnic] Israel" (Rom 11:24–26),[145] (3) a figurative number of post-70 CE ethnic Israelites who became *Christos*-followers, (4) a figurative number representing the complete number of God's people (cf. "the complete number" still to be fulfilled in the fifth seal; 6:9–11), and (5) a figurative number that represents all of the redeemed who are "formed as an army to conduct ironic holy war" (Bauckham).[146]

Bauckham's view, while not supersessionist, does affect how one categorizes the Apocalypse's eschatology. Given that Bauckham envisions God's final victory being achieved in conjunction with human agents, Revelation more so then would reflect prophetic eschatology, rather than

143 It should be noted that the list of tribes in 7:4–8 varies from other lists found in the Hebrew Bible.

144. Beale, *Revelation*, 416–23.

145. Beale dismisses the "all Israel" correlation since Rev 7:3–8 is only speaking of a remnant of Israel (*Revelation*, 416).

146. Beale, *Revelation*, 422. See Bauckham's argument in *Climax of Prophecy*, 217–29.

apocalyptic eschatology, since apocalyptic eschatology depicts God's final victory being achieved through his direct intervention (e.g., 20:7–10), without the aid of human agents (e.g., the 144,000).

Of these five options, only the fourth garners supersessionist interpreters who, like Beale, claim that the 144,000 symbol "is another example of the ways that Christians are portrayed in the Apocalypse under the OT guise of the true people of God, the true Israel."[147]

My interpretive approach incorporates the first two options mentioned by Beale. I view the 144,000 as a *figurative* number of a remnant of ethnic Israelites which I correlate with the "eschatological miracle" approach for interpreting Paul's phrase "all Israel" (Rom 11:26). Stated more simply, I view the 144,000 as being figurative of *non-Jesus-following ethnic Jews of an "Abrahamic faith" lineage.* John's 144,000 represent the final cohort of this faith lineage. As such, the 144,000 are part of the remnant of Israel, or what might be called the "true Israel," which has existed since Abraham's day. John appears to depict these 144,000 "Abrahamic-faith" Jews as being protectively sealed at the start of the seven eschatological trumpet judgments.

In what ways could one see John's 144,000 as being in theological continuity with Paul's true remnant of Israel (Rom 9:6–8)? First, Paul claims that not all of ethnic Israel is automatically part of Abraham's faith lineage when he writes that "not all of Abraham's children are his true descendants" (Rom 9:7). Second, Paul identifies Abraham's true Jewish descendants as being ethnic Jews (circumcised) who display an "Abrahamic faith" (Rom 4:11–17): Paul states that Abraham is "the ancestor . . . of the circumcised [i.e., ethnic Israel] who are not only circumcised but who also follow the example of the faith that our ancestor Abraham had before he was circumcised [i.e., the remnant of ethnic Israel]" (Rom 4:12). Each of these pre-*Christos*-era Jews, like Abraham, also have had their unconditional trust in God "reckoned to [them] as righteousness" (Rom 4:3; cf. Gen 15:6). Thus, they along with their final cohort (the 144,000) comprise part of Abraham's descendants who will be as numerous as the stars in fulfillment of God's unconditional Abrahamic covenant in Gen 15.

In this post-*Christos* era, Paul asserts that Abraham's faith-descendants also now include non-Jews (uncircumcised) who have put their unconditional trust in God's Son, the Jewish *Christos* (Rom 9:24–33).[148] In

147. Beale, *Revelation*, 418.

148. There are at least five intersections between the Genesis 15 covenant and Paul's theology that, when taken together, imply that, in Paul's mind, gentile inclusion

sum, one might even say that the Pauline statement that people "are saved by grace through faith" (Eph 2:8) also holds true in the pre-*Christos* era, not least for ethnic Jews. If so, then, God's gracious initiative of salvation becomes realized (1) for *post-cross* Jews and non-Jews whose "Abrahamic faith" rests upon Jesus as the crucified and resurrected seed of Abraham (Gal 3:16), and (2) for *pre-cross* and *post-cross* non-Jesus following ethnic Jews whose "Abrahamic faith" focused/focuses instead upon the God who unconditionally promised to make Abraham's "offspring/seed" into a great nation (Gen 12:1–3), one as numerous as the stars (Gen 15:5).

Given the foregoing, one can correlate John's cohort of 144,000 "Abrahamic-faith" Jews with Paul's "all Israel" who will experience eschatological salvation at the *parousia* of Jesus the *Christos* (Rom 11:26),[149] but with one caveat: Paul's phrase "all Israel" cannot then refer to every individual ethnic Jew. Rather, "all Israel" would then have reference only to the "true Israel" (Rom 9:6), that is, to the remnant of ethnic Israel (i.e., Jews of "Abrahamic faith"). Such a view mirrors Fitzmyer's contribution to the "eschatological-miracle" approach for interpreting Rom 11:26. He claims that "all Israel" refers in diachronic fashion to the faithful Jews of all time (pre- and post-cross) and/or in synchronic fashion to the faithful Jews (post-cross) who are alive when Jesus the *Christos* returns.[150]

---

is intrinsic to God's unconditional promises to Abraham: (1) Abraham's faith is the model for gentile faith (Gen 15:6; cf. Rom 4:1–5); (2) Abraham's uncircumcised state (Genesis 15) removes the necessity of gentile observance of Torah/Jewish identity marker observance (Rom 4:9ff); (3) God's unconditional promise of innumerable biological descendants (Gen 15:5), is extrapolated by Paul also to include uncircumcised gentiles (Rom 4:10–25); (4) While faith in YHWH's promise is the basis for Abraham's covenantal arrangement, for gentiles it is faith not only in YHWH but also in his promised one, the Lord Jesus Christ (Rom 4:24–25); (5) The peace with God, which ensues (Rom 5:1), is not simply existential (inner experience), nor fraternal (social relationships), but is forensic (a state): a state of permanently peaceful relations with the God of Abraham.

149. For a discussion of five interpretive approaches to Paul's phrase "all Israel," see Zoccali, *Whom God Has Called*, 91–117. For my interaction with Zoccali's discussion, see Korner, *Origin and Meaning of Ekklēsia*, 229–34. Zoccali reviews five approaches: (1) "eschatological miracle" (e.g., Fitzmyer, *Romans*, 623); (2) ecclesiological (e.g., Wright, *Paul and the Faithfulness of God*, 2.1239–46 and 2.1251); (3) Roman mission (e.g., Nanos, *Mystery of Romans*, 239–88); (4) two-covenant (e.g., Gager, *Reinventing Paul*, 128–42); and (5) total national elect (e.g., Ridderbos, *Paul*, 354–61).

150. "Eschatological-miracle" scholars have at least two foundational assumptions: (1) Israel's hardening is a temporary state of affairs, and (2) Israel's final salvation is an "eschatological miracle" which occurs only after the full number of gentiles have been saved. There are three sub-sets of this view: (1) "all" means the whole nation but

It would be fair at this point to ask whether John interweaves an Abrahamic covenantal motif elsewhere in the Apocalypse. If so, then my connection of an Abrahamic-faith motif with John's 144,000 gains more plausibility. Aune does in fact point us in that direction. He writes that the "great multitude" vision (7:9–17), which immediately follows the 144,000 text block (7:1–8), serves to reinforce

> the fulfillment of the promise to Abraham, which had two distinct traditional aspects: (1) *The promise of innumerable descendants* . . . (2) *The promise that Abraham would be the father of many nations.* . . . This passage implies that the promise to Abraham has been fulfilled . . . [through] the spiritualization of the promise to Abraham [as] found in Rom 9:6–13 [and] in Gal 3:16 [where] Paul interprets the 'offspring' of Abraham to mean Christ."[151]

Given Aune's observation, it seems plausible to suggest that if both pericopes (7:1–8, 9–17) are interpreted through the lens of an Abrahamic covenant motif, then they evidence greater narratological and theological unity such that the 144,000 become a sub-set of the "great multitude," while at the same time being differentiated as the eschatological cohort of the "true Israel," that is, of the pre- and post-cross non-Jesus-following ethnic Jews who exhibit "Abrahamic faith."

What are some interpretive implications of the above conclusion for how one reads John's apocalypse? Theologically, John's identification of the New Jerusalem with "the bride, the wife of the Lamb" (21:9, 10) would then mean that the twelve gates of the city, which represent the twelve tribes of Israel (21:12, 13), symbolically depict *both* pre-*Christos*-era *and* *Christos*-era "Abrahamic-faith" Jews as living eternally in God's presence. In addition to non-Jesus-following Jews, John also implicitly depicts Jesus-following Jews and non-Jews as comprising the New Jerusalem/bride of the Lamb. He does this through his identification of the

---

not to each member ("everyone"), (2) "all" means every individual Jew (e.g., Jewett, *Romans*, 702), and (3) "all Israel" refers either in diachronic fashion to the faithful Jews of all time and/or in synchronic fashion to the faithful Jews alive when the *Christos* returns (e.g., Fitzmyer, *Romans*, 623). Irrespective of which sub-set one chooses, the one presupposition that all "eschatological-miracle" scholars hold in common is that Israel's salvation follows rather than precedes the salvation of the gentiles. Such a view runs counter, however, to the universalism prevalent among Jews in Paul's day in which gentiles were seen to come to salvation only *after* Israel had already done so (see further in Donaldson, *Judaism and the Gentiles*).

151. Aune, *Revelation 6–16*, 466 [author's emphasis].

twelve-fold foundation of the city with the twelve apostles of the Lamb (21:14), who symbolically represent all *Christos*-followers.

Narratologically, John arranges two scenes between the sixth and seventh seals to champion his Jewish heritage rather than to supersede it (7:1–8, 9–17). John places the 144,000 text block (7:1–8) immediately after the conclusion of the sixth seal narrative (6:12–17). This serves to answer the question that is left hanging in 6:17: "the great day of their wrath [i.e., God and the Lamb] has come, and who can stand?" Within 7:1–8, John identifies a heavenly and an earthly cohort who stand victorious in the midst of God's wrath. In 7:1, John describes a heavenly cohort of four angels who stand and silence the winds of the earth. This earthly silence facilitates the protective sealing of the 144,000 (7:2–8). If this earthly silence corresponds to the heavenly silence of the seventh seal (8:1), then the sealing of the 144,000 occurs just prior to the blowing of the six trumpets which release divine judgment upon the earth, the sea, and the trees (8:5—9:21). In 14:1–5, John re-describes the earthly cohort of the 144,000 and emphatically answers the question of 6:17 by depicting them as standing victorious with the Lamb on Mount Zion after the completion of the eschatological woes (14:1). The 144,000 are called the "first fruits" of those "who have been redeemed from the earth" (14:3), a particularly apt description if they represent the faithful Abrahamic remnant of Israel. Rev 14:1–5 is John's second depiction of the return of the Lamb. The first is in the sixth Seal (6:16, 17), with two more potential iterations of "the End/Day of the Lord" in 19:11–16 and 20:9–11.

It is worth noting at this point, that the image of the Lamb standing victorious with the "true Israel" on Mount Zion contrasts starkly with the prior scene of the dragon/serpent/Satan standing on the shore of the sea (12:18) after having been thwarted in his attempt to kill the *Christos* who was born to a woman, ostensibly "Israel" (12:1–6). In the next scene (13:1–10), the dragon empowers a human agent, the seven-headed sea beast, "to make war on the saints and to conquer them" (13:7). But the hearer/reader is not left in despair because John has already envisioned them as conquerors who stand victorious even in death (7:9–17). Thus, John reminds his hearers/readers that even after death God's people of all ethnicities will forever stand victorious with the Lamb before the throne of grace.

From the foregoing, it becomes obvious that John's use of the 144,000 imagery finds its roots in a Jewish heritage. This becomes even more evident relative to chapter 7 given that there are Hebrew Bible and

Jewish antecedents for John's three images of the four winds of the earth, the protective nature of seals for God's servants, and the arrangement of God's people by ancient Israel's tribal formats. Ronald Herms provides a helpful overview which I replicate below.[152]

Table 1 John's Images that Reflect Hebrew Bible and Early Jewish Traditions

Revelation 7:1–4	HB Traditions	Early Jewish Traditions
"the four winds of the earth"	Ezek 37:9; Dan 7:2; Zech 6:5–6	1 *En.* 18:1–4; 76:1–14; 4 *Ezra* 13:5
"the seal of God"[153]	Gen 4:15; Exod 28; Ezek 9:2–6	*Pss. Sol.* 15:6–9; 4 *Ezra* 6:5; 8:53; CD 19.12
"the 144,000"	Num 1; 10	1QM 3.13–14; 5:1–2

The 144,000 and the "great multitude" are set within different textual units that are differentiated by the clause "after this/these thing(s) I saw" (7:1, 9). This clause functions throughout Revelation in a technical literary fashion as a textual demarcator. Thus, the 144,000 and the "great multitude" can be said to be continuous with, yet differentiated from, each other in some fashion. In chapter 8, I will provide a more detailed literary rationale for why the clause "after this/these things(s) I saw" can function as a structural demarcator for dividing Revelation's entire visionary episode (i.e., 1:9—22:20) into major blocks of thematically interrelated minor visions (e.g., Rev 7:1–8; 7:9—15:4). The clause "after this/these things(s) I saw" serves this same structural function in visionary texts of Hebrew prophetic and Jewish apocalyptic literature.[154]

Working within the above structural paradigm, which I call "textual blocking," one can suggest at least two conclusions relative to the visionary block of the 144,000 (7:1–8). First, the 144,000 can be identified as being either a sub-group of, or the same group as, the "great multitude" (7:9–17) if, in similar fashion to using LEGO© blocks, one (anachronositically) "snaps" the textual block of the 144,000 (7:1–8) "on top of"

152 Herms, "Psalms of Solomon," 77.

153. Herms helpfully notes the difference between the word "seal" as "a positive term for the faithful" (Rev 7:2–5, 8; 9:4) and the word "mark" which is used "exclusively as a negative term for those who resist God" (Rev 13:16, 17; 14:11, 14; 16:2; 19:20; 20:4) ("Psalms of Solomon," 77).

154 See especially chapter 8 in the section entitled The Jewish Literary Structure of John's Apocalypse.

the vision of the "great multitude" (7:9–17). The "great multitude" scene (7:9–17), which is demarcated by occurrences of the clause "and I saw" (7:9 and 8:1–2), is the first minor vision within its major textual block (7:9—15:4) (which ends at the next occurrence of the clause "after these things I saw" in 15:5). Using this literary principle of "textual blocking" reinforces a theological continuity between the very Israelite symbol of the 144,000 with the very multi-ethnic symbol of the heavenly "great multitude."

A second conclusion that results from the principle of "textual blocking," is that "snapping" the vision block of the 144,000 (7:1–8) onto "the top of" the "great multitude" minor vision (7:9–17) confirms that a concurrent chronology is assumed between the heavenly silence that follows the opening of the seventh seal (8:1) and the earthly silence of the stilled winds (7:1).[155] This may be the "cipher for this heavenly calm" which Wall decries that "John does not provide for the reader."[156] Thus, the visionary block that recounts the protective sealing of the 144,000 (7:1–8) can be said to form an interlocking parenthesis between the sixth seal (6:12–17) and the visionary block that incorporates references to divinely initiated judgments in the seven trumpets and seven bowls (7:9 —15:4). In sum, as an interlocking parenthesis, the 144,000 can be said to answer the question asked in 6:17 ("who can stand?") and anticipated in 8:1 ("what does the silence mean?").[157]

This brief survey of two Hebrew Bible *topoi* (lampstand/*menorah*, twelve tribes), that are transformed by John, affirms his Jewishness, re-inforces how integrally he socially identifies with his Jewish heritage, demonstrates his use of Jewish interpretive techniques (inner biblical exegesis),[158] even for the purpose of self-anchoring, and reflects how

155. Mounce makes note of the similarity between the heavenly silence of 8:1 with the earthly silence implied in the stilled winds (7:1–3) (*Revelation*, 170).

156. Wall, *Revelation*, 122.

157. Scholarship generally affirms 7:1–17 as being an interlude or parenthesis which establishes who will stand during the eschatological woes of the sixth seal (see Mounce, *Revelation*, 154; Aune, *Revelation 6—16*, 479; Beale, *Revelation*, 405). However, this parenthetical answer should be limited to 7:1–8 (*vision block #3*) since 7:9–17 belongs to the initial *individual vision* of the subsequent *vision block*. (i.e., 7:9—15:4).

158. Russel L. Meek helpfully differentiates between inner biblical exegesis and allusion: "The primary difference in these two methodologies is that inner-biblical exegesis argues that the receptor text has in some way modified the source text, whereas inner-biblical allusion argues that the receptor text alludes to the source text with no attempt at modification" ("Intextuality, Inner-Biblical Exegesis, and Inner-Biblical

deeply versed in a Jewish heritage John's audience is and, thus, how meaningful these symbols of their Jewish literary and cultural heritage would have been to them.

Allusion," 290).

5

John's Ekklēsiai *as Semi-Public Associations*

THE TWO GREEK TERMS *synagōgē* and *ekklēsia* were used by Jews and non-Jews to identify the gatherings, and sometimes, the communities of non-civic groups. One sub-set of a non-civic group is an association. Early Christ-follower *ekklēsiai* bear resemblance in many respects with associations that proliferated in the ancient Mediterranean world, and especially in the Greek East, not least Asia Minor, during the first century. Philip Harland, Richard Ascough, and John Kloppenborg are key contributors to the study of associations.[1] Philip Harland identifies at least five types of non-civic associations based upon their principal social networks: (1) household connections; (2) ethnic or geographic connections; (3) neighborhood connections; (4) occupational connections; and (5) cult or temple connections.[2]

Ascough argues that "association" is a meta-category within which various taxonomical sub-sets are included based on factors such as kinship, neighborhood, ethnicity, occupation or cultic expressions.[3] Thus, under the *taxon* "association" are subsumed particular types of associations, such as Jewish groups (e.g., the Covenanters of Qumran, the

1. See, for example, Ascough, Harland, and Kloppenborg, eds., *Associations in the Greco-Roman World* (2012). Separately, see Kloppenborg, "Edwin Hatch," 231; Ascough, *Paul's Macedonian Associations* (2003); McCready, "*Ekklēsia* and Voluntary Associations," 59–73; and Harland, *Associations*, 106, 182; Harland, *Dynamics of Identity*, 44–45.

2. Harland, *Associations*, 29. See also Instone-Brewer and Harland, "Jewish Associations in Roman Palestine," 202, 203.

3. Ascough, "What Are They Now Saying," 207–44.

Theraputae of Egypt, the *ekklēsia* in Alexandria [Philo, *Virt.* 108]),[4] Gre-co-Roman voluntary groups (e.g., *thiasoi, collegia, synodos, koina*), and Christ-follower groups (e.g., *ekklēsiai, hoi hagioi, synagōgai*). Ascough's more recent claim that "association" is a meta-category is an evolution-ary development from his earlier work that originally supported, with modification,[5] Wayne Meeks's ground-breaking study of ancient non-civic models for the organization of Paul's *ekklēsiai*.[6] Meeks's model suf-fers in its utilization of a four-fold sociological model that reified the terms synagogue[7] and association as alternative categories,[8] along with the household,[9] and philosophical schools.[10]

Ascough now resists any sharp dichotomy between "associations" and "synagogues." While the *taxon* "association" is a helpful heuristic category, consonant with Ascough, Kloppenborg observes that the com-munal complexity of Christ-follower communities cannot be accounted for simply by the definitional boundaries of "association." He argues that Graeco-Roman associations are "good to think with," not necessarily be-cause Christ groups were typical associations, but because "we have rich data from ancient associations that can generate heuristic questions for interrogating the data from Christ groups."[11]

4. For example, see Tellbe, *Paul between Synagogue and State*, 24–63.

5. Ascough, *What Are They Saying* (1998). While Meeks viewed "synagogue" and "association" as being distinct and separate categories, with "synagogue" best repre-senting Christ-follower groups, Ascough originally argued in the other direction that "association" was a better category than "synagogue."

6. Meeks, *First Urban Christians* (1983).

7. Some ways in which Christ-follower *ekklēsiai* are said to demonstrate affinity with synagogal gatherings include worship gathering function such as the reading and interpretation of Scripture, communal prayer, and commensality (1 Cor 11:17–34; 14:26), the settling of legal affairs within the community (1 Cor 6:1–7) (Meeks, *The First Urban Christians*, 80–81). However, Hugo Mantel notes twelve similarities be-tween diasporic Jewish synagogue communities and Greek and Egyptian voluntary associations ("Men of the Great Synagogue," 82–91). Examples include correlations in titles for association officials (e.g., *archisynagōgēs, presbyteros, grammateus*), judicial independence, regulatory *nomoi*, and penalties for disregarding *nomoi*.

8. For updated perspectives on Meeks's proposals, see both Edward Adams ("First-Century Models," 60–78), and John Kloppenborg ("Greco-Roman *Thiasoi*," 191–205).

9. See Kim, "Paul and Politics" (2010).

10. Edward Adams provides a concise survey of those scholars who suggest that Greek philosophical schools are a good paradigm for understanding how Paul orga-nized his *ekklēsiai* ("First-Century Models," 73–74).

11. Kloppenborg, "Membership Practices," 187.

The category "association" is purely a heuristic category for the purpose of noting similarities and differences among many small-group phenomena in the ancient Mediterranean world. Ancient associations are semi-public institutions. Semi-public associations restricted communal participation to members and sympathizers only. By way of review, Anders Runesson helpfully clarifies the three social levels on which "religion" "played out" in antiquity: "a. Public level (civic/state/empire concerns); b. Semi-Public level/Association level (voluntary groups/ cults and their concerns); c. Private level (domestic, familial concerns)."[12] With respect to Runesson's three categories, Christ-follower associations were semi-public groups irrespective of whether they self-designated as *synagōgai* or *ekklēsiai* or even *hoi hagioi*.[13]

Political Terminology and Associations

The use of the word *ekklēsia* as a permanent group identity by early Christ-followers is unattested in Greco-Roman literary,[14] epigraphic,[15] and papyrological[16] records or in other Jewish literary works.[17] As previously indicated, there does appear, though, to be one Jewish synagogue association in Egypt (early first century CE) that "beat early Christ-followers to the punch," so to speak, in adopting *ekklēsia* as a permanent

12. Runesson, "Christian Mission," 205–47, esp. 213.

13. For a discussion of the term *hoi hagioi* as a group designation see chapter 1, pp. 19–22 on the definition of the term "Christian."

14. There are over 1,062 mentions of the word *ekklēsia* in Greek literary sources (fifth century BCE to third century CE). None refer to a collective identity of a non-civic group, or to the name of the semi-public assembly of a non-civic group.

15. An electronic search of the over 2,100 epigraphic occurrences of the lexemes ἐκκλησία, ἐκκλησίη, ἐκλησία, ἐκκλεσία, ἐκλισήα, and ἐγκλησία (fifth century BCE to the eleventh century CE) through the Packard Humanities Institute does not turn up any evidence of a Greco-Roman non-civic group self-identifying collectively as an *ekklēsia*. At most, only three inscriptions use *ekklēsia* as the name of the ritual assembly of a non-civic association (*IDelos* 1519; *Samos* 119; *Sinuri* 73/8).

16. Within the papyrological evidence, there are at least thirteen extant documents written by voluntary associations. Of these thirteen, only one refers to an assembly convened by the association (P.Mich.:5:243; 14–37 CE), but the Greek word used is *syllogos* and not *ekklēsia*. See the edition of P.Mich.:5:243, 244 in Boak, *Papyri from Tebtunis* and in Boak, "Organization of Gilds in Greco-Roman Egypt."

17. The word *ekklēsia* occurs with frequency in Jewish Second Temple literary works: LXX (103x); Ben Sira (13x); Philo (23x); Josephus (48x). In all instances, except in Philo's *Virt.* 108 and *Deus* 111, *ekklēsia* is not used as a permanent collective identity for a sub-group of Israelites or Jews.

group identity. Philo appears to write of a non-civic *ekklēsia* association in Alexandria which took responsibility for the initiation and religious instruction of Egyptian converts (*Virt.* 108) and/or for religious "talk and study" (*Deus* 111).[18] The only examples of early Christ-follower communities that self-identified in an ongoing fashion as an *ekklēsia* are Pauline, Johannine,[19] and Matthean sub-groups.[20] Thus, at least four sub-groups of Christ-followers (Pauline, Matthean, and both "Johannine") positioned themselves distinctively in Greco-Roman society through their metaphorical embodiment of two key elements of a Greek *polis*: its leadership structure and its *ekklēsia*.

Wayne McCready's work on the socio-political missional relevance of Paul's trans-locally connected *ekklēsiai* associations within Greco-Roman culture also has relevance for our understanding of John's trans-locally connected Roman Asia *ekklēsiai*.[21] McCready sees the familiarity of the term *ekklēsia* as having facilitated missional success for Christ-followers because of that term's socio-political familiarity with

---

18. See Korner, "*Ekklēsia* as a Jewish Synagogue Term: Some Socio-Political Implications," 140–61.

19. I use the term "Johannine" for the sake of convenience here to refer to the authors of the Johannine epistles and to the book of Revelation, not necessarily implying thereby that both sets of literary works are written by the same "John."

20. The word *ekklēsia* is not used in writings attributed to the apostle Peter (1 and 2 Peter). In other New Testament writings the word *ekklēsia* is used with four different meanings. *Ekklēsia* is used (1) as a title for the semi-public, ritual assembly or meeting of early Christ-followers (1 Cor 11:18; 14:19, 28, 34, 35; Jas 5:14[?]; Heb 12:24); (2) for the collective sum of all Christ-followers while gathered together in assembly (Col 4:15: "Nympha and the *ekklēsia* in her home"; cf. Matt 18:17 [2x]; Rom 16:3–5; 1 Cor 16:19; Jas 5:14[?]); (3), as a collective designation for those self-same Christ-followers even when not gathered in assembly (e.g., Rom 16:16, 23; 1 Cor 1:2; 4:17; 10:32; 12:28; 2 Cor 1:1; 8:1, 18, 19, 23, 24; Gal 1:2, 13, 22; Phil 3:6; 1 Thess 1:1; 2:14; Phlm 2; 3 John 9; Rev 1:4, 11, 20; 2:1, 7, 8, 11, 12, 17, 18, 23, 29; 3:1, 6, 7, 13, 14, 22; 22:16) and (4) as a reference to the supra-local, or universal *ekklēsia*, of which regional *ekklēsiai* are local manifestations (e.g., Matt 16:18; 1 Cor 12:27, 28; Eph 1:22; 3:10, 21; 5:23–32; Col 1:18; 1 Tim 3:15). New Testament uses of the word *ekklēsia* accord with Greco-Roman usages in never designating a building as an *ekklēsia*.

21. John Kloppenborg provides an extensive list of scholarly resources relative to understanding the *ekklēsiai* of early Christ-followers as a Greco-Roman voluntary association ("Membership Practices" 187 n. 13).

Greco-Roman outsiders,[22] especially those with prior experience of associational life:[23]

> It makes eminent sense that voluntary associations offered an initial reference point that placed churches comfortably within the parameters of Graeco-Roman society—especially when the Jesus movement consciously and deliberately wished to appeal to gentiles. Indeed, the diversity of voluntary associations was an attractive feature, for it allowed experimentation and development by the *ekklēsiai* while at the same time providing a special type of belonging that created a form of community definition that was distinct from the larger society.[24]

As I have already mentioned, ancient associations commonly used political terminology. Paul Foucart is one of the first to note that "associations imitated the structure of the *polis* ["city-state"[25]]. Kloppenborg uses Foucart's observation to suggest that a Greco-Roman association could be called a "city writ small." Even Roman associations (the *Romaioi*) within Greek *poleis* used "mini-city" terminology.[26] Harland notes the mimesis of civic titles by associations in their use of civic terms, some of which Christ-follower associations also used, such as "'overseer' or 'bishop' (*episkopos*),[27] 'elders' (*presbyteroi*), 'servant'/'deacon' (*diakonos*), and 'patroness' (*prostatis*)."[28]

22. McCready states that "the point to be emphasized is that the concept of *ekklēsia* as a vehicle for claiming universal salvation was matched with a social institution capable of transcending a local village, town, or city to unite the church into a collective whole" (*"Ekklēsia* and Voluntary Associations," 69).

23. Inscriptional evidence for associations paints a picture of them as "groups of people gathering and organizing themselves into an extended family" for the fulfillment of a number of functions such as "athletics, sacrificing to a god, eating a common meal, and regular socializing, . . . [even] for decent burial of members" (McCready, *"Ekklēsia* and Voluntary Associations," 62).

24. McCready, *"Ekklēsia* and Voluntary Associations," 69–70.

25. The confluence of the three civic terms (*boulē, dēmos, ekklēsia*) within one inscription indicates a population center called a *polis* ("city-state").

26. See Onno van Nijf, "Staying Roman" (2012).

27. See also p. 29 n. 8 for Kloppenborg's citation of Edwin Hatch's claim that "ἐπίσκοπος [overseer/ 'bishop'] . . . along with ἐπιμελητής was a key title for a financial administrator in associations and in the *polis*" ("Edwin Hatch," 214).

28. Harland, *Associations*, 182 (see 299 n. 4 for the actual epigraphic references). Harland notes further: "the internal organization of many associations and guilds mirrors civic organization, with positions of leadership including secretary (*grammateus*), treasurer (*tamias*), president (*epistatēs*), and superintendent (*epimelētēs*; cf. Poland,

As McCready suggests and Kloppenborg clarifies, there were many positive socio-political benefits that accrued to ancient associations in their use of civic terminology as titles for their association officers. Kloppenborg contends that civic mimesis allowed many non-elites, whose socio-economic status excluded them from participation in the *boulē* and other official political offices, to gain socio-religious status within the confines of "a *polis* writ small." Mimesis also provided an implicit critique of official civic structures that followed the Roman *ordo* with its hierarchical, and thus restrictive, political power structure.

This mimicry of civic titles by associations did not, however, necessarily express anti-Roman ideology. Ascough notes, firstly, that even though associations "often took their nomenclature from the civic institutions [it was] more often not in direct competition but in the sense of 'imitation as flattery.'"[29] Thus, political mimicry may reflect a desire to replicate Athenian-style *dēmokratia* within a non-civic context. Second, there are numerous examples of Hellenistic-era associations self-presenting as "mini cities" well before the rise of Roman hegemony in the Greek East. Thus, one can assume that the use of "mini-city" terminology and structures by associations during Roman rule also would not have developed out of any anti-Roman sentiments either.

At the most, I would suggest that any inherent rhetoric of resistance one might attach to the mimesis of political institutions by non-civic associations would first and foremost have been directed against municipal-level expressions of oligarchic privilege and social-political hierarchy, rather than against the Roman *imperium*. It would appear that one could logically extend this rhetorical conclusion to how Roman authorities would have viewed Christ-follower associations that self-identified collectively as an *ekklēsia* (e.g., in Roman Asia) and which internally appropriated civic titles for their association officers (e.g., *episkopos, presbyteros, diakonos*).

Political Relevance of *Ekklēsiai* in Asia Minor

Having seen the rhetorical value that accrued to associations in their use of civic terminology, to what degree then would Christ-followers associations's adoption of an *ekklēsia* identity have been relevant for their public

---

Geschichte, 376–87)" (*Associations*, 106).

29. Ascough, "Voluntary Associations," 159 n. 47.

witness within Asia Minor in particular? Some scholars have suggested that civic *ekklēsiai* in Asia Minor during the first century CE had little political relevance, being shuffled to the margins of political power as honorific institutions that simply "rubber stamped" the decisions of the ruling oligarchs.

At least three factors challenge such an assumption. First, inscriptions of civic *ekklēsiai* in Asia Minor evidence the democratic practice of three of the four jurisdictional responsibilities of the classical Athenian citizenry: legislative authority, executive power, and judicial oversight.[30] The fourth, foreign policy initiatives, is absent in first-century CE inscriptions but is implied in later epigraphic evidence from the Asia Minor city of Termessos (second century CE). Onno van Nijf claims that Termessos "was technically still a democracy."[31] In terms of legislative authority, Termessos had a regular assembly (*ennomos ekklēsia*) wherein recommendations of the *boulē* were considered by upwards of 4,500 citizens.[32] With respect to formal jurisdictional responsibilities, the citizenry (*dēmos*) continued to debate issues that were not uncommon for the classical Athenian *ekklēsia*, known as the *ekklēsia kyria*.[33] Van Nijf cites examples such as "the appointment of magistrates, financial affairs, civic subdivisions (including the introduction of new *phylai*), construction works (roads and cisterns), food-supply, and the organization of games and festivals."[34] Foreign policy initiatives were also decided in the *ekklēsia* gatherings in Termessos, as is evidenced in the decisions to provide auxiliary troops and to send embassies to Rome.

Paul's *ekklēsiai* socially mirror what the classical Athenian *ekklēsia* represented socio-politically, especially in his Galatian *ekklēsia* in Asia Minor. In line with classical Athenian *dēmokratia*, Paul enjoins his Galatian *ekklēsia* to facilitate unrestricted social interaction for its members irrespective of socio-economic status and ethno-religious background (i.e.,

---

30. Glotz, *Greek City*, 162.

31. Nijf, "Public Space," 234.

32. *TAM* III.1. Van Nijf notes that the theatre in which the *dēmos* met in assembly contained seating for *c.* 4,500 people ("Public Space," 234).

33. The principal *ekklēsia* of classical Athens (*ekklēsia kyria*) had an all-embracing program which included: votes of confidence (ἐπιχειροτονία; *epicheirotonia*) with respect to the magistrates (*archontes*); discussion of military preparedness and of issues related to food security, consideration of accusations of high treason (εἰσαγγελίαι; *eisangeliai*), reports of confiscated property and of determinations made with respect to disputed inheritance claims (Glotz, *Greek City*, 85; cf. *AP* 43.4–6).

34. Nijf, "Public Space," 234.

Gal 3:28).[35] In this injunction Paul goes one step further than did Greek *poleis*. Not dissimilar to the practice of some Greco-Roman associations, he appears also to grant unrestricted membership rights to women and to slaves (Gal 3:28; 1 Cor 7:17–24).[36] There is no direct evidence by which to suggest that John's *ekklēsiai* also incorporate unrestricted social interaction into their communal and *polis* engagements, but if, as my earlier review of dating options for John's Revelation suggests, John's *ekklēsiai* may have been in some historical continuity with Pauline *ekklēsiai* that were located in the same cities of Roman Asia, then the postulate of some continuity in their socio-political practices is at least a possibility.

35. Robert Jewett states that the guiding principle behind Paul's honor system was not "love patriarchalism," that is, benefaction based upon hierarchical social stratification (65–66), but "agapic communalism" (*Romans*, 69). "Agapic communalism" means "owing nothing to anyone, except mutual love among equals" (Rom 13:8a). Agapic communalism levels the socio-economic playing field, so to speak, between the "administrative slaves" and aristocratic patrons within Paul's *ekklēsiai* (*Romans*, 60–61, 64–66; On Rom 16:10–11, see Jewett, *Romans*, 952–53, 965–68).

36. For an assessment of the degree to which Pauline *ekklēsiai* affirmed leadership positions for slaves, see the archaeologically sophisticated study by Katherine Shaner (*Enslaved Leadership in Early Christianity* [2018]) and my online review of her book, in particular my critique of her translation of *episkopos* in 1 Corinthians as "bishop" (*Review of Biblical Literature*, March 7, 2019).

6

Ekklēsia *as a Jewish Synagogue Term*

THE NOT INSIGNIFICANT DEGREE to which both John and Paul use Jewish and Hebrew thought patterns and literary allusions would have had particular relevance within Roman Asia, not least in the Lycus River Valley region (e.g., Laodicea, Colossae), given the substantial Jewish population there. The ensuing discussion will suggest that their Roman Asia *ekklēsia* communities could very well have been perceived, in non-supersessionist fashion, as being *Jewish synagogue associations*, not least by non-Jesus-following Jews, and perhaps even by Greco-Roman outsiders.[1] At the very least, John's and Paul's *ekklēsia* associations demonstrate social identification with Jewish ethnicity, culture, peoples, and synagogue terminology.

Having already explored correlations between Christ-follower *ekklēsiai* and Greco-Roman civic and non-civic *ekklēsiai* (e.g., Harland, Ascough, Kloppenborg, McCready), it remains next to assess what correlations exist between Christ-follower *ekklēsiai* and Jewish synagogue entities in the land (public synagogues) and in the diaspora (semi-public synagogues).

Jewish Synagogue Terms

In their 2008 synagogue sourcebook, Runesson, Binder, and Olsson include the word *ekklēsia* as being one among upwards of twenty-two

---

1. For fuller discussions on *ekklēsia* as a Jewish synagogue term, see Korner, *Origin and Meaning of* Ekklēsia, 81–149; Korner, "*Ekklēsia* as a Jewish Synagogue Term: Some Implications," 53–78; Korner, "*Ekklēsia* as a Jewish Synagogue Term: A Response," 127–36; and Gruen, "Synagogues and Voluntary Associations," 125–31.

terms used for Jewish assemblies and assembly places.[2] They use the English word "synagogue" as an umbrella term for at least twenty-two different Greek and Hebrew words that were used by Jews in the promised land and/or in the diaspora to describe five different synagogal entities: (1) a public/civic gathering in the land for administrative, judicial, religious, economic, and/or social activities (e.g., *synagōgē*),[3] (2) public or semi-public buildings (e.g., *proseuchē*,[4] *synagōgē*,[5] *bet ha-midrash*,[6] *bet mo'ed*,[7] *bet knesset*), (3) a temporary community identity (*synagōgē*) when gathered for public or semi-public purposes, (4) the meeting of a semi-public association (e.g., *syllogos*,[8] *synagōgē*[9]), and (5) a collective designation for a semi-public association in the diaspora (*ekklēsia*,[10]

2. Runesson, Binder, and Olsson, *Ancient Synagogue*, 159–63, 328, esp. 10, n. 21.

3. Levine, *Ancient Synagogue*, 29.

4. Runesson, Binder, and Olsson observe that Philo's use of *proseuchē* for the meeting places of Alexandrian Jews appears to be a regional synonym in Egypt for *synagōgē* (*The Ancient Synagogue*, 188). A *proseuchē* is some sort of physical structure in which Jews assemble for prayer (Philo, *Legat.* 132) and/or for public decision making (Josephus; in Alexandria [*C. Ap.* 2.10]; in Judea [*Vita* 276—81, 294—95]).

5. Philo uses *synagōgē* for the assembly place of the Essenes in *Hypoth.* 7.11–14. Philo claims that the Essenes were found in many cities and villages in Judea (*Hypoth.* 11.1).

6. In *m. Ter.* 11:10 the *bet hamidrash* is a building: "They may kindle oil of priest's due, that must be burnt, in the synagogues (*bate kenesiot*) and in houses of study (*bate midrashot*) and in dark alleys and for sick people by permission of a priest" (cf. Runesson, Binder, and Olsson, *Ancient Synagogue*, 105; cf. also Runesson, *Origins of the Synagogue*, 223–34).

7. The Hebrew phrase *bet mo'ed* (meeting house) is used in the War Scroll (1QM 3.3–4) of the sectarian community's (Essenes?) assembly place. Runesson, Binder, and Olsson claim that it "translates well into Greek as *synagōgē* . . . . It is probable that *bet mo'ed* represents the earliest known Hebrew term for synagogue" (Runesson, Binder, and Olsson, *ASSB*, no. 38).

8. *Syllogos* is not specific to, nor identifying of, any particular socio-religious group. Rather, *syllogos* is strictly a sociological term that means "a meeting for a specific purpose, whether for deliberations, consultations, etc. There is some kind of mutual activity" (Runesson, Binder, and Olsson, *Ancient Synagogue*, 201). The Therapeutae met for a *syllogos* ("general assembly") every seventh day (Philo, *Contemp.* 30–33; 30–45 CE).

9. Binder classifies the Essenes as "what we might imprecisely label 'sectarian synagogues'" (Binder, *Into the Temple Courts*, 24). Runesson contends that the Pharisees also could be considered as a Judean (synagogue) association (*Origins of the Synagogue*, 486).

10. Philo's *ekklēsia* in *Virt.* 108 appears to be an official collective, whether a meeting or a non-civic group, that represents the *politeia* of Alexandrian Jews for

politeuma[11]). I follow their lead in this volume by also using the English term "synagogue" as a global reference to all terms used by Jews when describing their meetings, their communities, or their meeting places (e.g., *syllogos, synagōgē, ekklēsia, proseuchē*). I also concur with their conclusion that mentions of *ekklēsia* in Jewish sources were not simply anachronistic references to a Greek civic institution.[12]

Anders Runesson gives further nuance to his synagogue taxonomy of twenty-two terms, by clarifying that there are also two types of synagogue institutions: public and semi-public.[13] Jewish public/civic synagogue gatherings addressed a broad range of issues relevant to all members of a regional community, usually in rural Judea, while semi-public synagogue gatherings were "members-only" meetings of a voluntary association usually within an urban setting in the diaspora.[14] In his Christian origins work, Runesson heuristically examines Christ-follower *ekklēsiai* through the rubric of semi-public association synagogues.[15]

The Second Temple context of *ekklēsia* usage by *intra muros* groups within pluriform Judaism(s) helps clarify how both Paul and John were able to address their ethno-religious conundrum of needing to find a distinctive group identity that could incorporate both Jewish and non-Jewish Christ-followers as one sub-group of the Jesus Movement.[16] It is important to note that their new group identity was not needed for the purpose of distinguishing their Christ-followers from pluriform

---

the purpose of providing ethno-religious instruction for Egyptian converts (Korner, "*Ekklēsia* as a Jewish Synagogue Term: Some Implications," 66–68).

11. Josephus speaks of Jews in Alexandria constituting a *politeuma* which in some fashion mirrors Greek governance models (e.g., monarchies, oligarchies; *Contra Apion* 2.164–65; cf. *Ant.* 1.13) and Greek community organizations (*Ant.* 1.5).

12. For a list of all Greek words used of Second Temple synagogues see Runesson, *Origins of the Synagogue*, 171–73.

13. Runesson, *Origins of the Synagogue* (2001).

14. See p. 14 where Runesson helpfully clarifies the three social levels on which 'religion' "played out" in antiquity ("Christian Mission," 213).

15. Runesson, *Origins of the Synagogue*, 171–72, 356–57. Two examples of association synagogues in the land of Israel are Philo's reference to the Essenes (*Prob.* 80—83), and the community associated with the first-century CE synagogue in Jerusalem mentioned in the Theodotus inscription (*CIJ* II 1404; see Kloppenborg, "Dating Theodotus (*CIJ* II 1404)"). An example of a semi-public Jewish association from the diaspora is Acts's mention of the "synagogue of the Freedmen" (Acts 6:9). See further in Runesson, "Rethinking Early Jewish–Christian Relations," 112.

16. Regarding the focus of ancient Mediterranean cultures on the collective (dyadic) rather than on individuals, see, Malina, *New Testament World*, 62.

Judaism(s).[17] Their group identity needed to affirm both Greco-Roman and Jewish cultural roots for the purpose of placing non-Jews qua non-Jews into theological continuity with Torah-observant Jews qua Jews.[18] *Ekklēsia*, with its linguistic roots *both* in Greek civic politics *and* in Jewish public and semi-public synagogue assemblies, would have served their ideological needs well. I explore the ideological benefits for Pauline *ekklēsiai* in much greater depth in my monograph on the origin and meaning of *ekklēsia* in the early Jesus movement.[19] In this volume on Revelation, I evaluate and apply those insights to John's seven Roman Asia communities to help discern the potential religio-political benefits they garnered through their corporate designation as *ekklēsiai*.

Aside from Jewish Christ-followers, there are at least five other ancient Jewish sources that use *ekklēsia* as a descriptor for a Jewish synagogue entity. These five sources use *ekklēsia* for regional/local synagogue entities, whether public or semi-public. Ben Sira and Josephus each use the term *ekklēsia* to describe a public/civic assembly in Judea. Philo twice mentions a non-civic *ekklēsia* that is associated with Jews in Egypt. One of his mentions is of a publicly accessible *meeting/assembly* that was sponsored by a "members-only" association. The other mention is of a semi-public "members-only" *association* which may have collectively self-designated as an *ekklēsia*. The (pre-)Covenanters of Qumran, a subgroup of the Essenes, adopted the Hebrew word *qhl (qāhāl)* as a group designation for their semi-public association. The Hebrew word *qāhāl* is always translated as *ekklēsia* in the Septuagint (LXX). The LXX uses the term *ekklēsia* in a supra-local/national sense as a corporate designation for the gathered nation of Israel during the desert wanderings (*ekklēsia* [of Israel]). In the following sections I discuss in greater detail each of these five *ekklēsia* usages in Jewish sources.

17. Philip Esler is one example of a Pauline scholar who contends that the term *ekklēsia* was chosen expressly to distinguish Christ-followers from their Jewish roots, that is, from "the Synagogue" (*Conflict and Identity in Romans* (2003)).

18. See p. 25 n. 92 for my definition of what I mean by the phrase "gentiles qua gentiles."

19. Korner, *Origin and Meaning of* Ekklēsia, 81–149.

Judean Public *Assemblies* Named *Ekklēsia*?
(Sirach, Josephus)

The Judea of Ben Sira's timeframe (ca. 198 BCE) appears to have contained public assemblies of Jews that were called *ekklēsiai*. The Greek text of Sirach uses *ekklēsia* to translate the Hebrew word *qhl* in Ben Sira, which is used to refer to publicly accessible assemblies of regional communities.[20] These public *ekklēsiai* address juridical, political, and religious issues within regions of Judea.[21] Sirach's Judean *ekklēsiai* accord closely with Lee Levine's definition of a public synagogue assembly and/or building, but Levine fails to include *ekklēsia* as a synagogue term in his seminal work on the ancient Jewish synagogues.[22]

The question here, as it will also be when we look at Josephus's use of *ekklēsia*, is whether Ben Sira's *qhl* was actually known as an *ekklēsia* by his intended audience—Hellenistic Judeans of the early second century BCE. In other words, is the word *ekklēsia* in Sirach *emic* (local and authentic) or *etic* (non-local and synonymous) terminology?[23] If *etic*, then Ben Sira's grandson, who translates the Hebrew text of Ben Sira into Greek (Sirach; ca. 132 BCE), is translating *qhl* with a Greek term (*ekklēsia*) more familiar to his intended Egyptian audience. In this case, then, Sirach is making its readers view Ben Sira's Judean *qhl* through the lens of a civic *ekklēsia* in the Greek East, or of a Jewish *ekklēsia* in Egypt. An *ekklēsia* reference in 1 Maccabees suggests the probability that Sirach's translation represents

20. Sirach writes of public *ekklēsiai* in Judea nine times (15:5; 21:17; 23:24; 24:2; 34[31]:11; 33:19; 38:33; 39:10; 44:15) (24:2 may only refer to a heavenly *ekklēsia*).

21. Sirach's Judean *ekklēsiai* are functionally similar to first-century CE rural Judean synagogues, that is, public synagogues. For example, politically, Sirach's *ekklēsiai* are civic venues where the views of respected community members are voiced (15:15; 21:17; 38:33) and where honor and praise is bestowed upon the blameless (34:11). Judicially, an adulterous woman can be judged εἰς ἐκκλησίαν (23:22–24).

22. Even Levine's *opus magnum* on ancient synagogues does not appear to include a discussion of *ekklēsia* as a synagogal entity (*Ancient Synagogue*, esp. 763–96 [Subject Index]).

23. Kenneth Pike first used the neologisms "*emic*" and "*etic*" from analogy with the linguistic terms "phonemic" and "phonetic." He states that "descriptions or analyses from the *etic* standpoint are 'alien' in view, with criteria external to the system. *Emic* descriptions provide an internal view with criteria chosen from within the system. They represent to us the view of one familiar with the system and who knows how to function within it himself" (*Language in Relation to a Unified Theory*, 153; see also, Pike, *Emics and Etics* [1990]). Within the context of *ancient* societies, DeConick helpfully describes an *emic* term as "a word actually used by ancient people to describe their experiences" ("What Is Early Jewish and Christian Mysticism?" 2).

an authentic use of *ekklēsia* for a public assembly of Jews in the increasingly hellenized Judea of the early second century BCE.[24] The *ekklēsia* mentioned in 1 Macc 14:19 was convened in Jerusalem for the purpose of allowing the Spartans to present condolences to Simon Maccabeus on the passing of his brother Jonathan (c. 141 BCE). This Jerusalem *ekklēsia* is a public/civic assembly.[25] When Ben Sira's grandson emigrates from Judea to Alexandria only nine years later and there translates *qhl* with the word *ekklēsia* he may have done so because the institution of the public *ekklēsia* existed in Judea, specifically in Jerusalem.

Josephus uses the word *ekklēsia* forty-eight times in reference to a public gathering.[26] Nine of those usages are for a public assembly in the Second Temple period.[27] It is possible that Josephus is using *ekklēsia* provincially, or in *etic* fashion, for the sake of his Roman reading audience.[28] However, it is just as possible that *ekklēsia* is *emic* terminology used by Jews during Josephus's day since his usage does not differ substantially from the public *ekklēsiai* described in Sirach and 1 Maccabees. If Josephus uses *ekklēsia* in *emic* fashion, then he implies that local Jewish communities in Judea met *en(eis) ekklēsia(n)* ("in an assembly named

24. 1 Maccabees mentions two public *ekklēsiai* in Judea. One is a more *ad hoc* gathering (1 Macc 5:16) while the other appears to be a permanent civic institution (1 Macc 14:19).

25. 1 Macc 14:19.

26. Josephus uses the word *ekklēsia* with at least three meanings: (1) for the physical assembling of all Hebrews/Jews in a particular region (*Ant.* 3:84: "He called the multitude into an assembly [*ekklēsia*]"; also *War* 7:412); (2) to indicate the assembly of a sub-group of a larger group (*Ant.* 6:222: "and after coming to Samuel and finding an assembly [*ekklēsia*] of prophets of God"; also *Ant.* 8:222; 16:393); and (3) to imply that once an *ekklēsia* is dispersed it no longer exists institutionally (*Ant.* 3:306: "when the assembly [*ekklēsia*] was dispersed, they [the men], their wives, and children continued the lamentation"; also *Ant.* 8:122).

27. Josephus speaks nine times of public *ekklēsiai*, eight times of one in Jerusalem (*Ant.* 12.164, Joseph Tobiad; *Ant.* 13.216, Simon Maccabeus; *Ant.* 16.62, Herod; *Ant.* 16.135, Herod; *Ant.* 16.393, Herod; *Ant.* 19.332, Simon; *War* 1.550, Herod; *War* 1.654) and once of a public *ekklēsia* in Jericho (*War* 1.666, Salome).

28. Donald Binder helpfully differentiates between anachronism, provincialism, and bias (*Into the Temple Courts*, 89). "Anachronism" is the practice of interpreting earlier architectural and literary artefacts from the perspective of later evidence. "Provincialism" involves the attribution to other geographical regions, or social groupings, the socio-cultural realities of one's own geo-political region. "Bias" entails the interpretation or revision of source material for the purpose either of supporting one's pre-existing suppositions or of creating new ideologically motivated conclusions.

ekklēsia") within a *proseuchē* or a *synagōgē*,[29] that is, within a communal structure that facilitated Jewish public life. As already mentioned, such public *ekklēsia* gatherings would have addressed issues related to local political, administrative, economic, judicial, and religious matters.

Egyptian Semi-Public *Associations* Named *Ekklēsia*? (Philo)

Philo's writings (30–45 CE) turn our gaze away from Judea, and the public/civic *ekklēsiai* described by Sirach and Josephus, towards Egypt. Philo mentions two usages of the term *ekklēsia* for Jewish synagogue entities that perhaps were located in Alexandria: (1) a public *ekklēsia* ("meeting") hosted by a semi-public association; and (2) a semi-public association that designates itself as an *ekklēsia*, probably even before Christ-follower communities began to do so.

Philo notes, firstly, that community meetings named *ekklēsia* were hosted by a semi-public Jewish association that Philo calls *hieros syllogos* ("sacred gathering/congregation").[30] *De Specialibus legibus* 1.324–25 reads, "Thus, knowing that in assemblies (*en tai ekklēsiai*) there are not a few worthless persons who steal their way in and remain unobserved in the large numbers which surround them, it [the law] guards against this danger by precluding all the unworthy from entering the holy congregation (*hierous syllogou*)."[31]

In *Spec.* 1.324–25, Philo mentions an assembly of Jews (*ekklēsia*) which is attended by "worthless" persons who, conversely, are prevented from entering the holy congregation (*hieros syllogos*). The key question for our purposes here is whether Philo is referring to ancient Israelite practice or to the contemporary practice of his day? Peder Borgen states that "he has his own contemporary situation in mind" given the fact that in *Spec.* 1.345 Philo says, "*we*, the pupils and disciples of Moses [emphasis mine]."[32]

---

29. Josephus mentions a purpose-built structure for public communal gatherings located in Judea which is designated as a *proseuchē* (*Vita* 276—81, 294—95) (cf., *ASSB*, no. 22).

30. The Special Laws (*De specialibus legibus*) book 1, sections 324–25.

31. *ASSB*, no. 210.

32. Borgen, *Philo of Alexandria*, 256.

If *Spec.* 1.324–25 refers to Philo's contemporary situation then the *ekklēsiai* are publicly accessible meetings of a group that calls itself "the holy congregation" (*hieros syllogos*).[33] These meetings (*ekklēsiai*) are identified by Runesson, Binder, and Olsson as being "some form of synagogue fellowship," that is, Sabbath assembly.[34]

Philo notes, secondly, that a contemporaneous semi-public synagogue association within the Jewish Quarter of Alexandria permanently self-designated themselves as an *ekklēsia*.[35] In *Virt.* 108 Philo refers back to Deut 23:8–9 on how sojourners are to be treated, specifically new converts: "If any of them should wish to pass over into the Jewish community [τὴν Ἰουδαίων πολιτείαν], they must not be spurned with an unconditional refusal as children of enemies, but be so favoured that the third generation is invited to the congregation [εἰς ἐκκλησίαν] and made partakers in the divine revelations [λογῶν θειῶν] to which also the native born, whose lineage is beyond reproach, are rightfully admitted."[36]

Philo appears to describe this Alexandrian *ekklēsia* as being some sort of contemporaneous official collective,[37] most likely a non-civic group that represents the *politeia* of Alexandrian Jews for the purpose of providing ethno-religious instruction to new Egyptian converts ("partakers in the divine revelations/words").[38] Philo, then, can be said not only to acknowledge the possibility of individual Egyptians converting

33. Runesson, Binder, and Olsson note that "The Greek words *hieros syllogos* (without definite article) could also be translated as 'a holy congregation'. Philo often returns to this allegorical interpretation of Deut 23 frequently using the word *ekklēsia* and sometimes also *syllogos*." By translating *hieros syllogos* as "a holy congregation," they remove the impression that *hieros syllogos* is a sub-category of *ekklēsia* (*The Ancient Synagogue*, 260).

34. Runesson, Binder, and Olsson, *Ancient Synagogue*, 260.

35. Runesson, Binder and Olsson suggest one more instance (*Deus* 111) of Philo using *ekklēsia* in reference to a group in Egypt that was contemporaneous with his day (*ASSB*, no. 203, see esp. the "Comments" section). For an extensive assessment of Philo's *ekklēsia* usage in *Deus* 111, see Korner, *Origin and Meaning of* Ekklēsia, 141–45.

36. *ASSB*, no. 203; translation by Runesson, Binder and Olsson.

37. A number of Philo scholars assert that Philo writes *Virt.* 108 as instruction for his contemporary Alexandrian readership (Borgen, *Philo of Alexandria*, 249; Wilson, *Philo of Alexandria*, 65). For a contrary view see, Trebilco, "Early Christians," 448.

38. In *Virt.* 108 Philo refers to Deut 23:8 on how sojourners are to be treated. Therein he enjoins his fellow Jews to focus their *philanthropia* upon one specific subset of Egyptians—new converts (*epēlutai*)—who are to be invited into the congregation (*eis ekklēsian*). For a complete discussion on Philo's use of οἱ ἐπηλύται for proselytes (*Virt.* 102) see Borgen, *Philo of Alexandria*, 256–59.

to the πολιτεία of the Alexandrian Jews, but that along with their new religio-ethnic identity they are also incorporated into a new semi-public association that self-designates as an *ekklēsia*. The practice of "initiating" Egyptian converts in this Alexandrian *ekklēsia* is congruent with religious activities described in Egyptian *proseuchai*, that is, "prayer halls."[39] Philo does not use the term *synagōgē* for the structure within which Egyptian Jews meet for their religious, political, social, and financial practices. Rather, Philo substitutes *proseuchē* as a regional Egyptian synonym. The word *synagōgē* is used more commonly of Jewish communal buildings within the land of Palestine.

The Supra-local *"Ekklēsia* of Israel" (LXX) and Local *Ekklēsiai* in Asia?

There is another Jewish use of the term *ekklēsia* that makes one wonder whether John reinforces a supersessionist agenda at the institutional level. John addresses his Roman Asia communities with the same Greek term (*ekklēsia*) that is also used in the LXX (Septuagint) for the ethno-religious nation of Israel. Given that Paul does the same thing, then perhaps scholarly reflections on the supersessionist intent relative to Paul's use of the word *ekklēsia* also have application for our assessment of John's use of the term *ekklēsia*.

Paul Trebilco is of the opinion that this terminological move does not reflect a supersessionist impulse. Trebilco suggests that since "both ἐκκλησία and συναγωγή were terms from the LXX for the 'assembly' of Yahweh.[40] . . . Jewish Christian Hellenists could use ἐκκλησία to claim theological continuity with the OT people of God, without thereby saying that other Jews [who designated their gatherings/buildings as *synagōgai*] were not the OT people of God."[41] Trebilco's conclusion relative to Hellenistic Jewish Christ-followers in Jerusalem no doubt also applies to diasporic Jewish perceptions of Christ-follower *ekklēsiai*.

---

39. The "instruction" mentioned in *Virt.* 108 seems to imply contemporary Alexandrian practice which is reminiscent of Philo's descriptions of the activities in the prayer halls/*proseuchai* (Runesson, Binder, and Olsson, *Ancient Synagogue*, 263).

40. There are two words for "assembly" in the Hebrew Bible, *qāhāl* and *ʿēdâ*. The LXX uses *ekklēsia* only when translating *qāhāl*, but uses *synagōgē* when translating both *qāhāl* and *ʿēdâ*.

41. Trebilco, "Early Christians," 458–59.

There is another Jewish sub-group, however, who can be said to be culpable of reinforcing a supersessionist ideology through their adoption of a group designation that is the Hebrew equivalent for the LXX's *ekklēsia* (of Israel). The (pre-)Covenanters of Qumran, a sub-group of the Essenes, adopted the Hebrew word *qhl* (pronounced *qāhāl*) as a group designation for their semi-public association. This usage is found within the late-second-century BCE document called "Some of the Works of the Law"[42] (4QMMT; *Miqsat Maʿase Ha-Torah*).[43] This use of *qhl* is found in 4QMMT,[44] the Damascus Document (CD),[45] 4Q396, and 1QSᵃ.[46] It is not found in the Community Rule (1QSerek), where *yahad* is the Covenanters's self-designation of choice.[47] The Hebrew word *qhl* is always translated as *ekklēsia* in the Septuagint (LXX).

But what might have been a rationale for the (pre-)Covenanters of Qumran to self-identify in permanent fashion with (or as) the *qāhāl* (a.k.a. LXX *ekklēsia*) of Israel? Unlike Trebilco's non-supersessionist interpretation of Jerusalem Christ-followers using *ekklēsia* as a group identity, the Qumran Essenes did have a pre-existing supersessionist ideology which their mimicry of the *ekklēsia* of Israel would have reinforced. The (pre) Covenanters's (*intra*-Jewish) polemic against other Jewish sub-groups,

---

42. Paul uses phraseology that is extant elsewhere only in one of the (pre-)Covenanters's writings. Martin Abegg notes three terminological convergences between Paul and 4QMMT, all the while taking heed to avoid the interpretive pitfall identified by Samuel Sandmel as "parallelomania." Parallelomania, in essence, assumes that correlation entails causation (Sandmel, "Parallelomania," 1–13). The most significant parallel with 4QMMT is Paul's phrase ἔργα νόμου ("works of the law"; Rom 3:20; Gal 2:16 [3x]; 3:2, 5, 10) which Abegg claims "is likely a translation of מעשי התורה, found in all of ancient Hebrew literature only at 4QMMT C 27 (4Q398 14–17 ii 3)" ("4QMMT," 139).

43. There are at least three general theories as to the literary intent of the sectarian document known as 4QMMT: (1) historic extramural polemic, (2) contemporary extramural polemic, or (3) contemporary intramural paraenesis. For examples of specific correlations between the authorial community of 4QMMT and the temple establishment, see Hogeterp, *Paul and God's Temple*, 79–81.

44. Fabry "קָהָל," In *TDOT* 12.559.

45. Within CD, *qĕhal* occurs at 7:17 ("the King is the assembly"), 11:22 ("trumpets of the assembly"), and 12:6 ("he may enter the assembly").

46. The Deuteronomic tradition of associating *qhl* (LXX *ekklēsia*) with a continuing group identity for the community of Israel, as opposed simply with a temporary assembly for the community, is evident in 1QSᵃ 2.4 and 4Q396 1–2i line 40 (Fabry, *TDOT*, 12:559).

47. Fabry notes that the root קהל occurs *c.* fifty times, but "strikingly, it does not occur at all in 1QS." (*TDOT* 12:559).

possibly even against the temple establishment in Jerusalem (e.g., 4QMMT), demonstrates that Jewish ethnicity was insufficient grounds by itself for a Jewish person's inclusion in the Covenanters's semi-public association named *qhl*.

Johannine *Ekklēsiai* as Semi-Public Synagogue Associations

When it comes to the *intra*-Jewish implications of John collectively addressing his seven groups of Christ-followers as *ekklēsiai*, there are at least two ways in which Roman Asia non-Jesus-following Jews may have viewed that institutional move. First, if Philo's mention of Jewish *ekklēsiai* in Egypt is indicative of a broader use of the word *ekklēsia* within the diaspora for Jewish associations, then John's communities could have been perceived in non-supersessionist fashion as trans-local extensions of a Jewish synagogal entity, that is, of *semi-public* Jewish associations named *ekklēsia*.

Second, if the lack of literary and epigraphic evidence for Jewish *ekklēsia* associations in Greece and Asia Minor means that *ekklēsia* largely was "free" as a diasporic group designation, and if there were public *ekklēsiai* in Judea, as Josephus claims, then non-Jesus-following Jews could have perceived John's *ekklēsiai* as being semi-public extensions of *public* Jewish society in the diaspora. This would have presented John's *ekklēsiai* as diasporic "satellites" in relation to other Judean public *ekklēsiai*. John's *ekklēsiai* would then have been viewed as *loci* for the full expression of all facets of Jewish life, including its ethno-religious, social, political, economic, and judicial dimensions.

Such a publicly oriented self-presentation would have received even greater reinforcement if Roman Asia Jews saw in John's *ekklēsiai* an allusion to the supra-local *ekklēsia* of Israel from the desert tradition (e.g., Deut 23:4). In this regard, then, Jews could have perceived John's *ekklēsiai* of *Christos*-followers as implicitly laying claim to being the full expression of the ethno-religious, social, political, economic, and judicial dimensions of Judean life within Roman Asia.

As with Philo's Jewish *ekklēsia* association (*Virt.* 108), John implicitly encourages individual Jews and non-Jews to submit to a Jewish πολιτεία ("constitution"), but, by contrast, not to one in Alexandria. Rather, John subsumes his *ekklēsia* associations under the πολιτεία of the New

Jerusalem above (Rev 21—22), so to speak.[48] In so doing, John not only envisioned his community members as being the earthly representatives/citizens (cleruchy) of a heavenly Jewish eschatological *kosmos-polis*, but also as gaining a new religio-ethnic sub-group identity, an association that both names itself and its regularly convened assembly an *ekklēsia*.

In sum, I would suggest that irrespective of whether John's communities were perceived as "satellites" of Judean public *ekklēsiai* or as diasporic semi-public Jewish associations, his designation of them as *ekklēsiai* would have served to minimize Jewish perceptions of his communities as being "other" relative to "Judaisms" within the matrix of pluriform Second Temple Judaism (and vice versa). The widespread use of *ekklēsia* terminology within the Greco-Roman and Jewish worlds would have granted John's Roman Asia associations an increased missional relevance and would have served, not least at the institutional level, to locate them socially with (not separated from) Jews, Jewishness, and "Judaism."

Conclusions: Johannine *Ekklēsiai* as Jewish Synagogue Associations?

One could conclude from the foregoing discussion that the mere fact of a Jewish semi-public association sub-group adopting *ekklēsia* as a group identity (e.g., Pauline, Johannine, and Qumran communities) does not determine whether or not that is a supersessionist move. Rather, it is the ideological expressions of that *ekklēsia* community that form the basis upon which one is able confidently to place them into the supersessionist camp.

It would seem, rather, that Paul's and John's strategy of naming their multi-ethnic associations as *ekklēsiai*, and thus making them also perceivable as Jewish synagogue associations, helped them to solve a key ethno-religious conundrum: If gentiles could not collectively assume the designation "Israel," but yet, through faith in the Jewish *Christos*, could share in historic Israel's covenantal benefits, then their designation of their multi-ethnic communities as *ekklēsiai* provided each of them with an inherently Jewish identity other than "Israel" by which they could institutionally integrate gentiles qua gentiles into theological

---

48. A similar metaphorical statement could be made of Paul's *ekklēsia* given his injunction to them to submit to "the Jerusalem above" (Gal 4:26).

continuity with Torah-observant Jews qua Jews.[49] In other words, by assigning *ekklēsia* as the group designation for their Christ-follower communities, gentiles could become part of the *qāhāl* (*ekklēsia*) of Israel even though they are not part of the ethnic '*am* (nation) of the Jewish people (i.e., Israel).[50] This being the case, it would seem that John's affirmation of a collective *ekklēsia* identity for each of his Roman Asia addressees problematizes scholarly suggestions, at least on the institutional level, that Christ-follower *ekklēsiai* were "parting ways" with the *Ioudaioi* (Jews),[51] that is, with Judaism(s), "Jewishness," or Jewish organizational forms.[52]

49. See p. 25 n. 92 for my definition of what I mean by the phrase "gentiles qua gentiles."

50. The closest the LXX comes to implying that non-Jews were considered to be a part of the *qāhāl*/*ekklēsia* is in 2 Chr 30:25. Therein, Hezekiah's Passover celebrations in Jerusalem are attended by, among others, "the strangers (οἱ προσήλυτοι) that came from the land of Israel." While the Greek term (προσήλυτοι) infers that these were proselytes rather than non-Torah-observant gentiles, the underlying Hebrew (וְהַגֵּרִים) allows for non-proselyte gentile participants (e.g., Lev 25:47).

51. As note earlier in this study, I use the term "Jewish" rather than "Judean," in contradistinction to Steve Mason's approach ("Jews, Judeans, Judaizing, Judaism," 457–512). For a judicious critique of Mason's position, particularly as it relates to (1) Mason's "terminological distinction between ancient contexts . . . and the late antique and modern situation," and (2) "the name of the place associated with Jew," see Runesson, "Inventing Christian Identity," 64–70.

52. For suggestions that the ways parted by the end of the first century CE, see the essays in Dunn, ed., *Jews and Christians*. For opinions that Christ-followers and Jews continued to exhibit social interaction in their dealings with one another even into the Late Antique period, see the collection of essays in Becker and Reed, eds., *The Ways that Never Parted*. See also, Spence, *The Parting of the Ways*.

7

John's Ekklēsiai *as*
Jewish *"City Writ Large"*

Ekklēsiai as Cleruchies of the *Kosmos-Polis*
New Jerusalem

JOHN'S CONCEPTION OF AN eschatological city called the New Jerusalem would particularly have resonated with a broader Jewish audience, especially the large Jewish populace in the Lycus river valley (e.g., Laodicea).[1] One could say that John's *ekklēsiai* (chs. 2—3) are presented as being the multi-ethnic earthly representatives of a heavenly *kosmos-polis* that is called "the New Jerusalem" (chs. 21—22). Assuming such an ambassadorial self-presentation, John's *ekklēsiai*, consonant with (earlier) Pauline *ekklēsiai*, could have been perceived by Greco-Romans as implicitly claiming a role as metaphorical cleruchies (colonies) of the "New Jerusalem"/"Jerusalem above."[2]

A cleruchy was an ancient Athenian colony in which the cleruchs, or settlers, maintained their political allegiance to Athens and retained their Athenian citizenship. Two Athenian cleruchies (Delos, Samos)[3]

---

1. With respect to Laodicea, Josephus states that, since the time of Antiochus III the Great (early second century BCE), it consisted of a predominantly Jewish population (*Ant.* 12.3.4), while Cicero notes that Flacco confiscated a large amount of gold (9 kg) which was destined for the temple in Jerusalem (*Pro Flacco* 28—68).

2. Rev 21:2, 10; Gal 4:26.

3. Samos is an island near the coast of Asia Minor, across the Aegean Sea from Athens. Samos has long-standing ties with Athens, not least as a cleruchy (365 BCE). Schweigert notes that "there were three cleruchic expeditions to Samos: 365/4, 361/0,

are associated with inscriptional evidence of a Greco-Roman association that names its semi-public assembly an *ekklēsia* (*IDelos* 1519 [167/6 BCE]; *Samos* 119 [n.d.]).[4] This background suggests that the confluence of a semi-public association using *ekklēsia* terminology, whether for their members-only assembly (Delos, Samos) or as the collective designation for the group itself (Johannine and Pauline *ekklēsiai*), would have positioned that association well to be perceived by Jews and Greco-Romans as a group of people who are ideologically committed to the socio-political health of their *polis* ("city-state") through the inculcation of democratic ideals within their association and through their social and political interactions with(in) the *polis*.

It is helpful at this point to take a look at extant Jewish apocalypses in John's day, which inform our understanding of how Jewish members of John's *ekklēsiai* may have perceived his leveraging of Jewish hopes via his presentation of an eschatological *kosmos-polis*. It needs to be remembered, though, that social identification is not determinative by itself of whether John is using those Jewish hopes either supersessionally or integrationally (a.k.a. non-supersessionally).

New Jerusalem as "the Land"

There are a number of shared motifs between the roughly contemporaneous books 4 *Ezra* and Revelation.[5] Four motifs of note are: messiah, city, land, and paradise.[6] One of the most striking is the common conception of the "city as land." In 4 *Ezra* 7:26, the expectation of divine holiness

---

and 352/1" ("Athenian Cleruchy on Samos," 194–98). Iain Spence notes numerous instances in Samos's history which demonstrate its enduring commitment to Greek democratic rule (*Historical Dictionary of Ancient Greek Warfare*, xxix, xxxv, 188).

4. (1) *IDelos* 1519 recounts the successful outcome of a decision reached in the *ekklēsia* ("assembly") of the Tyrian association of merchants, shippers, and warehousemen to send an embassy to Athens for permission to construct a sanctuary for Herakles. See discussions of *IDelos* 1519 by Kloppenborg ("Edwin Hatch," 231) and Harland (*Associations*, 44–45, 111). (2) *Samos* 119 is an inscription wherein mention is made of a gymnastic association that gathers (*synagō*) *eis ekklēsian* within the *palaistra* of the *gerousia* in order to enact an honorific decree (*psēphisma*) for a benefactor (*euergetēs*). See earlier publications of *Samos* 119 by Girard ("Inscriptions de Samos," 480) and Robert ("Inscriptions de Lesbos et de Samos," 476–77).

5. *OTP* 1.520.

6. See especially Table 19.1 in Jonathan Moo's essay "4 Ezra and Revelation 21:1—22:5: Paradise City," 168–74.

throughout the land is given new direction towards an expectation of a revelation of a new land: "For behold, the time will come when . . . the city which now is not seen shall appear, and the land which now is hidden shall be disclosed."[7] The phrase "unseen city" is generally taken to refer to the New Jerusalem.[8] The identity of the hidden land appears to be integrally tied with that of the "unseen city" since they both occur in parallelism with each other. One result of this parallelism relates to the presumed preexistence of both. 2 Baruch, which exhibits "some form of interdependence" with 4 Ezra also affirms the preexistence of the heavenly city but identifies the date of its creation with that of paradise (2 Bar. 4:2–3).[9] Michael Stone notes that the expression "land which is now hidden" is "unparalleled" in the Hebrew Bible or Jewish Second Temple literature.[10]

Within 4 Ezra, the land is "intimately connected with the survivors and is the locale of the messianic kingdom."[11] Since paradise and the heavenly Jerusalem are occasionally mentioned side by side, some (e.g., Gunkel, Box, and Baldensperger) equate "the land" here with "paradise."[12] Stone, though, sees this as being dubious since none of those references to paradise actually call it "land."[13] At best, Stone sees in 4 Ezra an analogous approach to an eschatologization of the "land."[14]

Three other options present themselves. First, the expression "land which is now hidden" may relate to the changing of the foundations of the earth at the eschaton. A second possibility sees this "hidden land" in parallel to the field Ardat, the place to which Ezra must go to view the heavenly Jerusalem, for "no work of man's building could endure in a

7. 4 Ezra is dated to around 90 BCE. Since the Babylon of 4 Ezra is thought to be a cryptic reference to Jerusalem then the introductory phrase of the book, "in the thirtieth year after the destruction of our city" dates 4 Ezra to roughly thirty years after the destruction of Jerusalem (cf. OTP 1.520).

8. This notion occurs elsewhere in 4 Ezra—8:52; 10:27, 42, 54 ("the city") and 10:44; 13:36 ("Zion"), especially in Vision 4 (e.g., 10:27, 42, 44, 54). Michael Stone notes that "the world to come or paradise is often talked of as heavenly Jerusalem" ("Qumran und die Zwölf," 134–46).

9. Collins, Apocalyptic Imagination, 212. In 2 Bar. 4:2–3 this heavenly city was already created when God created paradise.

10. Stone, Fourth Ezra, 214.

11. Stone, Fourth Ezra, 214. Cf. 4 Ezra 9:8; 12:34; 13:48. See also 2 Bar. 59:10.

12. See Stone, Fourth Ezra, 214 n. 52 for citation details.

13. Stone, Fourth Ezra, 214 n. 52.

14. Stone, Fourth Ezra, 214 n. 52.

place where the city of the Most High was to be revealed" (10:54).[15] A third possibility presented by the parallelism of the "unseen city" with that of the "hidden land" may be that the heavenly city expected in 4 *Ezra* is not just a replacement for the earthly city of Jerusalem but also for the very land upon which it sits, and possibly for the entirety of the promised land itself. Of particular note is that in 4 *Ezra* this land is already existent and awaits only its revelation to the chosen people during the time of the Messiah's temporary four-hundred-year earthly reign (7:28). After the Messiah's death the world will return to its primeval state for seven days "as it was at the first beginnings" (7:29, 30). In somewhat of a reversal, *Urzeit* will have become *Endzeit*. Then the resurrection of the righteous and unrighteous will take place followed by their judgment at the judgment seat of the Most High (7:31–44).

There are at least three ways in which the descent of the New Jerusalem in Rev 21 and 22 is analogous to the "unseen city" of 4 *Ezra*. First, Revelation mentions its *descent* as still future, *not* that its *creation* is still future. As such, the preexistence of Revelation's New Jerusalem in heaven appears to be assumed.[16] Second, the heavenly city of Revelation also serves as the replacement for the earthly Jerusalem as God's eternal dwelling place.

Third, by virtue of its gargantuan dimensions (approx. 2,200 km cube), the New Jerusalem may even implicitly be the replacement for the very land itself. Jewish Second Temple literature portrays the restoration of the promised land (*Endzeit*) in terms of supernatural fecundity reminiscent of the Garden of Eden (*Urzeit*).[17] John's integration of paradisiacal descriptions with those of the New Jerusalem may be an attempt to unite the two metaphors of heavenly city and earthly paradise which 2 *Baruch* views as being separate. Furthermore, the view espoused in *Jub.* 8:19 that

15. Stone, *Fourth Ezra*, 214.

16. Celia Deutsch notes that "the notion of a pre-existent Jerusalem is paralleled by the rabbinic concept of the seven things created before the word: Torah, repentance, Paradise, hell, the Throne, the heavenly Temple and the name of the Messiah; cf *b. Pes.* 54a; *Ned* 39b; also *Gen R.* I.4." She also cites E. Lohmeyer (*Die Offenbarung des Johannes*, 162) who states that the concept of an eternal city occurs in Egyptian, Persian, and Roman religion, while Babylonian religion also affirmed a heavenly city that was the image of the earthly city ("Transformation of Symbols," 118 n. 73).

17. For example, 1 *En.* 10:19 "And in those days . . . every seed that is sown on her [the earth], one measure will yield a thousand (measures) and one measure of olives will yield ten measures of pressed oil." Also, 2 *Bar.* 29:5–8 "The earth will also yield fruits ten thousandfold."

the Garden of Eden is "the holy of holies and the dwelling of the LORD" adds another layer of fulfillment to the cubic-shaped New Jerusalem. As John describes it to his Jewish-Christian readers, this paradisiacal city in which God now dwells is very reminiscent of the primordial bliss and bounty of the Garden. In this way it may also very well be metaphorical of the very "earth/land/promised land" (*ha eretz*) upon which it sits and, consequently, from which supernaturally eternal fecundity results (e.g., 22:1–5).[18]

New Jerusalem Supersedes Imperial Rome

It can be safely assumed from the apocalyptic imagery in John's letter that he is not interested in having his seven *ekklēsiai* maintain theological continuity with (earlier) Pauline *ekklēsiai* in their enactment of a socio-ethnic form of *dēmokratia*. In fact, the positive fashion in which the *ekklēsia* identity of his communities may have been viewed in the political culture of Roman Asia would only have served to undermine John's apocalyptic polemic. As such, John would have required an offsetting counter-imperial identity. He succeeds in this with his depiction of the New Jerusalem which, in its descent to earth at the end of human history (ch. 21), eternally supersedes Babylon (ch. 18), the symbol of Rome and its rulers (ch. 17).

John's New Jerusalem is depicted as a cubic-shaped *polis* that extends 2,200 kms in each direction (21:9, 10, 16). Thus, it is not difficult to imagine that the gargantuan dimensions of the eschatological Jewish *kosmos-polis* would have been viewed as counter-imperial imagery that takes aim at the highest political target—the Roman religio-political *imperium* and its pantheon of deities. In this respect, the New Jerusalem lays claim to re-placing Rome as the ruling *polis* of the *oikoumenē* ("the inhabited world"). This counter-imperial ideology would have been particularly poignant for Revelation's Jewish readership if Revelation was written during or

18. Revelation's vision of the New Jerusalem, though, does depart from that of 4 *Ezra* in two key ways. First, while in both books the "unseen city" comes down to earth in conjunction with the Messiah's reign, in Revelation this messianic reign does not appear to begin until after the first earth and heavens are destroyed (21:1, 2). Second, the messianic figure of 4 *Ezra* does not accord with the divine deliverer of Revelation, who is variously depicted as: (1) the Lion of the tribe of Judah and the Root of David (5:5); (2) the Lamb who was slain (5:9); (3) the Word of God (19:11); and (4) the King of kings and the Lord of lords (19:16).

soon after the Judean revolt (66–70 CE), when Jerusalem and its temple were destroyed at the hands of Caesar Vespasian's son Titus.

John did not leave the defeat of Rome only to the imagination through his symbolic representation of a hegemonic New Jerusalem. John also depicts the actual fall of Rome itself through symbolic imagery. John makes quite clear to his hearers/readers that the goddess Roma is a woman named "Babylon" (ch. 17).[19] This Babylon/goddess Roma represents either the city of Rome (17:18),[20] especially "in all her prosperity gained by economic exploitation of the Empire,"[21] or the Roman religio-political ideology, including its imperial cults,[22] which fuels that drive towards exploitative domination.[23]

There were a number of imperial cults in Roman Asia prior to, and during, John's day. If John's letter is dated to Nero's timeframe, there is some doubt, though, as to whether the Roman imperial cult can be the focus of John's religio-political critique. S. R. F. Price's research indicates that, prior to the Flavians (69 CE), only two of the seven cities in which Christ-follower *ekklēsiai* were located would have had a provincial imperial cult; these being Pergamum, dedicated to Rome and Augustus (29 BCE), and Smyrna, dedicated to Tiberius, Livia, and the Senate (23 CE).[24] Of additional import is the fact that although the collective nature of the imperial cult accommodated for images of Nero, no temples or shrines are specifically devoted to Nero.[25] How might one then explain the prom-

19. Bauckham, *Theology*, 17; Aune, *Revelation* 17—22, 925, 927. For descriptions of Roma worship among temples in Roman Asia, see Simon, *Rituals and Power*, 40–43, 252, 254.

20. In *Sib. Or.* 5:155–61 (c. 70–115 CE) "Babylon" is a code name for Rome. In 1 Peter (60s CE), which is also addressed to Christ-follower communities in Roman Asia, as well as to provinces beyond (e.g., Pontus, Bithynia, Cappadocia), "Babylon" is used as a cryptic reference for Rome (5:13).

21. Bauckham, *Theology*, 36. See also Bauckham, *Climax of Prophecy*, 338–83.

22. Ittai Gradel highlights how emperor worship reflected "an honors-for-bene-factions structure found in all relationships between parties of vastly unequal power and social standing in Roman society" (*Emperor Worship and Roman Religion*, 26). Divinity is one of degree, a sliding scale based on status earned, and not one of kind, an essence that creates an absolute dividing line between divine and human realms.

23. Beale, *Revelation*, 859; Runesson, "Was There a Christian Mission," 205–47.

24. See the "Catalogue of Imperial Temples and Shrines in Asia Minor" in Price, *Rituals and Power*, 249–74.

25. G. van Kooten notes that, "In Asia, there is no evidence that a separate provincial imperial cult was devoted to Nero, . . . after Gaius there was no other provincial imperial cult established in Asia for over 40 years. . . . For nearly sixty years—from 26

inence of ostensible Neronian allusions in Revelation? But I am getting ahead of myself. What do I mean by Neronian allusions in Revelation?

John appears to reinforce his counter-imperial message by way of allusion to two of Nero's architectural wonders. Both structures were built in Rome in the aftermath of the great fire in 64 CE. They are Nero's massive Golden House, and the colossal 120-foot-high statue of himself in the entrance hall of the Golden House. Nero's Colossus, as the statue was called, was styled after the Sun god Helios. In Rev 13 John describes an image, or statue, of the seven-headed beast. Throughout chapters 13—20 the image or statue of the beast is always spoken of in the singular. Van Kooten claims that, "This seems to signal that Revelation does not oppose the manifold images of the imperial cult, but opposes one particular image, that of Nero's Colossus in Rome."[26]

Nero's Golden House, or Domus Aurea, is described by Suetonius (*Nero* 31 1–2) as being adorned with precious jewels, gold overlays, ivory ceilings, moving panels, and a circular dining room with a revolving roof that was synchronized with the movement of the heavens.[27] This architectural marvel was located right in the very heart of Rome.[28] It spanned the Esquiline and Palatine Hills, the site of Nero's previous palace, but went beyond that to occupy most of the Caelian Hill as well. When it was finally completed Nero is reported to have said, "Good, now I can at last begin to live like a human being."[29] Popular opinion in Rome was scandalized by Nero's extravagance. In his epigrams, Martial summarizes some of that feeling: "One house took up the whole city of Rome" (*Liber de Spectaculis* 2.4). Suetonius mentions a popular warning about the

---

CE until the reign of Domitian in the late first century CE—Asia had two provincial cults [i.e. Pergamum and Smyrna] but was not successful in establishing a third" ("The Year of the Four Emperors," 232). See also, Friesen, *Twice Neokoros*, 27–28.

26. Kooten, "The Year of the Four Emperors," 232.

27. Suetonius (*Nero* 31 1–12) states that "A huge statue of Nero, 120 feet high, stood in the entrance hall; and the pillared arcade ran for a whole mile. An enormous pool, more like a sea than a pool, was surrounded by buildings made to resemble cities and by a landscape garden consisting of plowed fields, vineyards, pastures and woodlands. Here every variety of domestic and wild animals roamed about. Parts of the house were overlaid with gold and studded with precious stones and mother of pearl. All the dining rooms had ceilings of fretted ivory, the panels of which could slide back and let a rain of flowers, or of perfume from hidden sprinklers, fall on his guests. The main dining room was circular, and its roof revolved slowly, day and night, in time with the sky. Sea water, or sulfur water, was always on tap in the baths."

28. See further in Klingman, *The First Century*, 300.

29. Suetonius's Latin phrase reads, "quasi hominem tandem habitare coepisse."

tyrannical nature of the house itself: "Rome has become a house; citizens, emigrate to Veii. But watch out that the house does not extend that far too" (*Suetonius, Nero* 31).

If one reads John's description of the golden New Jerusalem (21:18, 21) with an eye to Nero's Golden House, then, as van Kooten suggests, "Revelation reads . . . as a 'tale of three cities.'"[30] Rome, the "great city,"[31] is fated to be destroyed by fire,[32] the earthly Jerusalem, the "holy city," will be trampled underfoot,[33] and the "city of God, the new Jerusalem" will come down out of heaven (the sky?) from God.[34] Given the New Jerusalem's construction entirely out of pure gold (21:18), one could say that John rhetorically presents it as the true "Domus Aurea" or "Golden House."

Overall then, one could say that John's expectation in chapter 18 that Babylon (Rome) will be destroyed once more, and for the last time, by fire, along with his description in chapter 21 of the massive New Jerusalem as "golden," can be "read as a deliberate undermining of Nero's new Rome, which has at its heart his 'Golden House.'" John's New Jerusalem does more than depict the supersession of imperial Rome. It also depicts the fulfillment of the Jewish hope of a New Jerusalem, not least as it is described in the book of Ezekiel, the post-exilic Hebrew prophet.

The Cubic New Jerusalem Fulfills Ezekiel's Temple-City

The metaphorical depiction of God's people/*ekklēsiai* as "*THE* heavenly city writ large" represents more than simply political ideology against the *imperium*. It is also an ethno-religious ideology that would have broadly resonated with a Jewish audience by John's depiction of his eschatological city through the lens of Jewish tropes and motifs.

As I have already shown, the first way in which Revelation interconnects its seven *ekklēsiai* with a Jewish heritage is by using the imagery of a hegemonic *polis* called "the New Jerusalem." The expansive size of the eschatological Jerusalem reinforces Jewish Second Temple conceptions

30. Kooten, "The Year of the Four Emperors," 226.

31. Rev 16:19; 17:18; 18:10, 16, 18, 19, 21 (perhaps also 11:8).

32. Rev 17:16; 18:8.

33. Rev 11:2.

34. Rev 3:12; 21:2, 10 (cf. 22.19). The Greek word *ouranos* can be translated "heaven" or "sky" (see 6:13).

of Jerusalem's centrality as the "navel/center of the earth"[35] while at the
same time exponentially revisioning previous Jewish depictions of an
ostensible eschatological New Jerusalem, particularly the one found in
Ezek 40—48[36] and in the seven Dead Sea scrolls which collectively are
referred to as the "Description of the New Jerusalem" (DNJ).[37]

With respect to Ezekiel's temple-city, there are at least three points
of contact between it and the New Jerusalem of Revelation. First, both
temple-*poleis* are associated with a mountain. Ezekiel's city rests on a
"very high mountain" (Ezek 40:2), while John views the descent of the
New Jerusalem from the vantage point of a "great, high mountain" (Rev
21:9). Second, as with Ezekiel's temple-city (Ezek 48:30–35), the New Jerusalem also has twelve gates, three per side, upon which are written the
names of the twelve tribes of Israel (21:12, 13).[38] John, however, does not
inform the reader as to the order in which the named gates are arranged.
Third, both Ezekiel and John record the fact that God's glory now dwells
eternally with humanity. In phraseology reminiscent of Ezek 43:1–7,
John notes that: "the home of God is among mortals, He will dwell with
them" (21:3, 4) and "the throne of God and of the Lamb will be in it [the
city], and his servants will worship him" (22:3–4).[39]

There are also at least three points of departure between the temple-
cities described in Ezekiel and Revelation. First, the name "YHWH is
There" rather than "Jerusalem" is expressly associated with Ezekiel's
temple-city. Second, Katheryn Pfisterer Darr claims that by listening
carefully to Ezek 47:1–12 "we cannot avoid hearing the silence concerning any paradisiacal transformation of land lying beyond the perimeters

35. Jerusalem is called the "navel of the earth" in *Jub.* 8.19 and is said to be situated
in the "middle of the earth" in 1 *En.* 26.1, *Sib. Or.* 5.249, and *Arist.* 83. As already mentioned, in the Hebrew Bible, Jerusalem is the city which is implicit in the descriptor
"the navel/center of the earth" (Isa 24:13; Ezek 38:12).

36. A square wall surrounds the outer court of the temple (40:5). It measures 500
cubits (approx. 0.25 km) on each side (42:15–20; 45:2). Beyond this, the wall of the city
itself forms an immense square 4,500 cubits on each side (approx. 2 km), with three
gates per side.

37. See p. 18 n. 61 for my discussion of which Qumran manuscripts comprise DNJ.

38. Each gate in Ezekiel's temple-city is named after one of the tribes of Israel
(48:30–35). For more details on Ezekiel's temple-city, see Vawter and Hoppe, *Ezekiel*,
210.

39. Ezekiel records that "the glory of the Lord filled the temple . . . 'this is the place
of my throne and . . . where I will reside among the people of Israel forever'" (Ezek
43:5, 7).

of Israel's territory."[40] By contrast, the New Jerusalem with its expansive walls depicts the extension of paradisiacal restoration beyond the limits of the promised land and to the very ends of the earth itself. Consonant with Ezekielian ideology, however, the mention of *walls* implies what John elsewhere makes explicit: the ungodly are left outside the boundaries of John's eschatological temple-city (21:8; 27; 22:15), even as godly gentiles/nations are granted entrance (21:24–26). A third variance involves Ezekiel's understanding of the land as an extension of temple land.[41] Ezekiel's temple vision revolves around the "main themes of separation and gradation"[42] such that there are "degrees of holiness [which] depend upon the distance from the center."[43] Thus, one might picture a proportional relationship in which "YHWH's holiness extends outward, in zones of decreasing holiness, making the temple holy and the land pure."[44]

John's vision of the New Jerusalem stands in stark contrast to Ezekiel's temple-land ideology. The fact that John did not see a temple in the city, but rather that he claims that "the Lord God Almighty and the Lamb are its temple" (22:21), implies that God's glory and concomitant holiness extends in an undiminished fashion throughout the length, breadth and height of the city. One's distance away from the throne of God (22:1–5), the spiritual epicenter of the New Jerusalem, is not reflective of differing degrees of holiness.

Like Ezekiel's temple-city, the ideal city in the surviving fragments of the DNJ also is not specifically named.[45] Although little of the structural details of the temple survive, the city's gates, wall, towers, and dwellings, to name a few examples, are explained. The outer wall of the New Jerusalem measures 140 *ris* on the east and west by 100 *ris* on the north and south.[46] This translates into a modern equivalent of 26 kilometers

40. Darr, "The Wall Around Paradise," 278.

41. Stevenson, "The Land is Yours," 2.

42. Greenberg, "Design and Themes," 192. Greenberg sees gradation evident in the temple proper, for example, "by the successively narrowing entrances to its inner parts" (ibid., 193).

43. Stevenson, "The Land is Yours," 3.

44. Stevenson, "The Land is Yours," 3.

45. Michael Chyutin has attempted a hypothetical reconstruction of the surviving fragments into a twenty-two-line, twenty-two-column scroll that he calls the "New Jerusalem Scroll" ("New Jerusalem," 71–97; Chyutin, *New Jerusalem Scroll* [1997]).

46. The *ris* measures 352 cubits. A cubit in the New Jerusalem Scroll is most likely

by 18.5 kilometers. Although a population estimate of 650,000 has been suggested for the ideal "Jerusalem" of the DNJ, its physical footprint is still a far cry from the 2,200 km length, width, and height attributed to each wall in "John's" New Jerusalem.[47]

The Cubic New Jerusalem as Heavenly Temple-*Polis*

John communicates Jewish ethno-religious ideology in his depiction of his multi-ethnic *polis* as a Jewish sanctuary.[48] The cubic form of John's "*kosmos-polis*" is reminiscent of the cubic shape ascribed to the Holy of Holies in the Israelites's desert tabernacle[49] and in the Solomonic Temple in Jerusalem.[50] This implicit identification of the New Jerusalem with the Holy of Holies is made more explicit for John in chapter 21. In 21:2, which is the start of the final *individual vision* of Revelation, John describes seeing "the holy city . . . coming down out of heaven [or sky] from God, prepared as a bride" and mentions hearing that this "holy city" as "the tabernacle of God is [now] with people." This final *individual vision* (21:2—22:20) seems to have two dramatic movements. The first visionary movement (21:2–8) gives a summary overview of all of the key elements that are described in more detail in the second visionary movement (21:9—22:20). This two-fold literary strategy within only a single *individual vision* is reminiscent of John's textual blocking literary strategy throughout the entire vision episode in which the sixth seal

---

the old royal cubit measuring seven handbreadths (i.e., 21 inches) (Chuytin, *New Jerusalem Scroll*, 70).

47. Within the expansive wall is a residential and temple area. The temple compound by itself is almost twice the size of the city of Jerusalem as it existed during the time of the Scroll's composition. The residential area of the city contains 240 residential blocks, each with 120 houses. This equates to a total of 28,800 homes. The number of couches in the dining room indicates that upwards of twenty-two residents were envisioned per home (5Q15 ii.11). This produces a minimum population estimate of 633,000 inhabitants.

48. John notes that he "saw no temple in the city, for its temple is the Lord God the Almighty and the Lamb" (21:22), that holiness extends to all parts of the temple-city ("nothing unclean will enter it"; 21:27), that only the pure will enter the city (21:27; 22:3, 14, 15), and that the (chariot) throne of the God and of the Lamb is set within its midst (22:3, 4).

49. In Exod 26:15–30 the vertical boards of the tabernacle are described as being 10 cubits high.

50. 1 Kgs 6:20 describes the inner sanctuary as being 20 cubits cubed. See further Briggs, *Jewish Temple* (1999).

(6:12–17) concisely overviews the key elements associated with divine judgment and consummation, which are then progressively re-described in ever-expanding detail in the rest of the vision episode (7:1—22:20). Thus, 21:2–8 concisely describes the consummation of salvation-history through the descent of the "holy city" (21:2–3) to the final instantiation of holiness throughout the new creation when God's presence visibly and experientially: (1) redeems humanity's suffering with eternal comfort and reward (21:4–7), and (2) judges rebellious humanity with their removal into the lake of fire (21:8; cf. also 20:12–15; 22:15).

Jan Fekkes III notes six temple motifs that extend throughout the city which together imply that God's holiness spreads throughout the new creation, that is, the cubic *polis*:[51] (1) since there is no temple in the city, God's Shekinah glory encompasses the city itself (21:22–23; 22:5); (2) the bringing of gifts to the New Jerusalem by the nations is a tradition normally associated with the temple in Jerusalem (21:26; cf. 4:10);[52] (3) the continuity of worship is evident in that it proceeds on an uninterrupted basis day and night; it is not limited to daylight "hours" (21:25; cf. 7:15a); (4) purity laws related to how one approaches God and enters the temple are now extended throughout the city (21:27); (5) 22:3b–5 reveals the eternal priesthood that serves God in the temple-city (cf. 1:6; 5:10; 7:14–15; 20:6); and (6) John's temple-city incorporates the motifs of the water and the tree of life (22:1–2), which are so central to Ezekiel's temple-city (Ezek 47:1–12).

John's New Jerusalem is thus depicted as the eschatological fulfillment of the Jewish hope for a renewed and purified temple.[53] This hope is found in Jewish writings such as the apocalyptic works of 1 *Enoch*,[54]

---

51. Fekkes, *Isaiah and Prophetic Traditions*, 99–101.

52. Ps 68:29 emphasizes this tradition: "Because of your temple at Jerusalem, kings bear gifts to you." An interesting parallel to Rev 21:26 is 2 Macc 5:16, in which Antiochus's despoiling of the temple involves the removal of "votive offerings which other kings had made to enhance the glory and honor of the place."

53. See Gärtner, *The Temple* (1965).

54. In the Book of Dreams (1 *En.* 85—90), Enoch sees an eschatological city situated on a mountain which has no tower (temple). In both 1 *Enoch* and Revelation there is no temple. This implies in each case that the *entire city* will be the sanctuary of God; 1 *Enoch* does not portray its city as a people, though.

4 *Ezra*,[55] 2 *Baruch*,[56] the Qumran sectarian work 4QFlorilegium,[57] and the non-sectarian,[58] non-eschatological[59] Temple Scroll (11QTemple).[60] Additionally, the implied conclusion that John's temple-*polis* replaces "heaven"[61] is in continuity with Jewish portrayals of heaven as a temple.

55. *4 Ezra* 7:26: "the city which now is not seen shall appear, and the land which now is hidden shall be disclosed." The "unseen city" is generally taken to refer to the New Jerusalem. This notion occurs elsewhere in *4 Ezra* (8:52; 10:27, 42, 54 ["the city"] and 10:44; 13:36 ["Zion"]), particularly in Vision 4 (e.g., 10:27, 42, 44, 54). Michael Stone also notes that the expression "land which is now hidden" is "unparalleled" in the OT or Jewish Second Temple literature (*Fourth Ezra*, 214).

56. *2 Baruch*, which exhibits some form of interdependence with *4 Ezra*, also affirms the preexistence of the heavenly city and temple but identifies the date of its creation with that of paradise (*2 Bar.* 4:2–3) and its revelation to take place in the *eschaton* (Collins, *Apocalyptic Imagination*, 212).

57. 4QFlorilegium (4Q174) speaks of an eschatological temple personally built by the hands of the Lord (מקדש אדם; "the place/temple of Adam"; 4Q174 3.vii). Unlike Rev 21:24, 4Q174 does not envision foreigners co-existing with God and his saints.

58. Yigael Yadin maintains that the Temple Scroll is the product of Qumran sectarians ("Temple Scroll," 32–49). The contrasting position is capably summarized by H. Stegemann ("Literary Compositions of the Temple Scroll," 123–48).

59. 11QTemple is presented as a direct revelation from YHWH to Moses—as written Torah. As such, the temple in 11QT is not eschatological. It represents an "ideal temple, apparently . . . [the one] the Israelites should have built after their entrance into the land of Canaan" (Maier, "Temple," 925). See also, Maier, "Architectural History," 24–25 and Stegemann, "Literary Compositions of the Temple Scroll," 123–48.

60. As is the case with DNJ and Ezek 40—48, the name Jerusalem does not occur in the Temple Scroll (11Q19, 11Q20). The sanctuary complex consists of three concentric squares that represent graduated concentric areas of holiness spreading outwards from the holy of holies in the center. The first is the inner court, or court of priests. It measures 300 cubits on each side, if one includes the gateway building on each side of the square (11Q19 19.6; 20.4; 34[?]—38.11; 46.2). The middle square, which measures 500 cubits per outer side is for ritually clean men (11Q19 38.12—40.5, 7). Its size matches that of the entire temple in Ezekiel's vision (chs. 40—48). The outer court, or court of Israel, which is for ritually clean men and women, encompasses the other two courts. It measures 1,700 cubits per outer side, giving a total perimeter of 6,800 cubits (11Q19 21.3–4; 22.13–15; 37.19; 40.5—45.2; 46.3; 4Q365 28.ii; see also, Maier, "Architectural History," 24–25).

61. John locates the throne of God and of the Lamb within the New Jerusalem before which "his servants will worship him . . . reign forever and ever" (Rev 21:5). Prior to the eschatological consummation of all things (6:12—22:21), John had located the throne of God "in heaven" (4:1—5:14, esp. 4:1).

This "heaven-as-temple" imagery is found in 1 *Enoch*,[62] the *Testament of Levi*,[63] 3 *Baruch*,[64] and Songs of the Sabbath Sacrifice.[65]

The Cubic New Jerusalem as the *Future* Covenantal People of God

But John goes one exponential step further than simply re-visioning Jewish hopes of an eschatological city that is at the same time *ha eretz* (the land), the temple/Holy of Holies, and "heaven." John is not interested only in demonstrating that the New Jerusalem is an eschatological place for the covenantal people of God. In Rev 21:9–10, John implicitly identifies the New Jerusalem itself as *being the people of God*, that is, "the bride, the wife of the Lamb" (21:2, 9, 10).[66] In a brilliant twist of plot, one could say that in the *eschaton* the "people of God" will become the "place of God."[67] Thus, not only is the curse removed, but the consequences of the curse are removed: the people of God will never be expelled from paradise, because the people of God have in fact *become* the restored paradise, known as the New Jerusalem. Additional reinforcement for this concept of people as place is found in the fact that Jesus speaks of the *ekklēsiai* (22:16) and that "John" speaks of the "bride" (22:17) in two antiphonally

62. The Book of Watchers (1 *En.* 1–36) describes a heavenly sanctuary, modeled on the Herodian Temple, through which Enoch travels on his way to God's presence so as to intercede for the Watchers (fallen angels).

63. *The Testament of Levi* (second century BCE) "originally included three heavens, although in some forms of the text (α) 3:1–8 has been modified and expanded in order to depict seven heavens" (*OTP* 1.788). The uppermost heaven is the dwelling of God (*T. Levi* 3:4). This contrasts with John's portrayal of the entire cubic New Jerusalem as being the dwelling of God.

64. 3 *Baruch* (first to third centuries CE) appears to presume a cultic temple given the priestly role of the archangel Michael.

65. In the Songs of the Sabbath Sacrifice (4Q400–407), heaven is depicted as a temple wherein the angels officiate the liturgy. Members of the community participate in the heavenly liturgy offered by the angels when they participate in the worship of the community (see Newsome, *Songs of the Sabbath Sacrifice* [1985]).

66. Rev 21:9, 10 reads, "Then one of the seven angels . . . came and said to me, 'Come, I will show you the bride, the wife of the Lamb.' And in the spirit he carried me away to a great, high mountain and showed me the holy city Jerusalem coming down out of heaven from God."

67. Robert H. Gundry claims that "John wanted his Christian readers . . . to see in the New Jerusalem, not their future dwelling place, but—what was even more heartening—their future selves and state" ("New Jerusalem," 264).

connected pericopes (22:16 and 22:17–19). This provides exegetical support for viewing John's addressees (the seven *ekklēsiai*) as being part and
parcel of John's symbolic portrayal of the "bride of Christ" as the New
Jerusalem.

John further reinforces the Jewish heritage of his seven *ekklēsiai* by
portraying his New Jerusalem as the culmination of God's salvation history through at least two of its other architectural features: the twelve
gates and the twelve-fold foundation. The twelve gates represent the
twelve tribes of Israel (21:12, 13). The twelve-fold foundation of the New
Jerusalem represents the twelve apostles of the Lamb (21:14, 19–21).[68]
Taken together these features could then be said symbolically to represent the union of the old and new covenant people of God into one
eternal Jewish *polis*.[69]

The metaphorical portrayal of the seven *ekklēsiai* in Roman Asia as
"*the* Jewish temple-city writ large" also serves the author's ethno-religious
purposes. He is able to affirm that Jewishness is intrinsic to the ethno-
religious makeup of his seven diasporic *ekklēsiai* in the *eschaton* and
beyond, even into eternity. It is in Revelation that we see the convergence
of supersessionist counter-imperial and a potentially non-supersessionist
pro-Jewish ideology within a single literary work and in a sustained and
visually engaging manner.

The Cubic New Jerusalem as the *Present* Covenantal People of God

If in fact the New Jerusalem in Revelation accords with 4 *Ezra's* view of
the eternal eschatological city as having already been created, but which
is invisible and yet to be visibly revealed, then could it be that the New
Jerusalem is *already* invisibly present upon the earth? If the New Jerusalem is to be equated not least with the future people of God ("the bride,
the wife of the Lamb"; 21:9, 10), then it may also be that the New Jerusalem presently dwells *invisibly* on the earth in the form of the universal
ekklēsia/Body of the Jewish *Christos* (1 Cor 12:27, 28). This possibility
has been asserted as early as the patristic era beginning with Origen,

---

68. Draper, "Twelve Apostles," 41–63.

69. The city gates each have the name of one Israelite tribe inscribed upon them.
Each of the twelve foundations has the name of one of Jesus's apostles inscribed upon
them (Rev 21:12–14).

who considered that "the new heaven and the new earth" (21:1) already began at Christ's resurrection and that the "church" is the "holy city, New Jerusalem" (21:2). Others who variously assert this type of inaugurated eschatology include Cyprian, Victorinus, Tertullian, Eusebius, Tyconius, and, most famously, Augustine in his *City of God*.[70]

There appear to be some clues in John's description of the throne room vision (Rev 4 and 5) that indicate that the people of God are *invisibly* present. One's identification of the twenty-four elders is the *crux interpretum* for this possibility. If they are to be identified with the *ekklēsia* universal, then John's eschatology parallels the Pauline inaugurated eschatology (e.g., Eph 2:3–10).[71]

The vision of the twenty-four elders who encircle the throne of God has given rise to many different proposals as to their identification and purpose. Prior to surveying the interpretive options, it may be best to summarize their depiction in Revelation. They are called *presbyteroi* ("elders") and they sit on twenty-four thrones around the throne of God (4:4; 11:16). They wear crowns of gold and are clothed in white garments (4:4).

Although not without its problems, the interpretation that is most consonant with other usages of the number twelve in the book of Revelation, is that the twenty-four elders are seen as having reference either to the collective people of God themselves[72] or to "the heavenly representatives of the elect."[73] Neither of these two possibilities need necessarily be seen as mutually exclusive options. The fact that angels are intimately identified with the corporate people of God whom they represent is clearly taught in chapters 2 and 3 wherein the seven stars, which are held in the hand of the glorified Christ, are said to represent "the angels of the seven churches" (1:20). In this regard, it is not hard to see why the twenty-four elders could be the angelic representatives of the corporate Body of Christ, whose identity is inextricably intertwined with the saints whom they represent.

70. For details see Kovacs and Rowland, *Revelation*, 222–25.

71. For correspondences between Rev 20 and some of the major features of Paul's eschatological perspectives, see Page, "Revelation 20," 31–43.

72. Cf. Swete, *Apocalypse of St. John*, 68–69. In this regard, the number twenty-four would be the sum of a twelve plus a twelve; the twelve tribes, which represent the old covenant people of God (cf. 21:12—the twelve gates of the New Jerusalem with the names of the twelve tribes of Israel on them) plus the twelve apostles of the Lamb (cf. 21:14, 19–20) whose names are written on the twelve foundations of the New Jerusalem) who represent the new covenant people of God.

73. Cf. Hurtado, "Revelation 4—5," 113.

Identifying the twenty-four elders with *Christos*-followers and/or the angelic representative of each *ekklēsia* of *Christos*-followers is also consistent with the witness of Revelation further on. In John's final visionary segment (21:2—22:20), the New Jerusalem is integrally identified with the bride, the wife of the Lamb (21:9, 10). Earlier, within the "marriage supper" pericope (19:1–9) John implicitly identifies the bride of the Lamb as being "the saints" who are dressed in the white garments of their righteous deeds. In 21:11–14 John correlates God's saints both past and present with two sets of twelve that form the very architecture of the city itself. As I just mentioned, the first set of twelve appears to represent the old covenant saints of God, given that the twelve gates of the New Jerusalem are each named after one of the twelve tribes of Israel. The second set of twelve appear to be the new covenant saints of God, given that the twelve foundations of the city are each inscribed with one of the names of the twelve apostles of the Lamb.

There are other interpretive options for the twenty-four elders, however. One option is that the twenty-four elders are the heavenly counterparts of the leaders of the twenty-four priestly courses of the Second Temple, which is described in 1 Chr 23:6 and 24:7–18.[74] Another option identifies the elders with the twenty-four divisions of musicians, descendants of Levi, who prophesied with lyres, harps, and cymbals (1 Chr 25:1–31; cf. 35:15; Ezra 2:41; 3:10; Neh 7:44). One wonders, though, whether the distinctively Jewish nature of these last two options would have made the symbol of the twenty-four elders less readily understandable for the non-Jewish members of John's *ekklēsiai*.

The twenty-four elders are said to "encircle" the throne (4:3; *kuklōthen*). The word *kuklōthen* is used with just such a meaning in 3 Kgdms 5:4; Sir 50:13; Zech 2:5; and 4 Macc 5:1.[75] The concept of "encirclement" of the throne, however, is unique to the book of Revelation.[76] This depiction, in Revelation, of heavenly beings *encircling* the throne of God departs from conventional biblical imagery. In 1 Kgs 22:19, Elijah "saw the LORD sitting on his throne, with all the host of heaven standing beside

74. For example, Mounce (*Revelation*, 135–36) and Charles (*Revelation*, 1:131–32) support this view.

75. For example, 4 Macc 5:1 reads: "The tyrant Antiochus, therefore, sitting in public state with his assessors upon a certain lofty place, with his armed troops standing in a circle (*kuklōthen*) round him . . ."

76. R. H. Charles notes that "This conception of a heavenly divan composed of four and twenty Elders is not found in existing Jewish literature" (*Revelation*, 1:128).

him to the right and to the left of him." In Dan 7:9 thrones are set up near (but not encircling) the throne of God, probably for the purpose of judgment.

This dearth of encirclement imagery is also evident in Jewish Second Temple literature. Aune notes that in *Sepher ha-Razim* 1.8, seven overseers are said to sit on seven thrones while further in 5.3–4 "twelve princes [are] seated upon magnificent thrones [in the fifth heaven], the appearance of their thrones is like that of fire."[77] But no attribution of encirclement is evident in their arrangement. This is also true of other passages in which the term "thrones" is used metaphorically for members of the angelic host, perhaps indicating a form of dominion that is subordinate to that of the Lord.[78]

It may be that the supposed "throne" ceremony, as reconstructed by Chyutin in the Dead Sea scroll named "Description of the New Jerusalem" (DNJ), may inform this "encirclement" concept somewhat, at least insofar as it relates to thrones *facing* the throne of God. The "throne" ceremony involves a throne in the Great Hall upon which the high priest sits subsequent to his crowning. This throne faces towards the Holy of Holies within which resides the ark of the covenant, that is, the cherubim throne of YHWH. This ritual union of priestly and kingly privilege in the priestly seat or throne inherently conjoins the concept of kingly rule with that of priestly atonement.

If John was aware either of the distinctive theology of the non-sectarian DNJ, or of its content, then John's portrayal of the twenty-four elders seated on thrones facing the (cherubim) throne of God would find some Jewish precedent. If so, then the implicit messianic connotations in the priest-king of the DNJ would have been used to good advantage by John in highlighting the "spiritual pedigree," so to speak, of the twenty-four elders. In this regard, they too are portrayed as priest-kings (Rev 5:9; also 1:6) by virtue of the atoning sacrifice and kingly authority of the messianic Priest-King, the Lamb of God. This spiritual "transaction" is implicit in the song of Rev 5:9, 10 ("You were slain and purchased for God with your blood men from every tribe and tongue and people and nation. You have made them to be a kingdom and priests to our God; and they will reign upon the earth"). If this song of the twenty-four elders in 5:9–10 is in some fashion self-referential then the twenty-four elders

77. Aune, *Revelation 1—5*, 286.

78. For example, *T. Levi* 3:8; *Asc. Isa.* 7:27; *T. Adam* 4:8; *Apoc. Elijah* 1:10; 4:10; 2 *Apoc. En.* (Rec. J) 20:1.

represent more than just angelic beings but also exalted humanity, that is, the redeemed old and new covenant people of God of all ages.

Additionally, the imagery of the twenty-four elders sitting on thrones, whether as the redeemed of the Lamb themselves or simply as their angelic representatives, is congruent with Revelation's description of the saints of God as a "a kingdom and priests to serve his God and Father" (Rev 1:6; cf. also 1 Pet 2:9, 10, which calls its Asia Minor addressees "a royal priesthood"). Like the DNJ, this description of *Christos*-followers in Rev 1:6 as ruling priests is metaphorically reinforced in Rev 4 through the picture of the twenty-four elders being seated on thrones that surround the throne of God.

If one reads the initiatory throne-room scene (Rev 4—5) with an eye to the concluding New Jerusalem scene (Rev 21—22), then, a multivalent picture of the redeemed people of God unfolds. If the *visible* New Jerusalem (a.k.a, the bride of Christ) which encircles God and the Lamb and their throne in the *eschaton* (21:22; 22:3) is already evident *invisibly* in the initiatory throne-room scene (chs. 4 and 5), then not just the twenty-four elders but also the rainbow would function in some fashion as symbolic imagery for the people of God (i.e., the universal *ekklēsia*/"church") encircling the throne of God.

The anomalous rainbow in Rev 4 makes more sense if one envisions John's portrayal of the people of God as a New Jerusalem whose walls are made out of jasper, clear as crystal (21:11, 18). If one then imagines what would happen when a bright light (the glory of God) shines out through the clear (prismatic) walls (21:23) in all directions, one would expect to see a rainbow encircling those (prismatic) walls. This image unifies the constellation of symbols for the people of God in Revelation— (1) the throne encircled by twenty-four elders and a rainbow, and (2) the New Jerusalem with its twelve gates and twelve-fold foundation. This ostensibly dual depiction of the people of God as being both a *present* (chs. 4 and 5) and a *future* (chs. 21 and 22) Jewish *kosmos-polis* hints at a theological unity with the Pauline inaugurated eschatology regarding the already/not yet status of individual Christ-followers (e.g., Eph 2:3–10). In John's corporately focused schema, his inaugurated eschatology entails the people of God (old and new covenant) as already being *invisibly* and mystically embodied as the New Jerusalem upon earth (the universal *ekklēsia*/"church"), and as being *visibly* revealed as the New Jerusalem in the *eschaton* at Christ's *parousia*.

John's portrayal of Christ-followers as living architecture is not without precedent beyond the writing of other Christ-followers. The Covenanters at Qumran partially mirror Revelation's conception of people as *polis*. In their pesher on Isa 54:11 (4QpIs^d, 4Q164), the Covenanters interpret the sapphire foundation stones of Isaiah's ideal Jerusalem (54:11) as referring to their community (4Q164 1 ii).[79] This symbolism is not dissimilar to John's depiction of the twelve apostles of the Lamb as forming the twelve-fold foundation of the New Jerusalem. Each layer of the apostolic foundation represents a different precious stone (21:14, 19–21).[80] While the Covenanters view their community as only being the ideal Jerusalem's foundation, John views all *Christos*-followers as comprising the entire city (22:9, 10). This aligns with Paul's theology of the twelve "apostle-prophets" (Eph 2:20; 3:5) forming the foundation of the living temple, the universal *ekklēsia*.[81]

A second way in which the Covenanters portray their community as living architecture is in their self-identification as the Jewish temple. In 1QS and CD the sect describes themselves as "a holy house."[82] An amplification of this impulse is found in 1QS 8.5–6. Therein, the "council of the Community" is called "a holy house for Israel [i.e., temple] and the foundation of the holy of holies of Aaron (קודש קודשים לאהרון)."

This Qumranic identification of people as sacred space is not a future expectation, however. They claimed it as a living reality that they embodied when they gathered. But their self-portrayal as a living temple was polemical in nature, even supersessionally so. The Covenanters apparently saw themselves as the living replacement for the corrupt temple and its establishment.[83] John's identification of his Christ-followers as the new temple/Holy of Holies may also have held polemical intent. If John

---

79. 4Q164 1 ii reads, "[Its interpretation:] they will found the council of the *yachad* ["community"], the priests and the people . . . the assembly of their elect."

80. Draper, "The Twelve Apostles," 41–63.

81. John unites into one sacred space (21:9, 10) all faithful non-messianic Jews (the twelve tribes), represented symbolically as the twelve gates of the New Jerusalem (Rev 21:1, 13), and all multi-ethnic Christ-followers (21:24–27), whose twelve apostles are symbolically portrayed as the twelve foundations of the *polis* (21:14).

82. "Holy house": 1QS 5.6; 8.5, 9; 9.6; 22.8; CD 3.19; 20.10, 13. "City of iniquity": 1QpHab 10.10. See Dimant, "Qumran Sectarian Literature," 514.

83. David Aune claims that the Covenanters's self-identification as a temple of God was "an intermediate situation in which they rejected the existing temple cult and lived in expectation of the rebuilding of the true and unpolluted eschatological temple" ("Qumran and the Book of Revelation," 641).

writes in a post-70 CE world, his polemic is obviously then *not directed against the Jerusalem temple*, since decades earlier it had been destroyed by the Romans. John's post-70 CE portrayal of all Christ-followers as a living temple-city would primarily then have been *counter-imperial* rhetoric. John's depiction of the continuation of the (now destroyed) temple *invisibly* as the living temple(-city) known as the New Jerusalem/universal *ekklēsia* takes rhetorical aim directly at Roman perceptions of victory over the Jewish people through their destruction of the physical temple in 70 CE.

The almost unimaginable size of John's New Jerusalem reinforces the world-encompassing nature of this new living temple/people of God. As mentioned, in Hebrew and Jewish Second Temple writings, historic Jerusalem was seen as being the "navel of the earth."[84] John's New Jerusalem takes that imagery to a whole new level. His living temple-*polis* is not just the "navel" but the whole "body," so to speak. This cube-shaped "mother of all cities" encompasses a large portion of the entire *oikoumenē* ("inhabited world") of the Roman empire. The 2,200 kilometer long, wide, and high walls of the New Jerusalem exponentially exceed any Jewish temple-city described in Ezek 40—48,[85] in the non-sectarian collection of Dead Sea scrolls called Description of the New Jerusalem,[86] and the Temple Scroll (11QT),[87] or in Book 5 of the *Sibylline Oracles*.[88] There is no Greek or Roman parallel for the size of John's walled city-state (approx. 5 million km²). The largest Greek hegemonic city-state was the unwalled territory controlled by Sparta (8,000 km²).[89]

84. Jerusalem is called the "navel of the earth" in *Jub.* 8:19 and is said to be situated in the "middle of the earth" in 1 *En.* 26.1, *Sib. Or.* 5.249, and *Arist.* 83. In the Hebrew Bible, Jerusalem is the implied city identified as "the navel of the earth" in Ezek 38:12.

85. The outer courts of Ezekiel's temple-city measure 500 cubits by 500 cubits (Ezek 42:16–20). Ezekiel uses the royal cubit (52 cm) instead of the standard cubit (45 cm). Thus, the area of the temple-city measures 50.6 km².

86. *DNJ* is non-sectarian with an early- to mid-second-century BCE compositional date. The residential area totals 28,000 homes with a minimum population of 633,000 people. This New Jerusalem measures 471 km² (26 kilometers by 18.5 kilometers) (Chyutin, *New Jerusalem Scroll*, 70ff).

87. See Stegemann, "The Literary Compositions of the Temple Scroll," 123–48.

88. Book 5 of the *Sibylline Oracles*, which dates from the late first century CE, presages somewhat John's concept of an enormous eschatological Jerusalem. In *Sib. Or.* 5.252 the future wall of Jerusalem is said to extend outwards even to the city of Joppa on the Mediterranean coast.

89. Mogens Hermann Hansen discusses four hegemonic *poleis*: Sparta, Kyrene, Thessalonike, and Demetrias, the last two of which grew by synoikism, not by conquest

John's presentation of his heavenly *polis* as a walled territorial state differs in one other respect from Greek conceptions of a *polis*. Hansen observes that Greeks never attempted "to unite all the city-states and create one large territorial state."[90] Even if one considers imperial Rome as a territorial state, that state is not contained within walls. Although an ancient reader would not have had the benefit of modern cartography and thus would not have known that the dimensions of John's walled *polis* geographically subsume the city of Rome,[91] John's readers in Roman Asia may very well have understood the counter-imperial implications of its gargantuan size, not least relative to the extension of God's sovereignty over Roman Asia. John's description of the descent of the New Jerusalem from heaven (Rev 21:2, 9–11) is in stark contrast to his depiction of the catastrophic fall of Rome (named as Babylon; 18:1–24). In John's symbolic universe, Rome is now a "crater," so to speak, rather than the "navel" of his eschatological religio-political universe.

While the geographic spread of John's New Jerusalem communicates Jewish counter-imperial dominance, what does its unfathomable height imply? One might (anachronistically) call this Jewish *polis* the "mother of all skyscrapers."[92] The wall's height implies the protection of the holy city from all unholiness. Not even a bird could accidentally defile the temple-city's holiness. The heavenly reach of the walls also implies a union of the holy city with all of creation. Celia Deutsch suggests that the cube-shaped New Jerusalem "bridges the gulf between the heavenly and the earthly; Heaven and earth become one."[93]

("Hellenic Polis," 150). Hegemonic *poleis* were ruled from the center even if their territory consisted of a number of independent *poleis* (Hansen, "Hellenic Polis," 150).

90. Hansen notes that "one important point emerges with unerring certainty: the Hellenic world remained a world of *poleis* and no attempt was ever made to unite all the city-states and create one large territorial state like that created in the 19th century. To the Greek mind such an idea was as remote as, e.g., the abolition of slavery" ("Hellenic Polis," 150).

91. As "the crow flies," the distance from the city of Jerusalem, the "navel/center of the earth" (Ezek 38:12), to the city of Rome measures about 1,400 miles/2,240 km.

92. The great height of John's New Jerusalem is concordant with the hope expressed in *Sib. Or.* 5:414–28: "the city which God desired ... more brilliant than the stars and sun and moon ... [a] great and immense tower [temple] over many stadia touching even the clouds and visible to all" (5.420–25). In *b. Bat.* 75b, the future Jerusalem is said to incorporate a thousand towers, gardens, palaces, and mansions each the size of Sepphoris. Jerusalem is said to extend to a height of 4.8 km.

93. Deutsch, "Transformation of Symbols," 111.

Not only is John's identification of his Christ-followers as a living temple not without precedent in the Jewish world, his identification of them as a *polis* is also not without precedent, but this time in the Greek world.[94] Stoics espoused two types of ideal *polis*. First, in *Republic*, Zeno "proposes an ideal communist city, all of whose citizens are wise,"[95] but this *polis* does not encompass the *oikoumenē*; it is located in a regional territory.[96] Second, Cicero, the Roman Stoic, expands the reach of Zeno's ideal *polis* to include the entire *kosmos*.[97] It needs to be noted though that John's metaphorical transformation of an entire socio-religious group (e.g., the *ekklēsiai* of Roman Asia) into a *kosmos-polis*, so to speak, goes well beyond Stoic, Cynic[98] and Epicurean[99] conceptions of a universal commonwealth.

Relative to the ethical makeup of the *dēmos* in the New Jerusalem, John is at odds with Cicero but he sides with Zeno. Cicero's *kosmos-polis* includes the wise, but "also includes the vicious and the stupid."[100] John demurs. He conceives of a virtuous *polis* community which excludes "those who practice abomination and lying" (Rev 21:27). John concretizes a *kosmos-polis* that Cicero can only abstractly conceive. John depicts a virtuous *dēmos*, consisting of at least seven earthly cleruchies (*ekklēsiai*), which together comprise a *polis* that stretches all the way to Rome.

By symbolically portraying his seven *ekklēsiai* as the "heavenly Jewish city writ large" (the eschatological New Jerusalem), John delivers a two-pronged ideological attack against the religio-political entity that is

94. There are some Greek enactment decrees in which the *politai* of a *polis* self-depict as a *polis* (*ISE* 53, *SEG* 33:317 and *SEG* 33:391).

95. Morrison, "Utopian Character," 249.

96. Daniel S. Richter questions scholarly assertions that Zeno envisaged "a cosmopolitan 'world-state' coterminous with the *oikoumenē*" and suggests that he, like Plato and Aristotle, attempted "to perfect the institution of the classical *polis*" (*Cosmopolis*, 62).

97. Cicero states that "the universe is as it were the common home of gods and men, or a city that belongs to both" (*ND* II 154; trans. Schofield, *Stoic Idea*, 65).

98. Cynic civic ideology views every person as a "citizen of the *kosmos*," or as Diogenes defined himself, as a κοσμοπολίτης, and claim an intimate relationship with the founders of the *kosmopolis* itself, that is, the gods (D.L. 6.37, 72). See Gillihan, *Civic Ideology*, 108.

99. Gillihan notes that Epicureans simultaneously affirmed the value of the Athenian *polis*, and later Greek and Roman empires, while critiquing their inadequacies, and concurrently seeking to establish alternative societies congruent with their alternative civic ideology (*Civic Ideology*, 97).

100. Morrison, "Utopian Character," 249.

Rome, and against the gods that purportedly give the *imperium* its power. This being the case, then John's social identification of not least his seven *ekklēsiai* as the heavenly and eternal Jewish "city-state" does not have as its primary rhetorical purpose the communication of a supersessionist agenda in which John's Christ-followers replace Israel through their metaphorical appropriation of Jewish institutions and symbols. Rather, John's metaphorical appropriation of Jewish institutions and symbols serves a counter-imperial purpose in demonstrating that God's chosen people (of the Abrahamic, Mosaic, and *Christos*-centric covenants) will supersede all forms of socio-political power and empire in the age to come (chs. 21, 22), and perhaps have already done so in the present age through the resurrection and exaltation of the Jewish *Christos*, the royal Davidic Lion of Judah, who is the sacrificial Lamb for all of humanity (chs. 4, 5).

8

John's Ekklēsiai

Jewish Literary Contexts

IN THE INTRODUCTION I cited Greg Carey's observation that "Revelation
stand[s] in a tradition of Jewish visions about Imperial rule."[1] In the previous chapter I noted the counter-imperial implications of "Jewish visions about Imperial rule." In this chapter I explore more fully the literary
contexts of the Hebrew Bible and of Second Temple Judaism, especially
visionary writings, that form a crucial foundation from which better to
understand how Revelation correlates with Jewish theology, terminology,
imagery, and apocalyptic genre. Carey notes some specific examples of
Jewish literary elements in John's Apocalypse: "John himself is Jewish.
His name is Jewish. The letters to the seven churches assume that the
addressees are Jewish, . . . there has been no split between the followers
of Jesus and 'Judaism,' . . . John builds his Apocalypse upon the foundation of Jewish Scriptures." I will unpack these various literary correlations
beginning with the Jewishness of John.

Jewishness of John the Author

The author of Revelation calls himself a "servant" of God (1:1; a Hebrew
Bible title of honor as well as a self-designation of the apostle Paul [e.g.,
Rom 1:1]) and a "brother" of those he addresses (1:9). The simplicity of
his self-description ("John"; 1:4, 9; 22:8) implies that he was so well known
to his seven *ekklēsiai* that he needed only to mention his first name. His

---

1. Carey, "Book of Revelation," 159.

acquaintance with the condition of the seven *ekklēsiai* of Asia Minor is evident in the seven letters he transcribed (2:1—3:22). John's familiarity with the Hebrew Bible, as evidenced by his numerous allusions, parallels, and "echoes," along with his use of numerous semitisms, presumes John's Jewish-Christian background.[2] His prophetic status is implicitly assumed given his description of Revelation as a "prophetic book." The majority of scholars suggest that "John" is not the apostle John, but rather a "John" who served in some capacity as an itinerant prophet, possibly even belonging to a circle of prophets (22:9, 16). Second-century CE authors, however, widely identified the "John" of Revelation with John the apostle, the son of Zebedee (e.g., Justin Martyr, *Dial.* 81.4; Irenaeus, *Haer.* 4.20.11).

The Jewish Literary Structure of John's Apocalypse

The question of how the visionary content in the book of Revelation is organized is critical to any interpretation of the Apocalypse. If one looks for structural cues for this very Jewish Apocalypse within visionary texts of Hebrew and Jewish visionary literature (e.g., Hebrew Bible prophets, Jewish apocalypses) then greater clarity arises as to how the events described in the vision episode of the Apocalypse inter-relate with one other. Before exploring further the two literary devices that David Aune affirms recur throughout Hebrew and Jewish visionary literature, I will review other structural approaches. One approach is to use implicit indicators as structural organizers. Examples of this approach involve

---

2. One example of a Hebrew Bible parallel is how the ten plagues of Egypt form the basis for descriptions of divine judgment in the seven trumpets and seven bowls. There are no explicit quotations of Hebrew Bible texts in the book of Revelation, however. The number of allusions are said to vary from 1,000 instances (Waal, *Openbaring van Jezus Christus*, 174–241) down to 195 occurrences (Dittmar, *Vetus Testamentum in Novo*, 263–79).

chiasm,[3] intercalation,[4] recapitulation, or more precisely, reiteration,[5] encompassing,[6] and cycles of worship/judgment/worship.[7] Another approach emphasizes the use of explicit textual indicators such as: "in the

3. See Kenneth Strand's chiastic model for the Apocalypse ("Chiastic Structure," 401–8; Strand, "Eight Basic Visions, 107–21). Paul Rainbow reviews some chiastic options within, but not for the entire text of, Revelation (*Pith of the Apocalypse*, 29–44). Predating both, N. W. Lund suggests a chiasm reflecting an A-F, F1-A1 outline (*Chiasmus in the New Testament*, 325–26).

4. R. J. Loenertz states that John "narrates in two episodes (A and A1) what is in reality a continuous movement, a single scene, and between the two he inserts another scene (B-intercalated). He thus requires us to see the combined passage A-B-A1 as an indivisible whole so as to avoid separating from one another the two fragments (A and A1) of a single scene" (*Apocalypse of St. John*, xviii–xix). Elisabeth Schüssler Fiorenza also emphasizes this technique of intercalation of texts (*Book of Revelation*, 172). Her resultant outline uses a concentric-symmetry pattern of A B C D C1 B1 A1 (*Book of Revelation*, 175; Cf. also Schüssler Fiorenza, "Composition and Structure, 364).

5. Scholars who discern reiteration (sometimes incorrectly called "recapitulation") claim that each successive series of seven seals, trumpets and bowls deals with the same events, either in whole or part, rather than representing a strict succession of events. Some supporters of this view include: Hendriksen, *More Than Conquerors* (1967); A. Y. Collins, *Combat Myth* (1976); Michaels, *Interpreting the Book of Revelation* (1992). Michaels prefers the term "reiteration" in lieu of "recapitulation," due to "its rather different use by Irenaeus, in the sense of going over the same ground again with opposite results" (*Interpreting the Book of Revelation*, 54, n. 5).

6. Lambrecht, "A Structuration of Revelation 4, 1—22, 5," 77–103. Lambrecht asserts that "through his encompassing technique the author of Rev. combines recapitulation and progression" (ibid., 103). Thus, the seal and trumpet septets demonstrate linear progression in that they are open-ended and "contain all that follows: A seals: 4, 1—22, 5 ; A trumpets : 8, 1—22, 5 ; and A bowls : 11, 15—22, 5" (ibid., 87). But at the same time reiteration is evident in his outline by a three-fold repetition of the same letters. In this regard, "A A A mean introduction; B B B mean the six first plagues; and C C C the global end-event" (ibid., 89).

7. Craig Koester claims that "the body of work consists of six cycles . . . [that] typically begin in the presence of God (5:1–13; 8:2, 6; 15:1, 5–8), then depict a series of threats, and conclude in the presence of God (8:1, 3–5; 11:15–18; 19:1–10)" (*Revelation*, 113). He notes that the four numbered groups of seven scenes (seven messages, seals, trumpets, bowls) and the two unnumbered scenes (11:19—15:4; 19:11—22:5) each follow that same cyclical pattern (*Revelation: A New Translation*, 113–14).

Spirit";[8] "what is now and what will take place later";[9] "come and see";[10] "earthquake";[11] and the number "7." Some scholars create an overall sevenfold outline for the Apocalypse within which is included the explicit references to the seven *ekklēsiai*, the seven seals, the seven trumpets and the seven bowls.[12] Some outlines with less than seven major sections still create seven sections within each major textual section.[13] And, finally, some incorporate both above approaches and arrive at an overall septenary outline for the Apocalypse within which is incorporated a sevenfold structure for a number of those self-same sections.[14]

8. The Apocalypse is divided into four segments based on the occurrence of the phrase "in the Spirit" at 1:10; 4:2; 17:3 and 21:10. Cf., Tenney, *Interpreting Revelation*, 32–41; Roberts, *Revelation to John*, 21–23; Smith, "Structure of the Book of Revelation," 373–93; Michaels, *Revelation*, 26–32.

9. Walvoord, *Revelation of Jesus Christ* (1966). His futurist interpretation rests upon the assumption that chapters 2—3 represent "what is now" (i.e., the seven churches in John's era) and that chapters 4—22 represent "what will take place later" (i.e., the church in the future) (see esp. pp. 47—49).

10. Ladd (*Revelation*, 14–17) divides the book of Revelation into four visions, each of which is introduced by the invitation to "come and see" (1:9; 4:1; 17:1; 21:9).

11. Bauckham, "Eschatological Earthquake," 224–33. Bauckham identifies two implicit references (4:5: thunder and lightning only; 20:11: the earth and sky flee) and five explicit references (6:12; 8:5; 11:13, 19; 16:18) to the eschatological earthquake in the Apocalypse. He sees it playing "a distinctive role in the structure of the book" ("Eschatological Earthquake," 224). I would suggest that 18:10 is another potential implicit reference to the "great earthquake" (Babylon falls within the space of one hour).

12. An influential treatment is given by R. H. Charles (*Revelation of St. John* [1920]). Structural details are given in 1:xxiii–xxviii; see also, Hendriksen, *More than Conquerors*, 16–21. Hendriksen sees seven sections that historically "run parallel to one another. Each of them spans the entire dispensation from the first to the second coming of Christ." Rather than simply a sevenfold overall structure, Swete argued for a plan based on fourteen sections which represents a doubled seven (*Apocalypse of St. John*), xxxviii–xxxix.

13. Farrer, *Rebirth of Images*, 45. He divides Revelation into six major sections with each section itself having a sevenfold division. A. Y. Collins (*The Combat Myth*, 19; Collins, *Crisis and Catharsis*, 149) uses Farrer's sixfold structural proposal but adds her own refinements such as a prologue and an epilogue. See Rainbow, who identifies seven visions within chs. 6—22 (*Pith of the Apocalypse*, 34—41).

14. Commentators who note a doubled septenary as an organizational structure in Revelation include: Moulton, *Modern Reader's Bible* (1907); Lohmeyer, *Die Offenbarung des Johannes* (1926); Rissi, *Zeit und Geschichte*, 9–26; Lilje, *Das Letzte Buch der Bibel*, 11–14. Some scholars go beyond a doubled septenary and suggest *seven* series of seven (within the framework of the prologue and epilogue): Loenertz, *Apocalypse*, 3–35; Bowman, "The Revelation to John," 436–53 and *First Christian Drama* (1955). He sets his 7 x 7 structure within the context of a first-century CE dramatic motif.

Problematic Assumptions of a Linear Reading

Another factor in developing a structure is the interpreter's choice as to whether they envision a linear or a reiterative reading of the visionary content. Linear readings—the best-selling dispensational book series *Left Behind* being one example—appear to prioritize at least two hermeneutical presuppositions. First, a linear reading uses the final form of the text of Revelation. Second, a linear approach adopts a left-to-right reading strategy of the final form of the text. This reading strategy has as its underlying assumption that the order in which John recorded his visions also represents the order in which those visions's events will occur. This might be a legitimate reading strategy for the book of Revelation, but it is not a *necessary* strategy, nor even necessarily the *best* strategy for reading Revelation.

When deciding upon the most appropriate reading strategy, at least, two questions need to be asked when interpreting the events described in Revelation's vision episode. First, must one assume that the events are literal and not symbolic? Idealist interpreters like G. K. Beale remind us that Revelation is highly symbolic and not necessarily literal. All of the visionary elements may not have particular reference to specific historical or eschatological events at all.

Second, must one assume that the chronology of events can only be represented by a linear unfolding? But why assume this? Many scholars affirm reiteration (or recapitulation) within the text. As already noted, examples include Adela Yarbro Collins, Merril Tenney, and J. Ramsay Michaels. There are at least three eschatological events in Revelation that appear to be re-described four different times from different narratological angles. These three eschatological events are: (1) the "great earthquake"; (2) the final battle, otherwise known as "Har-Mageddon"; and (3) "the Day of the Lord/return of Jesus the *Christos*." Jan Lambrecht calls these eschatological events, "global end events."[15]

In the ensuing discussion, I will demonstrate how three Jewish visionary literary devices not only provide structure for the vision episode in the book of Revelation, but also create a framework for making interpretive sense of multiple descriptions of what may very well be only

---

For an eclectic combination of both authors that incorporates Loenertz's view for the purpose of refining Bowman's proposal, see the discussion by Spinks, "Critical Examination," 211–22.

15. Lambrecht, "A Structuration of Revelation 4, 1—22, 5," 77–103.

singular events. This repetitive reality challenges linear readings of the events within Revelation's vision episode. I have summarized below in bullet form the multiple descriptions of the three eschatological "global end events" identified above.

1. **Four "Armageddons"?**

   • 9:13–21 [sixth trumpet] 200 million horsemen from east → 1/3 humanity killed

   • 16:12–16 [sixth bowl] Kings of the east meet kings of the whole world → Har-Magedon

   • 19:17–21 Beast and the kings of the earth and their armies → "Great supper of God"

   • 20:7–10 Satan and Gog and Magog "gather for war . . . on the broad plain"

2. **Four *Earthly* Earthquakes?** (chs. 6, 11, 16, 18[?])

   • Four **earthly (bolded)** and three heavenly alternating earthquakes?

     i. **6:12**; 8:5; **11:13**, 19; **16:18**, 19; **18:10** (implied?; cf. 11:13 Babylon)

     ii. Only the earthly earthquakes are called the "great earthquake"

3. **Four Finales/Returns?**

   • 6:12–17 (sixth seal) → "great day of the wrath [of God and the Lamb]"

   • 14:1—15:4 → the Lamb on Mt. Zion, earth judged, "anti-Beast" saints in heaven

   • 19:11–21 → the Word of God waging war with the Beast and his armies

   • 20:9–11 → Devil cast into lake of fire, the great white throne judgment

Three Jewish Literary Devices for Vision Structuration

In order for any structure credibly to account for the multiple descriptions of singular events, one must have a consistent hermeneutic by which to delineate structural divisions in the vision episode of Revelation. In other words, unless there is one recurring principle for determining structural divisions, any resulting outline is subject to the criticism of being too subjective and/or arbitrary with respect to identifying textual demarcators that account for reiteration. This does raise the question, though, as to whether there is such a thing as an "objective" reading of Revelation's visionary text? I have suggested in a previous article that an "objective" reiterative reading is possible if one organizes Revelation's content around the textual placements of three visionary literary devices.[16]

The three visionary literary devices that divide the visionary episode of Revelation (1:9—22:20) are: the "space/time referent" (Rev 1:9, 10) and the two Greek clauses *kai eidon* ("and I saw") and *meta touto/ tauta eidon* ("after this/these thing[s] I saw"), and their variations. The linguistic equivalents of these three literary devices also occur throughout visionary literature in the Hebrew Bible (Ezekiel, Zechariah, Daniel),[17] as well as in Jewish Second Commonwealth (1 *Enoch*, 4 *Ezra*, 2 *Baruch*), and early Christian (*Ascension of Isaiah*, *Shepherd of Hermas*), apocalyptic literature.

Within Jewish apocalypses, the clause "after this/these things I looked (and behold)" first appears unequivocally in the Animal Apocalypse (1 *En.* 85—90), which is dated ca. 165-161 BCE.[18] This practice is not evident again until the late first-century CE apocalypses of 4 *Ezra* and 2 *Baruch*.[19] Another literary connection between the book of Revelation

16. Korner, "And I Saw," 160–83.

17. The only place in the Hebrew Bible where it may occur is in Dan 8:3, 4 although the Hebrew to Greek correspondence in v. 3 is not as direct as one would hope.

18. Charles notes Ethiopic equivalents for the clause "After these things I saw" (*Revelation*, 1.106) at 89:30 ("After that, I saw"); 89:19 ("thenceforth I saw"); 89:54 ("Thereafter I saw"); 89:72 ("Thereafter I saw") (Cf. also, Tiller, *Commentary on the Animal Apocalypse*, 148-217). The *vision episode* of the Book of Watchers (1 *En.* 14—36) only contains one occurrence of "after these things I saw" (32:1) but the Greek does not read *meta tauta eidon* (*kai idou*) (Cf. Black and Denis, eds., *Apocalypsis Henochi Graece*, 36).

19. Given the fact that another literary genre (i.e., "the parables"; 1 *En.* 38—44; 45—57 and 58—69) is mixed within the *Similitudes of Enoch*, these three visionary literary conventions, by themselves, do not solely determine a structural outline for 1 *En.* 39:3—71:17. A good example of this is found in the "second parable" (45:1—57:3), which actually straddles three *vision blocks* (41:1—51:5; 52:1—56:8; and 57:1-3). The other *vision blocks* in the *Similitudes* are initiated at 40:1 and 71:1. The actual phraseology reflected in the text varies: a) "And after that, I saw" (40:1 and 41:1); b) "After those days . . . my eyes saw" (52:1); c) "And it happened afterward that I had another vision"

and Zechariah (1:7—6:15) is that they both express a prophetic text in terms of visionary revelation.[20]

Already in 1920, R. H. Charles affirmed the structural value of the two Greek literary devices for identifying a structure for the vision episode in Revelation: "The clause [i.e., *kai meta tauta eidon (kai idou)*] with or without the *kai idou always introduces a new and important vision* in our Apocalypse. . . . Generally *similar and closely related* sections, paragraphs and clauses are introduced by *kai eidon*. . . . These formulae are characteristic of apocalyptic literature, and imply an ecstatic condition. They are not, however, so carefully distinguished in other authors as in our Apocalypse."[21]

The "space/time referent" determines the textual length of the vision report (1:9—22:20). It indicates the start of the vision report by indicating the "where" and/or the "when" of the Seer's physical body at the moment the visionary episode began in his life: "I, John . . . was on the island of Patmos. . . . On the Lord's day I was in the spirit . . ." (Rev 1:9, 10). (See my complete review of space/time referents in HB and Jewish visionary literature in Appendix 2.)

Major sub-divisions of thematically interrelated content are created at each occurrence of an "after this/these thing(s) I saw" clause.[22] I call these major sub-divisions *vision blocks*. There are six *vision blocks* in the vision report (1:9—3:22; 4:1—6:17; 7:1–8; 7:9—15:4; 15:5—17:18; 18:1—22:20). (See further in Appendix 3.) Minor sub-divisions within each *vision block* are created at each occurrence of an "and I saw [and behold]" (*kai eidon [kai idou]*) clause. I call these minor sub-divisions *individual visions*. There are forty *individual visions* in the vision report. (See further in Appendix 3.)[23]

These *individual visions* form the basis from which one can demonstrate that the Jewish literary technique of chiasm and concentric

---

(57:1); d) "It happened after this . . . And I saw" (71:1). Since "After this he showed me" (66:1) is a third person reference it does not qualify as a *vision block* initiator.

20. See Zech 1:7—6:15 where visionary revelation is specifically coupled with a prophetic "word of the Lord."

21. Charles, *Revelation*, 1:106; author's emphasis.

22. Variations of *vision block* demarcators are *(kai) meta tauta/touto eidon (kai idou)* (4:1; 7:1, 9; 15:5; 18:1).

23. The clause *kai eidon (kai idou)* ("and I saw [and behold]") actually occurs forty-four times in Revelation. However, since four of the forty-four occurrences of the clause *kai eidon* have modifiers such as "when I saw" or "which I saw" I count only forty *individual visions* within vision episode of Revelation.

symmetry is at work within the *vision blocks*. The chiastic/concentric centerpoints of each *vision block* serve a narratological function. Taken together, their centerpoints function as a type of shorthand, or "reader's digest" version, if you will, of the overarching narrative of the vision episode. Each literary centerpoint of four *vision blocks* identifies one of the key actors in the grand eschatological drama of human redemption that was begun at creation and brought to fulfillment in the new creation (Rev 21—22). The key actors introduced at the textual centerpoint of four *vision blocks* (*VB*) are, in order: (1) the Lion who is the Lamb, that is, Jesus the Jewish *Christos*/Messiah (*VB#2*, 4:1—6:17); (2) two of Christ's three earthly adversaries: the Sea Beast and the Land Beast/False Prophet (religio-political heads of state) (*VB#4*, 7:9—15:4); (3) the third of Christ's three earthly adversaries: Babylon, the Prostitute, (socio-religious institution of the state) (*VB#5*, 15:5—17:18); and (4) Christ's heavenly adversary: the Dragon/Ancient Serpent/Devil/Satan, (VB#6, 18:1—22:20).[24]

The "Jewish" Structure of the Book of Revelation

Although the clause *meta tauta eidon* (and its variations) is acknowledged as an identifier of new and important visions by other scholars, neither Charles[25] nor any other commentator[26] that I investigated uses it to organize the visionary section of Revelation (1:9—22:20). Even though some commentators do use *kai eidon* (and its variations) as a structural indicator of minor visions, they do so only within select sections of the Apocalypse. Specifically, they use *kai eidon* for structuring sections in

24. See Appendices 4–8 for diagrammatic representations of the chiastic/concentric symmetry organization of *vision blocks* 2, 4, 5, and 6.

25. For example, between the prologue and the epilogue, R. H. Charles divides his structure into seven sections at 1:4; 2:1; 4:1; 6:1; 21:9; 20:11; and 21:5a. Thus, only once does his sevenfold structure coincide with an occurrence of *meta tauta eidon* (i.e., 4:1), even though, ironically, Charles emphatically claims that *meta tauta eidon* has significant value for identifying a structure for Revelation (*Revelation*, 1:106).

26. A sampling of other commentators who, to varying degrees, affirm the structural value of the clause *meta tauta eidon* (and its variations) include (in ascending chronological published order): Swete, *Apocalypse of St. John*, 66; Beckwith, *Apocalypse of John*, 494; Charles, *Revelation*, 1:cxxxiv and 1:106; Allo, *Saint Jean, L'Apocalypse*, cli; Kiddle, *Revelation of St. John*, 79; Farrer, *A Re-birth of Images*, 47–49; Farrer, *Revelation of St. John the Divine*, 87; Pohl, *Die Offenbarung des Johannes*, 1.158, n. 160; Massyngberde-Ford, *Revelation*, 70; Beasley-Murray, *Book of Revelation*, 111; A. Y. Collins, *Combat Myth*, 14–16; Morris, *Revelation*, 84; Thomas, *Revelation 1—7*, 333–34; Aune, *Revelation 1—5*, 279–80, 338; Mounce, *Revelation*, 117, n. 1; Beale, *Revelation*, 316–17.

Revelation which do *not* contain the seven numbered elements of the seals, trumpets, and bowls.[27] Thus, for example, Adela Yarbro Collins uses *kai eidon* occurrences to organize 12:1—15:4. But selective organization like this is arbitrary since the clause *kai eidon (kai idou)* occurs *throughout* the entire text of Revelation. A systematic application of *both* Greek phrases as structural identifiers for the *entire* vision-oriented text of the Apocalypse had not yet been fully explored until my *Novum Testamentum* article (2000).[28] While there are other verbal forms for "seeing" used in Revelation (e.g., *deiknumi, blepō, theoreō* and other *horaō* forms), I suggest that they are only used in a descriptive sense for visual seeing. I contend that only the 2nd aorist active indicative first person singular form of *horaō* (i.e., *eidon*) is used in a technical literary sense for textual demarcation within visions.[29]

The Apocalypse can be said to have a seven-fold structure with my structural proposal. Surrounding the six *vision blocks* of the vision episode (1:9—22:20) is a non-visionary epistolary framework with an introduction (1:1–8) and conclusion (22:21). This epistolary framework becomes the seventh literary section of the Apocalypse. Additionally, if one has a predilection for biblical numerology, then the forty *individual visions* may have interpretive significance. The number "forty" in Scripture not infrequently indicates key transitional moments in God's salvation history (e.g., forty-year exodus, multiple forty-year segments in Moses's life, Jesus's forty-day temptation). If one associates the concept of "transition"

---

27. For example, Loenertz (*Apocalypse*, vi, 128–37) divides 19:11—22:5 into seven sections; Jacques Ellul also finds seven visions within the text of 19:11—22:5 (*Apocalypse*, 42–43); Harold W. Hoehner also affirms the technical function of *kai eidon* as well as *meta tauta eidon* for vision identification, but primarily within 19:1—22:5, rather than with their structural application to the entire text of Revelation ("Evidence from Revelation 20," 247–48). Farrer delineates seven visions within 12:1—15:1 (*A Rebirth of Images*, 47–48); Bowman ("The Revelation to John," 436–53) uses *kai eidon* (or its perceived equivalents) to provide structure for his "unnumbered" Acts IV (11:19—15:4), VI (17:1—20:3, 7–10) and VII (20:4–6, 20:11—22:5); Michael Wilcock gives the "unnumbered" section of 13:1—15:4 a sevenfold structure (*I Saw Heaven Opened*, 114–15).

28. Korner, "And I Saw," 160–83.

29. These verbs of "seeing" (other than *eidon*) occur as follows in Revelation according to NA28: (1) *Blepō*, 1:12; 3:18; 11:9; 18:9, 18; 22:8 (2x); (2) *deiknumi*, 1:1; 4:1; 17:1; 21:9, 10; 22:1, 6, 8; (3) *Theōreō*, 11:11, 12; (4) *horaō* (e.g., *eiden*), 1:7, 19, 20; 11:19; 12:1, 3, 13; 17:6, 8, 12, 15, 16, 18; 18:7; 22:4, 9; and (5) the particle *idou* which may also be used to denote the act of seeing, 1:7, 18; 2:19, 22; 3:8, 9, 20; 4:1, 2; 5:5; 6:2, 5, 8; 7:9; 9:12; 11:14; 12:3; 14:1, 14; 16:15; 19:11; 21:3, 5; 22:7, 12.

as an intentional message behind John's creation of forty *individual visions*, and then if one couples that with the concept of "incompletion" associated with the number "six," then perhaps John is communicating that transition to heavenly consummation comes only after the conclusion of the sixth vision block and the arrival of the "block-buster" event of God's redemptive story—the return of Jesus the *Christos* and the corporate resurrection of God's faithful into eternal glory.

When one demarcates the text of Revelation's vision episode at each occurrence of the three literary devices then the following structure emerges:

I. *Prologue* (1:1–3)

II. *Epistolary Benediction* (1:4–8)

III. *Vision Block* #1 (1:9—3:22) The Seven Letters
    "Space/time referent" (1:9–12) with *kai eidon* at 1:12

IV.   *Vision Block* #2 (4:1—6:17) The Six Seals
    meta tauta eidon kai idou at 4:1
        eleven *individual visions* (*kai eidon* [*kai idou*])

V. *Vision Block* #3 (7:1–8) The 144,000 Sealed
    meta touto eidon at 7:1
        two *individual visions* (*kai eidon* [*kai idou*])

VI. *Vision Block* #4 (7:9—15:4) The Seventh Seal /
  the Six Trumpets/the Seventh Trumpet/the Seven Bowls
    meta tauta eidon kai idou at 7:9
        twelve *individual visions* (*kai eidon* [*kai idou*])

VII.   *Vision Block* #5 (15:5—17:18)
The Seven Bowls and Babylon Described
    kai meta tauta eidon at 15:5
        four *individual visions* (*kai eidon* [*kai idou*])

VIII. *Vision Block* #6 (18:1—22:20) Babylon Falls
  and New Jerusalem Descends
    meta tauta eidon at 18:1
        ten *individual visions* (*kai eidon* [*kai idou*])

IX. *Epistolary Postscript* (22:21)

Three Jewish Literary Devices for a Reiterative Structure: Textual Blocking

Even though David Aune also affirms the organizational value of the two visionary literary devices within the vision episode (1:9—22:20; *kai eidon* and *meta touto/tauta eidon*), he contends that it is written linearly in chronological sequence. In fact, he attributes this linear chronological progression of the text precisely to occurrences of the clauses *kai eidon* and *meta touto/tauta eidon*.[30] I will suggest the exact opposite. I contend that reiterative progression can be demonstrated through John's use of the clause *meta touto/tauta eidon* (and its variations). Additionally, I will show that a chiastic organization within each *vision block* can be demonstrated through John's use of the clause *kai eidon* (and its variations).

What might a reiterative structuration of the visionary content of the Apocalypse look like in light of the textual placements of the three visionary literary devices? I say "might look like." I do not suggest that my reiterative arrangement of the *vision blocks* is the only possible way to interpret the structural data. But I do believe that it is the best one, particularly with respect to creating an integrated narrative in which the storyline progresses at one literary level while the interrelationship of the events within that storyline unfolds at another literary level (i.e., the interrelationship of the three global end-events).

The interpretive principle that I call "textual blocking" allows one to reorganize *vision blocks* #2–6 in such a way as to account for the reiteration of the three global end-events from differing perspectives. Textual blocking is an organizational approach that is not unlike some TV shows, which, for the sake of increasing viewer interest, choose not to recount a story in linear fashion (e.g., like a documentary), but rather recount the unfolding story from different angles by using foreshadowing, flashbacks,

---

30. Aune writes, "This artificial literary unity has been imposed on numerous discrete units that have been paratactically linked together in an apparently chronological order; i.e., if the phenomenon of recapitulation is present, it lacks any clear formal literary indications of its presence or (perhaps more likely) belongs to an earlier level of composition than that now extant in Revelation. John occasionally links major segments of text together in artificial chronological sequence using the temporal phrase 'after these things' (4:1; 7:1, 9; 15:5; 18:1; 19:1). More frequently (nearly 40 times) [in actual fact, 44 times] he uses the paratactic phrase *kai eidon* 'and I saw' usually intending temporal sequence and appropriately translated by the RSV as '*then* I saw'" (*Revelation* 1—5, xciii).

and even flash-sideways. Revelation is a visual journey; reiteration creates a much more engaging journey for the "viewer."

Textual blocking affirms, firstly, that the order in which John saw the *visions* occur is demonstrated through a linear arrangement of the six *vision blocks* laid end to end. Textual blocking also affirms, secondly, that the order in which the *events* within those *vision blocks* are said to occur (whether symbolically or eschatologically) is reiterative. Thus, it will be seen that the linear arrangement of the six *vision blocks* spreads the multiple occurrences of Armageddon (4x), the "great earthquake" (4x), and the finale of human history (4x) across *multiple vision blocks*. However, if one "snaps" *vision blocks* on top of one another, much like one would do when building with, say, LEGO® blocks, then the inter-relationships of other events associated with the multiple occurrences of a singular event can be more readily discerned. One example is how textual blocking interconnects the destruction of Jerusalem (VB#4→11:13; second woe/sixth trumpet; cf. 9:12) and Babylon (VB#5→16:19; seventh bowl; VB#6→18:10; second woe[?]) as concurrent events during the singular "great earthquake" of the eschatological sixth seal (VB#2→6:12).

Textual Blocking and Three Reiterative Global End-Events

I turn now to a more detailed exploration of the reiterative interconnection of all three key global-end events. First, I will identify in bullet form where each global end-event occurs within the various *vision blocks*. Second, I will explore where each *vision block* best seems to "snap" onto another *vision block* for the purpose of reiteratively providing more expansive detail of the same event/theme that is found earlier in John's apocalyptic narrative.

Four "Armageddons"

1. *Vision Block #4 (7:9—15:4)*

   • 200 million horsemen from east, 1/3 humanity killed → sixth trumpet (9:13–21)

2. *Vision Block #5 (15:5—17:18)*

   • Kings of the east meet kings of the whole world at Har-Mage-don (Armageddon) → sixth bowl (16:12–16)

3. *Vision Block #6 (18:1—22:20)*

- "Great supper of God": Beast, the kings of the earth, and their armies → 19:17–21

4. *Vision Block #6 (18:1—22:20)*

- Satan and Gog and Magog "gather for war . . . on the broad plain" (Har-Magedon?) → 20:7–10 (chiastically paired with 20:1–3)

Four Earthly Earthquakes

1. *Vision Block #2 (4:1—6:17)*

- "a great earthquake" → sixth seal (6:12–17)

2. *Vision Block #4 (7:9—15:4)*

- "a great earthquake" (11:13) → second woe/sixth trumpet

3. *Vision Block #5 (15:5—17:18)*

- "a great earthquake" (16:18, 19) → seventh bowl

4. *Vision Block #6 (18:1—22:20)*

- "Woe, woe, the great city, Babylon . . . for in one hour your judgment has come" (18:10; implied earthquake?) → second woe(?), thus, sixth trumpet?

Four Finales

1. *Vision Block #2 (4:1—6:17)*

- "the great day of their wrath [God and the Lamb]" → sixth seal (6:12–17)

2. *Vision Block #4 (7:9—15:4)*

- Lamb on Mt. Zion with 144,000, earth-dwellers judged, saints harvested and sinners trodden in winepress of God's wrath (14:1—15:4) → seven bowl angels (15:1, chiastically paired with seven trumpet angels [8:2–5])

3. *Vision Block #5 (15:5—17:18)*

- Word of God treads winepress of God's wrath (19:11–16) by waging war against the Beast, the kings of the earth, and their armies (19:17–21)

4. *Vision Block #6* (18:1—22:20)

- Babylon destroyed (18:10), Beast and False Prophet thrown into the lake of fire (19:19, 20), Satan and Gog and Magog devoured by fire from heaven (20:9), the devil is thrown into the lake of fire (20:10), the "great white throne" judgment of "the dead" (20:11)

The above overview shows that the structure derived from the three Hebrew/Jewish visionary literary devices provides a consistent hermeneutic whereby to demonstrate how reiterated events contribute to a greater cohesion of a multivalent storyline. However, it still remains to "place" the six *vision blocks* on top of one another in such an order as to make narratological sense, not only of the three repeated global end-events, but also of the three sets of seven judgment sequences (the seven seals, trumpets, and bowls).

Textual Blocking and Telescopic Reiteration of the Sixth Seal

An overview of the key message of each *block* of interrelated *visions* (i.e., *vision block*) within John's vision episode can be stated as follows. *Vision block* #2 (4:1—6:17) moves from the seven-sealed scroll in the throne room to the opening of the sixth seal (6:12–17) by the Lamb (6:1a). In the sixth seal are described in concise fashion the global end-events of the *eschaton* that precede the *parousia* of the Lamb as the Lion ("the wrath of God and the Lamb"; 6:17).

The four subsequent *vision blocks* simply re-describe the *eschaton* and *parousia* that are envisioned in the sixth seal by offering greater details. As such, the four *vision blocks* directly and indirectly "snap" onto the *individual vision* of the sixth seal (6:12–17; *kai eidon*). In this way John is able progressively to reiterate in expansive ways the sixth seal's "reader's digest" version of eschatological global end-events. *Vision block* #4 (7:9—15:4) is the central section of the vision episode (1:9—22:20). *Vision block #4* contains the seventh seal (which is synonymous with the sixth seal), the six trumpets (8:5—9:21) and the seven bowls (15:1) and concludes with heavenly consummation (15:2–4), which is prefigured in the heavenly consummation of the seventh trumpet (11:15–19).

Vision block #4 "snaps" directly onto the sixth seal (6:12–17), which is the last *individual vision* of *vision block* #2. Vision Block #5 (15:5—17:18) is the penultimate *vision block* of the vision episode. It reiterates in greater detail the seven bowl judgements (15:5—16:21) that are only foreshadowed in the appearance of the seven bowl angels in 15:1 (the second last *individual vision* of *vision block* 4). *Vision block #5* "snaps" directly onto the seven bowl angels *individual vision* (15:1), and thus indirectly back to the sixth seal through *vision block #4*.

Vision block #6 (18:1—22:20) is the concluding *vision block* of Revelation's vision episode. It reiterates in greater detail how humanity experiences the heavenly consummation described in 15:2–4 (the concluding *individual vision* of *vision block #4*). *Vision block #6* describes the fall of Babylon (ch. 18) and the descent of the New Jerusalem (chs. 21 and 22). *Vision block #6* "snaps" directly onto the heavenly consummation *individual vision* (15:2–4), and thus indirectly back to the sixth seal through *vision block #4*.

The overview above of how *vision blocks* reiterate global end-events by "snapping" onto each other depicts an organizing principle that I call "telescopic reiteration."

"Telescoping" is the first word of my phrase telescopic reiteration. I affirm the basic insight of R. L. Thomas and before him, of J. Loenertz, that the seventh seal and the seventh trumpet function as narratological junction points, or umbrella terms, for all the visionary content that preceded them and for all which succeeds them.[31] Thomas calls this principle "telescoping," while Loenertz calls it "dove-tailing."

My point of departure with both Thomas and Loenertz, though, is that rather than assuming that the seventh seal represents a progression of events that occur *after* the sixth seal, I assume that the seventh seal represents a progression of events *within* the sixth seal. In other words, the seventh seal functions as an expansive reiteration of the concise details in the sixth seal. Thus, the events in the seventh seal do not happen *after* those of the sixth seal. Rather, the seventh seal: (1) happens *concurrently* with the sixth seal; (2) implicitly incorporates all of the events which occur *after* the sixth seal (i.e., the seven trumpets and seven bowls); and (3) is in fact re-describing the same events of the sixth seal, but from different angles and with progressive expansion.

In other words, I suggest that the sixth seal is recounting in shorthand, or in "reader's digest" form, the *eschaton* and that the rest of the visionary content is simply reiterating, in progressive fashion, the concise

31. Thomas, *Revelation 1—7, Revelation 8—22* (1992/1995) and Loenertz, *Apocalypse of Saint John* (1949).

sixth seal events, but with expansive detail. The "empty" seventh seal (8:1, 2), then, functions as an umbrella "term" (1) for the seven trumpets and the seven bowls that follow and (2) for the sixth seal (6:12–17) that precedes it. Thus, the *eschaton*'s cataclysmic events telescope out of the sixth seal while all the while being reiterated with each progressive vision of judgment in the seven trumpets and seven bowls.

In the diagrammatic depiction of telescopic reiteration below I use what appears to be LEGO® blocks that are being snapped on top of one another. Even though I risk (appropriately) being labelled "anachronistic," in the interest of clarity, I chose a LEGO®-block style of representation as a visual aid for better understanding what might be going on in John's vision episode (1:9—22:20).

Telescopic reiteration is demonstrated in the "snapping" of *vision blocks* 3–6 (7:1—22:20) on top of the sixth seal (6:12–17) (and upon each other) for the purpose of demonstrating that the seven trumpets and seven bowls are actually re-describing from different angles the same events and eschatological timeframe of the sixth seal (see the diagram below and also in Appendix #3). More specifically, telescopic reiteration uses four *vision blocks* (#3 to #6) and three *individual visions* (6:12–17; 15:1; 15:2–4) to reiterate the global end-events of the eschatological sixth seal (6:12–17) through the "wide angle lens" perspective of the seventh seal (8:1), which in its role as an umbrella term for the sixth seal, is a two-stage "telescope" that reveals, firstly, the six trumpet judgments (8:2—11:14) and then, out of the seventh trumpet (11:15–19), it reveals, secondly, the seven bowl judgements (15:5—16:21).

Telescopic reiteration accounts well for (1) why the seventh seal and the seventh trumpet are each literarily separated from their previous six elements (the six seals and six trumpets); and (2) why the seventh seal and the seventh trumpet each have a more heavenly perspective than their previous six elements. It should be noted, though, that the seventh bowl is unique among all of the judgment elements (seals, trumpets, and bowls) in that it merges heavenly and earthly perspectives into one final scene of judgement finalized (16:17–21). In the seventh bowl, for the first and only time in Revelation, the heavenly earthquake is merged with the earthly "great earthquake." This "great earthquake" is accompanied with some of the same cataclysmic events that are found in the sixth seal (i.e., islands and mountains disappearing). Thus, telescoping concludes with the seventh bowl, while the seventh bowl revisits/reiterates where eschatological judgment first began, that is, in the sixth seal.

My argument that the seventh trumpet (11:15–19) telescopically and implicitly includes the seven bowls is literarily reinforced by its addition of a fifth element to the storm theophany (11:19), which is unique relative to the previous storm theophanies (4:5, throne; 8:5, 6 trumpets). The seventh trumpet storm theophany adds the occurrence of "great hail" (11:19). If Bauckham is correct in his claim that the "great hail" of the seventh trumpet (11:19) is the heavenly representation of the earthly "great hail" that falls (16:21) in the seventh bowl judgment (16:17–21), then the earthquake in the seventh trumpet theophany (11:19) is the heavenly representation of the "great earthquake" of the seventh bowl (16:18, 19).[32] And since the seventh bowl reiterates similar events to those found in the sixth seal (islands, mountains), one can postulate that the seventh trumpet, which telescopically includes the seventh bowl, is also reiterating the finalized judgment pictured in the sixth seal ("wrath of God and the Lamb").

GRAMMATICAL AND HISTORICAL SUPPORT FOR TELESCOPIC REITERATION

There is also a serendipitous piece of grammatical support for my assertion that the rest of the vision episode after the sixth seal is actually a reiteration of the sixth-seal global end-events, but from expanded and differing perspectives. This grammatical anomaly is found in 7:1, immediately following the sixth seal *individual vision* (6:12–17). At 7:1 we encounter a new *vision block* of two thematically related *individual*

32. Bauckham, "Eschatological Earthquake," 227–28. Bauckham's interlocking principle appears to follow Loenertz's concept of "dovetailing" (*Apocalypse*, xv). Loenertz describes dovetailing as follows: "the seventh homogeneous section of each of them belongs equally to the septenary following whereof it forms the initial section" (ibid., xv). Thus, for example, "the appearance of the seven [trumpet] archangels forms part, at one and the same time, of the septenary of the seals, as its final section, and of that of the trumpets, as its preliminary section"(ibid., xv). John's placement of the seventh seal (8:1) in a different *Vision Block* (7:9—15:4) than that of the six seals (4:1—6:17) would seem to emphasize this double link. Thomas refines Loenertz's approach with his concept of "telescoping" (*Revelation 1—7, Revelation 8—22*, 1:43 and 2:534). He uses "telescopic" terminology to describe a perceived interlocking pattern such that the seventh of each septenary is like the joints of a telescope which when extended reveal more and more detail. My article generally affirms Thomas's "telescopic" principle but challenges his linear chronology by reiteratively organizing his telescopic content ("And I Saw," 176–83). Specifically, I suggest that the seventh seal is an *expansive reiteiration* of the sixth, rather than iterating *subsequent* events to the sixth seal.

visions (*vision block #3; 7:1–8*). *Vision block #3* begins with the anomalous clause "after *this thing* I saw" (7:1), rather than the normal clause "after *these* things I saw." If, in 7:1, John is intentional in his avoidance of his usual plural phrase ("after *these things* I saw"), is he then implying that the eschatological content from 7:1 to the end of the vision episode (22:20) is *only* replicated in the sixth seal ("*this* thing" [*touto*]), and not also in all the first five seals ("these things" [*tauta*])? If so, then when John says "after *this thing* I saw" (7:1), he is indicating that everything which follows the sixth seal events (7:1—22:20) represents *the same timeframe as the sixth seal events*.

This grammatical interpretation gains reinforcement in the fact that the events described in the first five seals could have been perceived as already having been fulfilled prior to the composition of the Apocalypse. The first five seals symbolically speak of military conquest, civil/international war, food shortages, widespread disease, wild animals, and martyrdom. The eschatological "great earthquake" of the sixth seal would have held historical relevance for Asia Minor residents. In 17 CE an earthquake devastated four of the seven cities in which Revelation's *ekklēsiai* lived (Thyatira, Sardis, Philadelphia, and Laodicea), and the earthquake of 60 CE ended up re-devastating Laodicea.

TELESCOPIC REITERATION AND ESCHATOLOGICAL IMMINENCE

By way of summary, if one interprets the content of the vision episode in Revelation through the lens of telescopic reiteration, then John's vision episode suggests that there are no necessary events still yet to occur (i.e., any visionary elements recorded *after* the sixth seal) before the *eschaton* begins with its unfolding of global end-events. Given the assumption that the entire content of Revelation after the sixth seal telescopically reiterates the *eschaton* initiated with the sixth seal, John's structural organization reinforces the expressed sense of imminence that he explicates elsewhere for his contemporary audience (i.e., 1:1, 3; 22:7, 12, 20).

This structurally reinforced sense of imminence would have allowed John's *ekklēsiai* to see themselves as already being in the "last days" even while they yet await the "last day/Day of the Lord." This theological perspective would parallel Peter's use of the phrase "last days" in his sermon in Acts 2. Therein, Peter analogizes the coming of the Holy Spirit with visible signs like tongues as paralleling the prophet Joel's description of supernatural events that would herald the start of the "last days." Thus, Peter clearly implies that the coming of the Holy Spirit (and the invisible birth of the universal *ekklēsia*) on the day of Pentecost (Acts 2:14–21) initiated "the last days" envisioned in the book of Joel (2:28–32).

Allow me to restate in a concise manner how the eschatological sixth seal reiterates a sense of imminence relative to Christ's return within the assumptions of my literary framework: if, *firstly*, one views the first five seals as only describing historical events that recur prior to the *eschaton*, and that may have been seen as having already occurred prior to and during the timeframe of John's addressees in Roman Asia, and, *secondly*, if the sixth seal is the only eschatological seal in *vision block #2* (4:1—6:17), and, *thirdly*, if the rest of the vision episode in Revelation (7:1—22:20) is simply reiterating telescopically the same eschatological timeframe of the sixth seal but does so through progressively expansive re-descriptions of the concise global end-events concisely depicted in the sixth seal, then, *fourthly*, John's seven *ekklēsiai* may very well have viewed themselves as being on the cusp of the *eschaton*, or perhaps even already within the *eschaton*.

The textual blocking diagram below depicts how the *vision blocks* can be re-arranged so as to demonstrate telescopic reiteration (i.e., the reiteration of the sixth-seal events through their telescopically expansive re-descriptions in the seven trumpets and the seven bowls).

TELESCOPIC REITERATION DEPICTED

Figure 1

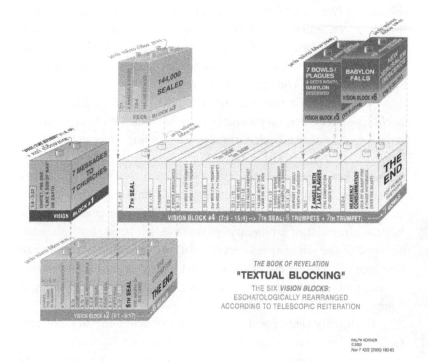

THE BOOK OF REVELATION
"TEXTUAL BLOCKING"
THE SIX *VISION BLOCKS*:
ESCHATOLOGICALLY REARRANGED
ACCORDING TO TELESCOPIC REITERATION

TEXTUAL BLOCKS AND CHIASTIC "SHORTHAND"

As I have briefly indicated, chiastic organization is a well-documented literary technique found within Jewish writings, not least the Hebrew Bible and the New Testament. Thus, it is not surprising if we should also find it reflected in the book of Revelation.[33] A chiasm is a literary structure in which the central emphasis/climax of a narrative is found in the center of the story, not at the end of the story as is usually the case in Western literary works. The literary (and narratological) centerpoint of a bounded text emerges with the division of that text into multiple text units based on their alignment along the lines of thematic continuity. The theme of each text unit that is situated prior to the pivotal/central

---

33. See p. 141 n. 3 for my previous references to Kenneth Strand and Lund regarding their chiastic approaches to Revelation.

text (e.g., text unit A) is repeated in reverse order on the opposite side of the textual centerpoint (e.g., text unit A^1). But the opposite text unit (A^1) generally has progressed the theme of the initial text unit (A). A chiasm has two parallel narratological centerpoints, or "peaks" (e.g., E, E^1) while "concentric symmetry" has one narratological centerpoint, or "peak" (e.g., E). One way of depicting this type of textual organization is through diagrams that reflect a Mayan step pyramid ("chiasm") or an Egyptian pyramid ("concentric symmetry").

Chiastic organization is found within four of Revelation's six *vision blocks*. The Greek visionary literary device *kai eidon* ("and I saw"), and its variations, demarcates each narratological stepping stone in the chiastic "pyramid" that arises within those four *vision blocks*. The diagram immediately below portrays the chiastic/concentric organization of *vision blocks* 2, 4, 5, and 6 (see also Appendices 4–8). But there is an unexpected discovery that surprises the ancient hearer (and modern reader). The thematic content of the four literary "peaks" together summarizes the entire storyline of the vision episode of Revelation (1:9—22:20). Together the four "peaks" of *vision blocks* #2, 4, 5, and 6 provide a shorthand version or "snapshot" version of the five key actors in John's grand eschatological drama.

The literary centerpoint of the concentric symmetry in *vision block* #2 (4:1—6:17) portrays Christ the Lamb of God (6:1a) as the only one who is worthy of judging the forces of evil through his opening of the seven-sealed scroll. The two chiastic centerpoints of *vision block* #4 (7:9–15:4) display the Sea Beast (13:1–10) and Land Beast/False Prophet (13:11–18) as fitting objects of the wrath of the Lamb. The two chiastic centerpoints of *vision block* #5 (15:5—17:18) focus on Babylon the Great and her judgment via the eschatological "great earthquake." The two chiastic centerpoints of *vision block* #6 (18:1—22:20) focus on Christ's spiritual antagonist, Satan, who is the final object of the wrath of the Lamb. John has created a literary masterpiece through his use of this Jewish organizational technique. His readers/hearers need simply to "skim read" the literary mountain peaks of each *vision block* for a summary synopsis of the key theologically significant participants in the cosmic struggle between the kingdom of God and the kingdom of Satan.

CHIASTIC ORGANIZATION AND A NON-LITERAL MILLENNIUM

Another interpretive implication of reading *vision block* #6 in chiastic fashion relates to the thorny issue of the chronology of the events in chapters 19—22. If the various textual segments/*individual visions* that result from "and I saw" placements are meant to be read in chiastic pairs (e.g., 18:1—19:10 and 21:2—22:20) then their order is not meant to communicate a chronological/linear reading of the events described in *vision block* #6. This has particular application to the two *individual visions* at the chiastic "peak," which together describe Satan's activity during a thousand-year/millennial timeframe (20:1–3; 20:4–10). In other words, the textual location of the two central *individual visions*, then, is not intended to communicate that the millennium only begins after the return of the King of Kings (19:11–16), and the defeat of the two Beasts and the kings of the earth (19:17–21). Rather, the central textual location of the two millennium-focused *individual visions* communicates how very central the role of Satan was and will be in the drama of salvation history.

This "Satan-focused" chiastic "peak" in *vision block* #6 facilitates realized millennialism/a-millennialism in at least five ways. First, the millennium/thousand years becomes a symbolic (not literal) number for the timeframe during which Satan has waged war against *Christos*-followers beginning with the resurrection of Jesus the *Christos* (as the Lamb of God) and ending with the return of Jesus the *Christos* (as the Lion of Judah). In this regard, the millennium becomes a symbol of the age of human history during which the universal *ekklēsia* of God exists. So, one could also then equate the "great tribulation" (7:14) with the millennium as the era of "church history," so to speak.

Second, the reference to Satan being "bound for a thousand years" would then refer to the triumph of Jesus over Satan through the cross and resurrection.[34] Satan is now a defeated foe whose activity will be eternally curtailed at the return of Jesus (20:10), but who, just prior to that, will "be set free for a short time" not least "to deceive the nations in the four corners of the earth . . . and gather them for [the final] battle [of Har-Megiddo/Armageddon] (20:7–8)." I have already suggested that this

---

34. See Beale's informative excursus on the phrase "one thousand years" (*Revelation*, 1017–21). He suggests that since "the three elements of the binding of the evil heavenly beings, the messianic reign, and a thousand-year epoch are found together nowhere in Jewish writings outside Rev. 20:1–6 . . . [they] indicate that Christ's death and resurrection have inaugurated both the binding of Satan and the era of the saints' reign with Christ" (*Revelation*, 1021).

final battle is referenced previously at least three times (8:13–19 [sixth trumpet]; 16:12–16 [sixth bowl]; 19:17–21).

Third, the phrase "the first resurrection" then becomes a reference to the bodily resurrection of Jesus in which he corporately also raised spiritually and corporeally (but not yet bodily) all the "saints of God" past, present, and future to his resurrection. Such a conception would correspond with the Pauline "already/not yet" eschatological schema in which all saints past, present, and future were corporeally co-raised spiritually (but not yet bodily) with Christ (Eph 2:8–10; 4:9–11).

Fourth, the centrality of Satan comes to the fore as the key antagonist who deserves eternal judgment (20:10) because of his unrelenting warfare against God, his *Christos*, and "God's people, the city he loves" (20:9; i.e., the New Jerusalem, a.k.a. the universal *ekklēsia* of God). With his being cast live into the lake of fire (20:10), we see the finalization of judgment against the "unholy trinity," so to speak (the two Beasts and Satan).

Fifth, it becomes possible that the casting of the "unholy trinity" into the lake of fire is a simultaneous event due to the translational ambiguity of the Greek syntax in 20:10b. A simultaneous timeframe mitigates against the need to read the *individual visions* within Rev 19—20 in linear chronological fashion and reinforces the value of a chiastically reiterative reading of those *individual visions*. English translations usually read "where the beast and the false prophet *had been thrown*" (past tense). However, there is no *eimi* verb ("to be") in the Greek text. The syntax simply reads "where also the beast and false prophet." Thus, one could read the intent of the syntax as implying that Satan is thrown into the same location where the beast and the false prophet end up after the final battle against the "King of Kings" and his army (19:19). Thus, if the two battles in 19:19 and in 20:8–10 are in fact one battle reiterated from different perspectives, then the casting into the lake of fire of the anti-*Christos* "unholy trinity" is in fact a simultaneous action, which the flexible syntax of 20:10b reinforces.

The diagram below illustrates how reading *vision blocks* 2, 4, 5, and 6 through Jewish literary eyes brings to the fore the five key actors in John's cosmic apocalyptic drama. The concentric symmetry of *vision block #2* highlights the legitimacy of the Lamb as Judge while the chiastic organization of *vision blocks* 4, 5, and 6 highlights the Lamb's four adversaries (the Sea Beast, the Land Beast, Babylon, and Satan).

LITERARY MOUNTAIN PEAKS OF VISION BLOCKS 2, 4, 5 & 6:
THE LAMB AND HIS 4 KEY ANTAGONISTS
(SATAN, BEAST, FALSE PROPHET, BABYLON)

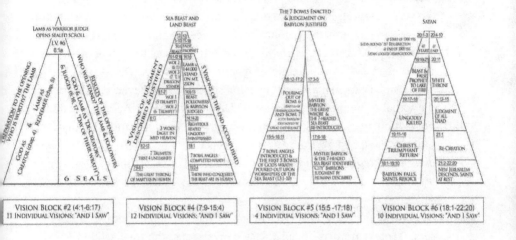

Perhaps, by way of a very loose summary, I can conclude this section on John's use of the three Jewish visionary literary devices for the structural organization of his vision episode by saying:

> If you understand the structure of the Book of Revelation within the historical and literary context of Hebrew Bible prophetic literature and Second Temple Jewish apocalypses, and if you use three of their literary devices to organize the Apocalypse's visionary content, then you will not be *Left Behind* interpretively, but rather you will have joined me in saying that "I saw . . . a visionary literary device for the telescopically reiterative structuration of the book of Revelation."

The Genre of John's Apocalypse?

The lack of scholarly consensus on historical-critical questions such as dating and authorship is also evident when one approaches the question of the literary nature of the book of Revelation. The question of the genre of the Apocalypse is still not settled to the complete satisfaction of scholarship. The internal evidence of the book of Revelation attests to three literary elements: letter, apocalypse, and prophecy.

Is Revelation a Jewish Letter?

In its final form the book of Revelation is presented as a circular letter to the seven churches of the Roman province of Asia (1:4, 5: "John, to the seven churches . . ."). Its epistolary framework is evident in 1:4–8 and, at the very least, 22:21 ("The grace of the Lord Jesus be with all"). Revelation 1:9—22:20 recounts the visionary experience of John. Within the visionary text, specific messages are written in letter format to each of the seven churches (2:1—3:22). In spite of its circular function, David Aune sees the epistolary format as possibly being superficial and even secondary to the actual content of the Apocalypse. He notes that: "the Apocalypse does not exhibit an epistolary structure, with the exception of the framing text units in 1:4–8 and 22:10–21. In this respect the Apocalypse is unique: *no other apocalypse is framed by epistolary conventions*, for the pseudonymity of other apocalypses would necessitate a fictional receiver as well as sender."[35]

Although Aune is correct in saying that no other apocalypse has its *complete* text framed by epistolary conventions, the final section (78—86) of the Jewish apocalypse 2 *Baruch* is set within an epistolary format.[36] While I follow all commentators in affirming an epistolary framework for the book of Revelation, I will use the placement of visionary literary devices as a basis from which to argue that Revelation's concluding text unit (e.g., 22:10–21 [Aune]) should be amended to include only 22:21. This then results in the epistolary framework of Revelation as comprising 1:4–8 and 22:21.

Revelation as a Covenant Letter to the Jewish Diaspora in Roman Asia

The anomalous epistolary framework of Revelation's covenant-based apocalypse[37] may reflect a Jewish epistolary sub-genre—a "covenantal letter to the diaspora."[38] Donald Verseput states that a covenantal letter to the diaspora evinces a tone of consolation in light of future hope. Such a

35. Aune, *New Testament*, 240 (author's emphasis).

36. 2 *Bar.* 78:1 begins, "The letter of Baruch, the son of Neriah which he wrote to the nine and a half tribes . . . which were across the river"; 2 *Bar.* 86:1 concludes, "When you, therefore, receive the letter, read it carefully in your assemblies."

37. See my previous discussion of Strand's view of the covenantal format of the Apocalpyse in p. 141 n. 3.

38. Verseput, "Genre and Story," 96–110.

letter has six characteristics: (1) "an authoritative center, typically Jerusa-lem"; (2) "consoled the assembled communities in the Jewish Diaspora"; (3) "in the midst of the affliction"; (4) "occasioned by their evil circum-stance"; (5) "admonished them regarding their covenant responsibilities"; and (6) "in hope of the expected restoration."[39]

Verseput identifies five extant texts of this sub-genre of Jewish epistolary literature: Jer 29:1–23; The Epistle of Jeremiah; 2 Macc 1:1–9; 1:10–2:18; 2 *Bar.* 78—86, and the epistle of James.[40] The underlying mo-tivation that spawned this "peculiar sub-genre," as Verseput puts it, is the prevalent notion within Second Temple Judaism that "the very existence of the Jewish Diaspora was . . . evidence of divine displeasure from which only national repentance and divine mercy could bring relief."[41] He notes that in each of the five Jewish textual examples cited "the specific content of the instruction varies, but the tone of consolation in tribulation and the appeal to the motivational power of the future hope remain constant."[42] The tone of present consolation in light of future hope is clearly intrinsic to the symbolic message of the book of Revelation. However, the note of God's displeasure with his covenant people is distinctly lacking.

With respect to Verseput's six genre characteristics, five are clearly expressed within the Apocalypse. The book of Revelation, as a "New Cov-enantal Letter to Diasporic *Christos*-followers," so to speak, would have: (1) "consoled the assembled communities in the Christian Diaspora" (the seven *ekklēsiai* [2:1—3:22]); (2) "in the midst of the affliction" (e.g., Smyrna [2:8–11] and Pergamon [2:12–13]); (3) "occasioned by their evil circumstance" (e.g., Philadelphia [3:7–13]); (4) "and admonished them regarding their covenant responsibilities" (e.g., Ephesus [2:1–7], Sardis [3:1–6], and Laodicea [3:14–22]); and (5) "in hope of the expected res-toration" (e.g., the concluding promises of eternal reward for each of the seven churches [2:7, 11, 17, 26–28; 3:5, 12, 21]).

One of Verseput's genre characteristics, however, is not explicit—provenance from Jerusalem—though it may be implicit. One can hardly call the Isle of Patmos an authoritative center from which John's "epistle"

39. Verseput, "Genre and Story," 99–101.

40. Verseput, "Genre and Story," 101–2. Verseput contends that "For James, as for the other writers of the sub-genre, the exilic existence of Israel was a painful ex-perience requiring perseverance in hope of God's ultimate triumph on behalf of his people" ("Genre and Story," 102).

41. Verseput, "Genre and Story," 100.

42. Verseput, "Genre and Story," 101.

was sent. But perhaps in the case of Revelation (and maybe even the epistle of James) it is not a geographical center (e.g., Jerusalem) but a person, as the authoritative representative of that center (e.g., an apostle-prophet), who fulfills that particular literary requirement in this possibly Jewish-Christian version of a "covenantal letter to the diaspora." This possibility is enhanced if the "John" of the Apocalypse is the apostle-prophet who was one of Jesus' twelve disciples.

Is Revelation a Jewish Apocalypse?

In approaching the question of what is constitutive of the Jewish apocalyptic genre, Paul D. Hanson highlights the need, in scholarly discussion, for making careful terminological distinctions between "apocalyptic genre," "apocalyptic eschatology," and "apocalypticism."[43] Aune's suggestion of one more category—"apocalyptic imagery"—is a helpful one.[44] These four categories prove especially valuable in the discussion of the Apocalypse's relationship to the Jewish apocalypses.

Apocalypse Defined

The apocalyptic genre is a literarily, and not a theologically, determined category. In his seminal study, John J. Collins identified the genre characteristics that are most germane to apocalyptic literature.[45] One of the primary defining characteristics of an apocalypse is the supernatural mediation of otherworldly realities by an otherworldly being, that is, an angel. In this regard, anything formally classified as apocalyptic has primary reference to the "revelation" of heavenly mysteries. Although these mysteries may be revealed symbolically, and even allegorically, they need not necessarily be of an eschatological nature. Rather, they may simply involve an attempt: (1) to communicate heavenly "revelations" of what is true throughout all of human history and not just in the *eschaton* (e.g., 1 *En.* 72—82; The Book of the Heavenly Luminaries); or (2) to explicate proper Christian living (e.g., the *Shepherd of Hermas*).

---

43. Hanson, *Visionaries and their Apocalypses*, 12.

44. Aune, *New Testament*, 227. See also Aune, "Qumran and the Book of Revelation," 2.624.

45. Collins, "The Jewish Apocalypses," 21–59.

While certainly characteristic of *all* apocalypses, a definition this general would cover a much wider corpus than just that of apocalypses. As such, Collins suggests that one needs to go beyond a definition based simply upon a revelation of heavenly mysteries to one in which content provides a differentiating factor between apocalypses and other literature. Thus, although Mounce surely overstates the case when he contends that "the genre apocalyptic . . . is always *eschatological*,"[46] eschatology is nonetheless one of its consistent characteristics. The Apocalypse Group of the SBL Genres Project (1979) under the chairmanship of J. J. Collins proposed a definition of "apocalypse" that is still foundational in scholarship today: "Apocalypse is a genre of revelatory literature with a narrative framework, in which a revelation is mediated by an otherworldly being to a human recipient, disclosing a transcendent reality which is both temporal, insofar as it envisages eschatological salvation, and spatial, insofar as it involves another, supernatural world."[47]

This definition is reflected in the paradigmatic grid (Appendix 1) developed by Collins for the classification of characteristic literary elements that comprise the genre apocalypse for Jewish writings.

Aune has used J. J. Collins's master paradigm of a *Jewish* apocalypse as an evaluative grid by which he compares the "Jewish-Christian" book of Revelation.[48] Revelation accords strongly with the thirteen generic categories of a Jewish apocalypse (see Appendix 1). Some would see circular reasoning evident in a classification of Revelation as an apocalypse, however, since the entire genre's designation is etymologically derived from *apokalypsis*, the first word of the Apocalypse (1:1).

One might ask why an apocalyptic genre designation for the Apocalypse has attracted so much controversy. While Jewish apocalyptic literature has found nourishment from a variety of sources, possibly even non-Jewish ones,[49] most would concur with the assessment of D. S. Russell that "there can be no doubt that the tap root, as it were, went deep down into Hebrew prophecy."[50] Thus, while Rowley correctly affirms that

46. Mounce, *Revelation*, 3 (author's emphasis).

47. Collins, "Introduction," 9. See also Hellholm, ed., *Apocalypticism in the Mediterranean* World (1989).

48. Aune, *Revelation* 1—5, lxxvii–lxxxix.

49. For example, some see apocalyptic literature as a Hellenistic phenomenon (e.g., Betz, "On the Problem," 134–56), or as a development from Iranian religion (e.g., Hultgård, "Persian Apocalypticism," 1:39–83).

50. Russell, *Method and Message of Jewish Apocalyptic*, 88.

"apocalyptic is the child of prophecy,"[51] Aune adds an important caveat: "Yet apocalyptic must be regarded, not simply as *the* successor of prophecy, but as one among many offspring."[52] This perceived literary continuity between Jewish apocalyptic literature and Hebrew Bible prophetic writings lends credence to Revelation's expressly prophetic self-designation (e.g., Rev 1:3).

There are others, however, who affirm a strictly apocalyptic designation for the book of Revelation.[53] In so doing they tend to deny it any prophetic character. This assumption of the mutually exclusive character of the apocalyptic and prophetic genres tends to raise the "theological stakes," so to speak. A denial of the Apocalypse's prophetic character is seen by some as placing into question the divine authority, and even the possible historicity, of the *apokalypsis* ("revelation, uncovering") contained within its text.

Perhaps as a way of redressing this angst, David Aune, in his commentary on Revelation, proposes a literary middle road in order to continue this genre discussion. He designates the book of Revelation as a "prophetic apocalypse," but one in which the prophetic and apocalyptic genres are seen as being mutually exclusive literary elements. Working from this assumption he textually separates the genres by means of a twofold diachronic history for the development of the text. Thus, his textual history begins with the apocalyptic material (the First Stage: 4:1—22:9) and concludes with the later addition of a prophetic framework (the Second Stage: 1:9—3:22; 22:10–21).[54] Aune does not appear to be entirely consistent in his proposal, however.[55]

---

51. Rowley, *Relevance of Apocalyptic*, 15.

52. Aune, *Prophecy in Early Christianity*, 114.

53. For example, Perrin, "Apocalyptic Christianity," 137.

54. Aune, *Revelation 1—5*, lxxxix: "the First Edition of Revelation (4:1—22:9) is clearly an apocalypse, while the expansions that were added in the Second Edition (1:1—3:22; 22:10–21) have a more clearly prophetic character."

55. To his original source-critical division of Revelation, Aune later adds 1:7–12a to, and removes 22:6–9 from, the First Edition (i.e., the apocalypse): "The First Edition consisted approximately of 1:7–12a and 4:1—22:5 and appears to have had a thoroughly apocalyptic orientation. . . . The Second Edition added . . . 22:6–21 (a concluding epilogue and an epistolary conclusion) [which] had a strongly prophetic and parenetic orientation" (*Revelation 1—5*, cxx; see also cxxiv).

Apocalyptic Eschatology Defined

Apocalyptic eschatology is "a set of ideas and motifs that may also be found in other literary genres and social settings."[56] Hanson contends that its rise "follows a pattern of an unbroken development from pre-exilic and exilic prophecy."[57] Generally, apocalyptic eschatology involves the theological description of various factors that constitute the final cosmic salvation of YHWH at the end of human history. The necessity of this salvation is presupposed by a "pessimistic eschatological dualism [such that] the present evil world order (controlled by the human collaborators of an evil supernatural being and his allies) will shortly be terminated by divine intervention and replaced with a new and perfect order."[58] This perspective is specifically found within "historical apocalypses" like the book of Daniel.

But this type of end-time scenario is not evident in all apocalypses. Collins contends that what is characteristic of "all the apocalypses, however, [is that they] involve a transcendent eschatology that looks for retribution beyond the bounds of history."[59] He sees this retribution as sometimes being located beyond the bounds of history but only insofar as it relates to the judgment of individuals after death (e.g., 3 *Baruch*, *Apocalypse of Zephaniah*). Thus, their judgment is not necessarily only effected at the end of history.

It is important to note, however, that these themes related to the judgment of the dead and the *eschaton* are not limited only to apocalyptic literature. Collins aptly summarizes the methodological challenge in identifying characteristics of a distinctly apocalyptic eschatology:

> The genre is not constituted by one or more distinctive themes but by a distinctive combination of elements, all of which are also found elsewhere. ... What is at issue here is the affinity between the eschatological allusions and the scenarios which are found in more elaborate form in the apocalypses. Affinities vary in degree, and, although the label "apocalyptic eschatology" may be helpful in pointing up the implications of some

---

56. Collins, *Apocalyptic Imagination*, 2.

57. Hanson, *Dawn of Apocalyptic*, 7–8.

58. Aune, *New Testament*, 227.

59. Collins, *Apocalyptic Imagination*, 11.

texts, we should always be aware that the adjective is used in an extended sense.[60]

Given the distinct possibility that apocalyptic literature stemmed from prophetic, it is perhaps appropriate at this point to note a distinction in their eschatology in relation to the time of YHWH's salvific intervention. Unlike apocalyptic eschatology, prophetic eschatology need not have reference only to the end of history. It may also describe salvific events within an era of human history, such as the Babylonian exile. Later in this chapter, I will summarize nine distinguishing characteristics between apocalyptic and prophetic eschatology.

Apocalyptic Imagery Defined

Aune defines apocalyptic imagery as "the language and conceptions of apocalyptic eschatology found in bits and pieces in a variety of ancient literary settings."[61] Thus, although these themes and motifs are found in a variety of literary settings, they are "no longer used in the context of a coherent apocalyptic world view."[62] These themes find expression, for example, in the notions of the visitation of God, the kingdom of God, the resurrection of the dead, and the tribulation.

J. J. Collins distinguishes two fundamental approaches used to ascertain this apocalyptic imagery.[63] In the tradition of the English-speaking world, as influenced by R. H. Charles, the sources of apocalyptic language were primarily sought within the context of Jewish literature.[64] But this approach tended to lose sight of the more foreign mythological and cosmological elements.

Contrasted to this is Hermann Gunkel's approach that focused on the elucidation of traditional, even mythological, materials ensconced within the apocalypses.[65] In highlighting mythological correlation to much of apocalyptic imagery, Gunkel demonstrated its symbolic and allusive nature. Thus, the principle that is said to govern much of apocalyptic

---

60. Collins, *Apocalyptic Imagination*, 12.

61. Aune, *New Testament*, 227.

62. Aune, "Qumran and the Book of Revelation," 624.

63. Collins, *Apocalyptic Imagination*, 14–19.

64. See esp. Charles's *Apocrypha and Pseudepigrapha of the Old Testament* (1913).

65. Gunkel, *Schöpfung und Chaos* (1895).

literature is not so much "Aristotelian logic but . . . [the principle of] the poetic nature of myth."[66]

Apocalypticism Defined

Apocalypticism is a socio-religious movement sharing a common apocalyptic worldview. It was neither "peculiar to a particular sect or the product of a single movement."[67] Rather apocalypticism was constitutive of "a distinctive worldview within Judaism" until at least the first century of the Common Era.[68] As such, it is neither tied to any one literary form nor limited to a particular theological tradition, since apocalyptic worldviews find expression in other literary genres (e.g., the *Sibylline Oracles* and the Pauline epistles). Instead, apocalypticism reflects *"forms of behavior* based on those beliefs"[69] which are a response to the social realities within which the literary community finds itself. This social location subsequently gives rise to literature that may incorporate either one, or both, elements of apocalyptic imagery and apocalyptic eschatology, or even come to reflect the genre "apocalypse" itself.

Challenges: Is Revelation an Apocalypse?

There are a number of objections raised with respect to an identification of the book of Revelation with the genre "apocalypse." I have already addressed the fact of Revelation's anomalous epistolary framework. In this section I will discuss three other objections.

First, even though the Apocalypse Group of the SBL Genres Project went through a lengthy two-stage process to define the apocalyptic genre, some scholars wonder whether, to some degree, the argumentation is inherently circular. For example, J. Ramsey Michaels comments: "Scholars assemble a group of documents suspected of belonging to a genre called apocalypse and list the common features of these documents to define the genre. For example, the definition quoted above appears to be tailored to fit the Book of Revelation, or at least to make sure of its inclusion."[70]

66. Collins, *Apocalyptic Imagination*, 17.
67. Collins, *Apocalypticism in the Dead Sea Scrolls*, 7–8.
68. Collins, *Apocalypticism in the Dead Sea Scrolls*, 7–8.
69. Aune, *The New Testament*, 227 (author's emphasis).
70. Michaels, *Interpreting the Book of Revelation*, 26.

Second, J. Kallas brings to light some discontinuities between Isra-elite and Jewish apocalyptic views on suffering. He states that Israelite-Jewish literature emphasizes God as the source of suffering while Jewish apocalyptic writings focus upon suffering as being arbitrary, malicious, and vindictive in its derivation from cosmic sources opposed to God.[71]

B. W. Jones, however, claims that Kallas's contrast of Israelite and apocalyptic perspectives on suffering is an oversimplification. Jones con-tends they are not mutually exclusive perspectives.[72] Aune also challenges Kallas's approach. He wonders, perhaps correctly, at the appropriateness of "arbitrarily selecting a feature of apocalyptic and elevating it to the status of the central, indispensable feature of the apocalypse genre."[73]

A third challenge that is sometimes brought forth relates to the use of pseudonymity in Jewish apocalypses. In Aune's comparison of the book of Revelation with Collins's comparative chart of thirteen genre characteristics of a Jewish apocalypse, pseudonymity is evident in all fif-teen Jewish apocalypses surveyed by Collins.[74] John's self-identification as a contemporaneous writer to the seven *ekklēsiai* makes the book of Revelation a singular exception to that rule. Collins does not see that as sufficient rationale for excluding Revelation from consideration as a Jewish apocalypse.[75] A lack of pseudonymity, however, is evident in the witness of a later "Christian" apocalypse, the *Shepherd of Hermas*. Thus, Aune suggests that since the Apocalypse and the *Shepherd of Hermas* are Christian, they should not then be subject to exclusion as an apocalypse simply because they lack what is essentially a characteristic of Jewish apocalypses.[76] Revelation does accord, however, with all of the other twelve characteristics of the Jewish genre apocalypse, whether explicitly or implicitly.

---

71. Kallas, "The Apocalypse–an Apocalyptic Book?" 74.

72. Jones, "More about the Apocalypse as Apocalyptic," 325–27.

73. Aune, *Revelation* 1–5, lxxxviii.

74. See Appendix 1, row 3.1 (*Manner of Revelation*) in Collins, "Jewish Apocal-pyses," 28.

75. Collins comments that "to make pseudepigraphy into the *sine qua non* of apocalyptic writing . . . is surely to overrate it. Pseudepigraphy is only one of several formal markers of the apocalypses and is by no means peculiar to the genre. It was basically a way of lending authority to a text [but] . . . not the sole basis of authority" (*Apocalyptic Imagination*, 270).

76. Aune, *Revelation* 1–5, lxxxviii.

A fourth factor to consider in one's designation of Revelation as an apocalypse, is the fact that the final form of the text contains prophetic self-designations. Examples of prophetic claims are found in: (1) 1:3, "Blessed is the one who reads the words of this prophecy"; (2) 22:7, "Blessed is he who keeps the words of the prophecy"; (3) 22:10, 18, "the words of the prophecy of this book"; and (4) 22:19, "takes words away from this book of prophecy."

As has been discussed, Aune approaches this prophetic self-designation from a diachronic perspective. His postulate of a three-stage historical composition of the text assumes redactional activity. However, the use of the verb *propheteuein* (10:11), in relation to a divine command to John "to prophecy," is somewhat anomalous if redactional activity is assumed in Revelation. This prophetic interjection does not appear to fit within the purportedly apocalyptic section of Revelation (4:1—22:5 [or 9]). Rather the verb *propheteuein* would seem to presuppose the prophetic nature of the *apokalypsis* of Jesus Christ (1:1).

Revelation 10:9–10 alludes to Ezek 2:8–13 in which Ezekiel, like John after him, is commissioned to the prophetic ministry by eating a scroll whose taste was "sweet as honey in my mouth." In John's case, however, the scroll's initial sweetness turns to bitterness in his stomach. The similarity between the two accounts strongly reinforces the possibility that John's eating of the little scroll is a symbolic acceptance of his prophetic commission. In this instance, Aune states that the verb *dei* ("one must, it is necessary") "suggests the unavoidable necessity of prophesying" and, in fact, may even carry with it the connotation of a divine commission.[77] That this is not the first time that John is considered to have prophesied within the vision is indicated by the use of *palin* ("again"; 10:11).[78] Thus, the command to "prophesy again" is a divine reaffirmation of John's previous commissioning in 1:10–20 and 4:1–2, "although the first commission includes the whole book and the second probably includes the remainder of the book from that point." Revelation 10 then

---

77. Aune, *Revelation 6—16*, 573. Aune asserts that "the term *dei* is sometimes used in literary accounts of divine commissions (Acts 9:6; 27:24) and is perhaps related to the theme of divine compulsion to proclaim the message of God sometimes expressed by prophets or attributed to them (Amos 3:7–8; Jer 4:19; 6:11; 20:7–9; *Sib. Or.* 3.162–64; *Eccl. Rab.* 8:1; 1 Cor 9:16–17)."

78. *Palin* may also mean "in turn" or "on the other hand" (BDAG, 753) but the context favors a translation of "again."

functions as a prophetic commissioning for the next phase of God's out-pouring of judgment.

Aune's acknowledgment of a prophetic commissioning in Rev 10 seems problematic given his identification of 4:1—22:5 [or 9] with the apocalyptic genre. One might ask how it is possible to see continuity be-tween John's prophetic commissioning in the prophetic framing section (1:9—3:22) with his recommissioning to that same prophetic call within the context of a purportedly apocalyptic section (4:1—22:5 [or 9])?[79]

Is Revelation a Jewish Prophecy?

In spite of the wealth of evidence presented for an apocalyptic classifica-tion of the Apocalypse's genre, the book's prophetic self-designation (1:3; 22:7, 10, 18, 19) still remains a challenge. How has scholarship sought to address this internal witness to the prophetic nature of the *apokalypsis 'Iesou Christou* (1:1)? Even if one is to assume redactional activity such that the prologue (1:1–8) and the epilogue (22:6–21 or 22:10–21 or 22:21) were subsequently attached to the vision report (1:9—22:5), the use of the verb *propheteuein* in 10:11 appears to presume the prophetic nature of the *apokalypsis* of Jesus Christ (1:1).

Attempts at harmonizing the prophetic and apocalyptic elements of the Apocalypse have been approached from numerous directions. John J. Collins, for example, claims that designating the Apocalypse as "Chris-tian prophecy is not wrong. . . . [Since] prophecy was a broad category in the Hellenistic and Roman worlds, it could encompass various kinds of revelation, including what we call apocalyptic."[80] Although Collins

79. Apparently the strongest evidence forwarded by Aune for the apocalyptic character of John's prophetic message in Rev 10 is in relation to his interpretation of the meaning of the preposition *epi* + the dative in 10:11. He notes two possible mean-ings: (1) "You must again prophesy *against* many peoples, and nations, and tongues, and kings"; or (2) "You must again prophesy *about* [or *concerning*] peoples, and na-tions, and tongues, and kings." Aune favors the more negative way of construing *epi* ("against" rather than "about") since he sees it "supported in part by the exclusively negative content of the scroll mentioned in Ezek 2:9–10 (to which this passage al-ludes)" (*Revelation 6—16*, 573). Translating *epi* as "against" is said to reflect "a more typically negative apocalyptic attitude toward the ungodly nations of the world" (*Rev-elation 6—16*, 573). While certainly a possible translation, Aune acknowledges that *epi* can also be legitimately interpreted to mean "about or concerning." This would then reflect "a relatively neutral, perhaps prophetic, attitude toward the nations" (*Revelation 6—16*, 573).

80. Collins, *Apocalyptic Imagination*, 269.

acknowledges a degree of commonality, he does not clarify the distinguishing characteristics between Christ-follower and Graeco-Roman prophecy. Since the epistolary framework of the Apocalypse incorporates an assertion of continuity between Christian and Hebrew Bible prophecy, an investigation of that continuity is worth pursuing.

Apocalyptic revelation does stand in some continuity with the pre-exilic and exilic prophetic revelations found within the Hebrew Bible.[81] However, from a Jewish literary perspective, Collins asserts that "Apocalypticism is not simply late prophecy, but is rather a new phenomenon of the Hellenistic age, which drew on many streams of tradition."[82] If the literary gap between Hebrew Bible prophecy and Second Temple apocalypticism is, in fact, as great as Collins claims, what type of prophecy might the Apocalypse represent, given its Jewish *Christos*-centered perspective (i.e., an *apokalypsis* of Jesus Christ [Rev 1:1])? How can one best account for the presence of these apparently dichotomous literary traditions in the book of Revelation?

New Testament Prophecy

Some assert that there is no inherently apocalyptic influence in the *apokalypsis* within the Apocalypse. Rather, it is claimed that the manner of revelation is expressed in line with that of either Christian or of classical prophecy (i.e., Hebrew Bible prophecy). Robert L. Thomas asserts that the "Apocalypse is the product of the NT gift of prophecy, administered by the Holy Spirit."[83] His nomenclature "NT prophecy" is somewhat problematic since the canon of the "New Testament" was not established until many years after the writing of the Apocalypse. He would be best served by perhaps using the phrase "Christ-follower prophecy" instead. Thomas's motive in this regard is to affirm the supernatural origin of the Apocalypse so as to distinguish it from "uninspired but similar works whose writers did, in fact, choose a particular genre."[84]

---

81. Aune asserts that "Apocalyptic literature is historically and genetically derived from the various revelatory media of ancient Israel, of which classical prophecy was the most important exemplar. . . . Yet apocalyptic must be regarded, not simply as *the* successor of prophecy, but as one among many offspring" (*Prophecy in Early Christianity*, 114).

82. Collins, *Apocalypticism in the Dead Sea Scrolls*, 7.

83. Thomas, *Revelation 1—7*, 25.

84. Thomas, *Revelation 1—7*, 29.

Given its self-proclaimed status as prophetic revelation, Thomas adduces thirteen characteristics of Spirit-inspired prophecy within the New Testament that he claims are also reflected in the book of Revelation.[85] Unfortunately, there are two ways in which he minimizes the force of his argument for the primacy of Christ-follower prophecy as the manner of revelation in the Apocalypse.

First, he does little to correlate each of the thirteen New Testament elements with specific examples from the book of Revelation. Second, although he claims that a better genre designation for the Apocalypse would be "visional-prophetic,"[86] his list does not include "visions" as a manner of New Testament prophetic revelation. This would seem to be a rather crucial factor since: (1) the Apocalypse is essentially a vision report; and (2) visions are the distinguishing characteristic in the manner of revelation for Jewish apocalypses, as Collins's *Semeia* paradigm demonstrates (which Thomas himself acknowledges).[87] Thus, the burden of proof is upon Thomas to demonstrate that "New Testament prophecy" is a more appropriate genre for visionary communication. This oversight implicitly weakens his case for an essentially prophetic nature of the *apokalypsis* within the Apocalypse.

However, even if one could demonstrate the correlation of Revelation with Christ-follower prophecy and of Christ-follower prophecy with visionary revelation, this would still not overcome the greatest weakness inherent in Thomas's approach. In his bid to establish the authoritative nature of the Apocalypse's content he is seeking to demonstrate that Revelation is an exemplar of *New Testament* prophecy. Unfortunately, unlike Hebrew Bible/Classical prophecy, Christ-follower prophecy lacked the inherently authoritative element of an unequivocal word from the Lord. Thomas even discusses this in point 11 of his thirteen-fold description: "For the most part, the NT prophet did not follow stereotyped oracular formulas. A noteworthy exception here is the use of the *tade legei to pneuma to hagion* ["thus says the Holy Spirit"] formula by Agabus and John. Aside from this rare indicator, Christian prophecy had to be recognized on other grounds."[88]

85. Thomas, *Revelation 1—7*, 25–28.

86. Thomas, *Revelation 1—7*, 29.

87. See Collins's paradigmatic chart ("The Jewish Apocalypses," 28) in Appendix 1. He does not dispute the fact that "for the apocalyptic communication the message was passed on . . . in the form of visions" ("The Jewish Apocalypses," 29).

88. Collings, "The Jewish Apocalypses," 28 n. 78.

The "other grounds" for prophetic recognition in the New Testament mandated congregational discernment with respect to the content of the prophet's message (1 Cor 14:29). Unlike a Hebrew Bible prophet, the Christ-follower prophet did not appear to have inherent authority by simple virtue of his or her personhood. In other words, his or her words, in and of themselves, did not hold inherent authority. This point is highlighted by the apostle Paul in 1 Cor 14:29 where he says that "two or three prophets should speak, and let the others discern."

Thomas fails to appreciate adequately the ramifications of this fact in relation to the resultant loss of inherent authority for the book of Revelation if it is generically identified with Christ-follower prophecy. The challenge in asserting the prophetic nature of the Apocalypse is to find a prophetic model by which the heavenly revelation is given authoritative status. The most obvious exemplar is Hebrew Bible prophecy. But Hebrew Bible prophecy had ceased by the time of the early Jesus Movement. Thus, the issue to address is whether there is an authoritative prophetic sub-genre within the early Jesus Movement. One option will be explored at the end of this section.

Although his argument is ultimately unsuccessful, Thomas's designation of the Apocalypse as being of the "visional-prophetic" genre does hold some promise. It highlights the need to harmonize more adequately the Apocalypse's self-proclaimed prophetic nature with its visionary manner of revelation.

Hebrew Bible Prophecy

F. D. Mazzaferri has argued that rather than being apocalyptic or related to Christ-follower prophecy, Revelation belongs to the literary genre of Hebrew Bible prophetic writings.[89] The Apocalypse's correlation with classical prophecy is elucidated under the rubric of form, content, and function. Within *form* are included elements such as the call narrative, which incorporates the introductory word and the commission. The ensuing revelation is verbally expressed through oracles of blessing and curses while non-verbal proclamation is accomplished through the medium of action and sign language. The *content* of classical prophecy is conditional rather than deterministic and as a result full restoration is available upon human repentance and obedience. The *function* of a

---

89. Mazzaferri, *Genre of the Book of Revelation*, 181–84.

prophet is to be YHWH's spokesperson by delivering his conditional word, whether it be for blessing or for calamity.

Critique of Mazzaferri's work centers primarily around his exclusion of "apocalyptic" from Revelation's genre. Beale notes that "though he is right to point out differences between Revelation and the pseudepigraphic Jewish apocalyptic genre, the two have much in common since both rely heavily on the OT, including Isaiah, Ezekiel, Daniel, and Zechariah."[90] In fact, Beale would go so far as to say that "along with Revelation, the earlier Jewish apocalypses could be *broadly* classed as 'OT prophetic-apocalyptic' works."[91]

However, one key difficulty in identifying the Apocalypse with the prophetic genre of the Hebrew Bible is the contention of some that this genre had ceased to exist approximately five hundred years prior to the composition of the Apocalypse. Moreover, Schüssler Fiorenza notes that the Apocalypse "should not be misunderstood as an only slightly Christianized form of Jewish [whether Hebrew Bible or Second Temple] apocalyptic theology but must be valued as a genuine expression of early Christian prophecy whose basic experience and self-understanding is apocalyptic."[92] The challenge then is to locate the Apocalypse in a category of the prophetic genre that is neither simply Hebrew Bible nor early Christ-follower, but is in some fashion a congruent balance of both. Where does one look for this prophetic amalgam? The three options below in varying degrees join the search for this literary "holy grail," so to speak.

Prophetic Letter

J. Ramsay Michaels describes the Apocalypse as a "prophetic letter" in an effort to do justice to the epistolary framework of the book of Revelation. He comments that regardless of "whether Revelation is taken as prophecy, letter, or prophetic letter . . . the 'I' style of this work should be taken seriously."[93] In this respect, as a good "listener" to the finished form of the text, we are enjoined to take seriously what V. Philips Long calls, the "truth claims" of the text. This means that one will at least *begin* the interpretive process of Revelation with an acceptance of its explicit claims of

---

90. Beale, *Revelation*, 37 n. 3.

91. Beale, *Revelation*, 37 n. 3.

92. Schüssler Fiorenza, "Apokalypsis and Propheteia, 114–15.

93. Michaels, *Interpreting the Book of Revelation*, 16.

prophetic proclamation (e.g., 1:3; 22:7, 10, 18, 19). One's subjective "truth values" will then be held in abeyance until evidence contrary to the "truth claims" is uncovered.[94]

However, Ramsay Michaels's preference for designating Revelation as a "prophetic letter" leaves out the possibility of an *apocalyptic* element within the Apocalypse. Is this a valid assumption? Since the content of the book provides the interpretive material, it seems appropriate to question the validity of an epistolary designation as being of prime import in genre designation.[95]

Prophetic–Apocalyptic

Beale approaches the search for an appropriate prophetic category for Revelation in a way that seeks to integrate its apocalyptic characteristics and content. He contends that "it is best to understand apocalyptic as an intensification of prophecy. . . . Apocalyptic should not be seen as too different from prophecy, though it contains a heightening and more intense clustering of literary and thematic traits found in prophecy."[96] Beale asserts that the word *apokalypsis* found in Rev 1:1 is a direct allusion to Dan 2, where the same word group is used of God's prophetic revelation to Daniel.[97] Similar to Daniel, Revelation pairs *apokalypsis* with prophetic self-designation (1:1, 3). Given this conjunction of "apocalypse" with prophecy, Beale states that "Revelation is best seen as fitting into the genre of OT prophetic-apocalyptic works, especially that of Ezekiel, Daniel, and Zechariah."[98] The force of Beale's argument is lessened though by his assumption that Daniel is an exemplar of Hebrew Bible prophetic-apocalyptic literature. The majority of scholarship demurs on this point since Daniel is considered an *ex eventu* ("after the event") work from the post-classical prophecy Maccabean era (167 BCE) and not from fifth-century BCE exilic Jews.[99] Furthermore, the *opinio communis* does not consider Ezekiel as an apocalyptic exemplar.

94. Long, "Reading the Old Testament as Literature," 89.

95. So also, Michaels, *Interpreting the Book of Revelation*, 32.

96. Beale, *Revelation*, 37.

97. Beale, *Revelation*, 181.

98. Beale, *Revelation*, 37.

99. Regarding the possibility of a fourth-century BCE compositional date for the entire Aramaic corpus of Daniel (2:4a—7:28), see my essay "The 'Exilic Prophecy' of Daniel 7," 333–53. I argue that the "little horn" of Dan 7 is one of Alexander the Great's

While having identified Revelation with the Hebrew Bible prophet-ic-*apocalyptic* works, Beale switches the terms and goes on to discuss Revelation as an apocalyptic-*prophetic* work. Perhaps he views the designations as interchangeable, but I, for one, view the *nomen rectum* as the primary genre identifier. Thus, his term reversal does cloud somewhat the precision of his discussion. Nonetheless, Beale's primary point is that this designation serves to "focus more on the source of revelation than does prophetic literature."[100] Although this emphasis is not absent in the Hebrew Bible prophetic literature (e.g., Isa 6; Ezek 1—2), in Revelation "it becomes the dominating focus in order to underscore the divine, heavenly source of revelation sent to the seven churches."[101]

Beale seeks to give clarity to his classification by stating that "The apocalyptic-prophetic nature of Revelation can be defined as God's revelatory interpretation (through visions and auditions) of his mysterious counsel about past, present, and future redemptive-eschatological history, and how the nature and operation of heaven relate to this."[102] While this definition reflects the book of Revelation, Beale's definition would have benefited from also demonstrating that the category "apocalyptic-prophetic" also represents accurately the content of the Hebrew Bible books he references.

Beale gives further refinement to the attempt by Carson, Moo, and Morris to integrate the three literary components of the book of Revelation. They describe Revelation as "a prophecy cast in an apocalyptic mold and written down in a letter form."[103] Beale adds social function as a corollary to their definition: "the most preferable view is that Revelation is 'a prophecy cast in an apocalyptic mold and written down in a letter form' in order to motivate the audience to change their behavior in the light of

---

Diadochoi/"Successors," Ptolemy I Soter of Egypt (reigned 323–282 BCE), but that the "little horn" of Dan 8 is Antiochus IV Epiphanes, the Seleucid king who desecrated the temple in Jerusalem (167 BCE). This historical background has literary implications for the genre of Dan 1—12. Aramaic Dan 7, which is an apocalypse by genre, now can be compositionally aligned with Aramaic Dan 2—6. This opens up the possibility that Aramaic Dan 2—7 together is an apocalypse, not simply historiography known as "Court Tales" (Dan 2—6). In this scenario, then, Hebrew Dan 8—12 would have to stand on their own merit for the genre designation "apocalypse."

100. Beale, *Revelation*, 38.

101. Beale, *Revelation*, 38.

102. Beale, *Revelation*, 38.

103. Carson, Moo, and Morris, eds., *Introduction to the New Testament*, 479.

the transcendent reality of the book's message."[104] In this regard, Beale's overall assessment of the Apocalypse finds its value in amalgamating the social function of an epistolary framework with the authoritative claims of a prophecy as clarified by the transcendent vision of an apocalypse. But, literarily, it does not seem very helpful to postulate a dual generic classification for the Apocalypse. It inevitably devolves into a literary "tug-of-war," so to speak, in which a dual genre inexorably pulls the discussion towards opposite poles when specific sections of Revelation are analyzed. Clarity would seem rarely to result.

Prophetic Apocalypse

Using terminology similar to that of Beale's "prophetic-apocalyptic," Aune suggests that the Apocalypse is best described as a "prophetic apocalypse."[105] He too broaches the question of whether the Apocalypse's genre is not a *mixtum compositum*. But contrary to Beale, Aune clearly delineates where the text of the Apocalypse shifts from the prophetic to the apocalyptic genre (and vice versa). In this regard, he opts for the literary middle road in an attempt to incorporate both genre designations for the Apocalypse.

Aune proposes that this *mixtum compositum* of prophetic and apocalyptic are of a mutually exclusive nature and as such cannot intermingle textually. In deference to this presupposition, he affirms a compositional history of Revelation in which the First Edition (4:1—22:5 [or 9]) is apocalyptic while the Second Edition (1:1—3:22; 22:6 [or 10]–21) has a more prophetic character. His diachronic approach to the text does affirm a literary unity for the finished product, but a unity that is purported only to be "artificial [and which] has been imposed on numerous discrete units that have been paratactically linked together in an apparently chronological order."[106]

Aune's motivation is laudable in that his "ultimate concern is not to atomize Revelation into a plethora of discrete textual units ... but rather to try to understand how and why a single author, John of Patmos,

---

104. Beale, *Revelation*, 39. Beale quotes Carson et al., *Introduction to the New Testament*, 479.

105. Aune, *Revelation 1—5*, lxxxix–xc.

106. Aune, *Revelation 1—5*, xciii.

brought Revelation into being."[107] It is this atomization of the text that has affected the intelligibility of some previous commentators. One example is R. H. Charles[108] whose "theories of radical displacement . . . [have allowed] the critic to rewrite the text in the way in which he or she thinks it should have been written."[109] Aune's source-critical presuppositions appear to combine the principles of a *revision theory*[110] with that of a *fragmentary theory*[111] since they "are not mutually exclusive theories . . . [and] can contribute to the unraveling of the various layers of tradition in Revelation."[112]

Nevertheless, Aune's attempt to textually separate the prophetic and apocalyptic elements of Revelation can be questioned on a few fronts. First, Biguzzi's criticism of Aune's diachronic proposal highlights two anomalies: "Synoptic sayings should only [then] be found in the second [i.e., prophetic] edition but cf. 1,7; 13,10; 16,15; formulae with *eidon* and/ or *ēkousa* [i.e., apocalyptic visionary devices] should only be found in the second edition, but cf. 1,12b.17; 22,8."[113]

Second, Aune's removal of a prophetic influence from 4:1—22:5 does not appear even to sufficiently take into account his own distinction between prophecy and apocalypticism. Contrary to apocalypticism, Aune states that prophecy does not see the wicked state of the unrighteous as irreversible and thus addressable only through eschatological judgment. Instead, he contends that prophecy leaves the door open for repentance on the part of the unrighteous and requires admonition and exhortation of the righteous to keep them faithful.

However, within the section of Revelation that Aune claims is an apocalypse (4:1—22:5), there does appear to be evidence of repentance on the part of the righteous not least in the episode of the "two witnesses" (11:1–13). The two witnesses are killed by "the beast that comes up from

107. Aune, *Revelation* 1—5, cxviii.

108. Charles, *Revelation* (2 vols.; 1920).

109. Aune, *Revelation* 1—5, cxviii.

110. Aune describes a *revision theory* as "a single extensive apocalyptic composition was subject to later editorial expansion; either an original Jewish apocalypse was transformed into Revelation by a Christian editor, or an original Christian apocalypse was revised and augmented by a later editor or series of editors" (*Revelation* 1—5, cxviii).

111. A *fragmentary theory* is defined as a proposal in which "various units of texts were joined together by John to form Revelation" (Aune, *Revelation* 1—5, cxviii).

112. Aune, *Revelation* 1—5, cxviii.

113. Biguzzi, Review of David E. Aune, *Revelation* 1—5, 584.

the Abyss" (11:7). After three and a half days they are raised back to life which elicits a reaction of terror from their enemies (11:11) and, no doubt, wonder as they view the ascension of the witnesses into heaven (11:12). It is at "this very hour" that a great earthquake destroys the city in which the enemies of the two witnesses dwell with the result being that "the survivors were terrified and gave glory to the God of heaven" (11:13). Admittedly, no indication is given of the duration of that repentance with respect to their concomitant lifestyle. But the very fact that repentance is recorded as an eventuality in the lives of some of the unrighteous mitigates against a purely apocalyptic eschatology within what Aune contends is the apocalyptic body of the Apocalypse (4:1—22:5). This eschatological *mixtum compositum*, so to speak, is even conceded by Aune when he says that there is a "juxtaposing [of] apocalyptic with prophetic elements throughout the entire composition."[114] But it would seem to me that the genre implication of that juxtaposition is not sufficiently correlated with his diachronic analysis of Revelation.

Another significant prophetic element in the Apocalypse surfaces in the contrast between the resurrection of Christ and the radical pessimism of apocalyptic literature. The resurrection of Christ is vividly portrayed in the Apocalypse in the vision of the Lamb "looking as if it had been slain" (5:6). This imagery, however, occurs within the apparently non-prophetic section of the Apocalypse. Schüssler Fiorenza claims that the centrality of the resurrection of Christ which (1) has ushered in the "onset of the last times" and (2) "stresses that God is acting in and through Jesus Christ in history," demonstrates that the Apocalypse is "substantially nearer to the God of the prophets than to the God of the apocalyptists."[115] Thus, the portrayal of Christ's resurrection with its concomitant assumption of ongoing redemption would appear to favor a prophetic emphasis.

This conclusion challenges Aune's structural proposal in which the vision of the Lamb (chs. 5 and 6) is said to occur within a strictly apocalyptic section of the book of Revelation. This appears to be especially problematic given Schüssler Fiorenza's concluding comment in relation

114. Aune, *Revelation* 1—5, xc. Aune explains the purpose of this apparent literary strategy: "by juxtaposing apocalyptic with prophetic elements throughout the entire composition, the author appears to have attempted to give a new lease on life to apocalyptic traditions that could not and did not long retain their vitality in early Christianity because of their indissoluble association with nationalistic myths connected with the royal ideology of ancient Israel."

115. Schüssler Fiorenza, "The Phenomenon of Early Christian Apocalyptic," 303–4.

to early Christian texts, including that of Revelation: "from a formal-structural point of view Christian apocalyptic texts are a part of Jewish apocalyptic but from an essential-theological point of view they differ substantively from Jewish apocalyptic speculation."[116]

Thirdly, as has already been suggested, Aune appears insufficiently to assess the impact upon his diachronic structure of the divine command for John "to prophecy" (10:11: *propheteusai*) which also is found within the apparently apocalyptic section. A related question arises with Aune's contention that the framing sections of the Apocalypse are prophetic. He does not give specificity as to which "prophetic" sub-genre they are most characteristic (e.g., Hebrew Bible or Christ-follower).

The Apocalypse as an Apocalyptic "Apostolic-Prophecy"

Thomas attempted to harmonize the visionary manner of the Apocalypse's revelation with its self-proclaimed prophetic nature by describing it as "visional-prophetic" in genre. I have suggested, however, that this attempt fell short since he correlated Revelation with the sub-genre of *New Testament* prophecy, which, in contrast to Hebrew Bible prophecy, lacks the inherently authoritative element of an unequivocal word from the Lord. While the authority of both was derivative, only a classical prophet appeared to claim an authority over the life of the covenantal community that presumed infallibility in his predictions and a necessary submission to his moral and spiritual pronouncements. In other words, unlike a classical prophet, the proclamation of a Christ-follower prophet, in and of itself, no longer held *inherent* authority within the covenant community. Describing the Apocalypse as New Testament prophecy results in an inherent loss of authority for its content.

Aune, while being true to the prophetic self-designations in the final form of the text, nevertheless deprived it of a comprehensive prophetic character with his diachronic approach. His restriction of the body of the Apocalypse (4:1—22:5 [or 9]) as solely apocalyptic literature necessarily delimited its prophetic content to the two framing sections (1:1—3:22; 22:6 [or 10]–21). His resultant genre designation "prophetic apocalypse," while possible, appears open to question given some of the paradoxical outcomes from the standpoint of exegetical (Biguzzi), and theological (Schüssler Fiorenza) concerns.

116. Schüssler Fiorenza, "The Phenomenon of Early Christian Apocalyptic," 304.

Aside from Aune, none of the other scholars examined above (i.e., Thomas, Schüssler Fiorenza, and Beale) make literary characteristics foundational to their analyses. Instead, they prioritize exegetical and theological considerations for a genre determination. However, this fails to respond directly to the literary basis upon which Collins defines the apocalyptic genre in *Semeia* 14. To assert a prophetic nature for the Apocalypse one must firstly demonstrate the inadequacy of the apocalyptic paradigm as it relates to the book of Revelation and, secondly, detail the Apocalypse's literary correlation with a prophetic paradigm. One challenge in this regard is in determining the prophetic sub-genre to which Revelation best corresponds.

To his credit, Aune has sought to be very precise in his attempt to categorize which elements in the Apocalypse are prophetic and which are apocalyptic. Unfortunately, Revelation ends up being divided into two apparently mutually exclusive textual components, with the apocalyptic section being accorded compositional primacy. The prophetic framing sections are implicitly assigned a secondary compositional and thus literary status.

KORNER'S GENRE: APOCALYPTIC APOSTOLIC-PROPHECY

In my search for greater precision in Revelation's genre designation, I will attempt to keep three priorities in balance: (1) the supernatural (not just literary) character of the *apokalypsis* recorded in the Apocalypse; (2) the implicit authority of this supernatural revelation as indicated in the text's prophetic self-designation; and (3) the visionary manner of the *apokalypsis* (whether angelically mediated or not) as being integral not just to apocalyptic literature, but also to prophetic literature.

The road forward in this venture lies in a threefold direction. Firstly, precise textual delimitation is crucial for an appropriate determination of the Apocalypse's genre. Aune's dichotomous division will be evaluated in light of three visionary literary conventions found within 1:9—22:20. These three literary devices are also found within Jewish apocalyptic and Hebrew prophetic literature. Within this wide body of literature it will be seen that they are consistently used for the provision of structure for vision-oriented texts.

The "space/time referent" is the most crucial of these three with respect to delimiting a text. Its structural significance has been neglected by previous scholarship.[117] Based on these three literary devices, the text of the Apocalypse cannot be divided at 4:1 for the purpose of genre differentiation. Instead, the literary function of the "space/time referent," specifically, requires that the entire text of Revelation from 1:9—22:20 be read (and heard) from the perspective of only one compositional timeframe, and thus, genre.[118] This delimitation then allows one to incorporate the prophetically explicit affirmations in 22:7, 10, 18, and 19 in one's consideration of the vision report's (1:9—22:20) literary genre. The prophetic self-identification moves one away from giving "apocalypse" primacy of place with respect to genre classification. As a result, I will suggest that Aune's categorization of the Apocalypse as a "prophetic apocalypse" is perhaps most appropriately reclassified as an "apocalyptic prophecy."

The second question to address then is, "Which sub-genre of prophecy best represents this 'apocalyptic prophecy' (1:9—22:20)?" While some deem Revelation to be an example of New Testament/Christ-follower prophecy (Thomas) or Hebrew Bible prophecy (Mazzaferri), I will suggest a third prophetic sub-genre: "apostolic-prophecy." An "apostolic prophet" is defined not only as one of the Spirit-anointed apostolic leaders of the new covenant community (e.g., Eph 4:11), but one who, like Hebrew Bible prophets, was perceived to be divinely authoritative in his verbal or written proclamations. The Eleven (the Twelve less Judas Iscariot) are the irreducible minimum as far as new covenant "apostolic prophets" are concerned. The phrases "the Eleven" and "the Twelve" communicate that only a limited number of people are eternally foundational to the universal *ekklēsia*.[119] It will be investigated whether it is possible to identify the Eleven and Paul as the foundational leaders of the universal community who rest upon Jesus Christ, himself, as the chief cornerstone (cf., Eph 2:19–22; 3:4–5).[120]

Of the three visionary literary conventions, the "space/time referent" will be seen to function beyond simply Jewish visionary *apocalyptic* literature. It is also found in Jewish *prophetic* literature, whether of a visionary or non-visionary nature (see Appendix 2). Appendix 2 identifies

---

117. See Korner, "'And I Saw,'" 162–72, 175–77.

118. For an analysis of "space/time referents" that occur within Hebrew prophetic and Jewish apocalyptic literature (visionary and non-visionary), see Appendix 2.

119. For example, 2 Pet 3:16 attributes scriptural status to the Pauline letters: "Paul . . . wrote to you, as also in all [his] letters . . . which the untaught and unstable distort, as [they] do also the rest of the Scriptures, to their own destruction."

120. This possibility is examined in greater detail in pages 194 to 197.

two variant forms of the "space/time referent": a generalized format used
in apocalyptic vision-oriented texts; and a more specific version used in
Hebrew Bible prophecy (whether visionary or only verbal). The "space/
time referent" of Revelation (1:9, 10) appears to synthesize both the generalized and specific versions within the phrase "on the imperial/lordly/
Lord's day" (*kyriakē hēmera*). This appears to reflect a distinctive modification to a typical "imperial space/time referent," wherein the dating of
a Hebrew prophetic vision is directly tied to the regnal chronology of a
king/suzerain (e.g., "In the third year of King Cyrus of Persia . . . on the
twenty-fourth day of the first month . . . I looked up and saw . . . "; Dan
12:1–5). As such, Revelation's distinctive "imperial space/time referent,"
while anchoring the prophetic nature of the vision in the Apocalypse, at
the same time maintains literary continuity with Jewish apocalyptic literature. This generically integrational "space/time referent" lends implicit
support to my alignment of Revelation's prophetic nature with the sub-
genre of "apostolic-prophecy"—such a designation aligns the "revelation
of Jesus the *Christos*" with the same implicit divine authority assumed in
Hebrew Bible prophetic proclamations (e.g., "thus says the LORD").

The third key question to address in an investigation of the Apocalypse as an "apocalyptic-prophecy" is how one defines "apocalyptic" in
relation to "prophecy." Categorizing a text as prophetic in genre does
not *ipso facto* exclude its incorporation of apocalyptic eschatology or
apocalyptic imagery as a central factor in how the inherently prophetic
message is communicated to its intended audience. Later in this section,
I will clarify more precisely the literary interplay between the prophetic
Apocalypse and its apparently apocalyptic eschatology.

Having argued against the *opinio communis* that "apocalypse" is
the primary genre designation for the book of Revelation, it remains to
examine the interpretive significance of its prophetic designation. The
question that will be addressed is whether the "apocalyptic prophecy" of
Revelation is in some fashion predictive. In other words, does the apocalyptic imagery have prophetic force, specifically as it relates to the predic-
tion of actual real space/time events intended to occur at some point in,
or still future to, John's era.

Both Jewish apocalyptic and Hebrew prophetic literature use the
three literary conventions for the provision of linear structure for their
vision reports/*vision episodes.*[121] John, however, appears to take literary li-

121. I define a *vision episode* as "a literary classification for a section of vision-
oriented text identified through a 'space/time referent'" ("And I Saw," 164). Thus, since

cense with this traditional usage in going beyond a simply linear chronology in his organization of the visionary components. He appears to use the three literary conventions to facilitate a reiterative relationship between the various major visions/*vision blocks* and minor visions/*individual visions* within Revelation's *vision episode* (1:9—22:20). This provides a basis upon which to postulate that the events of the sixth seal and forward are eschatological events, some of which were beginning to unfold in John's day, but yet which did not see full completion in John's day.

Prophetic Sub-Genre of the Apocalypse?

If the Apocalypse is first and foremost a prophecy, then it is important also to ascertain which prophetic sub-genre it belongs to. I have already addressed the inadequacy of attempting to identify Revelation with the sub-genres of either New Testament/Christ-follower or Hebrew Bible prophecy. I have also suggested the value of investigating whether any of the Hebrew Bible prophetic books might provide precedent for seeing for the book of Revelation as "apocalyptic prophecy." However, that question must remain, for the moment, a "project in waiting."

This section will explore the aforementioned third option for the prophetic sub-genre of the book of Revelation, one that nonetheless still exhibits a sense of continuity between the two Testaments: "apostolic -prophecy." Craig Evans notes that the close relationship between apostle and prophet is evidenced in the Hebrew Bible where, "by definition, prophets are those who have been 'sent' by Yahweh" (e.g., Isa 6:8; Jer 1:7; Ezek 2:3).[122] Even Moses, the great lawgiver and prophet, is said to have been "sent."[123] Evans also points out that similar terminology is used in the New Testament with respect to the Hebrew Bible prophets and the disciples/apostles of Jesus.[124] This "apostolic prophetic" language extends

---

there is only one "space/time referent" in Revelation (1:9, 10), this indicates that the rest of the Apocalypse (1:11—22:20) is one cohesive literary unit.

122. Evans, "Paul as Prophet," 763.

123. Cf. Exod 3:10, 12, 13, 14, 15; 4:28; 7:16; Deut 34:11. In later Jewish and Samaritan traditions Moses is identified as an "apostle/sent one" (*Mek. R. Sim. Yoh.* on Exod 3:10–11; *'Abot R. Nat.* A §1; *Exod. Rab.* 3.4 [on 3:12]; 3.14 [on 4:10]; *Memar Marqa* 5.3; 6.3).

124. For example, Matt 23:37; Mark 1:2; Luke 9:2; 10:3; 13:34; 22:35; John 1:6; 3:28; Rom 10:15.

even to later traditions where "apostle" is a term used for a prophet (cf. *Mek.* on Exod 12:1 [*Pisha* §1]).[125]

In seeking to identify a Christ-follower exemplar of the Apocalypse's prophetic sub-genre, Schüssler Fiorenza provides some promising insights. She points towards the apostle Paul as a key exemplar of the type of prophecy characteristic of the visionary *apokalypsis* of Christ (1:9— 22:20). First, I will examine the theological and literary affinities between the writings of the apostle Paul (initially excluding the deutero-Pauline writings) and the prophet John. Second, I will discusses the apostle Paul's prophetic status in comparison with the prophetic commissioning of Hebrew Bible prophets. Third, Paul's identification not just as an apostle nor simply as a prophet, but as an "apostle-prophet" will be suggested. Fourth, John's visionary experience will be compared with the prophetic call narratives of the Hebrew Bible, particularly Ezekiel's. Fifth, the question will be asked whether the implicitly authoritative status of Revelation implies that its author is not just a New Testament/Christ-follower prophet, but an "apostle-prophet" like Paul. Sixth, I will conclude with a look at the symbolic New Jerusalem's twelve-fold apostolic foundation (21:14). This metaphor of an apostolic foundation is also found in the (deutero-)Pauline letter to the Ephesians. Therein, "the apostles and prophets" are said to form the foundation of the universal *ekklēsia* (Eph 2:20; 3:5). I will explore any potential correlation between Paul and John in their use of "foundation" imagery as it is applied to themselves, and the other disciples/apostles of Jesus, for the depiction of their "apostolic-prophetic" status.

PROPHETIC SUB-GENRE OF THE APOCALYPSE IN LIGHT OF PAULINE WRITINGS

In affirming that Revelation accords with the prophetic character of the apostle Paul and his writings, Schüssler Fiorenza sees similarity in the *Sitz im Leben* of both authors's intended audiences. Some challenge this with their contention that the Apocalypse's theology and community structures are seen as not fitting the assemblies in Roman Asia to whom the book is addressed.[126] But Schüssler Fiorenza contends that it is John

125. In *Pisha* §1 God says to the prophet Jonah: "I have other apostles like you."

126. Schüssler Fiorenza ("Apokalypsis and Propheteia," 114 n. 24) refers to Satake (*Die Gemeindeordnung in der Johannesapokalypse* [1966]) as an influential example of

himself who should be seen as a Jewish Christ-follower rather than what she sees as being his largely gentile addressees. Thus, she claims that John's *apokalypsis* would still have found affinity with a Pauline Christian community familiar with Pauline (and deutero-Pauline) writings.

She notes four affinities between Revelation and the Pauline writings. The first highlights correspondences between the apocalyptic theology of the prophetic Revelation and Pauline writings. The second describes affinities with respect to prophetic functions. The third affirms Pauline influence in the epistolary framework of the Apocalypse. The fourth compares linguistic similarities between the two.

Firstly, J. Baumgarten identifies seven thematic motifs ("Themenkreise und Funktion") of Pauline (and deutero-Pauline) apocalyptic theology which are also evident within the book of Revelation.[127] These are: (1) expectation of the *parousia* and the final judgment; (2) resurrection and eternal life; (3) exaltation and translation; (4) angelology and demonology; (5) cosmos and new creation; (6) enthusiasm; and (7) imminent expectation. Sydney Page also postulates numerous points of contact between Pauline eschatology and Revelation, especially in chapter 20.[128] Some examples he cites are: (1) the two-stage defeat of Satanic powers;[129] (2) the correspondence between the restrainer in 2 Thess 2:6–7 and the binding of Satan (20:1–3);[130] and (3) the integration of "the concepts of judgment on the basis of works and judgment on the basis of grace" in the final judgment.[131]

Secondly, J. Panagopoulos discusses five functions of the prophetic word in early Christianity, which are significantly informed by Pauline (or deutero-Pauline) sources.[132] These are said to constitute: (1) an es-

---

this position.

127. Baumgarten, *Paulus und die Apokalyptik*, esp. 59–227.

128. Page, "Revelation 20," 31–43.

129. Page, "Revelation 20," 33.

130. Page, "Revelation 20," 34, 40–41. Page writes that "the parallels between the third vision in Revelation and what Paul says about the eschatological rebellion associated with the man of lawlessness are so numerous and so detailed that it is unlikely that they are coincidental. . . . Though differences do exist, they do not amount to contradictions and may largely be explained by the fact that Rev 20:7–10 is built on the prophecies concerning Gog and Magog in Ezekiel while the background for Paul's teaching in 2 Thessalonians 2 is to be found in the book of Daniel" ("Revelation 20," 41).

131. Page, "Revelation 20," 42.

132. Panagopoulos, "Die urchristliche Prophetie," 25–32.

chatological message; (2) concrete influences ("konkreten Wirkungen"); (3) the authoritative word of the Lord or his Spirit through revelation (e.g., dream, vision, auditory or direct encounter with the risen Lord); (4) encouragement/exhortation of the assembly (*paraklēsin* and *paramuthian*; 1 Cor 14:3); and (5) a diversity of forms and types ("Vielgestaltigkeit von *Formen und Typen*"). Again, the book of Revelation exhibits congruency with these Pauline prophetic functions.

Thirdly, aside from the Apocalypse's theological and thematic correlation with Pauline prophecy, the epistolary framework of the book of Revelation (especially 1:4–6 and 22:21) appears to imitate consciously that of a Pauline letter. Schüssler Fiorenza concurs with K. Berger in his assertion that there is a "great difference in form between the seven letters [2:1—3:22] and the epistolary framework of Rev."[133] This leads her to claim that "This difference in form underlines that John understands his prophecy not only in general as a prophetic letter but explicitly characterizes it as a circular, authoritative apostolic letter which is patterned after the already traditional Pauline letter form."[134]

A fourth affinity between the Apocalypse and Pauline writings involves linguistic considerations. The terms *apokalypsis* and *apokalyptein* occur rarely in the LXX,[135] only seldom in the Gospels[136] and, outside of the Gospels, almost exclusively within Pauline (or deutero-Pauline) literature.[137] Aside from 1 Pet 1:7, 13, the full phrase *apokalypsis 'Iesous Christou* occurs exclusively within Pauline and deutero-Pauline writings.[138] Only in Pauline writings is the full phrase used for a *visionary* revelation of Jesus Christ (i.e., Gal 1:12). Elsewhere it occurs in reference to the *parousia*.[139]

133. Schüssler Fiorenza, "Apokalypsis and Propheteia," 125.

134. Schüssler Fiorenza, "Apokalypsis and Propheteia," 125; see also p. 125 n. 54. See also my discussion on the possibility of seeing Revelation as "a covenant letter to the diaspora." Thus, Revelation may not just reflect only a Pauline epistolary format.

135. *Apokalypsis* does not occur in the LXX; *Apokalyptein*: LXX Deut 29:29; 1 Sam 3:7, 21; 2 Sam 7:27; Job 12:22; 20:27; Prov 25:9; Isa 22:14; 23:1; 40:5; 53:1; 56:1; Jer 11:20; 33:6; Dan 2:19, 22, 28, 29, 30, 47; 10:1; Amos 3:7.

136. *Apokalypsis* in the Gospels: Luke 2:32; *Apokalyptein*: Matt 10:26; 11:25, 27; 16:17; Luke 2:35; 10:21, 22; 12:2; 17:30; John 12:38.

137. *Apokalypsis*: Rom 2:5; 8:19; 16:25; 1 Cor 1:7; 14:6, 26; 2 Cor 12:1, 7; Gal 1:12; 2:2; Eph 1:17; 3:3; 2 Thess 1:7; 2:3; 1 Pet 4:13; Rev 1:1; *Apokalyptein*: 1 Cor 2:10; 3:13; 14:30; Gal 1:16; 3:23; Eph 3:5; Phil 3:15; 2 Thess 2:3, 6, 8; 1 Pet 1:5, 12; 5:1.

138. 1 Cor 1:7; Gal 1:12; 2 Thess 1:7.

139. I.e., 1 Cor 1:7; 2 Thess 1:7; 1 Pet 1:7, 13.

PAUL THE PROPHET AND HEBREW BIBLE PROPHETS

K. O. Sandnes claims that the apostle Paul "conceived of his apostolic commission to preach the gospel in prophetic terms."[140] Paul's autobiographical description of his Damascus road experience (cf. Acts 9:1–8) in Gal 1:15–16a reminds one, for example, of Jeremiah's prophetic call narrative.[141] It is this revelatory confrontation with the risen Lord in which Paul was commissioned to preach the gospel to the nations that demonstrates similarity with Hebrew Bible prophetic call narratives. Six correspondences are highlighted: "The basic structure, call, election, revelation, commission and definition of target group, corresponds to the basic structure of the commission texts of the OT prophets."[142] In this light, Paul's writings may be assumed to have an authority in the life of believers similar to that found in the OT prophets.

Schüssler Fiorenza also correlates Gal 1:15–16a with Hebrew Bible prophetic call narratives. Thus, Gal 1:16 relates the appearance of Christ to Paul (*apokalypsai ton huion autou en emoi*), which in 1:12 is directly attributed to divine revelation rather than to human intermediaries. Furthermore, she states that while Paul uses specifically Christian terms, he presents his apostolic call in an analogous manner to that of the call of a classical prophet (e.g., "set me apart, even from my mother's womb," "I did not consult flesh and blood"). As such, Schüssler Fiorenza claims that "John deliberately has chosen the title *apokalypsis Iesou Christou* in order to characterize his own experience as a Christian prophetic experience similar to the call-experience of Paul."[143]

PAUL THE "APOSTLE-PROPHET" AND NEW TESTAMENT PROPHETS

Notwithstanding this similarity with Hebrew Bible prophecy, Paul's prophetic authority is also seen as being greater than even that of a New Testament prophet: "If anyone thinks he is a prophet . . . let him recognize

---

140. Sandnes, *Paul-One of the Prophets?* 224.

141. Gal 1:15, 16a reads: "But when God, who had set me apart from my mother's womb and called me through his grace, was pleased to reveal his Son in me so that I might preach Him among the gentiles"; Jer 1:4, 5 reads: "Now the word of the LORD came to me saying, 'Before I formed you in the womb I knew you, and before you were born I consecrated you; I appointed you a prophet to the nations.'"

142. Sandnes, *Paul—One of the Prophets?* 4.

143. Schüssler Fiorenza, "Apokalypsis and Propheteia," 126.

that the things which I write to you are the Lord's commandment. But if anyone does not recognize this, he is not recognized" (1 Cor 14:37). It is Paul's apostolic commissioning that distinguishes him from a New Testament prophet and which is "something radically new compared to OT prophets."[144] In line with Sandnes one might, therefore, classify Paul as an "apostle-prophet"[145] and his writings as "apostolic-prophecy." But is "apostolic-prophecy" only a Pauline phenomenon? Perhaps in view of their alleged apostolic authorship, the Gospels of Matthew and John also provide a starting point as examples of "apostolic-prophecy." However, in raising this question, it is recognized that genre discussion is based upon form and content rather than authorship. As such, an investigation of this possibility goes beyond the bounds of this present study.

Schüssler Fiorenza contends that the "John" of the Apocalypse, unlike the Eleven, does not explicitly claim to derive his authority from personal fellowship with the pre-resurrected Jesus of Nazareth. Rather, the "John" of the Apocalypse is said to base his authoritative claim on a prophetic experience—the visionary *revelatory* experience of the *resurrected* Lord. This is similar to the basis upon which the apostle Paul also claimed apostolic status in, for example, 1 Cor 9:2 ("Am I not an apostle? Have I not seen the Lord?").[146] Hence, she argues that while "John's self-understanding and perception of authority . . . are not apostolic but prophetic,"[147] it is still viable to see his apostolic commission as being possible nonetheless.

If one assumes that this "John" was familiar with the whole of Paul's Corinthian correspondence, it would seem incongruous then that he would claim apostolic status in direct contradiction of Pauline claims to be the last of the apostles (1 Cor 15:7–9), especially given Schüssler Fiorenza's demonstration of "John's" literary indebtedness to the apostle Paul.

Is there evidence in the Pauline corpus that can more concretely connect Paul the prophet with Paul the apostle? The designation "apostle-prophet" for Paul seems to be warranted from two passages in the epistle to the "Ephesians"/"Laodiceans."[148] The (deutero-)Pauline epistle

144. Sandnes, *Paul—One of the Prophets?* 7.

145. Sandnes, *Paul—One of the Prophets?* 7.

146. In Gal 1:12 and 16 Paul also claims that a visionary *revelatory* experience of the *resurrected* Lord was the basis upon which he received an apostolic commission to preach the gospel to the nations.

147. Schüssler Fiorenza, "Revelation," 414.

148. For my discussion of Douglas Campbell's claim that the intended audience for

to the Ephesians appears expressly to use the term "apostle-prophet." The authenticity of Ephesians as a Pauline epistle has been questioned with respect to its address, vocabulary, style, and theological emphasis. But whether one holds to Pauline or deutero-Pauline authorship, Sandnes notes that the *opinio communis* is that at the very least "Ephesians should be considered as a witness from the apostle's vicinity, a circle or school deeply dependent on the apostle."[149] Some circumvent these concerns by affirming Pauline content that is perhaps composed by an *amanuensis*. If the letter is deutero-Pauline then a second-century compositional date is suggested, years *after* the book of Revelation was written. Thus, to use Ephesians as evidence for any argument related to Revelation is treading on potentially unstable ground. But it will be seen that, in regard to the foundational role of "the apostles and prophets," theological affinity between Ephesians and Revelation also finds some parallel in the sectarian literature of the Qumran community, literature that predates both New Testament documents irrespective of their compositional date.

In Eph 2:19–22 the community of Christ-followers is metaphorically described as "a holy temple in the Lord" and its spiritual leaders as "the foundation": "So then you are no longer strangers and aliens, but you are fellow citizens with the saints and members of the household of God, built upon the foundation of the apostles and prophets, Christ Jesus himself being the cornerstone, in whom the whole structure is joined together and grows into a holy temple in the Lord; in whom you also are built into it for a dwelling place of God in the Spirit."

The phrase "the apostles and prophets" (*tōn apostolōn kai prophētōn*) is found in both Eph 2:20 and 3:5. It is used of those who form the foundation of the universal *ekklēsia* with "Christ Jesus himself being the cornerstone." Two referents are possible. First, the phrase "the apostles and prophets" could indicate two different types of people ("the apostles as well as prophets"). Second, it could refer to one group comprised of one type of person ("the apostles who are also prophets" or simply "the apostle-prophets").

If the phrase *tōn apostolōn kai prophētōn* refers to two separate classes of people then who are the "prophets?" They could be either Hebrew Bible or Christ-follower prophets. Of these two, Sandnes excludes the Hebrew Bible prophets as a viable option "primarily because of the

---

Paul's ostensible epistle "to the Ephesians" was the *ekklēsia* in Laodicea, see p. 34 n. 9.

149. Sandnes, *Paul—One of the Prophets?* 225.

revelatory schema in Eph 3:5. The salvation-historical *nun* ('now') definitely forbids us interpret them as OT prophets."¹⁵⁰ Sandnes favors seeing New Testament/Christ-follower prophets being referenced in Eph 3:5 in continuity with Eph 4:11a.¹⁵¹ In this latter verse we find the phrase *tōn apostolōn kai tōn prophētōn*, which definitely refers to two separate classes of individuals—the apostles and the *Christ-follower* prophets.¹⁵² But Sandnes's conclusion can be questioned since in Eph 4:11b we find the same syntactical construction as in Eph 2:20 and 3:5 but yet which Wayne Grudem claims can be translated as a hendiadys. A hendiadys is two nouns which imply one group—"the shepherds who are also teachers" (*tous de poimenas kai didaskalous*). Grudem states that "it is clear that one group with only one component (or one person) is implied. . . . The 'pastors and teachers' are the same people but two different functions are named."¹⁵³

Thus, it is not improbable that the phrase *tōn apostolōn kai prophētōn* (2:20; 3:5) also is a hendiadys—"the apostles who are also prophets." The word *kai* is then to be taken epexegetically such that *prophētōn* defines and characterizes the first noun more precisely. This grammatical construction reflects the translational mandate of the Granville Sharp rule, although this rule does not specifically apply to nouns in plural form (i.e., Eph 2:20; 3:5).

The Granville Sharp rule states that when two personal nouns (singular in number, excluding proper nouns) are connected by a conjunctive *kai*, with the only the first noun having a definite article, then a single group comprised of only a single component is represented.¹⁵⁴ As

150. Eph 3:3, 5 reads ". . . by revelation there was made known to me the mystery . . . which in other generations was not made known to the sons of men, as it has *now been revealed to his holy apostles and prophets in the Spirit*" (3:5:) (*nun apekalyphthē tois hagios apostolois autou kai prophētaia en pneumati*).

151. Sandes writes, "In Eph 2:21–22 the growth of the community is based upon the gospel-preaching of 'the apostles and prophets' (v. 20). In Eph 4:11, however, the growth is due to the offices mentioned in v. 11. On the basis of this connection between the two paragraphs it is problematic to narrow the meaning of Eph 2:20 and 3:5 into apostles alone. It seems that the prophets mentioned are epexegetically referring to the apostles, but are the Christian prophets, as is the case in Eph 4:11" (*Paul—One of the Prophets?* 235).

152. Examples of those simply known as "apostles" would be Andronicus and Junias (Rom 16:7), and "prophets" would be Barnabas (Acts 13:1), Judas and Silas (Acts 15:32).

153. Grudem, *Gift of Prophecy*, 97.

154. Sharp, in his *Remarks on the Uses of the Definitive Article*, defines this first of

is readily evident, due to the plural form of the phrase *tōn apostolōn kai prophētōn*, this rule's application in Eph 2:20 and 3:5 is at best analogous and not definitive.

Within the same verse (4:11), three other types of divinely appointed people are identified for the purpose of "equipping the saints for ministry." In this case, each noun is preceded by a definite article, thus, indicating three different types of people are in view (*tous men apostolous, tous de prophētas, tous de euaggelistas*; "some as apostles, and some as prophets, and some as evangelists"). Therefore, one could say that in Eph 4:11a "the apostles" and "the prophets" are two separate types of people, not one person viewed from two perspectives ("the apostle-prophet").[155] This grammatical clarity in 4:11a contrasts sharply with the more ambiguous phrase *tōn apostolōn kai prophētōn* found twice in the previous two chapters (i.e., 2:20; 3:5).

Presumably, then, the author of Ephesians does not intend to reference two separate groups 2:20 and 3:5 since he could simply have added a definite article in front of "prophets" as he did a few verses later in 4:11. This being the case, then we have three types of people in view: a group of *ekklēsia* leaders known as "apostle-prophets" and two other types of *ekklēsia* leaders known separately as "apostles" or as "prophets." Grudem argues that categorizing *tōn apostolōn kai prophētōn* as a unique class of assembly leaders called "the apostle-prophets" is congruent within Pauline literature. He contends that in the Pauline corpus there is not a single unambiguous example in which two distinct *people* or classes of *people* (as opposed to *things*) are referenced when using only a single, initial article and joined by the conjunctive *kai*.[156] Thus, one could say that

---

six rules on the use of the article as follows: "When the copulative *kai* connects two nouns of the same case, [*viz.* nouns (either substantive or adjective, or participles) of personal description, respecting office, dignity, affinity, or connexion, and attributes, properties, or qualities, good or ill], if the article *ho* or any of its cases, precedes the first of the said nouns or participles, and is not repeated before the second noun or participle, the latter always relates to the same person that is expressed or described by the first noun or participle: i.e., it denotes a farther description of the first-named person . . ." (cited in Wallace, *Greek Grammar Beyond the Basics*, 271).

155. It is the express purpose of these less authoritative apostles and prophets to assist in the equipping of the saints "for the work of ministry, for building up the body of Christ, until we all attain to the unity of the faith and of the knowledge of the Son of God, to mature manhood to the measure of the stature of the fullness of Christ" (Eph 4:11–12).

156. Grudem, *Gift of Prophecy*, 100–101. He cites two examples from Acts in which this does occur (13:50 and 15:2).

Ephesians presents the first group ("apostle-prophets") as being foundational to the universal *ekklēsia* (2:20; 3:5) while the second set (4:11) fulfill similar functions but for regional *ekklēsiai* without the attendant spiritual authority characteristic of the first.

Grudem suggests that at least one of the four interpretive options for the word "foundation" (*themelios*) can refer to a group of apostles who are also prophets: (1) *themelios* has primary reference not to the apostles and prophets themselves but to their functions, such as preaching and teaching, receiving and proclaiming the gospel, or to their overseeing activity among the *ekklēsiai*; (2) *themelios* refers to the New Testament apostles and the Hebrew Bible prophets; (3) *themelios* refers to the New Testament apostles and the New Testament prophets as two separate groups; or (4) *themelios* refers to one group—"the NT apostles who are also NT prophets."[157]

Is there any other New Testament reference to people forming the foundation of the universal *ekklēsia*? The apostle Peter, for one, is a person metaphorically described as a foundational rock upon which Christ said he would build his *ekklēsia* (Matt 16:18). The book of Revelation also depicts people as a foundation of the universal *ekklēsia*, symbolized in the twelve-fold foundation (*themelios*) of the New Jerusalem (21:14). I will address this example further on in this section.

THE TWELVE AS "APOSTLE-PROPHETS"?

I would identify the eternally foundational group of "apostle-prophets" as being those disciples who were personally commissioned by Jesus and who were witnesses of him in his resurrected body. If the "John" of Revelation is included in the "twelve apostles of the Lamb," then he is to be identified with the apostle by the same name.

The question naturally arises as to who the twelfth member of this select group might be. The first eleven appear to be the disciples/apostles of Christ (excluding Judas Iscariot).[158] Given the twofold qualifications of an apostle (i.e., a witness of the resurrected Christ and one personally

157. Grudem, *Gift of Prophecy*, 83–105.

158. John P. Meier notes that "The close connection, if not total identification, between the Twelve and the apostles in later Christian thought is due mainly to the theology of Luke. In Luke's version of Jesus's selection of the Twelve (Luke 6:13), Jesus 'summoned his *disciples* (the larger group), and *from them* he chose *twelve*, whom he also named *apostles*'" ("Circle of the Twelve," 635–72) (italics are author's emphasis).

chosen by Christ himself), only one other person can be identified as the twelfth apostle of the Lamb—the apostle Paul.

If Paul is the twelfth apostle, then the selection of Matthias by the Eleven requires some investigation. This incident is found in Acts 1:15–26. Peter proclaims the need to maintain the number twelve with reference to "this ministry and apostleship from which Judas turned aside to go to his own place" (1:25). Peter states that the criteria for selection as the twelfth apostle is that the successful candidate must have followed Christ from the day of his baptism under John (Luke 3:21–23) to the day of his ascension after the resurrection (Acts 1:9). Two names were put forward: Joseph called Barsabbas and Matthias. Matthias was chosen by virtue of a drawing of lots.

Although the historicity of this action is not under consideration here, one wonders about its theological precision. First, Peter neglected one essential criterion evident in every apostolic selection: the Gospels report that it was Jesus himself who personally selected men to the group of twelve. The text in Acts does not indicate any involvement by the resurrected Jesus (e.g., through vision or prophecy) in the selection of Matthias. Rather, it appears that Peter's assumption of the need for a twelfth apostle brought him to take this matter into his own hands. The text neither affirms nor critiques Peter's action. It merely reports it and lets the reader judge the propriety of Peter's actions.

Second, the validity of Matthias's apostolic selection appears suspect in view of Saul's personal selection by the resurrected Christ. Christ personally appeared to Saul and commissioned him to the ministry of an apostle—a ministry with the same divine authority as that of the Eleven. In this light, only Saul (later called Paul) fulfilled the twofold criterion for the twelfth apostle, which may warrant his designation as one of the "apostle-prophets" (Eph 2:20; 3:5).

The above argument assumes that the term "the Twelve" is primarily attributive in its force. Meier contends, however, that "the Twelve" was initially used substantivally as a stereotypical expression for Christ's inner circle of disciples.[159] Thus, the actual number of disciples is not crucial

---

159. Meier describes "the way in which the nomenclature of the Twelve developed in the early church. As we can see from the independent witness of Paul, Mark, and John, 'the Twelve,' used absolutely as a substantive and not as an adjective modifying 'disciples' or 'apostles,' was the earliest designation of this inner circle. Far from 'the Eleven' being the early and natural way of referring to the circle when one member was missing, the phrase 'the Eleven' occurs only in the second-generation stage of the Gospel tradition" ("Circle of the Twelve," 662).

since "the Twelve" is also used of the Eleven. Rather, Meier purports that
it is the eschatological significance of the number twelve that forms the
background to the substantival use of "the Twelve." Commenting on Matt
19:28, Meier sees in this logion the transformation of "the Twelve" into
a symbolic group created by Christ "whose very number ... promised,
and ... began the regathering of the twelve tribes. Accordingly, within his
larger prophetic vision of God coming to rule Israel as king in the end-
time, Jesus promised in Matt 19:28 par. that his inner circle of the Twelve,
the prophetic sign and the beginning of the regathering of the twelve tribes,
would share in the governance (or judgment?) of the reconstituted Israel."[160]

However, the stereotypical nature of "the Twelve" notwithstanding, the very fact that a specific number is used to describe Christ's inner circle does not preclude a sense of limited participation within that
circle, even if its actual number exceeds twelve. This still allows, then,
for the apostle Paul's membership, even if Matthias's selection process is
theologically valid.

Meier observes that even though Paul was "clearly not one of the
Twelve" during Christ's earthly ministry, he "fiercely vindicated his right
to the title apostle (e.g., Gal 1:1, 17; 2:8; 1 Cor 9:1–2; 15:9; 2 Cor 1:1; 11:5;
12:11–12; Rom 1:1, 5)."[161] It is possible that, as the apostle to the gentiles,
Paul viewed his foundational role in the growth of Christ's *ekklēsia* in
analogous terms to the role the Twelve played in Christ's eschatological
vision of a reconstituted Israel. If in fact "the Twelve" was stereotypical
of a foundational group of disciples who "would share in the governance
(or judgment?) of the reconstituted Israel," then perhaps the apostle Paul
also placed himself among that number. His self-identification with
this eschatological "Twelve" may have implicitly served, in his mind, to
communicate that the boundaries of the "reconstituted Israel" are also
expanded to include the gentiles.

Meier, though, does not appear to allow for a distinct group known
as "apostle-prophets" whose spiritual authority was analogous to that assumed in "the Twelve." He observes that "what is beyond doubt is that in
the first Christian decades 'apostle' had a range of meanings that extended
far beyond the Twelve."[162] As has already been seen, however, the epistle

160. Meier, "Circle of the Twelve," 657–78. The regathering or reconstituting of
the tribes of Israel is already hoped for in HB and non-apocalyptic pseudepigraphic
literature (e.g., Tob 13; Sir 36:1–17).

161. Meier, "Circle of the Twelve," 640.

162. Meier, "Circle of the Twelve," 640.

of Ephesians would limit Meier's observation to those known simply as "the apostles" (4:11a). The phrase "the apostle-prophets" (2:20; 3:5) may then have implicit reference only to "the Twelve," whether that number is used literally or figuratively.

The prospect of John's membership in the Twelve is enhanced if the epistolary framework of Revelation is in fact an example of the epistolary sub-genre known as "a covenantal letter to the diaspora." One identifying characteristic of a covenant letter to the diaspora, which Revelation lacks, is an authoritative center from which John's "epistle" was sent. But perhaps in the case of Revelation, it is not a geographical center (e.g., Jerusalem, the center of the Jewish apostles) but a person, as the authoritative representative of that center (e.g., a Jewish apostle-prophet), who fulfills that specific literary requirement. If the "John" of Revelation was also to be identified with John, the son of Zebedee, one of the Twelve, then an explicit reference to Jerusalem as an authoritative center from which the "covenantal letter to the diaspora" would have been sent was even less necessary. The "apostle-prophet" John's obvious involvement in the core leadership of the Jerusalem church would have made any reference to Jerusalem redundant. Furthermore, if Revelation was written in the latter half of the first century CE, then any mention of Jerusalem would have been anachronistic given the dispersion of the Jewish *Christos*-followers from there following the Roman occupation of the city in 70 CE. If, however, one does not identify the "John" of Revelation as an "apostle-prophet," then given his self-identification as a prophet (10:1ff), one would need to place him among "the prophets" referenced in Eph 4:11a. The result of this, though, is that the authoritative spiritual status of the writer of Revelation is then undermined, which lessens his chance of being viewed as an authoritative replacement for Jerusalem of his ostensible covenantal letter to the seven diasporic *Christos*-following *ekklēsiai* in Roman Asia.

JOHN THE PROPHET AND THE HEBREW BIBLE PROPHETS

Not only does Paul's prophetic experience mirror the call of a Hebrew Bible prophet, but so also does John's. F. D. Mazzaferri claims that "John's Call Narrative [Rev 10:1–11] follows the ancient paradigm very faithfully indeed, except for the minor novelty of the angel [*angeles interpres*]."[163]

---

163. Mazzaferri, *Genre of the Book of Revelation*, 296.

He summarizes the most basic features of the Hebrew Bible prophetic paradigm that are elucidated by N. C. Habel in his classic analysis of the literary form of the prophetic call narrative.[164] They are: (1) the divine confrontation; (2) the introductory word; (3) the commission; (4) the objection; (5) the reassurance; and (6) the sign.[165] The first three characteristics predominate in John's prophetic commission (1:9–20; 10:1–11). Since John offers no protest to the divine call, the reassurance and the sign are superfluous.

But Mazzaferri goes beyond identifying John's commissioning with just the general characteristics of Hebrew Bible prophecy. He also identifies it with one specific Hebrew Bible prophet. He claims that not only is Revelation 10 "John's personal Call Narrative, patterned closely on the classical paradigm in general [but specifically on] Ezekiel's call in particular."[166] The most obvious similarity between the prophetic call narratives of Ezekiel and John involves their consumption of an opened scroll of prophecy (Ezek 2–3 and Rev 10). Aside from the parallel between their prophetic commissions, there are also correspondences between their literary formulae for the introduction of visionary experiences (e.g., an "imperial space/time referent"), as has been highlighted in my earlier review of the three visionary literary devices.[167]

JOHN THE "APOSTLE-PROPHET" AND NEW TESTAMENT PROPHETS

While it is evident that, for John, the authority of the *apokalypsis* (1:1) is explicitly connected with his encounter of the resurrected Christ (1:12–20), this does not necessarily mean that John's personal authority with the seven *ekklēsiai* of Roman Asia derives from that experience. In fact, his self-identification to the *ekklēsiai* by way of his first name, without any further identifying characteristics, would seem to favor a pre-existing intimate, if not even authoritative, status for John within those *Christos*-following communities. This would make superfluous any explicit statement by John as to his apostolic status.

164. Habel, "The Form and Significance," 297.

165. Mazzaferri, *Genre of the Book of Revelation*, 89–90. Cf. Habel ("The Form and Significance," 317–19) for how he defines each of the six elements of the call narrative.

166. Mazzaferri, *Genre of the Book of Revelation*, 295.

167. Although John also alludes to Ezekiel's prophecy (e.g., the vision of the New Jerusalem [Ezek 40—48; Rev 21:9—22:5]) this is not germane to the present discussion on correspondences in their prophetic call commissions.

The apparent breadth of John's identification with Pauline theological, thematic, literary, and linguistic characteristics would not only have
served to enhance the relevance of the Apocalypse's message to a Pauline
audience but may in fact even have served to reinforce a pre-existing
apostolic brotherhood with Paul. If this is the case, then this reinforces
a correlation of the diasporic "John" of the Apocalypse with the Judean
apostle John.

Regardless of whether the "John" of the Apocalypse is the apostle by
the same name, the fact remains that it is not unreasonable to assume an
implicit claim on his part to an apostolic authority similar to that of the
apostle Paul.[168] This implicit apostolic claim clarifies the prophetic sub-
genre to which the book of Revelation most closely adheres. A categorization of the "revelation of Jesus Christ" as an "early Christian" or "New
Testament" prophecy would only identify Revelation with the non-author-
itative version of prophecy described in 1 Cor 14:29.[169] John's visionary
message, however, appears to presume an authoritative status not unlike
that of an Hebrew Bible prophecy.

Given the correlation of John's *apokalypsis* to Pauline (and deutero-
Pauline) literary and theological features, John's prophetic writing may
also be reflective of the potential Pauline sub-genre that I call "apostolic
-prophecy." Mazzaferri claims that the uniqueness of John's prophetic
commission is without parallel: "John's call draws him close to the OT
prophets, but he does not share the experience even with the NT prophets. This sets him apart from the apocalypticists as well."[170] Placing the
Apocalypse within the very selective category of "apostolic-prophecy"
appears to do justice to this uniqueness. It also reaffirms the authoritative
status of its prophetic proclamations (e.g., 21:18, 19: "everyone who hears
the words of the prophecy . . . and adds to them, God will add to him the
plagues . . . and if anyone takes away from the words of the book of this
prophecy, God will take away his part from the tree of life").

John as one of the Twelve "Apostle-Prophets"

We also see a "foundation" (*themelios*; e.g., Eph 2:20) metaphor in the
book of Revelation wherein the foundation of the New Jerusalem is

168. 1 Cor 14:37–38 illustrates Paul's apostolic authority over a Christian prophet.

169. Cf. R. L. Thomas's argument for Revelation as New Testament prophecy. 1 Cor
14:29 reads "Let two or three prophets speak, and let the others weigh what is said."

170. Mazzaferri, *Genre of the Book of Revelation*, 296.

symbolically comprised of the twelve apostles of the Lamb. In the pericope beginning at 21:9, 10, an angel takes John to a high mountain in order to show him "the bride, the wife of the Lamb." Instead of being shown a vision of a person or of the people of God, John is shown the New Jerusalem coming down out of heaven. As indicated, this strongly implies that the New Jerusalem is not a place for people, but a people who are place.[171] By recounting this visionary experience, John is telling his seven *ekklēsia* that the New Jerusalem is a symbolic picture of themselves, and all other *ekklēsiai*, past, present, and future; in other words, the universal *ekklēsia* of Jesus the *Christos*.

John then goes on to describe the twelve gates and the wall of the city which has a twelve-fold foundation (21:14). Each of the twelve layers is comprised of a different precious stone. Upon each layer of the foundation is written the name of one of the twelve apostles of the Lamb. This accords very well with the (deutero-)Pauline reference to individuals called "the apostles and prophets" who are presented as being the foundation of the universal *ekklēsia* (Eph 2:20).

A. Y. Collins contests such a conclusion, though. She argues that the inscription of the twelve names of the apostles upon the twelve-fold foundation of the New Jerusalem lessens, if not even denies, the apostolic authority of the "John" of the book of Revelation since that description "is characteristic of a time in which the age of the apostles is past. It is unlikely that a living apostle would speak in such a way."[172] This is not a necessary assumption, though, as early Jewish precedents do exist.

This association of a spiritual community and its current leaders with "building" imagery is not simply a Christ-follower concept. The use of "temple" and "city" imagery for the people of God in Ephesians and Revelation has striking parallels in Essene sectarian literature. The community of Qumran saw themselves collectively as forming a temple of God and their spiritual leaders as forming the foundation of that temple. Their identification of themselves as a temple of God was "an intermediate situation in which they rejected the existing temple cult and lived in expectation of the rebuilding of the true and unpolluted eschatological temple."[173] This temple ideology is found in 1QS and CD. Therein, mem-

---

171. See also 21:1, 2 where the New Jerusalem is described as coming down from heaven "as a bride adorned for her husband."

172. A. Y. Collins, "Book of Revelation," *ABD* 5.694–708, esp. 702.

173. Aune, "Qumran and the Book of Revelation," 641.

bers of the sect refer to themselves as "a holy house" (i.e., a temple) and to their opponents, the "Searchers of slippery things," as "a city of iniquity."[174]

With respect to the council of the Essene community, the spiritual leaders of this "holy house," they themselves were also viewed as "the holy house of Israel" (1QS 8.5). Their primacy within the community is even further emphasized with their ensuing description as "the foundation of the holy of holies of Aaron" (1QS 8.5–6).[175] In 4QpIs^d (4Q164), which is a pesher on Isa 54:11, "the council of the Community, the priests and the people" are correlated with the sapphire foundations of the implied New Jerusalem.[176] The council of the *Yachad* was comprised of "twelve men and three priests, perfect from everything that has been revealed from all the law" (1QS 8.1, 2).[177] This demonstrates that the Essenes "tended to identify their community with the holy city, just as they did with the Temple."[178]

J. A. Draper concludes, on the basis of a comparison of Revelation (21:14; 19ff) with 1QS (The Rule of the Community) and 4Q164 (4QpIs^d), that both the author of Revelation and the Qumran community were heirs to a definite method of Hebrew Bible interpretation.[179] Revelation's parallel imagery with Qumran includes seeing the community of salvation as a holy building (21:9, 10) whose twelvefold leadership is its foundation (21:14) that is composed of precious stones (21:19–20). This common stock of imagery may even have implications for the apostolic nature of the prophecy called the *apokalypsis* (Rev 1:9—22:20).

The author of Revelation presumes a position of spiritual leadership, possibly even as an apostle-prophet, among the seven *ekklēsiai* of Asia Minor (1:1–8, 11). In light of Qumranic literature, it does not seem unreasonable that, while still alive, John could envision himself being part of the foundation of the New Jerusalem, that city which is identified so closely

174. "Holy house": 1QS 5.6; 8.5, 9; 9.6; 22.8; CD 3.19; 20.10, 13. "City of iniquity: 1QpHab 10.10. See further, Dimant, "Qumran Sectarian Literature," 514.

175. García Martínez and Tigchelaar, *Dead Sea Scrolls Study Edition*, 1.88, 89.

176. García Martínez, *Dead Sea Scrolls Translated*, 190.

177. García Martínez and Tigchelaar, *Dead Sea Scrolls Study Edition*, 1.89.

178. Murphy-O'Connor, "Jerusalem," 404. While affirming that "the 'temple' was used both at Qumran and in early Christianity as a metaphor for the community of salvation in the end time," Aune notes that "there is [no] indication that the temple-city in 11QT^a [nor] the city in DNJ [the "Description of the New Jerusalem"; 1Q32, 2Q24, 4Q554–555^a, 5Q15, 11Q18] . . . symbolizes their respective communities" ("Qumran and the Book of Revelation," 640).

179. Draper, "Twelve Apostles," 41–63.

with the people of God, "the bride, the wife of the Lamb" (Rev 21:9, 10). Given the evidence from Qumran, this conclusion is still possible even if one does not use Eph 2:19–22 and 3:5 as corroborative evidence that a *living* spiritual leader could form a part of the community of salvation.

LITERARY IMPLICATIONS OF THE APOCALYPSE AS "APOSTOLIC-PROPHECY"

If the sub-genre of "apostolic-prophecy" is an appropriate literary category for text written by an "apostle-prophet," and if the Apocalypse can be classified as an "apostolic-prophecy," then the Apocalypse is more than a record of an apocalyptic journey in which heavenly mysteries are revealed to the reader. Rather, the book of Revelation then assumes an inherently authoritative status with its readership; a status that is given reinforcement through Revelation's claims of eternal consequences for anyone who tampers with the written record of the *apokalypsis* of Jesus the *Christos* (22:18, 19).

A classification of Revelation as "apostolic-prophecy" also allows one to take seriously its claim to contain prophetically predictive elements ("the things which must soon take place" [1:1; 22:6]; "the things which will take place after these things"[1:19]). In line with the accountability of an Hebrew Bible prophet (Deut 18:20–22), John's prophetic call (10:11) would also be subject to similar scrutiny with respect to the fulfillment of any predictive prophecy. John wrote "the words of the prophecy of this book" (Rev 22:7, 10, 18, 19) to a specific community (the seven *ekklēsiai* of Roman Asia), who knew him so well that his epistolary benediction (1:4–8) only required his first name. This presumption of intimacy in their relationship would have exponentially increased John's sense of personal accountability to them for "words of the prophecy of this book" that he addressed to them. If it is also true that John assumed apostolic authority for the content of his Apocalypse, then, perhaps, in line with a Hebrew Bible prophet, he would have understood the personal consequences of unfulfilled prophecy. In this light, John's claim of predictive authority for his *apokalypsis* (1:1, 3, 19) lends greater credence to his prophetic message.

Revelation's Jewish Eschatology

Having explored the literary and narratological organization of John's Apocalypse earlier in this chapter, a theological task still remains. Does John's Apocalypse reflect Jewish apocalyptic and/or Hebrew prophetic eschatology?

Hebrew Prophetic Eschatology

Hanson notes that apocalyptic eschatology and prophetic eschatology "are best viewed as two sides of a continuum. The development from the one to the other is not ineluctably chronological, however, but is intertwined with changes in social and political changes."[180] Thus, Hanson suggests that it is in periods of history during which the community envisioned an improvement in their historical situation through human effort that their literature reflected a prophetic eschatology. By contrast, it is during periods of intense suffering, with its resultant loss of humanistic optimism, that a community defaulted to an apocalyptic eschatology. Hanson is appropriately careful to nuance his differentiation of the social circumstances behind the development of the two eschatologies. He reminds us that we need to keep in constant tension "the recognition that prophecy itself underwent many changes and that there are numerous striking similarities between late prophecy and early apocalyptic."[181]

All things considered, there is still a generally distinctive tone between prophetic and apocalyptic eschatology. Prophetic eschatology "was an optimistic perspective which anticipated that God would eventually restore the originally idyllic and pristine conditions by acting through historical processes."[182] In this respect, Hanson claims that what the prophet witnessed in the divine council he "translates into the terms of plain history, real politics, and human instrumentality; that is . . . how the plans of the divine council will be effected within the context of their nation's history and the history of the world."[183] Thus, the Hebrew prophet presented the unfolding of God's plans in terms that depicted divine intervention being effected through actual historical and political

180. Hanson, "Apocalypses and Apocalypticism," 281.

181. Aune, "Apocalypticism," 47.

182. Aune, "Apocalypticism," 47.

183. Hanson, *Dawn of Apocalyptic*, 11.

events and processes. Prophecy is essentially optimistic in its expectation of restoration within human history while apocalypticism is essentially pessimistic. Thus, apocalyptic eschatology presents the necessity of the future breaking into the present for the realization of restoration, while prophecy sees this future restoration as arising out of the present.[184]

With respect to corporate or national salvation, prophetic eschatology could profitably be understood in two related phrases: "last days/ end of days" and the "last day/the end/day of the Lord." As previously indicated, Peter aligns the coming of the Holy Spirit (and the invisible birth of the universal *ekklēsia*) on the day of Pentecost (Acts 2:14–21) with "the last days" (*eschatais hēmerais*) envisioned in the book of Joel (2:28–32). John appears to use a similar framework for his cosmic drama. His seven *ekklēsiai* could very well have viewed John's correlation of the Sea Beast and Babylon imagery with the Roman religio-political *imperium* as indicating that they were already living in the "last days" which just now awaited the "Last Day" of Christ's salvific *parousia*. This dual focus of immediate fulfillment but yet which still awaits ultimate fulfillment is consonant with Hebrew prophetic eschatology and in many respects with the sectarian eschatology of the (pre)Covenanters of Qumran.

Hebrew prophetic eschatology can be encapsulated in two Hebrew terms: *qets* ("end") and *aharit ha-yamim* ("end of days").[185] The *qets* is generally a specific, decisive event—the day of judgment. But this day of judgment is not usually seen as being the end of the world but rather as the end of "a world," that is, the end of Israel as an independent nation (e.g., Amos 8:2). Where cosmic judgment is found, the day of the LORD motif emphasizes both destruction of the wicked and exaltation of the LORD and deliverance of his faithful ones (e.g., Isa 2:10–22; 13:9–13; Zeph 1:14–16). The *aharit ha-yamim*, which originally was used of future turning points in Israel's history (e.g., Deut 4:30; 31:29), evolved into the expectation of a definitive transformation of Israel in the distant future (e.g., Isa 2; Mic 4). Daniel and Ezekiel broadened that time of salvation also to include the dramatic events that will lead up to the culminating

184. J. J. Collins states that "For the prophets the most significant action takes place on earth. Even if a decision is taken in the divine council, it is acted out on earth, in 'plain history.' For the apocalypticists, however, the most significant action takes place between heavenly mythological beings, in the conflict of God and Belial, Christ and Anti-Christ, angels and demons, sons of light and sons of darkness" ("Apocalyptic Eschatology," 30).

185. See further in Collins, "Expectation of the End in the DSS," 74–90 and Collins, "Eschatology," 256–61.

point of salvation. Daniel uses the Aramaic equivalent of "the end of days" in Nebuchadnezzar's dream of the four kingdoms and the final kingdom of God in heaven (Dan 2). Collins comments that in Ezek 38 "the end of days" is "the time when Gog invades Israel, and so is a time of distress, but one that culminates in the destruction of the invader."[186]

The Dead Seas Scrolls continue this broadening of the *aharit ha-ya-mim*. 4Q174 (Florilegium) explains Ps 2 as "a time of refining that comes . . . as it is written in the book of Daniel, the prophet." Catena[a] describes the testing and refining of the men of the *yachad* ("community") at the end of days, while 4QMMT indicates that the (pre)Covenanters were already in the time of testing.[187] Thus, Qumran sectarian expectations were that the "end of days" would be a time of incipient salvation, that is, "the last period of time, directly before the time of salvation."[188] The time of salvation is when messianic deliverance and conflict with Belial would occur.[189] It is of interest to note, though, that in the sectarian document 1Q28[a] (Rule of the Congregation), the future coming of the two messiahs, the priestly "messiah of Aaron" and of the royal "messiah of Israel," do not greatly affect societal conditions.[190]

Unlike prophetic eschatology, Collins contends that an apocalyptic worldview does not localize the restoration of idyllic bliss only within the context of communal fulfillment or of a future resurrection:

> Apocalyptic still deals with a communal context, whether it be the nation or, more often, the just. However, its concern has extended to the life of the individual. By its focus on heavenly, supernatural realities it provides a possibility that human life can transcend death, not merely by the future generations of the nation [which is the emphasis of prophecy] but by passing to the higher, heavenly sphere. It is this hope for the transcendence

---

186. Collins, *Apocalypticism*, 56.

187. See further in Collins, "Eschatology," 256–61.

188. Collins, "Eschatology," 258.

189. Cf. 1QS (1QSerek; Community Rule), CD (Damascus Document), 1QM (War Scroll).

190. For more detailed descriptions of the two messiahs of Qumran, see Collins, *Apocalyptic Imagination*, 160–66. The royal warrior messiah is often paired with, yet subordinated to, the priestly messiah (e.g., CD 12:22b—13:1a; 14:19; 19:11; 20:1; cf. 1QS 9:11). Both are human beings, not divine figures. The messiah of Aaron "will fill the same role in the community as the historical Teacher" (Collins, *Apocalyptic Imagination*, 164).

of death which is the distinctive character of apocalyptic over against prophecy.[191]

While certainly plausible, the confidence with which Collins holds forth transcendence of death as the *prima facia* characteristic of apocalyptic eschatology may be open to question given the limited scope of the literature surveyed. As previously indicated, Collins does not include any material earlier than the second century (e.g., the late prophetic books) nor later than the first century BCE (i.e., 4 *Ezra*, 2 *Baruch* and the Apocalypse of John). His main text is Daniel with supplementary material from the Qumran Scrolls, 1 *Enoch*, *Jubilees*, and the *Assumption of Moses*. Of course, given the controversy surrounding the dating of Daniel and Collins's use of Daniel as a *primary* witness for second-century BCE Jewish apocalyptic literature, one may question the conclusiveness of his observations.

When considering sectarian Qumran literature, Collins notes that the transcendence of death is not just a *future* reality, as in Dan 12, 1 *En.* 104:2, 6, and the *Similitudes* (1 *En.* 39:5). The Essenes believed that they experienced transcendence of death within the context of their *present* community. This may explain somewhat the dearth of references to the resurrection of the dead. In 1QH (1QHodayot^a) death is not a theological problem. Rather, the community's fellowship with the community of angels was used as evidence that it had already transcended death.[192] While Revelation affirms the physical resurrection of the body (20:4-6), a transformation of the earth (21:1), and the ushering in of a new age (21:2—22:20), all of which are reflective of apocalyptic divine intervention, one's *present* experience of the transcendence of death also receives emphasis (e.g., the New Jerusalem as the people and presence of God on earth).[193]

191. Collins, "Apocalyptic Eschatology," 30.

192. For example, even though the first three columns of 1QH have only survived in very fragmentary form, Collins translates 1QH iii.19-23 as "I give thanks to you, O Lord; For you have redeemed me from the pit; And from Sheol Abaddon you have lifted me up to the eternal height . . . to be stationed with the host of the holy ones; And to enter the fellowship with the congregation of the children of heaven; And you have apportioned to man an eternal destiny with the spirits of knowledge" ("Apocalyptic Eschatology," 72). Angelic presence in the community is reflected in 1QS^a ii.3-11: "No man who suffers from a single one of the uncleannesses that affect humanity shall enter their assembly. . . . For the holy angels are [a part of] their congregation" (Michael Wise et al., *Dead Sea Scrolls*, 146).

193. See chapter 7 (in the section entitled "The Cubic New Jerusalem as the Present Covenantal People of God"). For examples of the transcendence of death in heaven

Revelation and Jewish Apocalyptic Eschatology

David Aune notes nine features of apocalyptic eschatology upon which there appears to be general scholarly agreement.[194] Each is represented in John's Apocalypse. These are not exhaustive but illustrative of some of the distinctive perspectives of an apocalyptic eschatology: (1) a sharp distinction between the present age and the age to come (i.e., temporal dualism); (2) a pessimistic outlook with respect to this present age as opposed to an otherworldly hope focused on the future age to come; (3) a resultant radical discontinuity between this age and the age to come; (4) the periodization of history according to a predetermined plan (e.g., segments of four, seven, twelve); (5) angels and demons are introduced to explain historical and eschatological events; (6) an imminent divine intervention in history in which the reign of God is established and the present world order is destroyed; (7) this impending crisis is cosmic in scope and individual salvation or judgment is emphasized as opposed to a collective/corporate location of the individual (e.g., within Israel or the people of God); (8) God's cataclysmic intervention results in the salvation for the righteous which is depicted in terms of the *Urzeit* of the Garden of Eden; and (9) a new mediator for humanity with royal functions is introduced, otherwise known as a/the Messiah (*Christos*).[195]

Temporal Dualism

One of the essential characteristics of apocalypticism is a belief system according to which the cosmos is divided under two supernatural protagonists, God and Satan, who represent the moral qualities of good and evil, respectively. This cosmological dualism is limited in scope and time, however, since, in Jewish thought, God as the absolute Sovereign over all creation is in some fashion the originator of evil. Thus, like the dualism of ancient Iranian religion, the resultant moral dualism is *neither absolute nor eternal.*

This cosmological dualism expressed itself in three distinct ways in early Jewish apocalypticism.[196] Temporal dualism sharply distinguishes

---

before the *parousia* see: (1) the souls under the heavenly altar (6:9–11), and (2) the righteous multitude in heaven (7:9–17).

194. Aune, "Apocalypticism," 48.

195. Aune, "Apocalypticism," 48.

196. Aune, "Apocalypticism," 49.

between this age and the age to come. The belief in two successive ages only slowly unfolded in Judaism, but by the end of the first century it was well established (e.g., 4 *Ezra* 7:50: "The Most High has not made one Age but two"). Ethical dualism divides humanity into two mutually exclusive groups, the righteous and the wicked, who are seen to correspond to the supernatural powers with whom their allegiances lie. The War Scroll clearly reveals the Essene ethical dualism in which humanity is divided into two camps: the people of God and the Kittim (1QM 1.6; 18.2–3). Psychological dualism emphasizes an internalization of this dualism such that a struggle between the forces of good and evil ensues within the personhood of individuals. A Christ-follower example of this perspective is enunciated by the apostle Paul in Rom 6—8, wherein he ostensibly describes the believer's internal battle between flesh and spirit.

The book of Revelation clearly presumes a temporal dualism in which the forces of evil represented by the unholy trinity of Satan (12:3–17; 20:1–10), the Beast (13:1–10; 19:19–21) and the False Prophet (13:11–18; 19:19–21) lead ungodly humanity in battle against the holy Trinity of the Father (4:2–11), the Son (5:1–10; 19:11–16), and of the Spirit (4:5) and their saints (12:6–17; 13:7; 20:7–9).

Present Pessimism and Future Hope

One of the ramifications of a belief in temporal dualism, is a more pessimistic outlook on the redeeming qualities of this present age. This perspective represents apocalypticism well. This contrasts with the more optimistic outlook espoused within prophetic works. This apocalyptic pessimism is tempered with an equally confident emphasis on an otherworldly hope which is specifically focused on the future age to come.

This dual alignment of present-worldly pessimism with a next-worldly optimism is germane to the book of Revelation as well. The inevitability of divine wrath upon unrepentant humanity is pervasive in the seal, trumpet, and bowl judgments. The temporal inadequacy of this present age is implicitly affirmed in the description of the passing away of "the first heaven and the first age" (21:1). The idea that optimism can only be based on the expectation of a new age is expressly communicated in the depiction of a new heaven and a new earth (21:1) and the eternal New Jerusalem (21:9—22:20) in which "nothing unclean, and no one who practices abomination and lying, shall ever come into it" (21:27).

Radical Discontinuity between This Age and the Age to Come

This pessimism with respect to the viability of this present world order, translates into a vision of a radically discontinuous next world. One example of this is in Zech 14, where there is "the notion of a fundamentally different sort of cosmic and social order."[197] The various elements of this radical discontinuity within Zech 14 provide a metonymous template for understanding this phenomenon in apocalyptic eschatology generally. Zechariah 14 describes a cosmic and social order in which one's "experience of time, natural order, social existence, religious affiliation, even Yahweh's lordship, will be of a fundamentally different sort of form that which had existed earlier."[198]

This radical discontinuity is especially evident at the end of the book of Revelation, starting at chapter 21. Therein, a new cosmic and social order is presented in which: (1) time is no more (21:1);[199] (2) the old cosmos is supplanted with a new heaven and a new earth (21:1); (3) a new social order is established in which all of the ungodly are eternally exiled to the "lake of fire" (21:8; 22:15); (4) there is no longer any remnant of temple-centered worship (21:22: there is no temple in the city), and (5) the immediacy of YHWH's presence is the eternal experience of redeemed humanity (21:4, 22–23; 22:3–5).

A Periodization of History

The apocalyptic periodization of history proceeds from the underlying assumption that God's purposes will unfold according to a predetermined plan. This periodization is usually construed in segments of four (e.g., Dan 7:1–28), seven (e.g., Dan 9:25: seven weeks of years), or twelve (1 En. 89.51–72; 90.6–12).[200]

197. Petersen, "Eschatology" 578.

198. Petersen, "Eschatology," 578. See also Isa 65:17–25.

199. The destruction of time is implied in 21:1 in the ostensible destruction of the original created order, including its planetary movements, and its replacement by a recreated and eternal heaven/sky and earth.

200. Of the seventy shepherds in the Animal Apocalypse (1 En. 85—90), that together represent four different epochs in Israel's history, Tiller identifies the first set of twelve as the Babylonian period and the second set of twelve as the Seleucid period. The two sets of twenty-three shepherds are said to represent the Persian and Ptolemaic periods (Animal Apocalypse, 55).

This sense of predetermined timeframes prior to divine intervention is evident in Revelation with respect to the timing of cosmic transformation. Chronological markers such as three-and-a-half years/forty-two months/1,260 days are tied to eschatological portents of the divine timetable for ultimate deliverance (e.g., 12:14: the "woman" is kept safe in the desert for 1,260 days; 13:5: forty-two months is the time allotted to the Beast for his blasphemous reign).

While not necessarily reflective of historical periodization, the numbers four, seven, and twelve play a significant organizational and theological role in the Apocalypse. The seven seals and trumpets are grouped into two thematically connected sets of four and three judgments each. The number four is represented in the four living creatures (4:6–9). The number seven in its metaphorical use for "completeness" pervades the *apokalypsis* (e.g., seven lampstands, seven *ekklēsiai*, seven stars, seven seals, seven trumpets, seven bowls, seven horns and eyes of the Lamb). The number twelve as the sign of God's covenant people is evident in the twenty-four elders (4:4), the 144,000 (7:4–8; 14:1), the twelve gates of the New Jerusalem (21:12), and the twelve foundations of the city upon which are inscribed the names of the twelve apostles (21:14).

Angels and Demons

Not only does an apocalyptic eschatology introduce angels and demons to help explain historical and eschatological events, but a uniquely apocalyptic theme is the eschatological judgment of heavenly beings. This is clearly envisioned for Satan, the king of the kingdom of darkness, in his banishment to the lake of fire (20:10). His human cohorts meet a similar fate in 19:20. Implied in the finality inherent in these scenes of eternal punishment is the summary punishment of all of Satan's minions who also are a part of his evil kingdom.

Imminent Divine Intervention

Within an apocalyptic eschatology, God's intervention in human history is expected with a sense of imminence. This divine intervention will result in the establishment of God's reign and the destruction of the present world order. Two important corollaries with respect to the process of divine judgment need to be made.

First, while prophetic eschatology may picture God using oppressing nations to punish Jews for breaking the covenant (e.g., Amos 4—8), apocalyptic eschatology links the oppressing nations with cosmic powers that are opposed to God.[201] A second, and related, apocalyptic motif is that the defeat of these ungodly nations and the cosmic powers with which they are associated is accomplished by direct divine intervention without any human agency.[202]

Revelation explicitly conveys this sense of imminence in its opening verse: "The revelation of Jesus the *Christos* which God gave him to show his bond-servants, the things which must soon take place." The expectation of divine intervention without the aid of any human agency is clearly depicted in a variety of images. The most poignant image is of the heavenly army being led by the Word of God, who is called the King of kings and the Lord of lords, and who singlehandedly defeats the armies of the Beast (19:11–21).

Individual Salvation or Judgment is Emphasized

Although this impending crisis is cosmic in scope, an apocalyptic eschatology also emphasizes an individualistic aspect to human salvation or judgment. This contrasts with a prophetic eschatology in which the fate of the individual is inextricably linked with the fate of the collective or corporate group (e.g., the fate of Israel or of the people of God).

With respect to the prospect of individual salvation, Aune notes two key distinctives of apocalypticism over against that of the prophetic.[203] He contends, firstly, that apocalyptic salvation is always eschatological while that of the prophetic may simply have an earthly focus that emphasizes peace in the land or a return from exile with its concomitant restoration of political, religious, and social autonomy. Secondly, he states that while the prophetic may allow for the repentance of the wicked and subsequent

201. Evans and Flint, eds., *Eschatology, Messianism, and the Dead Sea Scrolls*, 2.

202. Michael E. Stone notes that the "worldview . . . [of] apocalypses tend to break the nexus of a directly operative causal relationship between human action and political events which lay at the basis of the Deuteronomistic literature and of the view of classical prophecy. . . . The progress and fate of the world are largely determined by superhuman forces; history is viewed as an overall process, with the vindication of God's righteousness only to be made evident at its termination" (*Jewish Writings of the Second Temple Period*, 384).

203. Aune, *Revelation 1—5*, lxxxix–xc.

mercy from YHWH, apocalyptic has no place for the repentance of the wicked. Rather, salvation is experienced only in the elimination of the wicked by YHWH so that the righteous remnant can enjoy the eschatological kingdom (sometimes pictured as Mt. Zion/Jerusalem).

While Revelation generally emphasizes the role of divine intervention in the salvation of the righteous and the elimination of the wicked, there does appear to be an opportunity for repentance given to humanity. This would mitigate somewhat an affirmation of an exclusively apocalyptic eschatology within the Apocalypse. Revelation 9:20, 21 laments the non-repentance of "the rest of mankind who were not killed by the plagues." But even in this negative assessment of humanity there is an implicit hope in it—repentance might actually have been their response. This implicit hope of repentance is given clearer voice in Rev 11:1–13. Therein the dwellers of "the great city, which is mystically called Sodom and Egypt" (11:8) experience "a great earthquake . . . [in which] seven thousand were killed . . . and the rest were terrified and gave glory to the God of heaven" (11:13). The act of giving glory to God implies a repentant heart, although, admittedly, that is not explicitly indicated in the text.

With respect to the judgment of individuals at the end of history, J. J. Collins differentiates apocalyptic and prophetic eschatologies in that "*all* the apocalypses . . . involve a transcendent eschatology that looks for retribution beyond the bounds of history (even if no reference to the end of history is made; e.g., 3 *Baruch, Apocalypse of Zephaniah*)."[204] This differentiates it from prophetic literature, which does not necessarily espouse this temporal perspective on retribution. The book of Revelation reflects the apocalyptic emphasis on retribution beyond the bounds of history in its final three chapters. Chapter 20 particularly emphasizes the horrible prospect of divine retribution upon those who remain unrepentant in its description of their eternal banishment to the lake of fire.

Salvation Is Depicted in Terms of Urzeit Fulfilled

This cataclysmic intervention of God in human history is also pictured in utopian terms for the righteous. God's salvation on behalf of his saints is depicted in terms reminiscent of the *Urzeit* of the Edenic paradise. Hanson argues that the transition from prophetic to apocalyptic eschatology is evident in Isa 55—66. In particular, Hanson claims that

204. Collins, *Apocalyptic Imagination*, 11.

the essential characteristics of apocalyptic eschatology are drawn together into a coherent whole in Isaiah 65: the present era is evil; a great judgement separating the good from the evil and marking the crossroads between the present world and the world to come is imminent; a newly created world of peace and blessing ordained for the faithful lies beyond that judgement. These teaching of world epochs, universal judgement, and a modified dualism are the basic components of later apocalyptic eschatology.[205]

If this is the case then the correspondence of Rev 21—22 with Isa 65 suggests a common apocalyptic eschatology. Isaiah 65:17 and 66:22 predict the creation of a new heaven and a new earth in which there is no sorrow (65:19) and no killing (65:24; the lion and the lamb lie down together). Life is extended (65:20) and a personal relationship with YHWH is reestablished (65:24; 66:23). The vision episode of the Apocalypse also presents the eschatological finale in terms of *Urzeit*. This is especially evident in the New Jerusalem *individual vision* (21:2—22:20). In this eternal paradise, which is established on the new earth (21:1), there also will be no sorrow (21:4) in light of an eternal personal relationship with the Lord of Glory (21:3; 22:3, 4). The clearest allusion to the *Urzeit* of the Garden of Eden is the reintroduction of the tree of life. It is now said to bear twelve kinds of fruit as it grows on either side of the street of the city down the middle of which flows the river of the water of life (22:1–2). The curse, which first came into existence because of humanity's sin in the Garden, is now abolished forever (22:3a). John's "great earthquake" (6:12; 11:13; 16:19) appears to be patterned after the Noachic flood that is eschatologized in Isa 24.[206]

A Messianic Expectation

During the Second Temple period two main types of messianic expectation were in circulation: restorative and utopian messianism. Restorative messianism placed its hope in a restoration of the Davidic reign in which the conditions of the present world would progressively reflect the idyllic model (*Pss. Sol.* 17). In this way, the nostalgic glories of the past are projected into the future. In contrast, utopian messianism anticipates a

---

205. Hanson, *Dawn of Apocalyptic*, 160. Cf. also p. 185.
206. See further in pages 223 to 228.

future world that exponentially surpasses anything experienced in the past. Rather than being focused upon a dynastic kingdom, this messianic expectation prioritized the coming of a single messianic king sent by God to restore Israel's fortunes. But not all Jewish eschatological writings emphasized a messianic intermediary for divine restoration. Thus, for example, no mention is made of a Messiah in Joel, Isa 24—27, Daniel, Sirach, *Jubilees*, 1 and 2 Maccabees, and the Book of Watchers (1 *En.* 1—36).

In the book of Revelation, the kingly messianic figure who restores the fortunes of God's people is depicted as a heavenly conquering rider on a white horse called "Faithful and True" (19:11), "The Word of God" (19:13), and the "King of kings and the Lord of lords" (19:16) who strikes down the ungodly nations with a sharp sword which issues out from his mouth (19:15). This kingly Messiah is none other than the Son of God himself.

Revelation: Hebrew Prophetic or Jewish Apocalyptic Eschatology

Although the book of Revelation does not exhibit an exclusively apocalyptic eschatology, the weight of evidence appears to favor a predisposition in that direction. Revelation's multiple correspondences with the nine distinctive elements of apocalyptic eschatology indicate that it is not inappropriate to designate the vision episode of the Apocalypse as an "*apocalyptic* prophecy." Schüssler Fiorenza succinctly summarizes the interplay between Revelation's essentially prophetic nature (i.e., genre) and its apocalyptic eschatology. She comments that "In Revelation apocalyptic imagery and patterns also serve prophetic admonition and interpretation."[207] This is seen in the initial *individual vision/vision block* (1:9—3:22) in which there is prophetic admonition and interpretation of the existing religio-political situations that John's seven *ekklēsiai* were facing. This inaugural prophetic emphasis is revisited in the final *vision block* (18:1—22:20) in which visionary promise and exhortation are prevalent. From a preterist perspective, Schüssler Fiorenza also contends that "the central chapters of Revelation (10—14) are explicitly characterized as prophetic interpretation of the Christian community's situation."[208]

---

207. Schüssler Fiorenza, "Composition and Structure," 357.
208. Schüssler Fiorenza, "Composition and Structure," 357.

If one considers my genre discussion together with this eschatology discussion, then my designation of the vision episode of Revelation as an "apocalyptic apostolic-prophecy" would not appear to be out of synch with the evidence examined.

Jewish Symbolism

John employs a broad spectrum of Jewish symbolism in his Apocalypse. This implies, at the very least, that John affirms an enduring value for Jewish social, religious, ethnic, and institutional realities from his day forward into the *eschaton*, and beyond. John's social identification with Jewish symbolism includes elements such as Jewish numerology (e.g., the numbers 6 and 7), *topoi* and tropes (e.g., apocalyptic imagery).

As with each preceding section, the question to be asked in this section is whether John's appropriation of Jewish symbolism reflects a desire to communicate how integral and enduring Jewishness is within his multi-ethnic *ekklēsiai* or, rather, to propagate an ideological agenda that displaces Jewish ethno-religious identity from his *ekklēsiai*.

Jewish Numerology and Gematria

John makes extensive use of numbers in symbolic fashion within his Apocalypse. The number seven identifies something as being complete or finished. This meaning is first evident in the number of days in the creation week, with the seventh day being "set apart" as a day of rest for Israel (Deut 5:12). Subsequent usages of the number seven in the Hebrew Bible are consistent with the theme of completion or finality. Examples of the number seven in the Hebrew Bible include: (1) seven pairs of clean animals are brought onto the Ark (Gen 7:2); (2) sacrificial animals need to be at least seven days old (Exod 22:30); (3) Joshua is commanded to travel around Jericho for seven days, and on the seventh day to circle Jericho seven times (Josh 6:3–4). Examples in the New Testament include: (1) Jesus makes seven "I am" statements in the Gospel of John; (2) forgiveness is to be granted "seventy times seven" (Matt 18:22); and (3) seven kingdom parables in Matt 13. John's use of the number seven in Revelation (fifty-four occurrences) is much more numerous than in the rest of the New Testament put together. Examples include: (1) God's judgment symbolized through seven seals, trumpets, and bowls; (2) seven letters to the seven angels of the seven *ekklēsiai* of Roman Asia; (3) the seven spirits before God's throne; and (4) the seven horns with seven eyes of the Lamb of God.

As I have noted, John's visionary episode within the Apocalypse is broken into six textual blocks. The number "six" is one number short of the number "seven," the number of completeness or perfectness. In this respect, John's delineation of only six *vision blocks* may be an implicit commentary on the incompleteness of John's visionary experience.[209] In other words, John's numerology implies that the Revelation isn't complete until the actual "revelation" (*apokalypsis*) of Jesus Christ at the end of human history. Thus, as I have already enunciated, the seventh *vision block* is none other than the "blockbuster" event of human history—the visible and actual return of Jesus the *Christos*.

At risk of unnecessary repetition, I will also revisit John's use of the number "forty." John delineates forty *individual visions* in the Apocalypse through the textual placement of "and I saw" clauses. The number "forty" can communicate that the time of testing and trials for the people of God is now completed.[210] I would suggest, though, that the theme of completion of a transitionary period in God's salvific history is more prevalent. Thus, for example, we find the number forty used in relation to transitionary timeframes such as (1) the days of rain associated with the Noachic flood, (2) the three timeframes of Moses life (Egypt, desert, exodus), (3) the years of David's reign (3 + 37 years), (4) the days of Jesus's testing in the desert, and (5) the days that Jesus walked on the earth after his resurrection.

For a Jewish hearer/reader the literary practice of associating symbolic meaning with specific numbers is a not unfamiliar practice. This practice is called "gematria." Richard Bauckham notes that "since the letters of both the Greek and the Hebrew alphabets were all used as numbers, it is possible to add up the numerical value of each letter of any Greek or Hebrew word an obtain the 'number' of the word."[211]

209. Massyngberde-Ford (*Revelation*, 48–49) emphasizes this point with her organization of the Apocalypse based on six series of six, "that is, a symbol of incompleteness congruous with the 666 . . . expressing a lack of fulfillment felt by the Baptist and his followers before the coming of Christ (13:18)."

210. John J. Davis surveys commentators who note that, within the Scriptures, the number "forty" assumes symbolic meanings such as "testing or trial" (Hartill) and "development of history, associated with salvation" (Gunner) (*Biblical Numerology*, 122–23).

211. Bauckham, *Climax of Prophecy*, 385.

The most obvious example of gematria in the book of Revelation, which was discussed in the first section of this book,[212] is John's encouragement to his *ekklēsiai* to "calculate the number of the beast" (13:18), which is said to be 666. If one uses the ancient practice of gematria, then the numerical value of the Hebrew letters which transliterate the Greek phrase *nerōn kēsar* (Nero Caesar) is 666.[213] If one transliterates the Greek letters for the word "Beast" (*thērion*) into Hebrew letters (*nwyrt*), then the numerical value also is 666.[214] Given that the number 666 is "the number of a human" (13:18), it may be that the triple reinforcement of the "sixness" of unredeemed humanity triply reiterates the fact that humanity, although created by God, is never capable ever of being divine or complete by itself.

Jewish Tropes and *Topoi*

John not only employs Jewish symbolism in his *apokalypsis*, but he also employs Jewish apocalyptic tropes and *topoi* that may very well have been familiar to his listening/reading audience.[215] One example of an apocalyptic trope is John's use of the expression "a complete number" with respect to the faithful of God. An example of an apocalyptic *topos* (tradition) is John's appropriation of the common stock judgment imagery of "blood and horses." The table below surveys some of the similar Jewish *topoi* and tropes found both in John's Apocalypse and in the Jewish apocalypse known as 4 *Ezra* (c. 90 CE).[216]

212. See the section in chapter 1, "Pre-70 CE Composition: Neronic."

213. The Hebrew letters that transliterate *nerōn kēsar* are *nrwn qsr* [nun, resh, waw, nun + qof, samekh, resh]. The numerical value of the Hebrew letters, in order, are 50+200+6+50+100+60+200 = 666 (Bauckham, *Climax of Prophecy*, 387). Some ancient manuscripts report the number of the Beast as being 616. If one transliterates "Caesar Nero" (*nerō kēsar*) into Hebrew letters then it adds up to 616 (*nrw qsr* [nun, resh, waw + qof, samekh, resh]).

214. The numerical value of each Hebrew letter is as follows: t = 400 + r = 200 + y = 10 + w = 6 + n = 50 = 666 (Bauckham, *Climax of Prophecy*, 389).

215. A topos is a traditional theme in literature, akin to an author's use of stock imagery known within a cultural context. A trope refers to a figurative or metaphorical use of a word or expression.

216. See Bauckham's extensive review of Revelation's use of Jewish *topoi* and tropes (*Climax of Prophecy*, 38–83).

Table 2 John's Apocalypse and 4 *Ezra*: Tropes and *Topoi*

A "complete" number of individuals (*trope*)	Rev 6:11 and 4 *Ezra* 4.35–36[217]
First beast is a sea beast (*topos*)	Rev 13:1–10 and 4 *Ezra* 6.49–53
Second beast is a land beast (*topos*)	Rev 13:11 and 4 *Ezra* 6.49–53
Blood up to the horses's bellies or bridles (*topos*)	Rev 14:20 and 4 *Ezra* 15.35[218]
Judgment equated with a book opening (*topos*)	Rev 20:12 and 4 *Ezra* 6.20
Image of a restored Jerusalem (*topos*)	Rev 21:1–5a and 4 *Ezra* 7.26; 10.49

Hebrew *Urzeit* as *Endzeit* in John's *Apokalypsis*

Comparatively few religious systems shared the views of ancient Mediterranean Jews and *Christos*-followers that since the created order had a beginning it must of necessity also have an end. This ideological understanding presented the completion of history in terms that reflected the idyllic conditions of earlier periods (e.g., the Garden of Eden before the fall, YHWH and Israel in the wilderness, and the golden eras of David

217. While speaking of Christ-follower martyrs who are under the altar of incense, John locates their eschatological vindication by God at the point at which "the number would be complete . . . who were soon to be killed as they themselves had been killed" (6:9–11). 4 *Ezra* 4.35–37 reads: "the souls of the righteous in their chambers ask . . . 'How long are we to remain here? . . . when the number of those like yourselves are completed." Two other Jewish apocalypses also appropriate this trope: (1) 1 *En.* 47.1–4 reads: "the holy ones . . . supplicate . . . because of the blood of the righteous . . . that justice may be done to them."; and (2) 2 *Bar.* 23.4–5a reads: "And for that number a place was prepared where the living ones might live and where the dead might be preserved. No creature will live again unless the number that has been appointed is completed."

218. Revelation 14:20b records the height and distance of the blood of judgement: "And the blood flowed from the winepress, up to the bridles of the horses, for 1,600 stadia." Only the height of the blood is recorded in the two Jewish apocalypses 4 *Ezra* and 1 *Enoch*. 4 *Ezra* (6 *Ezra*) 15.35–36 reads: "and there shall be blood from the sword as high as a horse's belly and a man's thigh and a camel's back" (6 *Ezra* is a later third-century CE Christian interpolation). 1 *Enoch* 100.3 (prior to first century CE) reads: "And the horse will walk up to its chest in the blood of sinners, and the chariot will sink up to its height." Only the distance of the blood is recorded in the rabbinic and Byzantine texts that post-date Revelation (e.g., *Ginza, y. Ta'an.* 4.8; *Lam. R.* 2:2.4; *Gitt.* 57a).

and Solomon). This schema in which the future is expected to exhibit parallels with the idyllic past is described in terms of *Urzeit* and *Endzeit*.[219]

In this regard, the conditions of eschatological salvation are usually pictured in terms of the *restoration* of primal conditions as opposed to the inauguration of a completely new epoch with no links to the past. Jewish and Christ-follower eschatology can be seen as "a mythical mode of understanding the complete realization of salvation as a *future* event or series of events which are, nevertheless, somehow linked to the *present*."[220] In Revelation, this *Urzeit/Endzeit* principle is applied to at least five images of heavenly consummation and of worldwide earthly judgment in the *eschaton*: the New Jerusalem, the "great earthquake," and the seven seals, trumpets, and bowls.

The New Jerusalem and the *Urzeit* of the Garden of Eden

Regarding final consummation, John depicts the *Endzeit* as entailing the re-creation of a new heaven (sky?) and a new earth and the visible revelation of a temple-city, the New Jerusalem. This *Endzeit* finds its *Urzeit* at the beginning of the Hebrew Bible in God's original creation—the paradisiacal Garden of Eden (Gen 3:23).[221] Some of the parallel imagery in Genesis and Revelation includes: (1) God dwelling face to face with human beings (Gen 3:8, 9 and Rev 21:3, 4); (2) gold of the highest quality (Gen 2:11, 12 and Rev 21:18); (3) a flowing river (Gen 3:10 and Rev 22:1; cf. Ezek 47:1–12); (4) the Tree of Life (Gen 3:9, 22 and Rev 22:2; cf. Ezek 47:11, 12); and (5) the removal of the Adamic "curse" (Gen 3:17 and Rev 22:3).

This eschatological New Jerusalem, however, is not just a container of a transformed *Urzeit* (e.g., the Garden). This Jewish *kosmos-polis* is itself transformed. It is not only characterized as an "un-city,"[222] but even

219. Hermann Gunkel postulates this perspective in *Schöpfung und Chaos* (1895).

220. Aune, "Eschatology," 594.

221. An association of the heavenly city with imagery reminiscent of the Garden of Eden or paradise was already common stock imagery in Jewish writings of John's day (cf. 2 *Bar.* 4.1–7 with the use of parallelism in *T. Dan.* 5.12).

222. There are four anomalous architectural features that point towards the "un-citylike" nature of Revelation's eschatological city: (1) it appears to contain only a single street (21:21); (2) explicit mention is made of the fact that John did not see a temple in the city (21:22); (3) it is built in the shape of a gargantuan cube (12,000 stadia high, wide, and long; 21:16); (4) unlike the temple-city of the DSS compilation

as a "non-city" by virtue of its implicit identification as "the bride, the wife of the Lamb" (21:2, 9, 10). As mentioned previously, the "people of God" have now become the "place of God."[223] Since God's people are now a paradisiacal place, they can never be expelled from the (eschatological) Garden. In their guise as the *polis* New Jerusalem, the eschatological "people of God" are forever in the presence of God. And, as the cubic *naos* New Jerusalem, the eschatological "people of God" forever *are* the presence of God.[224]

The "Great Earthquake" and the *Urzeit* of the Noachic Flood

Regarding John's "great earthquake," there are clear allusions to the *Urzeit* of the Noachic Flood and to its eschatologized "cousin" found in Isa 24. Even though the terror associated with John's "great earthquake" would been quite relevant to his *ekklēsiai* simply by virtue of their knowledge and experience of real earthquakes in Roman Asia, Galatia, and Phrygia, John still needed an earthquake motif that was universal and eschatological, though. The Noachic flood, which is eschatologically re-imagined in Isa 24, fits that bill perfectly and significantly better than other earthquake imagery found in the Hebrew Bible and Jewish Second Temple writings to which John could have alluded. Bauckham identifies four types of earthquake references: (1) a forerunner of God's coming (e.g., Mount Sinai; Exod 19:8; Ezek 38:19–23); (2) a key element in God's judgment of the wicked (*Sib. Or.* 3.675–93); (3) one among many natural disasters that together act as signs, or preliminary judgments, of the End

---

known as *Description of the New Jerusalem*, but like Ezekiel's temple-city (chs. 40—48), there are no human residences described in John's vision of the New Jerusalem.

223. Gundry claims that "John wanted his Christian readers . . . to see in the New Jerusalem, not their future dwelling place, but—what was even more heartening—their future selves and state" ("New Jerusalem," 264).

224. Gundry suggests that the New Jerusalem becomes "God's dwelling place in the saints rather than their dwelling place on earth" ("New Jerusalem," 256). This conception of God's people as symbolic architecture finds precedent in sectarian literature of the *yahad*, the community at Qumran. In 1QS and CD the sect refers to themselves as "a holy house" (1QS 5.6; 8.5, 9; 9.6; 22.8; CD 3.19; 20.10, 13). A clear identification of the community with the temple is found in 1QS 8.5–6 where the "council of the Community" is called "a holy house for Israel and the foundation of the holy of holies of Aaron" (קודש קודשים לאהרון). Aune claims that their self-identification as a temple of God was "an intermediate situation in which they rejected the existing temple cult and lived in expectation of the rebuilding of the true and unpolluted eschatological temple" ("Qumran and the Book of Revelation," 2.641).

(Mark 13:8; 2 *Bar.* 27:7; 4 *Ezra* 9:3); or (4) the final, great earthquake that destroys the old cosmos to make way for the new (4 *Ezra* 6.11–16; 1 *En.* 83.3–5; cf. Heb 12:27).[225]

Bauckham suggests that the earthquake of the Sinai theophany (Exod 19:8) is the model, or *Urzeit*, for the "great earthquake" of the Apocalypse. There are at least three shortcomings to his suggestion. First, the Sinai earthquake is only of a regional nature, while Revelation's earthquake is worldwide in scope. Second, the Sinai earthquake simply announces the coming of the LORD, while Revelation's earthquake is an instrument of the divine judgment. Third, the Sinai earthquake is non-eschatological, while Revelation's "great earthquake" is eschatological.

Contra Bauckham, I would forward another Hebrew Bible candidate for the *Urzeit* of the "great earthquake," which he does not address—the implied earthquake in the Noachic flood narrative (Gen 6—9). In Gen 7:11 the comment is made that in conjunction with the "waters from above" the "fountains of the great deep burst forth." This scenario would seem to imply some sort of worldwide earthquake that disrupted the earth's crust. In a previous essay, I explore how the worldwide implied earthquake in the Noachic flood narrative is transformed through Isa 24 into a worldwide eschatological earthquake.[226]

At least three substantive allusions to the Noachic flood are found in Isa 24—the waters from above,[227] an earthquake,[228] and an everlasting covenant.[229] These three flood allusions demonstrate that Isa 24 becomes a new *traditio* for the earlier *traditum* of the Noachic flood. Isaiah

225. Bauckham, "Eschatological Earthquake," 225.

226. Korner, "Great Earthquake," 143–70.

227. Unlike the Genesis flood account, in Isa 24 only (metaphorical) waters from above, but not from below, are mentioned (24:18b; "the windows of heaven were opened"). The Hebrew phraseology of Isa 24 (כִּי־אֲרֻבּוֹת מִמָּרוֹם נִפְתָּחוּ) is very similar to the Noachic flood account in Gen 7:11 (וַאֲרֻבֹּת הַשָּׁמַיִם נִפְתָּחוּ). Even though, in Isa 24:18 מָרוֹם is used instead of הַשָּׁמַיִם two factors favor its consideration as an intentional allusion to the Genesis account: (1) the same lexical substitution is made in Isa 24:21; (2) BHS comments that at v. 18 "frt ins (perhaps insert) הַשָּׁמַיִם" for מִמָּרוֹם.

228. In contrast to the Genesis account, but similar to Revelation's "great earthquake," the earthquake motif in Isa 24 is very prominent through the poetic representation of Isaiah's eschatological earthquake as being able to rend and shake the earth (24:1, 18b–20).

229. John D. Watts claims that Isa 24:5 has "obvious reference to the everlasting covenant [*berit ōlam*] of Gen 9:12[–17]" (*Isaiah* 1—33, 318). See also Sweeney, *Isaiah* 1—39, 322–23. The phrase *berit ōlam* occurs a further fifteen times in the Hebrew Bible. However, none refer to the Noachic flood or to worldwide judgment.

eschatologically transforms the Genesis account through what Fishbane calls inner-biblical aggadic exegesis.[230] Isaiah's new *traditum* of an eschatologized earthquake for divine judgment then finds a new *traditio* in Revelation's eschatological, worldwide "great earthquake" that symbolizes God's final judgment upon rebellious humanity. For ease of reference I have included two charts below that highlight the correlations between earthquake references found in Hebrew Bible and Jewish apocalyptic literary texts and the "great earthquake" references in Revelation.

There are three elements to Revelation's "great earthquake" (6:12, sixth seal): (1) worldwide divine judgment (e.g., earthly cataclysms); (2) an expressly eschatological timeframe ("the great day of their [i.e., God's and the Lamb's] wrath"; 6:17), and (3) an absence of water. It may be that because of God's promise not to use water for worldwide judgment again that a "fire" motif is correlated with the "great earthquake" as becomes evident in the reiteration of the sixth seal through the trumpets and bowls. Examples of fire judgments during the worldwide *eschaton* include the first trumpet (8:7), the sixth trumpet/second woe (9:18/11:5), and the post-millennial judgment of God (20:9). The chart below compares how John most closely appropriates Isa 24, rather than other Hebrew Bible or Jewish apocalyptic texts, as his literary precedent for Revelation's "great earthquake" imagery.

Table 3 Earthquake References in the Hebrew Bible[231]

Earthquake references with: 1) *divine judgment* **but** 2) no eschatological purview 3) no destruction by fire 4) no allusion to the flood	*Habakkuk* 3:6, A prayer set within the Mt. Sinai motif asking God to again come in power and plague pestilence. *Isaiah* 5:25, 30, A shaking/roaring in the land of Israel due to God's judgment through foreign invaders.

---

230. Fishbane, *Biblical Interpretation*, 429–31, esp. 408. *Traditum* refers to the original text. *Traditio* is the new text, to use Fishbane's terminology, which is created through aggadic exegesis. Aggadic exegesis refers to "the exegetical transformation of specific texts or traditions" (*Biblical Interpretation*, 380).

231. See the original chart in Korner, "The 'Great Earthquake,'" 152.

Earthquake references with:	*Judges* 5:4—5, After the defeat and death of Sisera, Deborah celebrates in song and recounts how God's presence at Mt. Sinai was accompanied by an earthquake and watery deluge.
1) *divine judgment*	
2) *allusion to the flood*	
but	
3) <u>no</u> eschatological purview	
4) <u>no</u> destruction by fire	
Earthquake references with:	*Joel* 2:10 *and* 3:16 [4:16], Set within the context of the "Day of the Lord," the earth is said to quake, the heavens to tremble, the sun and the moon to be darkened, and the stars to withdraw their shining.
1) *divine judgment*	
2) *eschatological* purview	
but	*Ezek* 38:18–23, God's day of wrath against Gog will result in a great shaking in the land of Israel.
3) <u>no</u> destruction by fire	
4) <u>no</u> allusion to the flood	*Zech* 14:4, God is depicted as splitting the Mount of Olives in two when he stands upon it at his appearing in judgment. This "earthquake," however, is analogized to the one experienced during the days of Uzziah, not to the one during the flood.
Earthquake references with:	*Isaiah* 24:18b–20; *cf.* 24:5, An "earth-rending" quake is part of God's judgment upon הָאָרֶץ ("the earth/land") when he comes to reign on Mt. Zion. This earthshaking judgment is said to derive from the inhabitants of the earth having broken God's "eternal covenant" with Noah (cf. Gen 9:16).
1) *divine judgment*	
2) *eschatological* purview	
3) *destruction by fire*	
4) *allusion to the flood*	

From the above chart one can see that, while eschatological elements of the sixth seal are found in Isaiah, Joel, and Ezekiel, it is only in Isa 24 that we find each of the three key elements associated with Revelation's "great earthquake" in conjunction with an explicit allusion to the Noachic flood. The correlation with Isa 24 would have been even more explicit if John's audience were familiar with the tendentious LXX version of Isa 24, since it creates an even more explicitly eschatological focus than does the Hebrew text.[232] LXX Isa 24 also develops a remnant theme (LXX

232. At least six eschatological motifs are much more predominant in the text of LXX Isa 24 than in the MT. These six motifs, in and of themselves, do not necessarily substantiate an eschatological agenda. However, when viewed together an intentional eschatological agenda for LXX Isa 24 seems inescapable. The six eschatological motifs are: (1) a universal scope and eschatological timeframe for divine judgment (LXX 24:1, 16); (2) transgression against YHWH himself as the rationale for the universal

24:14a), which is not found in 1QIsaᵃ and the MT.[233] Since only Isa 24 alludes to the Noachic flood, and since LXX Isa 24 adds a "remnant" theme (24:14a), it is possible that the eschatological remnant of LXX Isaiah is alluding back to the faithful remnant of Noah's family who survived the original (earthquake induced) flood.[234]

Our next step is to assess how closely John's earthquake *traditio* accords with any Jewish apocalyptic tradition before privileging Isa 24 as Revelation's *traditum*. The chart below demonstrates that the juxtaposition of God's judgment with an earthquake is indeed a standard apocalyptic motif. It is to be noted, however, that only one Jewish apocalypse (1 *En.* 1:3–9) includes each of the three criteria required of a *traditum* for Revelation's "great earthquake." One shortcoming, though, which Isa 24 does not suffer, is that 1 *En.* 1.3–9 does not frame that earthquake within an *Urzeit*, not least a Noachic one.

---

scope of divine judgment (LXX 24:5, 16); (3) a more specifically future focus to the judgment of God (use of the future indicative tense); (4) a righteous remnant theme (LXX 24:6, 13b, 14a, 23); (5) the eschatological hope/joy of the righteous remnant (LXX 24:14b–16); and (6) the godly as participants with God in final eschatological judgment and glory (LXX 24:16, 21, 23).

233. The LXX makes the "remnant theme" more explicit than do 1QIsaa and the MT. In v. 6 the LXX, 1QIsaᵃ, and the MT highlight that a curse consumes the earth because its inhabitants have sinned. As a result, judgment descends "and few people/ men are left." This "remnant" does not resurface again in 1QIsaa or the MT. As such, one is left wondering if the few who are left in v. 6 are simply finished off once the earthquake unleashes its fury upon the whole earth. However, the LXX (vv. 13b and 14a) "resurrects" the righteous remnant from its uncertain state as described in v. 6. Beginning with v. 14, the eschatological joy of the godly over the divine judgment of the ungodly is described ("these shall cry aloud and they that are left on the land shall rejoice together in the glory of the Lord"). But this joy is not limited to those who are only outside the promised land. The insertion of "the remnant" back into the text at LXX 24:14a ("and they that are left on the land") makes explicit, what was missing in 1QIsaᵃ/MT 24:14–16: God's judgment of the earth/land (הָאָרֶץ; vv. 1–13) also involves his eschatological salvation of a remnant (LXX 24:14).

234. Does the tendentious reading in LXX Isa 24:14 hint at flood elements? LXX variations from the Hebrew text of v. 14 (1QIsaᵃ and the MT) are highlighted in bold: "These **shall** cry aloud; [LXX adds: "**and they that are left on the land**"] shall rejoice together [LXX does not include "**from the west** (lit. "sea")]" in the glory of the LORD; [LXX adds: "**the water of the sea shall be troubled**"].

Table 4 Earthquake References Jewish Apocalyptic Literature[235]

Earthquake references with: 1) *divine judgment* 2) *eschatological purview* 3) *destruction by fire* **but** 4) <u>no</u> allusion to flood	1 *Enoch* 1.3–9, The Lord's coming is attended with fire, mountains falling, the earth being rent and universal judgment.
Earthquake references with: 1) *divine judgment* 2) *eschatological purview* **but** 3) <u>no</u> destruction by fire 4) <u>no</u> allusion to flood	1 *Enoch* 102.1, 2, The Lord's judgment results in the luminaries failing and the earth trembling. 2 *Baruch* 27.8, The sixth part of the tribulation in the "end of days" involves earthquakes. *Testament of Moses* 10.3–5, God's wrath is attended with the ends of the earth being shaken, the sun and moon being darkened, and the stars in disarray. *Apocalypse of Zephaniah* 12.1–8, The uprooting of trees in the time of God's wrath implies an earthquake.

The Six Seals and the *Urzeit* of the Exile

The first four seals draw heavily upon Zechariah, Ezekiel, and Leviticus for their compositional framework. The four horsemen allude to the book of Zechariah (1:7–21; 6:1–15). The colors of the horses in Zechariah and Revelation are almost identical. John, however, differs from Zechariah on two points. First, John depicts only an individual horse and rider, while Zechariah describes four groups of horses (1:7–1) and four groups of horses pulling chariots (6:1–15).[236] Second, John adds a metaphorical meaning to each color relative to the plague that each horseman introduces: "white for conquest, red for bloodshed (cf. e.g., 2 Kgs 3:22–23), black for famine (cf. Targ. Jer. 14.2), and pale green for death."[237]

235. See the original chart in Korner, "The 'Great Earthquake,'" 152.

236. Beale states, however, that "the difference is not significant, since John may have deduced by implication from Zechariah 6 that four riders were in the chariots. Also, Zechariah's summary of the four sets of horses as 'the four winds of heaven' may be another factor in John depicting only four horses" (Beale, *Revelation*, 378).

237. Beale, *Revelation*, 372.

The fourth seal is reminiscent of Ezek 14:12–23 (cf. Deut 32:23–25). The trials that come upon the unfaithful who have been sent into Babylonian exile by God are seen as "four evil judgments." In order, Ezekiel lists shortage of bread and "famine" (14:13), "wild beasts" (14:15), "sword" (14:17), and "death" (14:19). If John's four seals refer to world conditions that had already happened by the time of temple destruction, then the theological point of Ezek 14 is implicitly replicated by John. Beale notes that although the main emphasis of Ezek 14:21 is that "*all* Israelites will suffer persecution because of rampant idolatry (cf. 14:3–11)," the trials also function positively "to purify the righteous remnant by testing their faith (cf. 14:14, 15, 18, 20, 22–23)."[238] For John's purposes, Beale suggests that "the church community is the focus of the judgments, . . . yet the sphere of these calamities likely extends beyond the borders of the church to the whole world. . . . Believers need to understand the dual role of these calamities so that they can accept them in a positive manner as tools of sanctification, yet also realizing that these same trials are punishments upon unbelievers."[239]

Graeco-Roman backgrounds also inform one's interpretation of the four seals. The color schemes John uses for the four horses correlate with Graeco-Roman traditions relative to the meaning of colors viewed during the heavenly portents known as eclipses.[240] Graeco-Roman traditions also "heighten the identification of the rider [of the first seal] as representing forces of false prophecy and false messiahs" particularly if John's addressees connected the bow and crown as being "typical emblems associated with Apollo, . . . who was a god closely associated with the inspiration of pagan prophecy, . . . especially [in] Smyrna and Thyatira."[241]

The fifth seal highlights the sacrificial nature of those slain through its mention of an "altar" under which they lie. This altar is most likely not the brazen altar of sacrifice in the temple court but rather the golden altar of incense in the inner court, near the Holy of Holies.[242] The high priest would pour upon this altar the sacrificial blood of the Day of Atonement. Incense also was burned on it, which is specifically referenced in Rev 8:3–5. Therein, the incense of the altar symbolizes the prayers of the "holy ones" just prior to the blowing of the six trumpets that initiate the

---

238. Beale, *Revelation*, 372.

239. Beale, *Revelation*, 373.

240. Malina, *On the Genre and Message of Revelation*, 127.

241. Beale, *Revelation*, 378.

242. Beale, *Revelation*, 379.

first round of judgments upon "those who dwell upon the earth" (chs. 8 and 9). This association in Rev 8 of the altar with the prayers of the "holy ones" mirrors the fifth seal altar imagery of the martyrs praying to God for vengeance ("how long?"; 6:10).[243] Their prayers for vengeance are answered in the start of the seven trumpet judgments (8:5ff). There are extensive Jewish backgrounds that inform John's use of the "how long?" trope, some of which I have already discussed.[244]

In the sixth seal we find images of finalized eschatological judgment. I have already addressed the intertextual connections of John's "great earthquake" with the implied earthquake of the Noachic flood (7:14) through its eschatologization within the Isaianic "proto-apocalypse" (Isa 24—27). What remains then is a survey of John's other imagery of eschatological judgement in the sixth seal. John's reference to the sun and moon being darkened are firmly founded upon Hebrew Bible and Jewish writings.[245] Pre-exilic references include Isaiah's pronouncement of doom upon Babylon.[246] Exilic references include Ezekiel's targeting of Egypt (32:7-8). Jewish usages of the sun and moon motif as symbols of God's judgment include 1 En. 102.1-2[247] and T. Mos. 10.3-5.[248] John's use of the judgment motif of stars falling to earth[249] find precedent in Hebrew Bible[250] and Jewish Second Temple writings. The most influential Hebrew

243. The martyrs's question "how long?" hearkens back to Zech 1:12, where "how long?" is asked after the four groups of horses return from their patrolling of the earth/land and report that those nations who had persecuted Israel were enjoying peace. God replies that he will now judge those nations (Zech 1:13–16) and he uses those same horses as agents of that judgment (Zech 6:1–8).

244. See esp. Beale, *Revelation*, 392–94 and Bauckham, *Climax of Prophecy*, 38–83.

245. See esp. Patterson, "Wonders in the Heavens and on the Earth," 385–403.

246. Isaiah 13:10 reads, "The stars of heaven and their constellations will not show their light. The rising sun will be darkened and the moon will not give its light." See also references to sun and moon being darkened on the day of the Lord in Joel 2:10 and 3:16; Amos 5:18–20 and 8:9–14.

247. "In those days, when he hurls out against you terror of fire . . . . All the luminaries shall faint with great fear, the whole earth shall faint and tremble and panic."

248. *Test. Mos.* 10.3–5 (first century CE): "For the Heavenly One . . . will go forth from his holy habitation with indignation and wrath on behalf of his sons. And the earth will tremble, even to its ends shall it be shaken. . . . The sun will not give its light. And in darkness the horns of the moon will flee. It will be turned wholly into blood. Yea, even the circle of the stars will be thrown into disarray" (Charlesworth, ed., *OTP*, 1.932).

249. In Hebrew Bible and Jewish texts "stars" metaphorically represent heavenly powers of good (Judg 5:20; Dan 8:10) or evil (Deut 4:19; Isa 14:12; 24:21; 47:13; Jer 8:2; Wis 13:2; 1 En. 18.13–15; 21:3; Sib. Or. 5.511–30).

250. Joel 2:10 ("the day of the LORD is coming . . . and the stars withdraw their

Bible text is probably Isa 34:4.[251] John's reference to kings, rulers, and mighty/great ones is reminiscent of Isa 34:12 where the same groups of people suffer divine judgment in their role as key players in the corrupt systems of human governance.

Beale provides a helpful summary of the intertextual continuities between the six seals of Revelation and the apocalyptic discourse of the Synoptic Gospels. He observes that the Synoptics present "the following elements in similar order to Revelation 6: (1) deception, (2) wars, (3) international strife, (4) earthquakes, (5) famines, (6) persecutions, and (7) cosmic changes in the sun, moon, and stars."[252]

The Seven Trumpets and Bowls and the *Urzeit* of the Exodus

Given the numerous overlaps of imagery between the seven trumpets and seven bowls, I will compare them together. The *Urzeit* of the exodus motif, in particular, informs John's *Endzeit* judgment imagery inaugurated in the six trumpets (8:5—9:21) and seven bowls (15:5—16:21).[253] The seven bowl judgements begin with John reporting an appearance of "the temple (*naos*; 'sanctuary') of the tent of witness in heaven" (15:5; the start of *vision block* 5). This imagery hearkens back to the tabernacle of the exodus wanderings ("tent of witness") which was a portable shrine built according to the heavenly pattern (Exod 25:9) that only priests could enter. John prefaces this exodus motif (15:5) with the concluding *individual vision* (15:2-4) of *vision block* 4 (7:9—15:4). In his depiction of heavenly consummation for the saints (15:2-4) John parallels that victorious finale with the victory of Moses and the Israelites over Pharaoh at the Red Sea. The victorious saints in Revelation are also by a sea where they sing the song of Moses (and of the *paschal*/Passover Lamb). Even as the Israelites are saved by virtue of the blood of the *paschal lamb* (Exod 12:7) so too the saints in Revelation are victorious by the Lamb's blood (5:9-10). The victory over Pharaoh and the Sea Beast also alludes to God's victory at creation, when he created order and stability by containing the primordial monsters of chaos, the land Beast (Behemoth) and the sea Beast

---

shining"), Joel 3:16; 4:16 ("For the day of the LORD is near in the valley of decision. The sun and the moon are darkened, and the stars withdraw their shining").

251. Isa 34:4 reads, "and the powers of the heavens will melt, and the heaven will be rolled up like a scroll and all the stars will fall . . . as leaves fall from a fig tree."

252. Beale, *Revelation*, 373.

253. My overview follows that provided by Leonard Thompson (*Revelation*, 152–58).

(Leviathan). Thus, within John's narratological (but not *vision block*) unity of 15:2–5, these two pivot points of cosmic and earthly religious history are re-visited. At this climactic point of finalized divine judgment, however, the primordial images are redirected towards the cosmic and earthly enemies of God: the Sea Beast, the Land Beast, Babylon, Satan, and unrepentant humanity.

The earthly destruction of the seven bowl judgments revisits the destructive elements of the six trumpet judgments, but with heightened intensity (3/3 vs. 1/3 of the earth is affected, respectively). The bowls and trumpets mirror the plague judgments upon Egypt prior to the exodus. In contrast to the six seals and the six trumpets in which the "those who dwell upon the earth" are in view, the earthly objects of the bowl judgments are narrowed down to "those who had the mark of the Beast and who worshipped its image" (cf. also 13:14–17; 14:9–10). The phrase "those who dwell upon the earth" (*hoi katoikountes epi tēs gēs*) can be read as reflecting technical language used in the Isaianic "proto-apocalypse" (LXX Isa 24—27) for identifying the sum total of rebellious humanity (e.g., LXX Isa 24:6).[254]

The descriptions of the trumpets and bowls form something of an *inclusio* for God's finalized eschatological judgment. The first six trumpets (8:5—9:21) form the content for the "empty" seventh seal (8:1), which I suggest is an "umbrella term" for the sixth seal with its short and concise descriptions of eschatological cataclysmic events (6:12–17). The opening of the seventh seal is the final event confirming the Lamb's worthiness for enthronement. The seven bowls reaffirm the Lamb's worthiness and re-inscribe his power over all of creation, especially given their textual location immediately prior to the final defeat of the two beasts and Babylon (17:1—20:10). Thompson comments that "in the scenes of disaster, the

---

254. Isa 24:6 reads, "Therefore, a curse devours the earth, and those who live in it are held guilty. Therefore, the inhabitants of the earth are burned, and few men are left." LXX Isaiah uses the phrase *hoi katoikountes epi tēs gēs*, which is replicated throughout Revelation. Beale asserts that this phrase "is a technical term repeated throughout the book [of Revelation] for unbelievers who suffer under incipient divine judgment because they persecute God's people (6:10; 8:13) . . . (for the universal use of the phrase in the OT see Isa 24:6; 26:21)." The equivalent Hebrew phrase occurs with some frequency in the Hebrew Bible (e.g., Lam 4:12; Jer 1:14; 25:29, 30; 38:11; Ezek 7:7). The *hoi katoikountes epi tēs gēs* is also found throughout early Jewish apocalyptic literature, where it has a predominantly negative connotation in reference to the nations of the world (e.g., 1 *En.*37.2, 5; 40.6, 7; 48.5; 4 *Ezra* 3.12, 34, 35; 4.21, 39; 2 *Bar.* 25.1; 48.32, 40; 54.1).

pouring out of the bowls is linked to the beasts and to Babylon (esp. 16:2, 10–21) looking back to chapters 13—14 and ahead to chapters 17—18."[255]

The first five bowls allude back to the judgement motif of the Egyptian plagues which led to the release of the Israelites from Egypt and led to their exodus wanderings which culminated in their entrance into the promised land. We see close parallels to the Egyptian plagues in John's references to "a foul and painful sore" (bowl #1, 16:2; cf. Exod 9:10) and to the sea, rivers, and springs of water becoming like blood (bowls #2 and #3, 16:3 and 4; cf. Exod 7:14–21). The second (8:8–9) and third (8:10–11) trumpets mirror the second and third bowls in their emphasis on water being turned to blood, yet with only one-third of the waters being affected. The fourth trumpet mirrors the plague motif of the sun being darkened (8:12; one-third of the light of the sun, moon, and stars; cf. Exod 10:21), while the fourth bowl reverses that motif of darkness by describing how the light of the sun exhibits such extreme heat that people are "scorched with fire" (16:8–9).[256] The fifth bowl, however, replicates that plague of darkness on the kingdom of Pharaoh, which was so "weighty" that it could be felt (Exod 10:21), with a darkness upon the kingdom of the Beast that brings people to "gnaw their tongues in agony" (16:10–11). With the sixth bowl (16:12–16) we see a re-emergence of parallels with the six trumpets, specifically with the sixth trumpet (9:13–19). The sixth bowl describes "the kings of the whole world" crossing the Euphrates river and assembling "for battle on the great day of God the Almighty" (16:14) at a place that in Hebrew is called "Harmegedon" (16:16; cf. Zech 12:11). The sixth trumpet (i.e., second woe; 9:12) also mentions a countless horde crossing the Euphrates river, one that is numbered at 200 million strong and through which "a third of humankind was killed" (9:15).

With the seventh bowl, God's judgments upon humanity come to a close. It is noteworthy that now, for the first time, the earthquake of the heavenly theophany and the "great earthquake" on the earth merge into one judgment scene (16:18). Prior to this point, the "great earthquake" (6:12; 11:13) and the earthquakes of the heavenly theophanies (8:5; 11:19) alternated in their occurrences. When they merge in the seventh bowl, (1) Babylon's judgment by earthquake is completed (16:19), (2) the "huge hail (stones)" of the seventh Egyptian plague are replicated (16:21; cf. Exod 9:18–34) and (3) the disappearance of islands and mountains

255. Thompson, *Revelation*, 153.

256. Contrast the scorching of rebellious humanity by the sun with the protection from the sun that is granted to the faithful (7:16).

of the sixth seal (6:14) are revisited (16:20). One could say that, with the seventh bowl, John's vision has gone "back to the future" where the *eschaton* first began in the sixth seal.

However, it is worth noting that the hearer's/reader's journey back to sixth seal is not totally unexpected. John has foreshadowed that possibility from the sixth seal forward. The target(s) of the sixth seal's "great earthquake" (6:12) are identified as being Jerusalem (11:8; sixth trumpet/ second woe [cf. 8:13; 9:12]) and cities of all the nations, including Babylon (16:19; seventh bowl). The addition of the "heavy hail" to the seventh trumpet's heavenly storm theophany also finds reiteration in the final judgment mentioned in the seventh bowl which has "huge hailstones, each weighing about a hundred pounds" (16:21). Thus, this line of continuity (1) from the sixth seal's "great earthquake" to the sixth trumpet's "great earthquake," which is reiterated with climactic finality in the seventh bowl's "violent earthquake" and (2) from the seventh trumpet's "heavy hail" to the seventh bowl's "huge hailstones," suggests the possibility (3) that John's literary strategy reflects dovetailing[257] or telescoping such that the seventh element of the seals and of the trumpets are each like the joints of a telescope, which when extended reveal more and more detail.[258]

However, given that the seventh bowl revisits the sixth seal in its reiteration of the "great earthquake" and the disappearance of the islands and mountains, I have suggested that a more precise term for John's narratological strategy would be "telescopic reiteration." Thus, in this respect, the seventh heavenly trumpet, which is "empty" of earthly judgment content, functions as the second joint of John's visionary telescope of sixth seal events. This second joint encompasses the seven bowl judgments. In not dissimilar fashion, the seventh seal with its "empty" content of earthly judgment functions as the first joint of John's eschatological telescope. This first joint encompasses the ensuing seven trumpets and the seven bowls. In this regard, the "high power magnification" of the telescoping seventh seal reiterates the same eschatological events described with a more concise "wide-angle lens" perspective in the sixth seal. This suggests that John's seventh seal is equivalent to the sixth seal and functions narratologically as an "umbrella term" for the sixth seal.

---

257. Loenertz, *Apocalypse*, xiv–xvi.
258. See the description of "telescoping" by Thomas in *Revelation 1—7*, 43.

9

Conclusion

Post-Supersessionism and Revelation

I BEGAN THIS EXPLORATORY journey of reading Revelation post-supersessionally with an adapted translation of John's opening words in the first four verses of the Apocalypse:

> "The revelation ["apocalypse"/*apokalypsis*] of Jesus the [Jewish] *Christos*/Messiah, which God gave him to show his servants what must soon take place; he made it known by sending his angel to his servant, John, [a Jewish apocalyptic apostle-prophet], who testified to the word of God and to the testimony of Jesus the *Christos*, even to all [six *vision blocks* within the vision episode] that he saw [*eiden*]. Blessed is the one who [publicly] reads aloud [during an *ekklēsia*/"assembly"] the words of this [Jewish apocalyptic apostolic-]prophecy . . . for the time [of the "Last Day" (i.e., the completion of the telescopically reiterative sixth seal) of these "last days" (that began with the first five seals)] is near. John to the seven *ekklēsiai* [that is, the multi-ethnic *Christos*-following associations] in [the Roman province of] Asia." (Rev 1:1–4)

It is my hope that, having reached the conclusion of this journey, that greater *apokalypsis* has dawned, not only into the terms and concepts I injected into the first four verses of the Apocalypse, but particularly with respect to the foundational purpose of this apocalyptic journey, which is to assess the degree to which John inculcates a non-supersessionist perspective for his *ekklēsia* addressees. A key evaluative tool in this process was assessing how indelibly John incorporates social identification with Judaism(s), Jewishness, and Jewish institutions into his *apokalypsis* of the Jewish *Christos*, Jesus. Of even more import, however, is determining if there are examples of positive social interaction between non-Jesus following Jews and John's multi-ethnic *ekklēsiai*. If no examples are obvious, then a corollary focus is to evaluate whether social interaction was affirmed, either explicitly or implicitly.

If the evidence only points toward social identification, then the jury will ultimately remain out as to whether John identifies with Judaism(s), Jewishness, and Jewish institutions for the purpose (1) of *replacing* Israel with his multi-ethnic *ekklēsiai*/universal *ekklēsia* or (2) of *emplacing* his *Christos*-follower communities further into their Jewish heritage as God's covenantal people (without necessarily thereby superseding the legitimacy of Israel as a national identity for ethnic Jews who do not follow Jesus as the Jewish *Christos*).

Allow me to rehearse what I believe this journey has uncovered relative to examples of social identification and social interaction in John's ideological program and theological priorities. Regarding John's overall ideological program, John's extensive social identification does not seem to be explicit in its intent to communicate a supersessionist agenda. Rather, it would seem that John's strategy reflects more so a program of social identity construction using "the imitation of Jewishness as flattery."

There are three socio-political micro-identities within which John can nest his *Christos*-followers—Jew, Greek, and Roman. His use of the collective term *ekklēsia* as a group designation for his *Christos*-followers facilitates their socio-political identification with Jews and Greeks, but not with Romans. In fact, John seems intentionally to eschew socio-political identification with all things Roman (1) through the collective identification of his *ekklēsiai* as a gargantuan Jewish *kosmos-polis* that *visibly* supersedes the Roman religio-political *imperium* at the *parousia* of Jesus the *Christos*, and (2) which may have already *invisibly* inaugurated that supersession of the *imperium*, not least in respect of emperor worship. Rome's supersession by the collective body of God's first and new covenant faithful was accomplished through the resurrection of *Christos* the Lamb and the concomitant emplacement of his Body, the Bride of the *Christos*, not only *in* the Holy of Holies around the throne (the twenty-four elders and the rainbow; chs. 4 and 5) but also *as* the Holy of Holies through the universal *ekklēsia*'s guise as the temple-"non-city" called the New Jerusalem (chs. 21 and 22).

As we have seen, the collective self-designation of an ancient Mediterranean sub-group as an *ekklēsia* implicitly identifies them with two micro-identities: (1) "Greek," given Greek usage of *ekklēsia* to identify civic assemblies and the assemblies of non-civic associations during the Classic, Hellenistic, and Imperial periods in Greece and the Greek East, and (2) "Jew," given Jewish uses of *ekklēsia* in the writings not least of the LXX, Sirach, 1 Maccabees, Philo, and Josephus. Both of these socio-political micro-identities (Jew, Greek) would have facilitated the missional effectiveness of John's *ekklēsiai* in Roman Asia.

With respect to missional relevance for a Greco-Roman audience, an *ekklēsia* identity provided *Christos*-followers with an air of familiarity, especially to those outsiders who were familiar with associational life. An *ekklēsia* identity also provided *Christos*-followers with perceptions of being positive participants in the civic life of their *poleis*, particularly in the Asia Minor, where a "political culture" based on "the two-way socio-political street" of euergetism thrived. In their ambassadorial self-presentation as *ekklēsiai* of (and as) the New Jerusalem, John's *Christos*-followers could have been perceived by Greco-Romans as implicitly claiming a role as metaphorical cleruchies (colonies) of that New Jerusalem.[1] Thus, as a spiritual cleruchy, a *Christos*-follower *ekklēsia* would naturally be expected to abide by the *politeia* (constitution) and *politeuma* (governing authority) of its spiritual *kosmos-polis*. Given that this *polis* is Jewish, then one would expect coherence with existing Jewish socio-religious *praxeis*, which John clearly expects and inculcates into his *ekklēsiai*. We see repetitive expectations that faithfulness to the Jewish *Christos* entails a Jewish-like lifestyle of worship, humble submission, obedience to Torah/commandments, of public testimony by the faithful (chs. 4—5; 7:9–12; 12:17), of praise of God, and of repentance from activities that are *anathema* to Jews by the faithless (9:20–21; 11:13).

With respect to missional relevance among Jews, John's social identification with Jewishness would particularly have resonated with a Jewish audience, especially the large Jewish populace in the Lycus river valley (e.g., Laodicea). The fact that the word *ekklēsia* functioned as a Judean and Egyptian synagogue term (e.g., in Sirach, 1 Maccabees, Josephus, Philo) suggests that John's *ekklēsiai* could have been viewed by diasporic

1. A cleruchy was an ancient Athenian colony in which the cleruchs, or settlers, maintained their political allegiance to Athens and retained their Athenian citizenship.

Jews in Roman Asia as extensions of public Judean society. If a diasporic Jew had done so, then each Johannine *ekklēsia* could have been viewed as a diasporic "satellite" in relation to other Judean public *ekklēsiai*, thereby implicitly laying claim to being able to express all facets of Jewish life (ethno-religious, social, political, economic, and judicial dimensions). If diasporic synagogue authorities viewed John's *ekklēsiai* (1) as *intra*-Jewish associations and (2) as satellites of public Judean synagogues called *ekklēsia*, and (3) if they also viewed John, the Jewish apocalyptic apostolic-prophet, as being in some fashion an ambassadorial *archisynagōgos* ("synagogue ruler"), then (4) one can see how the potential of social interaction between non-Jesus following Jews and multi-ethnic *Christos*-followers moves from possibility towards probability.

Regarding John's theological priorities, I have exegetically reviewed two key passages in Revelation that appear to challenge any claim that John's social identification with Jewishness is for the purpose of further emplacing his *Christos*-follower associations into their Jewish heritage. They each contain statements about people who claim to be Jews "and are not" and who are said to be "a synagogue of Satan" (2:9; 3:9). I reviewed six interpretive options for those to whom John denies the ethnic identity *Ioudaios*. Of these five, only one has supersessionist overtones (i.e., Christ-followers are the true Jews). Given the valid points made by the other perspectives it would seem that the burden of proof lies upon those who defend a supersessionist perspective. Regarding, John's phrase "synagogue of *ho satanas*," it became clear that *synagōgē* need not refer to a Jewish building or gathering. *Synagōgē* was used as a descriptor for Greco-Roman assemblies and for Jewish *Christos*-follower assemblies and/or sub-group identities (e.g., the Nazoreans). Thus, here too John is not necessarily making a pejorative anti-semitic/Judaistic statement, but may simply be referencing an intra-*Christos*-follower conflict, not a conflict between his *Christos*-followers and non-Jesus-following Jews.

Again, although there does not seem to be any explicit indication of social interaction with non-Jesus-following Jews, there is another implicit factor that opens up the probability of such interaction, not least within Smyrna. This move to probability is centered in the interpretation of John's pejorative phrase "synagogue of Satan" as having direct reference *not* to non-Jesus-following ethnic Jews but rather either to gentile proselytes to Judaism(s) or to God-fearers in Smyrna who later became followers of Jesus as their Jewish *Christos* but yet who mandated Torah-observance for gentile *Christos*-followers in John's *ekklēsia*. These judaizing (righteous) gentile *Christos*-followers would not have been welcome in any Pauline *ekklēsia* and, by logical extension, one would expect the same with respect to John's *ekklēsiai*. As such, one can understand why these (righteous) gentiles would have formed their own association and not have named it *ekklēsia*. Given their Judaistic predilections, naming their association as a *synagōgē* would have been a natural move. The logic of such an institutional move would have been even more obvious to these diasporic judaizing *synagōgē* members if they were aware of the Nazorean *synagōgai* of Jewish *Christos*-followers in the promised land or of James's Torah-observant diasporic *Christos*-followers who may very well have met within a *synagōgē* (Jas 2:2). John's attribution of the descriptor "of Satan/satanic" to this Smyrnean *synagōgē* is contiguous with Paul's attribution of a satanic agenda to judaizing *Christos*-followers who were troubling his Galatian *ekklēsiai* with requirements of Torah-observance for gentiles (Gal 1:6–9; cf. 2 Cor 11:14).

The foregoing scenario, then, removes the need for assuming that there was such a social rift between the *ekklēsiai* in Smyrna and Philadelphia and non-Jesus-following Jews that one can do nothing other than assume that their two communities were socially bifurcated and, thus, no longer engaged in positive social interactions. This conclusion can be said to hold even in spite of later patristic evidence to the contrary that, in Smyrna, *Christos*-followers were persecuted by the Jewish community. Second-century patristic evidence does not necessarily mean that the same social conditions existed in John's day. Even if Revelation was written in around Domitian's reign, there is still a time, and, thus, a sociological, gap between Revelation's compositional date and later patristic evidence of more than three decades or later (e.g., Polycarp, Bishop of Smyrna). This chronological gap is sufficient to make more plausible a gregarious relationship between Jews and *Christos*-followers in the 90s CE, let alone in the 60s CE during Nero's reign. A fractured relationship soon after Domitian's reign gains credibility in light of Pliny's letter to emperor Trajan. In that letter, Pliny explains how he is managing the influence of the *Christos* "cult" in Bithynia through policy and practice. This early second-century CE political scenario, then, lends itself more readily to seeing how Jews in nearby Roman Asia, through self-preservationist impulses, would come to validate persecution of *Christos*-followers as a "due diligence" strategy that avoids having Roman authorities associate their synagogue communities with *Christos*-follower associations through perceptions of "guilt by association." Ongoing social interaction between these communities by this timeframe would seem less plausible.

John's extensive valuation of "all things Jewish" through his literary masterpiece adds another way in which John may be communicating an integrated socio-religious *ethos* between his *ekklēsiai* and non-Jesus following Jews (i.e., the *ekklēsia* of Israel). One of John's literary strategies entails his reiterative structuration of the vision episode in Revelation (1:9—22:20) through the use of three Jewish literary devices that are found within Hebrew prophetic and Jewish apocalyptic visionary literature. The principle I call "telescopic reiteration" allows John to embed a sense of imminence relative to the return of Jesus the *Christos*. This imminence would have provided implicit motivation for his *ekklēsiai* holistically to engage their civic and non-civic contexts in Roman Asia with the good news of Jesus, the resurrected sacrificial Lamb who is returning as a Warrior-Judge. The authority with which John wields the "pen" as his "sword" gains reinforcement if one designates Revelation's genre as an apocalyptic apostolic-prophecy, written in the guise of a covenant letter to the Jewish diaspora, by a Jewish apostle-prophet; that is, by one member of the New Jerusalem's twelve-fold foundation, specifically John, the disciple/apostle of Jesus.

Another one of John's literary strategies for embedding a Jewish socio-religious *ethos* among his *ekklēsiai* is through his use of Jewish inner-biblical exegesis to appropriate and transform Hebrew Bible and Jewish *traditums* into first-century CE *traditios* for his *ekklēsiai*'s Roman Asia contexts. John uses Jewish numerology, *topoi*, tropes, and interpretive principles (*Urzeit* and *Endzeit*) to instantiate Jewishness within his multi-ethnic *ekklēsiai*. John's symbolic connection of the seven *ekklēsiai* with seven golden lampstands or *menorot* (1:12, 20) implicitly identifies his multi-ethnic *Christos*-followers with ethnic Israel. This imagery does not necessarily imply replacement theology. Rather, John's *menorot* imagery may function theologically in similar fashion to Paul's imagery of *Christos*-following gentiles being *grafted into* the "tree" of Israel (Rom 11). Thus, socio-ethnic identities remain distinct within a Jewish covenantal union fashioned by the Jewish *Christos*.

All of John's theological, literary, and exegetical interpretive strategies only serve further to reinforce an inherently *Jewish collective identity* for his *Christos*-followers. They are not "Israel" but an *ekklēsia of* Israel in which gentiles *qua* gentiles are able to integrate into theological continuity with Torah-observant Jews *qua* Jews. Or, in other (Hebrew) words, in analogous fashion to the supra-local identity of God's people during the desert wanderings (i.e., the *ekklēsia* of Israel), gentiles can become part of the *qāhāl* (the socio-political *ekklēsia*/assembly [of Israel]), but not part of the *'am* (the ethnic people/nation of Israel).

In sum, throughout this journey I have explored numerous instances of social identification with Jews, Jewishness, and Judaism(s) that John employs in his *apokalypsis* of the Jewish *Christos*, Jesus. The key question that needs continually to be asked is whether John's social identification is for the purpose of further emplacing his readers/hearers into a Jewish heritage and into a Jewish literary universe (non-supersessionism) or is it for the purpose of replacing Jewish stories/*traditums* with re-imagined *traditios* specific to *Christos*-followers only?

Given the evidence I have explored, allow me at this final stage of my investigative journey to state my conclusion: I understand John's apocalyptic apostolic-prophecy which he calls the *apokalypsis* of the Jesus, the Jewish *Christos*, as being a non-supersessionst visionary drama that socially identifies his multi-ethnic *ekklēsiai* with the *ekklēsia* of Israel and perhaps even provides ideological bridges that hold the prospect of fostering social interaction between *Christos*-followers and non-Jesus following Jews.

The Genre "Apocalypse" and the Book of Revelation

THE BOOK OF REVELATION COMPARED WITH JEWISH APOCALYPSES OF THE SECOND TEMPLE PERIOD[1] Asterisks indicate either: (1) that an element is possibly, but not certainly, present; or (2) is implicit; or (3) is present in a very minor way.	Apoc. Zephaniah	Test. Abraham 10—15	3 Baruch	Test. Levi 2—5	2 Enoch	Similitudes of Enoch	Heavenly Luminaries	1 Enoch 1—36	Apoc. Abraham	2 Baruch	4 Ezra	Jubilees 23	Apoc. of Weeks	Animal Apocalypse	Daniel 7—12	Revelation 1:9—22:20
Manner of Revelation:																
1.1.1. Visions	x	x	x	x	x	x	x	x	x	x	x		x	x	x	x
1.1.2. Epiphanies	x														x	x
1.2.1. Discourse					x		x						x	x	x	x
1.2.2. Dialogue	x	x	x	x	x	x		x	x	x	x				x	x
1.3. Otherworldly journey	x	x	x	x	x	x	x	x	x							x
1.4. Writing							x						x	x	x	x
2. Otherworldly mediator	x	x	x	x	x	x	x	x	x	x	x	x	x	x	x	x
3.1 Pseudonymity	x	x	x	x	x	x	x	x	x	x	x	x	x	x	x	
3.2 Disposition of recipient	x	x	x	x					x	x	x				x	x

1. This chart is adapted from J. J. Collins's paradigm ("The Jewish Apocalypses," 28). This comparison of the book of Revelation with Jewish apocalypses is appropriated from Aune (*Revelation 1—5*, lxxxii–viii).

	1	2	3	4	5	6	7	8	9	10	11	12	13	14	15	16
3.3. Reaction of recipient			x	x	x	x	x	x	x	x	x			x	x	x
Temporal Axis																
4.1. Cosmogony					x					x	x					*
4.2 Primordial events			x			x		x	x	x	x					*
5.1 Recollection of past								x	x	x						x
5.2 *Ex Eventu* prophecy								x	x	x	x	x	x	x		*
6. Present salvation																
7.1 Persecution						x		x		x	x			x	x	x
7.2 Other eschatological upheavals				x		x	x	x	x	x	x	x	x	x	x	x
8.1 Judgment/destruction of the Wicked	x	x	x	x	x	x	x	x	x	x	x	x	x	x	x	x
8.2 of world	x			x			x						x			x
8.3 of otherworldly beings				x		x	*	x				x	x	x	x	x
9.1 Cosmic transformation				x	x	x	x	x	x	x	x	*	x	*	x	x
9.2.1 Resurrection						x				x	x			*	x	x
9.2.2 Other forms of afterlife	x	x	x	*	x	x	x	x	x			x	*	x		x
Spatial Axis																
10.1 Otherworldly regions	x	x	x	x	x	x	x	x	x	x	x			x	x	x
10.2 Otherworldly beings	x	x	x	x	x	x	x	x	x	x	x	x	x	x	x	x
11. *Paraenesis by Revealer*											x					x
Concluding Elements																
12. Instructions to recipient			x	x		x			x	x	x				x	x
13. Narrative Conclusion		x	x	x	x		x			x	x			x	x	*

APPENDIX #2

The "Space/Time Referent" in Jewish Visionary Literature

APPENDIX #2
"Space/Time Referent" Occurrences in Visionary Literature of:
(1) the HB prophets
(2) the Dead Sea Scrolls
(3) the Jewish Apocalypses
of the Second Temple period

Special Notations

(1) 1=year; 2=month; 3=day; 4=all three dates cited;

(2) "+" means visionary revelation is claimed but only verbal proclamation follows instead;

(3) "[x]" means a Heavenly Throne vision;

(4) "?" means "Date is implied from context";

(5) *Angeles Interpres*–"v" = part of a vision; "a" = angel only, no visionary imagery;

(6) Due to the fragmentary nature of the Apocalypse of Zephaniah it is not possible to determine if a space/time referent was used.

	A "Prophetic Superscription"?	1st person speech	Year/Month/Day dating*	Details of personal context ("space")	"Imperial" timeframe stated*	General space/time details only	Non-visionary verbal revelation	Waking visionary revelation	Night vision or dream revelation	*Angeles Interpres*
	Space/Time Referent Details						**Medium of Revelation**			
Isaiah 1:1	x				x		x	+		
Isaiah 6:1		x	1		x			[x]		
Jeremiah 24:1		x		x	x		x			
Ezekiel 1:1–4	x	x	4	x	x			[x]		
Ezekiel 8:1		x	4	x	?			[x]		v
Ezekiel 37:1		x		x		x	x			
Ezekiel 40:1		x	4	x	?		x			v
Daniel 7:1, 2a		x	1		x				x	v
Daniel 8:1		x	1		x			x		v
Daniel 9:1–21		x	1	x	x		x			v
Daniel 10:1–5		x	1	x	x			x		v
Amos 7:1–3	x							x		
Amos 7:4–6	x							x		
Amos 8:1, 2a	x							x		
Amos 9:1a	x							[x]		
Zechariah 1:7, 8		x	4		x				x	v
Zechariah 4:1, 2		x		x		x		x		v

(1)* 1=year; 2=month; 3=day; 4=all three dates cited; (2) "+" means visionary revelation is claimed but only verbal proclamation follows instead; (3) "[x]" means a Heavenly Throne vision; (4) "?" means "Date is implied from context"; (5) *Angeles Interpres*–"v" = part of a vision; "a" = angel only, no visionary imagery; (6) Due to the fragmentary nature of the Apocalypse of Zephaniah it is not possible to determine if a space/time referent was used.	A "Prophetic Superscription"?	1st person speech	Year/Month/Day dating*	Details of personal context ("space")	"Imperial" timeframe stated*	General space/time details only	Non-visionary verbal revelation	Waking visionary revelation	Night vision or dream revelation	Angeles Interpres
4Qvisions of Amram (4Q543—548)										
The introductory "space/time referent" is found in: 4Q543 frg.1 v.1–4; 4Q545 frg.1 i.1–4; and 4Q frg.1 v.1	x	x	1, 3	x	?				x	v?
The concluding "space/time referent" is found in 4Q547 frg.4 v.8		x		x		x			x	
1 Enoch 1—36 (Book of the Watchers)										
13:7–8		x		x		x			x	
14:1–8		x		x		x			[x]	v
1 Enoch 37—71 (Similitudes of Enoch)										
37:1, 2	x	x				x			?	
39:1–4a		x				x			[x]	v
60:1		x	4						[x]	v
65:1–5		x		x		x	?			Eno-ch
70:1–4a		x		x		x			[x]	v
1 Enoch 72—82 (The Book of Heavenly Luminaries/The Astronomical Book)										
72:1–3a		x				x	x			v
1 Enoch 83—84 (The Book of Dreams-part 1)										
83:1–3		x		x		x			x	
1 Enoch 85—90 (The Animal Apocalypse)										
85:1–3		x		x		x			x	
1 Enoch 91:12–17; 93:1–10 (Apocalypse of Weeks)										
No supernaturally initiated revelatory accounts and, thus, no "space/time referents"										

(1)* 1=year; 2=month; 3=day; 4=all three dates cited; (2) "+" means visionary revelation is claimed but only verbal proclamation follows instead; (3) "[x]" means a Heavenly Throne vision; (4) "?" means "Date is implied from context"; (5) *Angeles Interpres*–"v" = part of a vision; "a" = angel only, no visionary imagery; (6) Due to the fragmentary nature of the Apocalypse of Zephaniah it is not possible to determine if a space/time referent was used.	A "Prophetic Superscription"?	1st person speech	Year/Month/Day dating*	Details of personal context ("space")	"Imperial" timeframe stated* ("space")	General space/time details only	Non-visionary verbal revelation	Waking visionary revelation	Night vision or dream revelation	*Angeles Interpres*
2 Enoch [J]										
1:1–7	x	x	4	x				x	x	v
3:1		x		x			x		x	v
69:1–5		x	3	x			x		x	
70:3		x					x		x	
71:24–27		x		x			x		x	
72:1–3		x	1				x		x	v
Jubilees 23										
No supernaturally initiated revelatory accounts, thus, no "space/time referents"										
4 Ezra 3—14										
3:1—4:1	x	x	1	x			x		?	v
4:20–32		x		x			x		?	v
9:26–38		x		x			x	x		
11:1a		x					x		x	
12:51—13:3a		x		x			x		x	
2 Baruch										
5:5—6:4		x		x			x	x		
21:26—22:1		x		x			x	+		
35:1—36:1		x		x			x		x	
2 Baruch										
52:7b—53:1a		x		x			x		x	
3 (Greek Apocalypse of) Baruch [excluding the questionable two verses of the first introduction]										
1:1–3a		x		x			x	x		v
Apocalypse of Abraham										
10:1–4		x		x	x	x		[x]		a, v
Testament of Abraham 10—15										
No "space/time referent" since only 3rd person rather than 1st person narration										
Testament of Levi 2—5										
2:1–6	x		1	x					[x]	v

APPENDIX #3*

Textual Blocking and Telescopic Reiteration in Revelation

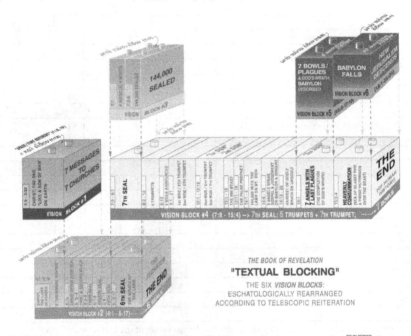

THE BOOK OF REVELATION
"TEXTUAL BLOCKING"
THE SIX *VISION BLOCKS*:
ESCHATOLOGICALLY REARRANGED
ACCORDING TO TELESCOPIC REITERATION

RALPH HOPNER
© 2002
Nov T 42/2 [2000] 160-83

* To view a color version of the Textual Blocking diagram above, see
https://www.academia.edu/43640216/Textual_Blocking_and_Chiasm_in_Revelation

248

Concentric Symmetry in VB 2:
The Lamb as Lion

*Special thanks to Caley Tse for transforming the diagrams in Appendices 4–8 into graphic form.

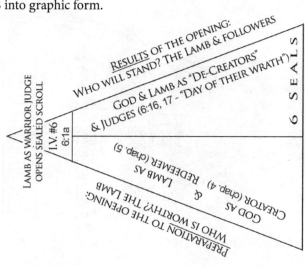

APPENDIX #5

Chiasm in VB 4: The Lamb's Religio-Political Antagonists (Two Beasts)

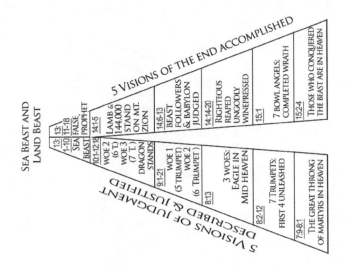

VISION BLOCK 4:
REVELATION 7:9–15:4
(12 INDIVIDUAL VISIONS; "AND I SAW")

Chiasm in VB 5: The Lamb's Socio-Religious Antagonist (Babylon)

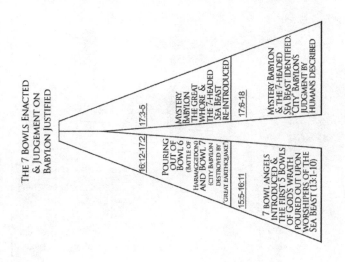

THE 7 BOWLS ENACTED & JUDGEMENT ON BABYLON JUSTIFIED

17:3-5
MYSTERY BABYLON THE GREAT WHORE & THE 7-HEADED SEA BEAST RE-INTRODUCED

17:6-18
MYSTERY BABYLON & THE 7-HEADED SEA BEAST IDENTIFIED. "CITY" BABYLON'S JUDGMENT BY HUMANS DESCRIBED

16:12-17:2
POURING OUT OF BOWL 6 (BATTLE OF HARMAGGEDON) AND BOWL 7 (CITY BABYLON DESTROYED BY "GREAT EARTHQUAKE")

15:5-16:11
7 BOWL ANGELS INTRODUCED & THE FIRST 5 BOWLS OF GOD'S WRATH POURED OUT UPON WORSHIPERS OF THE SEA BEAST (13:1-10)

VISION BLOCK 5:
REVELATION 15:5–17:18
(4 INDIVIDUAL VISIONS; "AND I SAW")

Chiasm in VB 6: The Lamb's Heavenly Antagonist (Satan)

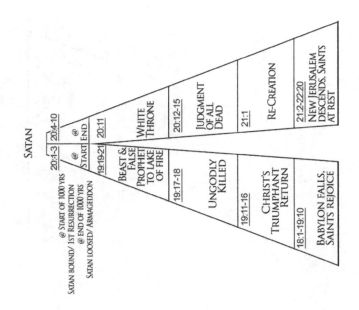

SATAN

20:1-3	20:4-10
@ START OF 1000 YRS	@
SATAN BOUND/ 1ST RESURRECTION	START END
@ END OF 1000 YRS	
SATAN LOOSED/ ARMAGEDDON	

BEAST & FALSE PROPHET TO LAKE OF FIRE — 19:19-21 | 20:11 — WHITE THRONE

19:17-18 — UNGODLY KILLED | 20:12-15 — JUDGMENT OF ALL DEAD

19:11-16 — CHRIST'S TRIUMPHANT RETURN | 21:1 — RE-CREATION

18:1-19:10 — BABYLON FALLS, SAINTS REJOICE | 21:2-22:20 — NEW JERUSALEM DESCENDS, SAINTS AT REST

VISION BLOCK 6:
REVELATION 18:1-22:20
(10 INDIVIDUAL VISIONS; "AND I SAW")

VB 2, 4, 5, 6: *Literary "Mountain Peaks"*

LITERARY MOUNTAIN PEAKS OF VISION BLOCKS 2, 4, 5 & 6:
THE LAMB AND HIS 4 KEY ANTAGONISTS
(SATAN, BEAST, FALSE PROPHET, BABYLON)

VISION BLOCK #2 (4:1–6:17)
11 INDIVIDUAL VISIONS: "AND I SAW"

LAMB AS WARRIOR JUDGE OPEN SEALED SCROLL
I.V. #6
6:1a

RESULTS OF THE OPENING:
WHO WILL STAND? THE LAMB & FOLLOWERS
GOD & LAMB AS "DE-CREATORS"
& JUDGES (6:16, 17 – "DAY OF THEIR WRATH")
6 SEALS

PREPARATION TO THE OPENING:
WHO IS WORTHY? THE LAMB
GOD AS CREATOR (chap. 4)
& LAMB AS REDEEMER (chap. 5)

VISION BLOCK #4 (7:9–15:4)
12 INDIVIDUAL VISIONS: "AND I SAW"

SEA BEAST AND LAND BEAST
5 VISIONS OF THE END ACCOMPLISHED
"5 VISIONS OF JUDGMENT DESCRIBED & JUSTIFIED"

THE GREAT THRONG OF MARTYRS IN HEAVEN

7 TRUMPETS
FIRST 4 UNLEASHED

3 WOES
EAGLE IN
MID HEAVEN

7 BOWL ANGELS
COMPLETED WRATH

THOSE WHO CONQUERED
THE BEAST ARE IN HEAVEN

RIGHTEOUS
& UNGODLY
WINEPRESSED

BEAST,
FOLLOWERS
& BABYLON
JUDGED

LAMB
& 144,000
STAND
ON MT.
ZION

BEAST
FALSE
PROPHET
DRAGON

VISION BLOCK #5 (15:5–17:18)
4 INDIVIDUAL VISIONS: "AND I SAW"

THE 7 BOWLS ENACTED
& JUDGEMENT JUSTIFIED

7 BOWL ANGELS
INTRODUCED &
THE FIRST 5 BOWLS
OF GOD'S WRATH
POURED OUT UPON
WORSHIPERS OF THE
SEA BEAST (13:1–10)

POURING
OUT OF
BOWL 6

MYSTERY
BABYLON
THE GREAT
WHERE &
THE 7-HEADED
SEA BEAST
RE-INTRODUCED

MYSTERY BABYLON
& THE 7-HEADED
SEA BEAST IDENTIFIED
CITY BABYLON'S
JUDGMENT BY
HUMANS DESCRIBED

VISION BLOCK #6 (18:1–22:20)
10 INDIVIDUAL VISIONS: "AND I SAW"

SATAN

SATAN BOUND: 1ST RESURRECTION
& END OF THRONES
SATAN LOOSED: ARMAGEDDON

BEAST &
FALSE
PROPHET
TO LAKE
OF FIRE

WHITE
THRONE

JUDGMENT
OF ALL
DEAD

RE-CREATION

NEW JERUSALEM
DESCENDS, SAINTS
AT REST

UNGODLY
KILLED

CHRIST'S
TRIUMPHANT
RETURN

BABYLON FALLS,
SAINTS REJOICE

Bibliography

Allo, Ernest Bernard. *Saint Jean, L'Apocalypse*. Paris: Librairie Victor Lecoffre, 1921.

Anderson, Paul N. "Anti-Semitism and Religious Violence as Flawed Interpretation of the Gospel of John." In *John and Judaism: A Contested Relationship in Context*, edited by R. Alan Culpepper and Paul N. Anderson, 265–311. Resources for Biblical Study 87. Atlanta: SBL, 2017.

Ascough, Richard S. "'Map-maker, Map-maker, Make Me a Map': Re-describing Greco-Roman 'Elective Social Formations.'" In *Introducing Religion: Festschrift for Jonathan Z. Smith*, edited by Willi Braun and Russell T. McCutcheon, 68–84. London: Equinox, 2008.

———. *Paul's Macedonian Associations: The Social Context of Philippians and 1 Thessalonians*. WUNT 161. Tübingen: Mohr-Siebeck, 2003.

———. "Paul, Synagogues, and Associations: Reframing the Question of Models for Pauline Christ Groups." *Journal of the Jesus Movement in Its Jewish Setting from the First to the Seventh Century* 2 (2015) 27–52.

———. "Voluntary Associations and the Formation of Pauline Christian Communities: Overcoming the Objections." In *Vereine, Synagogen und Gemeinden im kaiserzeitlichen Kleinasien*, edited by Andreas Gutsfeld and Dietrich-Alex Koch, 149–81. Tübingen: Mohr-Siebeck, 2006.

———. "What Are They Now Saying about Christ Groups and Associations?" *Currents in Biblical Research* 13.2 (2015) 207–44.

———. *What Are They Saying about the Formation of Pauline Churches?* Mahwah, NJ: Paulist, 1998.

Ascough, Richard, Philip Harland, and John Kloppenborg, eds. *Associations in the Greco-Roman World: A Sourcebook*. Waco, TX: Baylor University Press, 2012.

Aune, David E. "Apocalypticism." In *Dictionary of New Testament Background*, edited by Craig A. Evans and Stanley Porter, 45–58. Downers Grove, IL: InterVarsity Press, 2000.

———. "Dualism in the Fourth Gospel and the Dead Sea Scrolls: A Reassessment of the Problem." In *Jesus, Gospel Tradition and Paul in the Context of Jewish and Greco-Roman Antiquity: Collected Essays II*, edited by David Aune, 130–48. WUNT 303. Tübingen: Mohr Siebeck, 2013.

———. "Eschatology: Early Christian Eschatology." In *ABD* 2:594–608.

———. *The New Testament in Its Literary Environment*. Philadelphia: Westminster, 1987.

―――. *Prophecy in Early Christianity and the Ancient Mediterranean World*. Grand Rapids: Eerdmans, 1983.

―――. "Qumran and the Book of Revelation." In *The Dead Sea Scrolls after Fifty Years*, vol. 2, edited by Peter Flint and James C. VanderKam, 622–48. Leiden: Brill, 1999.

―――. *Revelation 1–5*. Word Biblical Commentary, vol. 52A. Dallas: Word, 1997.

―――. *Revelation 6–16*. Word Biblical Commentary, vol. 52B. Nashville: Thomas Nelson, 1998.

―――. *Revelation 17–22*. Word Biblical Commentary, vol. 52C. Nashville: Thomas Nelson, 1998.

Barclay, John. *Jews in the Mediterranean Diaspora (323 BCE–117 CE)*. Edinburgh: T. & T. Clark, 1996.

Barclay, William. *Letters to the Philippians, Colossians and Thessalonians*. Louisville, KY: Westminster John Knox, 1984.

―――. *The Revelation of John*. 2 vols. Philadelphia: Westminster, 1960.

Barthélemy, D., and J. T. Milik. *Qumran Cave 1*. DJD 1. Oxford: Clarendon, 1955.

Bauckham, Richard. *The Climax of Prophecy*. Edinburgh: T. & T. Clark, 1993.

―――. "The Eschatological Earthquake in the Apocalypse of John." *Novum Testamentum* 19 (1977) 224–33.

―――. "James and the Jerusalem Community." In *Jewish Believers in Jesus: The Early Centuries*, edited by Oskar Skarsaune and Reidar Hvalvik, 55–95. Peabody, MA: Hendrickson, 2007.

Baumgarten, Jorg. *Paulus und die Apokalyptik*. WMANT 44. Neukirchen-Vluyn: Neukirchener, 1975.

Beale, G. K. *The Book of Revelation: A Commentary on the Greek Text*. The New International Greek Testament Commentary. Grand Rapids: Eerdmans, 1999.

Beasley-Murray, G. R. *The Book of Revelation*. New Century Bible Commentary. Rev. ed. Greenwood, SC: Attic, 1978.

Becker, Adam, and Annette Yoshiko Reed, eds. *The Ways that Never Parted: Jews and Christians in Late Antiquity and the Early Middle Ages*. 2nd ed. Minneapolis: Fortress, 2007.

Beckwith, Isbon T. *The Apocalypse of John: Studies in Introduction with a Critical and Exegetical Commentary*. Grand Rapids: Baker, 1919.

Bell Jr., A. A. "The Date of John's Apocalypse: The Evidence of Some Roman Historians Reconsidered." *New Testament Studies* 25 (1979) 93–102.

Bernier, Jonathan. *Aposynagōgos and the Historical Jesus in John*. Biblical Interpretation Series, vol. 122. Leiden: Brill, 2013.

Betz, Hans Dieter. *Galatians*. Hermeneia. Philadelphia: Fortress, 1977.

―――. "On the Problem of the Religio-Historical Understanding of Apocalypticism." *JTC* 6 (1969) 134–56.

Biguzzi, Giancarlo. Review of David E. Aune, *Revelation 1–5*, *Biblica* 79.4 (1998) 582–85.

Binder, Donald. *Into the Temple Courts: The Place of the Synagogues in the Second Temple Period*. Atlanta: SBL, 1999.

Black, Matthew, and Albert-Marie Denis, eds. *Apocalypsis Henochi Graece; Fragmenta Pseudepigraphorum Quae Supersunt Graeca*. Leiden: Brill, 1970.

Blount, Brian K. *Revelation: A Commentary*. New Testament Library. Louisville, KY: Westminster John Knox, 2009.

Boak, Arthur. "Organization of Gilds in Greco-Roman Egypt." *TAPA* 68 (1937) 212–20.

————. *Papyri from Tebtunis, Part II: Michigan Papyri, Vol. V.* Edited by E. Husselman, A. E. Boak, and W. F. Edgerton. Ann Arbor, MI: University of Michigan, 1933–44.

Borgen, Peder. *Philo of Alexandria: An Exegete for His Time.* Supplements to Novum Testamentum 86. Leiden: Brill, 1997.

Boring, M. Eugene. *Revelation.* Interpretation Commentary Series. Louisville: John Knox, 1989.

Bowman, John Wick. *The First Christian Drama.* Philadelphia: Westminster, 1955.

————. "The Revelation to John: Its Dramatic Structure and Message." *Interpretation* 9.4 (1955) 436–53.

Boyarin, Daniel. *Judaism: The Genealogy of a Modern Notion.* Newark, NJ: Rutgers University Press, 2019.

————. "Semantic Differences; or, 'Judaism'/'Christianity.'" In *The Ways that Never Parted: Jews and Christians in Late Antiquity and the Early Middle Ages,* edited by A. Becker and A. Reed, 65–85. Tübingen: Mohr Siebeck, 2003.

Briggs, Robert A. *Jewish Temple Imagery in the Book of Revelation.* New York: Lang, 1999.

Bruce, F. F. *The Epistle to the Galatians.* New International Greek Testament Commentary. Grand Rapids: Eerdmans, 1982.

Buchanan, G. W. *The Book of Revelation: Its Introduction and Prophecy.* Mellen Biblical Commentary, New Testament series, vol. 22. Lewiston, NY: The Edwin Mellen Press, 1993.

Caird, G. B. *The Revelation of St. John the Divine.* Black's New Testament Commentaries. London: Adam and Charles Black, 1966.

Campbell, Douglas A. *Framing Paul: An Epistolary Biography.* Grand Rapids: Eerdmans, 2014.

————. *Paul: An Apostle's Journey.* Grand Rapids: Eerdmans, 2018.

Campbell, William S. "The Addressees of Paul's Letter to the Romans: Assemblies of God in House Churches and Synagogues?" In *Between Gospel and Election: Explorations in the Interpretation of Romans 9–11,* edited by Florian Wilk and J. Ross Wagner, with the assistance of Frank Schleritt, 171–95. Tübingen: Mohr Siebeck, 2010.

————. *Paul and the Creation of Christian Identity.* London: T. & T. Clark, 2006.

Carey, Greg. "The Book of Revelation as Counter-Imperial Script." In *In the Shadow of Empire: Reclaiming the Bible as a History of Faithful Resistance,* edited by Richard A. Horsley, 157–82. Louisville, KY: Westminster John Knox, 2008.

Carson, D. A., and D. J. Moo, and L. Morris, eds. *An Introduction to the New Testament.* Grand Rapids: Zondervan, 1992.

Charles, R. H. *Apocrypha and Pseudepigrapha of the Old Testament.* 2 vols. London: Oxford University Press, 1913.

————. *The Revelation of St. John.* 2 vols. The International Critical Commentary. New York: Scribner's Sons, 1920.

Charlesworth, James H., ed. *The Old Testament Pseudepigrapha,* vol. 1. New York: Doubleday, 1983.

Collins, Adela Yarbro. "Book of Revelation." In *ABD* 5:694–70.

————. "The Book of Revelation." In *Encyclopedia of the Dead Sea Scrolls,* vol. 2, edited by Lawrence G. Schiffman and James C. VanderKam, 772–74. Oxford: Oxford University Press, 2000.

————. *The Combat Myth in the Book of Revelation.* Missoula: Scholars, 1976.

———. *Crisis and Catharsis: The Power of the Apocalypse*. Philadelphia: Westminster, 1984.

Collins, John J. "Apocalyptic Eschatology as the Transcendence of Death." *Catholic Biblical Quarterly* 36.1 (1974) 21–43.

———. *The Apocalyptic Imagination: An Introduction to the Jewish Matrix of Christianity*. 2nd ed. Grand Rapids: Eerdmans, 1998.

———. *Apocalypticism in the Dead Sea Scrolls*. London: Routledge, 1997.

———. "Eschatology." In *Encyclopedia of the Dead Sea Scrolls*, vol. 1, edited by Lawrence G. Schiffman and James C. Vanderkam, 256–61. Oxford: Oxford University Press, 2000.

———. "Expectation of the End in the DSS." In *Eschatology, Messianism, and the Dead Sea Scrolls*, edited by Craig A. Evans and Peter Flint, 74–90. Studies in the Dead Sea Scrolls and Related Literature 1. Grand Rapids: Eerdmans, 1997.

———. "Introduction: Towards the Morphology of a Genre." *Semeia* 14 (1979) 1–20.

———. "The Jewish Apocalypses." *Semeia* 14 (1979) 23–44.

Chyutin, Michael. "The New Jerusalem: Ideal City." *Dead Sea Discoveries* 1 (1994) 71–97.

———. *The New Jerusalem Scroll from Qumran: A Comprehensive Reconstruction*. Journal for the Study of the Pseudepigrapha Supplement Series 25. Sheffield, UK: Sheffield Academic Press, 1997.

Darr, Katheryn Pfisterer. "The Wall around Paradise: Ezekielian Ideas about the Future." *Vetus Testamentum* 37.3 (1987) 271–79.

Davies, W. D. "Paul and the People of Israel." *New Testament Studies* 24 (1977) 4–39.

Davis, John J. *Biblical Numerology*. Grand Rapids: Baker, 1968.

Day, Peggy L. *An Adversary in Heaven: śāṭān in the Hebrew Bible*. Harvard Studies Monographs 43; Atlanta: Scholars, 1988.

DeConick, April D. "What Is Early Jewish and Christian Mysticism?" In *Paradise Now: Essays on Early Jewish and Christian Mysticism*, edited by April D. DeConick, 1–24. Symposium 11. Atlanta: SBL, 2006.

Deutsch, Celia. "Transformation of Symbols: The New Jerusalem in Rv 2,11–22,5." *Zeitschrift für Neuetestamentliche wissenschaft* 78 1/2 (1987) 106–26.

Dibelius, Martin. *James*. Hermeneia. Revised by H. Greeven. Translated by M. A. Williams. Philadelphia: Fortress, 1975.

Dimant, Devorah. "Qumran Sectarian Literature." In *Jewish Writings of the Second Temple Period*, Compendia Rerum Iudaicarum ad Novum Testamentum, Section Two, edited by Michael E. Stone, 483–550. Assen, NL: Van Gorcum, 1984.

Dittmar, Wilhelm. D. *Vetus Testamentum in Novo: Hälfte. Episteln, Apokalypse, Nachträge und Berichtigungen, Parallelen-Verzeichnis*. Göttingen: Vandenhoeck and Ruprecht, 1903.

Donaldson, Terence L. *Judaism and the Gentiles: Jewish Patterns of Universalism (to 135 CE)*. Waco, TX: Baylor University Press, 2007.

———. *Paul and the Gentiles: Remapping the Apostle's Convictional World*. Minneapolis: Fortress, 1997.

———. "Supersessionism and Early Christian Self-definition." *Journal of the Jesus Movement in Its Jewish Setting* 3 (2016) 1–32.

Draper, J. A. "The Twelve Apostles as Foundation Stones of the Heavenly Jerusalem and the Foundation of the Qumran Community." *Neotestamentica* 22 (1988) 41–63.

Duff, Paul. "'The Synagogue of Satan': Crisis Mongering and the Apocalypse of John." In *The Reality of the Apocalypse: Rhetoric and Politics in the Book of Revelation*, edited by David Barr, 147–68. Society of Biblical Literature Supplement Series 39. Atlanta: Society of Biblical Literature, 2006.

———. *Who Rides the Beast? Prophetic Rivalry and the Rhetoric of Crisis in the Churches of the Apocalypse*. Oxford: Oxford University Press, 2001.

Dunn, J. D. G. *The Epistle to the Galatians*. Peabody, MA: Hendriksen, 1993.

———, ed. *Jews and Christians: The Parting of the Ways A.D. 70 to 135*. Grand Rapids: Eerdmans, 1999.

———. "The Question of Anti-Semitism in the New Testament Writings of the Period." In *Jews and Christians: the Parting of the Ways, A.D. 70 to 135*, edited by J. D. G. Dunn, 176–211. Grand Rapids: Eerdmans, 1999.

———. *Romans*. 2 vols. Word Biblical Commentary 38A, B. Dallas: Word, 1988.

———. *The Theology of the Apostle Paul*. Grand Rapids: Eerdmans, 1998.

du Toit, Andries. "*Paulus Oecumenicus*: Interculturality in the Shaping of Paul's Theology." *New Testament Studies* 55 (2009) 121–43.

Eastman, Susan G. "Israel and the Mercy of God: A Re-reading of Galatians 6:16 and Romans 9–11." *New Testament Studies* 56.3 (2010) 367–95.

Eckhardt, A. Roy. *Elder and Younger Brothers: The Encounter of Jews and Christians*. New York: Scribner's Sons, 1967.

Ehrensperger, Kathy. *That We May Be Mutually Encouraged: Feminism and the New Perspective in Pauline Studies*. London: T. & T. Clark, 2004.

Eisenbaum, Pamela. *Paul Was Not a Christian: The Real Message of a Misunderstood Apostle*. New York: HarperOne, 2009.

Elderen, Bastiaan van. "Early Christianity in Transjordan." *Tyndale Bulletin* 45.1 (1994) 97–117.

Ellis, Nicholas J. "A Theology of Evil in the Epistle of James: Cosmic Trials and the Dramatis Personae of Evil." In *Evil in Second Temple Judaism and Early Christianity*, 262–81. WUNT 2, vol. 417. Tübingen, Mohr Siebeck, 2016.

Ellul, Jacques. *Apocalypse: The Book of Revelation*. Translated by G. W. Schreiner. New York: Seabury, 1977.

Esler, Philip. *Conflict and Identity in Romans: The Social Setting of Paul's Letter*. Minneapolis: Fortress, 2003.

Evans, Craig. "Paul as Prophet." In *Dictionary of Paul and His Letters*, edited by G. F. Hawthorne and R. P. Martin, 762–65. Downers Grove, IL: InterVarsity, 1993.

Farrar, Thomas J. "New Testament Satanology and Leading Suprahuman Opponents in Second Temple Jewish Literature: A Religion-Historical Analysis." *Journal of Theological Studeis* 70.1 (2019) 21–68.

Farrar, Thomas J., and Guy J. Williams. "Talk of the Devil: Unpacking the Language of New Testament Satanology." *Journal for the Study of the New Testament* 39 (2016) 72–96.

Farrer, Austin M. *A Re-birth of Images: The Making of St. John's Apocalypse*. London: Dacre, 1949.

———. *The Revelation of St. John the Divine*. London: Oxford University Press, 1964.

Fekkes III, Jan. *Isaiah and Prophetic Traditions in the Book of Revelation: Visionary Antecedents and Their Development*. Journal for the Study of the New Testament Supplement Series 93. Sheffield, UK: JSOT Press, 1994.

Feldman, Louis. *Studies in Hellenistic Judaism.* Arbeiten zur Geschichte des antiken Judentums und des Urchristentums, vol. 30. Leiden: Brill, 1996.

Fishbane, Michael. *Biblical Interpretation in Ancient Israel.* Oxford: Clarendon, 1985.

Fitzmyer, Joseph A. *Romans: A New Translation with Introduction and Commentary.* Anchor Yale Bible Commentary 33. New York: Doubleday, 1993.

Frankfurter, David. "Jews or Not? Reconstructing the 'Other' in Rev 2:9 and 3:9." *The Harvard Theological Review* 94.4 (2001) 403–25.

Floyd, Michael H. *Minor Prophets, Part 2.* FOTL 22. Grand Rapids: Eerdmans, 2000.

Friesen, Steven J. "Sarcasm in Revelation 2–3: Churches, Christians, True Jews, and Satanic Synagogues." In *The Reality of the Apocalypse: Rhetoric and Politics in the Book of Revelation,* edited by David Barr, 127–44. Atlanta: Society of Biblical Literature, 2006.

———. "Satan's Throne, Imperial Cults, and the Social Settings of Revelation." *Journal for the Study of the New Testament* 27.3 (2005) 351–73.

———. *Twice Neokoros: Ephesus, Asia and the Cult of the Flavian Imperial Family.* Leiden: Brill, 1993.

Gager, John G. *Reinventing Paul.* New York: Oxford University Press, 2000.

García Martínez, Florentino. *The Dead Sea Scrolls Translated: The Qumran Scrolls in English.* 2nd ed. Translated by Wilfred G. E. Watson. Leiden: Brill, 1996.

García Martínez, Florentino, and Eibert J. C. Tigchelaar. *The Dead Sea Scrolls Study Edition,* vols. 1 and 2. Leiden: Brill, 1997 and 1998.

Gärtner, Bertil. *The Temple and the Community in Qumran and the New Testament: A Comparative Study in the Temple Symbolism of the Qumran Texts and the New Testament.* Cambridge: Cambridge University Press, 1965.

Gaston, Lloyd. "Jewish Communities in Sardis and Smyrna." In *Religious Rivalries and the Struggle for Success in Sardis and Smyrna,* edited by Richard Ascough, 17–24. Guelph, ON: Laurier, 2005.

Gentry, K. L. *Before Jerusalem Fell: Dating the Book of Revelation.* Tyler, TX: Institute for Christian Economics, 1989.

Gillihan, Yonder Moynihan. *Civic Ideology, Organization, and Law in the Rule Scrolls: A Comparative Study of the Covenanters' Sect and Contemporary Voluntary Associations in Political Context.* Studies on the Texts of the Desert of Judah 97. Leiden: Brill, 2012.

Girard, Paul Frédéric. "Inscriptions de Samos." *Bulletin de correspondance hellénique* 5 (1881) 477–91.

Glotz, Gustave. *The Greek City and Its Institutions.* 1929. Reprint, New York: Barnes and Noble, 1969.

Gradel, Ittai. *Emperor Worship and Roman Religion.* OCM. Oxford: Oxford University Press, 2004.

Greenberg, Moshe. "The Design and Themes of Ezekiel's Program of Restoration." *Interpretation* 38.2 (1984) 181–208.

Grudem, Wayne A. *The Gift of Prophecy in 1 Corinthians.* Washington, DC: University Press of America, 1982.

Gruen, Erich. "Synagogues and Voluntary Associations as Institutional Models: A Response to Richard Ascough and Ralph Korner." *Journal of the Jesus Movement in its Jewish Setting* 3 (2016) 125–31.

Gundry, Robert H. "The New Jerusalem: People as Place, Not Place for People." *Novum Testamentum* 29.3 (1987) 254–64.

Gunkel, Hermann. *Schöpfung und Chaos in Urzeit und Endzeit*. Göttingen: Vandenhoeck & Ruprecht, 1895.

Guthrie, Donald. *New Testament Introduction: Hebrews to Revelation*. Downers Grove, IL: InterVarsity, 1962.

Habel, N. "The Form and Significance of the Call Narratives." *Zeithschrift für altetestamentliche Wissenschaft* 77 (1965) 297–323.

Hansen, Mogens Hermann. *The Athenian Assembly in the Age of Demosthenes*. Oxford: Blackwell, 1987.

———. "The Hellenic Polis." In *A Comparative Study of Thirty City-State Cultures: An Investigation*, edited by M. H. Hansen, 141–88. Copenhagen: Special-Trykkeriet Viborg a-s, 2000.

Hanson, Paul D. *The Dawn of Apocalyptic*. Philadelphia: Fortress, 1975.

———. *Visionaries and their Apocalypses*. Issues in Religion and Theology, vol. 4. Philadelphia: Fortress, 1983.

Harland, Phil. *Associations, Synagogues, and Congregations: Claiming a Place in Ancient Mediterranean Society*. Minneapolis: Fortress, 2003.

———. *Dynamics of Identity in the World of the Early Christians: Associations, Judeans, and Cultural Minorities*. London: T. & T. Clark, 2009.

Hellholm David, ed. *Apocalypticism in the Mediterranean World and the Near East*. Proceedings of the International Colloquium on Apocalypticism, Uppsala, August 12–17, 1979. 2nd ed. Tübingen: Mohr (Siebeck), 1989.

Hemer, Colin J. *The Letters to the Seven Churches of Asia in Their Local Setting*. 1986. Reprint, Grand Rapids: Eerdmans, 1989.

Hendriksen, W. *More Than Conquerors*. Grand Rapids: Baker, 1967.

Herms, Ronald. "Psalms of Solomon and Revelation 7:1–17: The Sealing of the Servants of God." In *Reading Revelation in Context: John's Apocalypse and Second Temple Judaism*, edited by Ben C. Blackwell, John K. Goodrich, and Jason Maston, 73–79. Grand Rapids: Zondervan Academic, 2019.

Hillhorst, A. "The Noah Story: Was It Known to the Greeks?" In *Interpretations of the Flood*, edited by Florentino Martinez Garcia and Gerard P. Luttikhuizen, 56–65. Leiden: Brill, 1998.

Hirschberg, Peter. *Das eschatologische Israel: Untersuchungem zum Gottesvolkverständnes der Johannesoffenbarung*. WMANT 84. Neukirchen-Vluyn: Neukirchener, 1999.

———. "Jewish Believers in Asia Minor according to the Book of Revelation and the Gospel of John. In *Jewish Believers in Jesus: The Early Centuries*, edited by Oskar Skarsaune and Reidar Hvalvik, 217–40. Peabody, MA: Hendrickson, 2007.

Hoehner, Harold W. "Evidence from Revelation 20." In *The Coming Millennial Kingdom: A Case for Premillennial Interpretation*, edited by Donald K. Campbell and Jeffrey L. Townsend, 235–62. Grand Rapids: Kregel, 1997.

Hultgård, Anders. "Persian Apocalypticism." *The Encyclopedia of Apocalypticism*, edited by John J. Collins, 1.39–83. New York: Continuum, 1998.

Hurtado, L. W. "Revelation 4—5 in the Light of Jewish Apocalyptic Analogies." *Journal for the Study of the New Testament* 25 (1985) 105–24.

Hvalvik, Reidar. "Jewish Believers and Jewish Influence in the Roman Church until the Early Second Century." In *Jewish Believers in Jesus: The Early Centuries*, edited by Oskar Skarsaune and Reidar Hvalvik, 179–216. Peabody, MA: Hendrickson, 2007.

Instone-Brewer, David, and Philip A. Harland. "Jewish Associations in Roman Palestine: Evidence from the Mishnah." *Journal of Graeco-Roman Judaism and Christianity* 5 (2008) 200–221.

Japhet, Sara. *I & II Chronicles: A Commentary*. Old Testament Library. Louisville, KY: Westminster John Knox, 1993.

Jewett, Robert. *Romans: A Commentary*. Hermeneia. Minneapolis: Augsburg/Fortress, 2007.

Jones, B. W. "More about the Apocalypse as Apocalyptic." *Journal of Biblical Literature* 87.3 (1968) 325–27.

Klingman, William K. *The First Century: Emperors, Gods and Everyman*. Edison, NJ: Castle, 1990.

Kallas, J. "The Apocalypse—An Apocalyptic Book?" *Journal of Biblical Literature* 86 (1967) 69–80.

Käsemann, Ernst. *Leib und Leib Christi*. Tübingen: Mohr-Siebeck, 1933.

Kiddle, Martin. *The Revelation of St. John*. The Moffatt New Testament Commentary. London: Hodder and Stoughton, 1940.

Kim, Ok-pil. "Paul and Politics: *Ekklesia*, Household, and Empire in 1 Corinthians 1–7." PhD diss., Drew University, 2010.

Kinzig, Wolfram. "The Nazoreans." In *Jewish Believers in Jesus: The Early Centuries*, edited by Oskar Skarsaune and Reidar Hvalvik, 463–87. Peabody, MA: Hendrickson, 2007.

Kloppenborg, John S. *Christ's Associations: Connecting and Belonging in the Ancient City*. New Haven, CT: Yale University Press, 2019.

———. "Collegia and *Thiasoi*: Issues in Function, Taxonomy and Membership." In *Voluntary Associations in the Graeco-Roman World*, edited by John S. Kloppenborg and Stephen G. Wilson, 16–30. London: Routledge, 1996.

———. "Dating Theodotus (CIJ II 1404)." *Journal of Jewish Studies* 51.2 (2000) 243–80.

———. "Edwin Hatch, Churches, and Collegia." In *Origins and Method: Towards a New Understanding of Judaism and Christianity*, edited by B. H. Maclean, 212–38. Sheffield, UK: JSOT Press, 1993.

———. "Greco-Roman *Thiasoi*, the *Ekklesia* at Corinth, and Conflict Management." In *Redescribing Paul and the Corinthians*, edited by Ron Cameron and Merrill P. Miller, 187–218. Early Christianity and Its Literature, no. 5. Atlanta: Society of Biblical Literature, 2011.

———. "Membership Practices in Pauline Christ Groups." *Early Christianity* 4.2 (2013) 183–215.

Koester, Craig. *Revelation and the End of All Things*. Grand Rapids: Eerdmans, 2001.

———. *Revelation: A New Translation with Introduction and Commentary*. The Anchor Yale Bible, vol. 38, part 1. New Haven, CT: Yale University Press, 2014.

Kooten, George H. van. "The Year of the Four Emperors and the Revelation of John: The 'pro-Neronian' Emperors Otho and Vitellius, and the Images and Colossus of Nero in Rome." *Journal for the Study of the New Testament* 30.2 (2007) 205–48.

Korner, Ralph J. "'And I Saw . . .': An Apocalyptic Literary Convention for Structural Identification in the Apocalypse." *Novum Testamentum* 42.2 (2000) 160–83.

———. "*Ekklēsia* as a Jewish Synagogue Term: A Response to Erich Gruen." *The Journal of the Jesus Movement in its Jewish Setting* 4 (2017) 127–36.

———. "*Ekklēsia* as a Jewish Synagogue Term: Some Implications for Paul's Socio-Religious Location." *The Journal of the Jesus Movement in Its Jewish Setting* 2 (2015) 53–78.

———. "The *Ekklēsia* of Early Christ-Followers in Asia Minor as the Eschatological New Jerusalem: Counter-Imperial Rhetoric?" In *Urban Dreams and Realities in Antiquity: Remains and Representations of the Ancient City*, edited by Adam Kemezis, 455–99. Mnemosyne Supplements: History and Archaeology of Classical Antiquity 375. Leiden: Brill, 2015.

———. "The 'Exilic Prophecy' of Daniel 7: Does It Reflect Late Pre-Maccabean or Early Hellenistic Historiography?" In *Prophets, Prophecy and Ancient Israelite Historiography*, edited by Mark J. Boda and Lissa M. Wray Beal, 333–53. Winona Lake, IN: Eisenbrauns, 2013.

———. "The 'Great Earthquake' Judgment in the Apocalypse: Is There an *Urzeit* for this *Endzeit*?" *Arc* 39 (2011) 143–70.

———. *The Origin and Meaning of* Ekklēsia *in the Early Jesus Movement*. Ancient Judaism and Early Christianity 98. Leiden: Brill, 2017.

———. Review of Katherine Shaner, *Enslaved Leadership in Early Christianity* in *Review of Biblical Literature*, March 7, 2019. https://www.academia.edu/38516539/RBL_review_of_Shaner_Enslaved_Leadership_in_Early_Christianity.

———. Review of William S. Campbell, *Paul and the Creation of Christian Identity*. Bryn Mawr Classical Review (2009.07.42). http://www.bmcreview.org/2009/07/20090742.html.

Köstenberger, Andreas. *A Theology of John's Gospel and Letters: The Word, the Christ, the Son of God*. Biblical Theology of the New Testament. Grand Rapids: Zondervan, 2009.

Kovacs, Judith and Christopher Rowland. *Revelation*. Blackwell Bible Commentaries. Oxford: Blackwell, 2004.

Kraabel, A. T. "The Roman Diaspora: Six Questionable Assumptions." *Journal of Jewish Studies* 33 (1982) 445–64.

Ladd, George Eldon. *Revelation*. Grand Rapids: Eerdmans, 1972.

———. *A Theology of the New Testament*. Rev.d ed. Edited by Donald A. Hagner. Grand Rapids: Eerdmans, 1993.

Lambrecht, Jan. "A Structuration of Revelation 4, 1—22, 5." In *L'Apocalypse johannique et l'Apocalyptique dans le Nouveau Testament*, edited by Jan Lambrecht, 77–103. Leuven: Leuven University Press, 1980.

Laughlin, Jack C., and Kornel Zathureczky. "An Anatomy of the Canonization of Asadian Genealogy: A Case Study." *Studies in Religion* 44.2 (2015) 233–52.

Levine, Lee. *The Ancient Synagogue: The First Thousand Years*. 2nd ed. New Haven, CT: Yale University Press, 2005. (First edition, 2000.)

Lightfoot, J. B. *Biblical Essays*. London: Macmillan, 1893.

Loenertz, R. J. *The Apocalypse of Saint John*. London: Sheed and Ward, 1947.

Lohmeyer, Ernst. *Die Offenbarung des Johannes*. Tübingen: Möhr, 1926.

Long, V. Philips. "Reading the Old Testament as Literature." In *Interpreting the Old Testament: A Guide for Exegesis*, edited by Craig C. Broyles, 85–124. Grand Rapids: Baker, 2001.

Lund, N. W. *Chiasmus in the New Testament: A Study in Formgeschichte*. Chapel Hill, NC: The University of North Carolina Press, 1942.

Maier, Johann. "The Architectural History of the Temple in Jerusalem in the Light of the Temple Scroll." In *Temple Scroll Studies*, edited by George J. Brooke, 24–62. Journal for the Study of the Pseudepigrapha Supplement Series 7. Sheffield, UK: JSOT, 1989.

———. "Temple." In *Encyclopedia of the Dead Sea Scrolls*, vol. 2, edited by Lawrence G. Schiffman and James C. VanderKam, 921–27. Oxford: Oxford University Press, 2000.

Malina, Bruce J. *The New Testament World: Insights from Cultural Anthropology.* Louisville, KY: Westminster John Knox, 2001.

———. *On the Genre and Message of Revelation.* Peabody, MA: Hendrickson, 1995.

Mantel, Hugo. "The Men of the Great Synagogue." *The Harvard Theological Review* 60.1 (1967) 69–91.

Marshall, John. *Parables of War: Reading John's Apocalypse.* Studies in Christianity and Judaism. Waterloo, ON: Wilfred Laurier University Press, 2001.

———. "John's Jewish (Christian?) Apocalypse." In *Jewish Christianity Reconsidered: Rethinking Ancient Groups and Texts*, edited by Matt Jackson-McCabe, 233–56. Minneapolis: Fortress, 2007.

———. "Who's on the Throne? Revelation in the Long Year." In *Heavenly Realms and Earthly Realities in Late Antique Religions*, edited by R. S. Boustan and A. Y. Reed, 123–41. Cambridge: Cambridge University Press, 2004.

Martin, Ralph P. *James.* Word Biblical Commentary 48. Waco, TX: Word, 1988.

Mason, Steve. "Jews, Judaeans, Judaizing, Judaism: Problems of Categorization in Ancient History." *Journal for the Study of Judaism* 38 (2007) 457–512.

Massyngberde Ford, J. *Revelation.* The Anchor Bible Commentary. Garden City, NY: Doubleday, 1975.

Mazzaferri, F. D. *The Genre of the Book of Revelation from a Source-Critical Perspective.* BZNW 54. Berlin: de Gruyter, 1989.

McCready, Wayne O. "*Ekklēsia* and Voluntary Associations." In *Voluntary Associations in the Graeco-Roman World*, edited by John Kloppenborg and Stephen G. Wilson, 59–73. London: Routledge, 1996.

McKnight, Scot. "Jesus and the Twelve." *Bulletin of Biblical Research* 11.2 (2001) 203–31.

———. *The Letter of James.* New International Commentary on the New Testament. Grand Rapids: Eerdmans, 2011.

Meek, Russel L. "Intertextuality, Inner-Biblical Exegesis, and Inner-Biblical Allusion." *Biblica* 95 (2014) 280–91.

Meeks, Wayne A. *The First Urban Christians: The Social World of the Apostle Paul.* New Haven, CT: Yale University Press, 1983.

———. "Man from Heaven in Johannine Sectarianism." *Journal of Biblical Literature* 91.1 (1972) 44–72.

Meier, John P. "The Circle of the Twelve: Did It Exist during Jesus' Public Ministry?" *Journal of Biblical Literature* 116.4 (1997) 635–72.

Meyers, Carol L., and Eric M. Meyers. *Haggai, Zechariah 1–8.* Anchor Bible Commentary 25B. New York: Doubleday, 1988.

Michaels, J. Ramsay. *Interpreting the Book of Revelation.* The Guides to New Testament Exegesis series. Grand Rapids: Baker, 1992.

———. *Revelation.* The IVP New Testament Commentary Series. Downers Grove, IL: InterVarsity, 1997.

Milik, J. T. "Description de la Jerúsalem Nouvelle (?)." *Qumran Cave 1.* Edited by D. Barthélemy and J. T. Milik. DJD 1. Oxford: Clarendon, 1955.

Mitchell, Stephen. "Festivals, Games, and Civic Life in Roman Asia Minor." *The Journal of Roman Studies* 80 (1990) 183–93.

Moo, Jonathan. "4 Ezra and Revelation 21:1—22:5: Paradise City." In *Reading Revelation in Context: John's Apocalypse and Second Temple Judaism,* edited by Ben C. Blackwell, John K Goodrich and Jason Maston, 168–74. Grand Rapids: Zondervan Academic, 2019.

Morris, Leon. *Revelation.* Tyndale New Testament Commentaries. Grand Rapids: Eerdmans, 1987.

Morrison, Donald R. "The Utopian Character of Plato's Ideal City." In *The Cambridge Companion to Plato's Republic,* edited by G. R. F. Ferrari, 232–55. Cambridge: Cambridge University Press, 2007.

Moulton, G. *The Modern Reader's Bible.* New York: Macmillan, 1907.

Mounce, Robert. *The Book of Revelation.* Rev. ed. New International Commentary on the New Testament. Grand Rapids: Eerdmans, 1998.

Murphy-O'Connor, Jerome. "Jerusalem." In *Encyclopedia of the Dead Sea Scrolls,* vol. 2, edited by Lawrence H. Schiffman and James C. VanderKam, 402–4. Oxford: Oxford University Press, 2000.

Murray, John. *Epistle to the Romans.* 2 vols. New International Commentary on the New Testament. Grand Rapids: Eerdmans, 1959 and 1965.

Mussner, Franz. *Der Galaterbrief.* HTKNT 9. 3rd ed. Freiburg: Herder, 1977.

Nanos, Mark. "Challenging the Limits that Continue to Define on Paul's Perspective on Jews and Judaism." In *Reading Israel in Romans: Legitimacy and Plausibility of Divergent Interpretations,* edited by Christina Grenholm and Daniel Patte, 212–24. Harrisburg, PA: Trinity, 2000.

———. "Introduction." In *Paul within Judaism: Restoring the First-Century Context to the Apostle,* edited by Mark Nanos and Magnus Zetterholm, 1–29. Minneapolis: Fortress, 2015.

———. *The Irony of Galatians: Paul's Letter in First-Century Context.* Minneapolis: Augsburg Fortress, 2002.

———. "The Jewish Context of the Gentile Audience Addressed in Paul's Letter to the Romans." *Catholic Biblical Quarterly* 61 (1999) 283–304.

———. *The Mystery of Romans: The Jewish Context of Paul's Letter.* Minneapolis: Fortress, 1996.

———. "Paul's Non-Jews Do Not Become Jews, But Do They Become 'Jewish'?: Reading Romans 2:25–29 within Judaism, alongside Josephus." *Journal of the Jesus Movement in Its Jewish Setting* 1 (2014) 26–53.

———. "To the Churches within the Synagogues of Rome." In *Reading Paul's Letter to the Romans,* edited by J. L. Sumney, 11–28. Atlanta: SBL, 2012.

Neufeld, Dietmar. "Christian Communities in Sardis and Smyrna." In *Religious Rivalries and the Struggle for Success in Sardis and Smyrna,* edited by Richard S. Ascough, 25–39. Studies in Christianity and Judaism/Etudes sur le christianisme et le judaïsme 14. Waterloo, ON: Wilfrid Laurier University Press, 2005.

Newsome, Carol. *Songs of the Sabbath Sacrifice: A Critical Edition.* Harvard Semitic Studies 27. Atlanta: Scholars, 1985.

Nijf, Onno M. van. *The Civic World of Professional Associations in the Roman East.* Dutch Monographs on Ancient History and Archaeology, vol. XVII. Amsterdam: J. C. Gieben, 1997.

———. "Public Space and the Political Culture of Roman Termessos." In *Political Culture in the Greek City after the Classical Age,* edited by Onno van Nijf and Richard Alston with the assistance of C. G. Williamson, 215–42. Leuven: Peeters, 2011.

———. "Staying Roman—Becoming Greek: Associations of *Romaioi* in Greek Cities." Paper presented at *Associations in Context,* Copenhagen Associations Project, Copenhagen, October 11–13, 2012.

Nongbri, Brent. *Before Religion: A History of a Modern Concept.* New Haven, CT: Yale University Press, 2013.

Page, Sydney H. T. "Revelation 20 and Pauline Eschatology." *Journal of the Evangelical Theological Society* 23/1 (1980) 31–43.

Pagels, Elaine. *Revelations: Visions, Prophecy, and Politics in the Book of Revelation.* New York: Penguin, 2013.

———. "The Social History of Satan, Part Three: John of Patmos and Ignatius of Antioch: Contrasting Visions of 'God's People.'" *The Harvard Theological Review* 99 (2006) 487–505.

Panagopoulos, J. "Die urchristliche Prophetie: Ihr Charakter und ihre Funktion." In *Prophetic Vocation in the New Testament and Today,* edited by J. Panagopoulos, 1–32. New Testament Supplement Series 55. Leiden: Brill, 1977.

Patterson, Richard D. "Wonders in the Heavens and on the Earth: Apocalyptic Imagery in the Old Testament." *Journal of the Evangelical Theological Society* 43.3 (2000) 385–403.

Perrin, Norm. "Apocalyptic Christianity." In *Visionaries and their Apocalypses,* edited by Paul D. Hanson, 122–40. Issues in Religion and Theology, vol. 4. Philadelphia: Fortress, 1983.

Petersen, David L. "Eschatology: Old Testament." In *Anchor Bible Dictionary,* edited by David Noel Freedman, 2:575–79. New York: Doubleday, 1992.

Pike, Kenneth. *Emics and Etics: The Insider/Outsider Debate.* Thousand Oaks, CA: Sage, 1990.

———. *Language in Relation to a Unified Theory of the Structure of Human Behaviour.* Preliminary edition. Dallas: Summer Institute of Linguistics, 1954.

Pleket, H. W. "Political Culture and Political Practice in the Cities of Asia Minor in the Roman Empire." In *Politische Theorie und Praxis im Altertum,* edited by W. Schuller, 204–16. Darmstadt: Wissenschaftliche Buchgesellschaft, 1998.

Pohl, Adolf. *Die Offenbarung des Johannes.* 2 vols. Wuppertal: R. Brockhaus, 1969 and 1971.

Poland, Franz. *Geschichte des griechischen Vereinswesens.* Preisschriften gekrönt und herausgegeben von der fürstlich Jablonowskischen Gesellschaft zu Leipzig 38. 1909. Reprint, Leipzig: Zentral-Antiquariat der Deutschen Demokratischen Republik, 1967.

Price, Simon R. F. *Rituals and Power: The Roman Imperial Cult in Asia Minor.* Cambridge: Cambridge University Press, 1984.

Prigent, Pierre. *Commentary on the Apocalypse of St. John.* Tübingen: Mohr Siebeck, 2001.

Rainbow, Paul. *Johannine Theology: The Gospel, the Epistles, and the Apocalypse.* Downers Grove, IL: InterVarsity, 2014.

———. *The Pith of the Apocalypse.* Eugene, OR: Wipf and Stock, 2008.

Rhodes, P. J. "Epigraphical Evidence: Laws and Decrees." In *Sources for the Ancient Greek City-State. Symposium August 24–27, 1994, Acts of the Copenhagen Polis Centre*, vol. 2, edited by M. H. Hansen, 91–112. Historisk-filosofiske Meddelelser 72. Copenhagen: Munksgaard, 1995.

Richardson, Peter. *Israel in the Apostolic Church.* Society for the Study of the New Testament Monograph Series 10. Cambridge: Cambridge University Press, 1969.

Richter, Daniel S. *Cosmopolis: Imagining Community in Late Classical Athens and the Early Roman Empire.* Oxford: Oxford University Press, 2011.

Ridderbos, Herman N. *Paul: An Outline of His Theology.* Translated by John Richard DeWitt. Grand Rapids: Eerdmans, 1975.

Rissi, Mathias. *Zeit und Geschichte in der Offenbarung des Johannes.* Zurich: Zwingli, 1952.

Robert, Louis. "Inscriptions de Lesbos et de Samos." *Bulletin de correspondance hellénique* 59 (1935) 471–88.

Roberts, J. W. *The Revelation to John (the Apocalypse).* The Living Word Commentary. Austin: Sweet, 1974.

Robinson, D. W. B. "The Distinction between Jewish and Gentile Believers in Galatians." *ABR* 13 (1965) 29–48.

Rojas-Flores, G. "The Book of Revelation and the First Years of Nero's Reign." *Biblica* 85 (2004) 375–92.

Rowland, Christopher. *The Open Heaven: A Study of Apocalyptic in Judaism and Early Christianity.* New York: Crossroad, 1982.

Rowley, H. H. *The Relevance of Apocalyptic.* New York: Association, 1963.

Rudolph, David. "Messianic Jews and Christian Theology: Restoring an Historical Voice to the Contemporary Discussion." *Pro Ecclesia* XIV.1 (2005) 58–84.

Runesson, Anders. "Behind the Gospel of Matthew: Radical Pharisees in Post-War Galilee?" *Currents in Theology and Mission* 37.6 (2010) 460–71.

———. "Inventing Christian Identity: Paul, Ignatius, and Theodotius I." In *Exploring Early Christian Identity*, edited by Bengt Holmberg, 59–92. Tübingen: Mohr Siebeck, 2008.

———. *The Origins of the Synagogue: A Socio-Historical Study.* Coniectanea Biblica. New Testament Series 37. Stockholm: Almqvist & Wiksell International, 2001.

———. "The Question of Terminology: The Architecture of Contemporary Discussions on Paul." In *Paul within Judaism: Restoring the First-Century Context to the Apostle*, edited by Mark Nanos and Magnus Zetterholm, 53–78. Minneapolis: Fortress, 2015.

———. "Rethinking Early Jewish–Christian Relations: Matthean Community History as Pharisaic Intragroup Conflict." *Journal of Biblical Literature* 127.1 (2008) 95–132.

———. "Was There a Christian Mission before the 4th Century? Problematizing Common Ideas about Early Christianity and the Beginnings of Modern Mission." In *The Making of Christianity: Conflicts, Contacts, and Constructions: Essays in Honor of Bengt Holmberg*, edited by Magnus Zetterholm and Samuel B. Byrskog, 205–47. Coniectanea Biblica. New Testament Series, 47. Winona Lake, IN: Eisenbrauns, 2012.

Runesson, Anders, Donald Binder, and Birger Olsson. *The Ancient Synagogue from Its Origins to 200 C.E.: A Source Book*. Ancient Judaism and Early Christianity, vol. 72. Leiden: Brill, 2008.

Russel, D. S. *The Method and Message of Jewish Apocalyptic*. Philadelphia: Westminster, 1964.

Sacchi, Paolo. "The Devil in Jewish Traditions of the Second Temple Period (c. 500 BCE–100 CE)." In *Jewish Apocalyptic and Its History*, translated by William J. Short, 211–32. Journal for the Study of the Pseudepigrapha Supplement 20. Sheffield, UK: Sheffield Academic Press, 1990.

Sanders, E. P. *Judaism: Practice & Belief, 63 BCE–66 CE*. Philadelphia: Trinity, 1992.

Sandmel, Samuel. "Parallelomania." *Journal of Biblical Literature* 81 (1962) 1–13.

Sandnes, Karl Olav. *Paul—One of the Prophets? A Contribution to the Apostle's Self-Understanding*. Wissenschaftliche Untersuchungen zum Neuen Testament. 2 Reihe. Tübingen: Mohr (Siebeck), 1991.

Satake, A. *Die Gemeindeordnung in der Johannesapokalypse*. WMANT 21. Neukirchen, 1966.

Schofield, Malcolm. *The Stoic Idea of the City*. 2nd ed. Chicago: University of Chicago Press, 1999.

Schüssler Fiorenza, Elisabeth. "*Apokalypsis* and *Propheteia*: The Book of Revelation in the Context of Early Christian Prophecy." In *L'Apocalyse johannique et l'Apocalyptique dans le Nouveau Testament*, edited by J. Lambrecht, 105–28. Leuven: Leuven University Press, 1980.

———. *The Book of Revelation: Justice and Judgment*. 2nd ed. Minneapolis: Fortress, 1998.

———. "Composition and Structure of the Book of Revelation." *Catholic Biblical Quarterly* 39.3 (1977) 344–66.

———. "The Phenomenon of Early Christian Apocalyptic: Some Reflections on Method." In *Apocalypticism in the Mediterranean World and the Near East*, edited by David Hellholm, 295–316. Proceedings of the International Colloquium on Apocalypticism, Uppsala, August 12–17, 1979. 2nd ed. Tübingen: Mohr (Siebeck), 1989.

———. "Revelation." In *The New Testament and Its Modern Interpreters*, edited by E. J. Epp and G. W. MacRae, 407–27. Philadelphia: Fortress, 1989.

Schweigert, Eugene. "The Athenian Cleruchy on Samos." *American Journal of Philology* 61.2 (1940) 194–98.

Shaner, Katherine. *Enslaved Leadership in Early Christianity*. Oxford: Oxford University Press, 2018.

Schrenk, Gottlob. "Was bedeutet 'Israel Gottes'?" *Judaica* 6 (1949) 81–94.

Schwartz, Daniel R. *Judeans and Jews: Four Faces of Dichotomy in Ancient Jewish History*. Toronto: University of Toronto Press, 2014.

Slater, T. B. "Dating the Apocalypse to John." *Biblica* 84 (2003) 252–58.

Soulen, R. Kendall. *The God of Israel and Christian Theology*. Minneapolis: Fortress, 1996.

Spence, Iain G. *Historical Dictionary of Ancient Greek Warfare*. Historical Dictionaries of War, Revolution and Civil Unrest 16. Lanham, MD: Scarecrow, 2002.

Spence, Stephen. *The Parting of the Ways: The Roman Church as a Case Study*. Interdisciplinary Studies in Ancient Culture and Religion 5. Leuven: Peeters, 2004.

Spinks, Leroy. "A Critical Examination of J. W. Bowman's Proposed Structure of the Revelation." *Evangelical Quarterly* 50.4 (1978) 211–22.

Stegemann, Hartmut. "The Literary Compositions of the Temple Scroll and Its Status at Qumran." In *Temple Scroll Studies*, edited by G. J. Brooke, 123–48. Journal for the Study of the Pseudepigrapha 7. Sheffield, UK: JSOT, 1989.

Stevenson, Kalinda Rose. "The Land Is Yours: Ezekiel's Outrageous Land Claim." Paper presented at the annual meeting of the Society of Biblical Literature, Denver, CO, November 2001.

Stone, Michael E. *A Commentary on the Book of Fourth Ezra*. Hermeneia. Minneapolis: Fortress, 1990.

———. "Qumran und die Zwölf." In *Initiation*, edited by C. J. Bleeker, 134–46. SHR 10. Leiden: Brill, 1965.

Strand, Kenneth. "Chiastic Structure and Some Motifs in the Book of Revelation." *Andrews University Seminary Studies* 16 (1978) 401–8.

———. "The Eight Basic Visions in the Book of Revelation." *Andrews University Seminary Studies* 25.1 (1987) 107–21.

———. "A Further Note on the Covenantal Form in the Book of Revelation." *Andrews University Seminary Studies* 21.3 (1983) 251–64.

Swete, Henry Barclay. *The Apocalypse of St. John: The Greek Text with Introduction Notes and Indices*. 3rd ed. Grand Rapids: Eerdmans, 1908.

Tajfel, H., and J. C. Turner. "An Integrative Theory of Intergroup Conflict." In *The Social Psychology of Intergroup Relations*, edited by S. Worchel and W. G. Austin, 33–47. Monterey, CA: Brooks, 1979.

Tellbe, Mikael. *Paul between Synagogue and State: Christians, Jews and Civic Authorities in 1 Thessalonians, Romans, and Philippians*. Stockholm: Almqvist & Wiksell International, 2001.

Tenney, Merrill C. *Interpreting Revelation*. Grand Rapids: Eerdmans, 1957.

———. *John: The Gospel of Belief*. Grand Rapids: Eerdmans, 1976.

Thiessen, Matthew. "Paul's Argument against Gentile Circumcision in Romans 2:17–29." *Novum Testamentum* 56 (2014) 373–91.

Thomas, Robert L. *Revelation 1–7, 8–22*. Chicago: Moody, 1992 and 1995.

Thompson, Leonard L. *Revelation*. Abingdon New Testament Commentaries. Nashville: Abingdon, 1998.

Thorsteinsson, Runar M. *Paul's Interlocutor in Romans 2: Function and Identity in the Context of Ancient Epistolography*. Coniectanea Biblica. New Testament Series 40. Stockholm: Almqvist & Wiksell, 2003.

Tiller, Patrick A. *A Commentary on the Animal Apocalypse of 1 Enoch*. Atlanta: Scholars, 1993.

Trebilco, Paul R. *Jewish Communities in Asia Minor Society*. New Testament Studies Monograph Series 69. Cambridge: Cambridge University Press, 1991.

———. *Self-designations and Group Identity in the New Testament*. Cambridge: Cambridge University Press, 2012.

Tucker, J. Brian. *Remain in Your Calling: Paul and the Continuation of Social Identities in 1 Corinthians*. Eugene, OR: Pickwick, 2011.

Vawter, Bruce, and Leslie J. Hoppe. *Ezekiel: A New Heart*. International Theological Commentary. Grand Rapids: Eerdmans, 1991.

Veelen, Ruth van, Sabine Otten, Mara Cadinu, and Nina Hansen. "An Integrative Model of Social Identification: Self-Stereotyping and Self-Anchoring as Two Cognitive Pathways." *Personal and Social Psychology Review* 20 (2016) 3–26.

Verseput, Donald J. "Genre and Story: The Community Setting of the Epistle of James." *Catholic Biblical Quarterly* 62.1 (2000) 96–110.

Vlach, Michael. *Has the Church Replaced Israel?* Nashville: Broadman and Holman, 2010.

Waal, C. van der. *Openbaring van Jezus Christus. Inleiding en Vertaling.* Groningen: de Vuurbaak, 1971.

Wall, Robert W. *Revelation.* New International Biblical Commentary. Peabody, MA: Hendrickson, 1991.

Wallace, Daniel B. *Greek Grammar beyond the Basics: An Exegetical Syntax of the New Testament.* Grand Rapids: Zondervan, 1996.

Walvoord, John F. *The Revelation of Jesus Christ.* Chicago: Moody, 1966.

Watts, John D. W. *Isaiah 1–33.* Word Biblical Commentary, 24A. Waco, TX: Word, 1985.

White, Ellen. *Yahweh's Council: Its Structure and Membership.* FAT 2/65. Tübingen: Mohr Siebeck, 2014.

Wilcock, Michael. *The Message of Revelation: I Saw Heaven Opened.* The Bible Speaks Today. Leicester, UK: InterVarsity, 1975.

Wilson, J. C. "The Problem of the Domitianic Date of Revelation." *New Testament Studies* 39 (1993) 587–605.

Wilson, M. "The Early Christians in Ephesus and the Date of Revelation, Again." *Neotestamentica* 39 (2005) 163–93.

Wilson, Walter T. *Philo of Alexandria: On Virtues.* Philo of Alexandria Commentary Series 3. Leiden: Brill, 2011.

Wise, Michael O., and Martin Abegg, Jr., and Edward Cook. *The Dead Sea Scrolls: A New Translation.* San Francisco: HarperSanFrancisco, 1996.

Wise, Michael O. "New Jerusalem Texts." In *Dictionary of New Testament Background*, edited by Craig A. Evans and Stanley Porter, 743–45. Leicester, UK: Downers Grove, IL: InterVarsity, 2000.

Wright, N. T. *The Climax of the Covenant: Christ and the Law in Pauline Theology.* Edinburgh: T. & T. Clark, 1991.

———. *The Letter to the Romans.* New International Bible Commentary 10. Nashville: Abingdon, 2001.

———. *Paul and the Faithfulness of God.* 2 vols. Christian Origins and the Question of God, vol. 4. Minneapolis: Fortress, 2013.

Yadin, Yigael. "The Temple Scroll—The Longest and Most Recently Discovered Dead Sea Scroll." *BAR* 10.5 (1984) 32–49.

Wall, Robert W. *Revelation.* New International Biblical Commentary. Peabody, MA: Hendrickson, 1991.

Zetterholm, Magnus. *Approaches to Paul: A Student's Guide to Recent Scholarship.* Minneapolis: Fortress, 2009.

Zoccali, Christopher. *Whom God has Called: The Relationship of Church and Israel in Pauline Interpretation, 1920 to the Present.* Eugene, OR: Pickwick, 2010.

Zuiderhoek, Arjan. "Oligarchs and Benefactors: Elite Demography and Euergetism in the Greek East of the Roman Empire." In *Political Culture in the Greek City after the Classical Age*, edited by Onno van Nijf and Richard Alston with the assistance of C. G. Williamson, 185–96. Leuven: Peeters, 2011.

———. "On the Political Sociology of the Imperial Greek City." *Greek, Roman and Byzantine Studies* 48 (2008) 417–45.

———. *The Politics of Munificence in the Roman Empire: Citizens, Elites and Benefactors in Asia Minor*. Greek Culture in the Roman World. Cambridge: Cambridge University Press, 2009.

Subject Index

Modern Authors Index

Index of Ancient Sources

CPSIA information can be obtained
at www.ICGtesting.com
Printed in the USA
FSHW012157301220
77051FS